✶

Clover Adams

A GILDED AND HEARTBREAKING LIFE

Natalie Dykstra

Houghton Mifflin Harcourt
Boston New York 2012

For information about permission to reproduce selections from this book,
write to Permissions, Houghton Mifflin Harcourt Publishing Company,
215 Park Avenue South, New York, New York 10003.

www.hmhbooks.com

Library of Congress Cataloging-in-Publication Data
Dykstra, Natalie.
Clover Adams : a gilded and heartbreaking life / Natalie Dykstra.
p. cm.
Includes bibliographical references and index.
ISBN 978-0-618-87385-2
1. Adams, Marian, 1843–1885. 2. Historians' spouses — United
States — Biography. 3. Adams, Henry, 1838–1918. 4. Women
photographers — United States — Biography. I. Title.
CT275.A34D95 2012   770.92 — dc23
[B]   2011028562

Book design by Lisa Diercks
Typeset in Fournier

Printed in the United States of America
DOC 10 9 8 7 6 5 4 3 2 1

In memory of Harriett M. Dykstra, 1930–2005

The moral is to make all one can out of life and live up
to one's fingers' ends.
— CLOVER ADAMS, JANUARY 1, 1882

All forms of decay knock at our gate and summon us to go out
into their wilderness, and yet every ideal we dream of
is realized in the same life of which these things are part.
— WILLIAM JAMES TO ELLEN HOOPER,
OLDEST NIECE OF CLOVER ADAMS, MAY 10, 1901

CONTENTS

+

PROLOGUE

THE AUTUMN OF 1883 was notably beautiful. Trees lining the streets of
Washington, D.C., seemed to hold on to their leaves, and as the season
deepened, roses and morning glories defied cooler temperatures, refusing to give up their last blooms. That fall Clover Adams celebrated her
fortieth birthday. Her husband, Henry Adams, the historian and a grand-
son and great-grandson of American presidents, had just finished writing
his second novel, *Esther,* and was again busy at his desk, poring over page
proofs for the first section of what would become his nine-volume *History
of the United States During the Administrations of Thomas Jefferson and
James Madison.* Most mornings, Clover rode her favorite horse, Daisy,
through the streets of the capital to enjoy what she called the "smiling
landscape," returning home to 1607 H Street with flowers for bouquets.
Their home faced south to Lafayette Square, with a view of the White
House in the background. The Square, also called the President's Park,
offered a shady retreat from southern heat, a place to stroll through ellip-
tical gardens on crisscrossing pathways lit by the yellowish glow of gas-
light. At the park's center a towering bronze of Andrew Jackson reared
up on horseback. Senators, vice presidents, cabinet secretaries, and military leaders occupied the stately federal-style homes that ringed the park.

Three years before, Clover and Henry had signed a lease for two hundred dollars a month for what they nicknamed the "little white house," asking its owner, William Corcoran, the banker, art collector, and philanthropist, to pay for renovations, including a brand-new stable and a large detached kitchen in back. Clover considered it a "solid old pile." With six bedrooms and a spacious library, the townhouse, built in 1845, was "little" only in comparison to the capital's grander homes, but it suited Clover's preference for what she called "coziness in the New England sense." Hand-carved mantels crowned fireplaces decorated with ceramic tiles. Carpets purchased on the Adamses' honeymoon to Egypt in 1872 covered the floors. An eclectic mix of Asian bronzes and porcelains were set on tables and shelves, and art, including Japanese hanging scrolls, sepia drawings by Rubens and Rembrandt, and watercolor landscapes by the English Romantics, adorned the walls. Elizabeth Bliss Bancroft, a near neighbor on H Street, once said to Clover, "My dear, I dislike auctions very much, but I mean to go to yours after you die."

Clover and Henry had married eleven years before, when she was twenty-eight and he was thirty-three, joining Hooper wealth to Adams political renown. In the close quarters of Boston Brahmin society, where they had both grown up, they were a likely—if not inevitable—match. If Clover could be an "undemonstrative New Englander," as she herself admitted, her practicality and quick wit tempered Henry's sometimes anxious nature. Together they enjoyed days of simultaneous fullness and leisure: a horseback ride in the morning, afternoons set aside for Henry's writing, tea promptly at five o'clock for visitors, then dinner and an evening's ride or a long stretch of reading by the fireplace. They collected art, traveled, gossiped about politics, supported various causes, and attended dinners and galas, which during the high time of the social season, from mid-October until Lent, took up many evenings. Of these years, Henry wrote, "This part of life—from forty to fifty—would be all I want."

A wide array of writers and artists, politicians and dignitaries, doctors and academics made their way to the Adamses' salon for food and talk. Presidents and their families made appearances. Elizabeth Adams knew it was her Aunt Clover "who brought people to their house and gave it its character and warmth." Henry James, who liked to stay with the Adamses for weeks at a time, at one point called Clover, with her satiric humor, "a perfect Voltaire in petticoats" and thought her an ideal specimen of a particular type of American woman—practical, honest, quick-thinking, with a streak of independence and rebellion. She read widely—George Sand, William Dean Howells, Henry James—and she took up Greek, tackling Plato and the Greek playwrights in the original language, a passion that never faded. Though Clover sometimes battled dark moods, she was no neurasthenic who took to her bed. She used her acerbic wit to maintain perspective and had the will to manage things to suit her. Athletic but petite, at five feet two inches in height, and her husband just an inch or so taller, Clover had the legs of all chairs and sofas shortened to better fit their personal proportions. When offered a seat, much taller guests, including the six-foot-two Oliver Wendell Holmes Jr., later a Supreme Court justice, would precipitously drop onto the low seating.

Clover reserved Sunday mornings not for church but for writing a letter—what she called her "hebdomadal drivel"—to her widowed father. Sometimes she despaired at how her writing failed to express all she wanted to say: "Life is such a jumble of impressions just now that I cannot unravel the skein in practical, quiet fashion. Oh, for the pen of Abigail Adams!" But Clover need not have been intimidated by her husband's great-grandmother. In fact, her father found it hard to comply with her request that he not read her letters aloud to family and friends—she told such interesting stories.

In early November of 1883, Clover reported that "our days go by quietly and pleasantly." The lively social season had not yet begun, though it would commence in the next month, when Congress returned to session. With no children of her own to take care of, with Henry busy at his desk, and with time on her hands, she turned once more to what had absorbed much of her attention during the summer. The previous May, she had started something new: she had begun taking and printing her own photographs. She delighted in every step of the process, from selecting a subject, through exposure of the negative, to the final print. She had shown interest in photography before, by collecting Civil War stereographs and small commercial photographs of the sights she wanted to remember from her Grand Tour through Europe in 1866. She'd spent hours looking at fine art in museums around the world, amassing with Henry a large collection of watercolors and charcoals, Japanese prints and ceramics. But taking a photograph was different from looking or collecting. With her portable five-by-eight-inch mahogany camera, Clover started making art, and the process was changing her life.

On a warm, windy November afternoon, just after lunch, she decided to photograph her beloved Skye terriers in the garden behind the townhouse. She draped a bed sheet over the back fence and positioned three chairs around a small dark table, complete with tea set — teapot, three cups and saucers, and a silver spoon. She placed each dog on a chair, somehow perching their front paws on the table and getting them to stay in position while she scrambled back to her camera. She took only one exposure with her new "instantaneous" lens, which didn't require the extended exposure of the usual drop lens. She made a careful entry in her small lined notebook where she listed her photographic experiments, giving the details: "Nov 5 — 1 P.M. — Boojum, Marquis & Possum at tea in garden of 1607 H. St. instantaneous, *not drop* shutter — stop no. 3." Later, with a different pen and in larger script, she commented on what she thought of the result: "extremely good."

That same afternoon, Clover loaded her black carriage with her camera, tripod, several lenses, a notebook, and a carefully packed set of glass negatives called dry-plate negatives because they'd been commercially prepared with light-sensitive chemicals. She rode out three miles to Arlington National Cemetery and stopped at a spot within view of General Robert E. Lee's former home. The new German minister's twenty-year-old wife, Madame von Eisendecker, whom Clover described as a young "Pomeranian blonde," tagged along. She had just come to America and wanted Clover, who was gaining a reputation around town for her portraits, to take her photograph. The two women arrived at the cemetery in midafternoon, and after setting up her equipment, Clover took two exposures of General Lee's house on the hill. But by "some crass idiocy," as she later explained, Clover ruined the pictures. After the first exposure, she'd forgotten to replace the glass negative at the back of the camera with another unused negative, something she had done several times before. Such mistakes irritated her. She crossed out the entry in her notebook with a large X. But she didn't give up. Late in the afternoon, she took a picture of a haunting landscape of soldiers' graves set against a background of trees. The tombs of those who died in the Civil War, the cataclysm that had profoundly shaped her generation and her own sense of America, rise up like unruly memories among the fallen leaves.

The next Sunday Clover wrote to her father that she'd spent "two good morning hours to develop photographs today," promising to send him a print or two. The complicated process of making a photograph — exposing the image, developing the negative, sensitizing the printing-out paper, making and developing the print — required patience and concentration. Kodak's promise ("You take the picture and we do the rest") was still five years away. When it came time to put prints in her album, Clover paired the image of her dogs at tea with the one of the Arlington graves, putting each in the exact middle of the page, so when the album was fully opened, the two images would be seen at the same time. On the left page, she wrote the dogs' names in the lower right-hand corner, beneath the photograph. She typically identified her photographs this way, with a quick description of who or what was pictured, the location, and sometimes the precise date or just the year. Beneath her image of the soldiers' graves on the right side, she wrote a Latin sentence meaning "You sleep in our memory." In the upper-right corner of the image itself, the only time she would write directly on a photograph, she included the last lines from the first act of Goethe's *Faust*, the book she had been reading aloud with Henry in the evening: "Ich gehe durch den Todesschlaf / Zu Gott ein als Soldat und brav" (I go to God through the sleep of death, / A soldier — brave to his last breath).

If Clover could be playful and mocking with her pictures, as with her "dogs at tea" photograph, a send-up of a social convention she occasionally found tedious, she could also evoke sadness or an intense feeling of loss. With her camera, she recorded her world for herself and for others to see, and in less than three years, her collection would grow to 113 photographs arranged in three red-leather albums.

But just when Clover discovered a powerful way to express herself, her life started to unravel. What had been a recurrent undertow of dark moods gathered force until she was engulfed by despair, "pulled down," in the words of a friend, as if by some unseen tide. On a gloomy Sunday morning in early December of 1885, two and a half years after she had first picked up her camera, Clover committed suicide by drinking from a vial of potassium cyanide, which she had used to develop her photographs. The means of her art had become the means of her death, a weapon she used against herself. The most dramatic moment of her life also became its most defining, cocooning her memory in the hush-hush of familial shame and confusion; when she was remembered at all, it was most often as the wife of a famous man or as a suicide.

Henry commissioned the sculptor Augustus Saint-Gaudens to create a bronze statue that would memorialize Clover. It was not intended to be a realistic image of her; instead Saint-Gaudens created a compelling and mysterious figure, draped and seated, which Henry informally called "The Peace of God." It is the only marker for her grave in Washington's Rock Creek Cemetery and Henry's only public tribute. He almost never spoke of her and did not even mention her in his Pulitzer Prize–winning autobiography, *The Education of Henry Adams*. Eleanor Shattuck Whiteside, a friend from school days, tried to find words to express her confusion at her friend's sudden death, writing to her own mother that "Clover's death has been a great shock and surprise to me. I can't get it out of my head . . . How often we have spoken of Clover as having all she wanted, all this world could give . . . It seems to me a kind of lesson on what a little way intellect and cultivation and the best things of this life go when you come to the heart of life and death. And yet they are all good things and the desired. And that's the puzzle."

Clover's life has remained half-illumined, a reflection of how others viewed her but not how she saw herself. But she left behind clues to what her friend called the "puzzle" of her life and of her death, clues in her many letters and, most eloquently, in her revelatory photographs, which invite the viewer to stand not on this side of her suicide, but on the other, the one she lived on. Her photographs range from portraits of her family and friends to moody landscapes, but in their composition and their arrangement in her albums, they always show her distinctive sensibility, allowing her vision of her world. Her story begins in Transcendentalist

Boston, with a privileged childhood shadowed by early losses. It moves on to the story of her iconic American marriage to a complicated, brilliant man who invented the study of American history, of their initial happiness, and of their inability, finally, to reach each other. Connection and disconnection, vitality and loss—these were deep currents in Clover's life, which she attempted to transform, as artists do, into something beautiful and something to be shared. To know the arc of her whole life, and to look closely at her photographs, is to give her back some measure of her full humanity.

PART I

A New World

I give thee all, my darling, darling child,
All I can give — the record of good things.
— ELLEN STURGIS HOOPER

CHAPTER I

"She Was Home to Me"

SHE WAS BORN Marian Hooper on September 13, 1843. But everyone called her Clover. For her mother, Ellen Sturgis Hooper, the arrival of this youngest daughter seemed unexpected and lucky, like a four-leaf clover. She delighted in telling stories of Clover's precocity, reporting how the baby, not yet a year old, would "stick out one finger and say 'Hark!'" She called the little girl with wide eyes "Clovy" and "my blessed Clover," telling her father that "Clover is inestimable." She admitted to a fierce maternal bond, an emotion not without peril, given that one in five children in midcentury America died before the age of five. But Ellen couldn't help herself. She was besotted with Clover, finding it hard to be away from her even for a short time. "I don't want to tend her all the time," she admitted to one of her sisters, "but I can't bear to lose an hour of her youthful foxiness."

Clover's mother, full of affection, was also known for her "wit, her sense of the ridiculous, her keen and quick perceptions." Though she'd been raised in enormous privilege, her manner was direct and democratic. One of her servants recalled that "Mrs. Hooper always appeared in her kitchen just the same as she did in company." A small woman, she spoke in a low, quiet voice. A lithographic portrait shows delicate features framed by raven hair that she carefully parted straight down the middle, in keeping with the style of the day. A hint of a smile doesn't undo the sadness in her shining dark eyes, which slant subtly downward.

But her sadness did not signal an overly delicate temperament. Clover's mother had strength and, more than that, a remarkable curiosity and capacity for learning. The feminist writer Margaret Fuller, two years older and her close friend, thought Ellen had a mind "full of genius" that was "exquisitely refined." Another friend observed that she was someone "whose character seemed in constant process of growth," attributing this capacity to her having "conquered . . . what is most difficult of all things to conquer—a constitutional tendency to depression." Her struggle, though "hard to bear," had "given depth and breadth and height to her character."

Ellen Sturgis was born in Boston in 1812 to a home marked by tragedy. She was the oldest daughter of Captain William Sturgis and Elizabeth Davis, the daughter of Judge John Davis, a U.S. district judge for Massachusetts. Captain Sturgis, who had been a "Cape-Cod boy," had decided, as had his father before him, "to follow the sea." He was an extraordinarily capable seaman, a kind of prodigy who commanded a large trading ship, the *Caroline*, between the Northwest Territories and China when he was not yet twenty. He was also gifted in languages and learned to speak with the fur-trading native tribes along the Pacific coast. By 1810, the year of his marriage, Captain Sturgis was a founding partner of Bryant and Sturgis, a firm that soon controlled over half the trade between Boston, the Northwest Territories, and China.

Six Sturgis children were born over the next fifteen years: William Junior, Ellen, Anne, Caroline, Mary, and Susan. Captain and Mrs. Sturgis prized education for all their children. William Junior went first to Sandwich Academy on Cape Cod, boarding with his mother's sister and her husband, the Reverend Ezra Goodwin. He continued on at the newly formed Round Hill School in Northampton in western Massachusetts, a boys' boarding school modeled after the German gymnasium. Ellen and her younger sisters were schooled in Hingham, fifteen miles south of Boston, at a boarding school run by two sisters, Elizabeth and Margaret Cushing. The curriculum in Hingham was similar to that of Round

Hill—Ellen studied Latin, French, chemistry, astronomy, rhetoric, and Greek history, which was her favorite subject.

Ellen was particularly close to her older brother. Reading before the age of five, William was by age ten studying with the young Harvard-educated Reverend Warren Goddard, an early convert to Swedenborgian theology. As a way to teach the classics, Goddard had his young students at Sandwich Academy copy out long passages from Homer and Shakespeare, a task William undertook with a meticulous hand. He reported back to his parents in Boston that he enjoyed his school "very much." "I want to stay here," William wrote, adding with a measure of pride that he had already translated "450 lines of Virgil."

But the enormous promise of the young man went tragically unfulfilled. In 1827, at sixteen, after attending Harvard for a single year, William Junior drowned in a freak accident on a mail boat off the coast of Provincetown, after being thrown overboard by a loose boom. Mrs. Sturgis reacted to the loss of her only son with unbridled grief. Her behavior over time became increasingly troubled, her letters a frantic sequence of random biblical quotations and spiritual sayings, a wrestling with darkness. Searching for some way to make sense of her loss, by 1831 Mrs. Sturgis withdrew from the family home at 52 Summer Street and lived instead with her sister and husband, who had no children, on Cape Cod, then in the Boston suburb of Brookline, as if the sight of her husband and children had become simply too painful to bear. Her daughters traveled back and forth between Boston and Brookline to see her. When Caroline, who was seven years younger than Ellen (and named after her father's first ship), visited her mother in Brookline much later, she found her "walking up and down her darkened rooms with her gaze bent upon the floor as if fixed there." From time to time, Mrs. Sturgis would return home, only to flee again, unable to endure for any length of time the emotional demands of family life.

Captain Sturgis forbade anyone to speak about the tragedy that had befallen his family. Practicality and a personal toughness had enabled him to survive the hardships he'd endured on the way to making his fortune. He was austere, not given to self-examination or outward expressions of personal feeling. He neither drank nor smoked, and though he had traveled the world, he collected no paintings or other artwork, a disinclination unusual for someone of his social standing and economic means. His motto for his children — one he enforced — was that they must learn to take care of themselves. His values had endowed him with tenacity and determination, but these qualities did little to help him understand his wife's behavior or comfort her in her distress. Captain Sturgis implored his wife to take her place beside him; at the same time, he remained uncomprehending of her unbounded grief for their son, so he turned to his daughters (and later his grandchildren) for consolation and a shared family life. In the mid-1840s, he bought a large summer house in Woburn, near Horn Pond, where he enjoyed being outdoors with his daughters and seven grandchildren and sailing on the pond.

The Sturgis sisters, grieving for their older brother and abandoned by their mother, looked to their oldest sister, Ellen, for solace. Though only fourteen years old at the time of her brother's death, Ellen stepped into the breach as best she could, and over the years she became a de facto mother figure for her younger sisters and a companion for her father, though she herself wrestled with melancholy and low moods. From time to time, Ellen tried to reason with her mother, attempted to understand her plight, but a request she made, to begin an undated letter reporting on family news, measures the distance that had grown between Mrs. Sturgis and her family: "Do take the trouble to read this," Ellen wrote her mother, clearly not sure whether Mrs. Sturgis would be interested enough to do so. Perhaps of most importance, Ellen urged her sisters not to take their mother's confounding behavior personally. She was particularly protective of Sue, her mercurial and sensitive younger sister, who was just six years old when their parents separated. "I have not seen her [Mother] for some time," Ellen explained to Susan on one occasion, preparing her for what she knew would feel like a rejection. "I do not think she feels able to write to you. I know you will feel very sorry to hear this, but you [must] remember Mother has had this depression before and when it is upon her, there is no certainty how long it may continue." Their mother would remain what Ellen aptly called "a mystery of sorrow."

Caroline was more pointed about the emotional temperature of her family life, once complaining to Margaret Fuller that the "moment I have anything to do with my own family it seems as if the blast of death had struck me & chilled me to the heart." Even Ellen, despite how she'd tried to nurture her sisters, did not escape Caroline's censure; she told Margaret Fuller that her father and her sisters "are really very kind but never for one minute loving."

In the early evening of Monday, September 25, 1837, Ellen Sturgis married Robert William Hooper at King's Chapel, the first Unitarian church in America. At twenty-five, she was somewhat older than the typical age at which women in her generation married. The young Reverend Ephraim Peabody, who that year was assisting the great Unitarian luminary William Ellery Channing at his nearby Federal Street Church, officiated at the simple ceremony.

There is no record of the Hooper courtship, though the two most likely met through their families. Robert was already a relation by marriage — his older brother, Samuel Hooper, had wed Ellen's younger sister Anne five years before. Ellen's elder by two years, Robert (whom Ellen often called William in her letters) was a good match from a prominent family, the seventh of nine children of John Hooper, the owner of the largest bank in Marblehead, Massachusetts. The Hoopers had been in America since 1635, and the family fortune was made in the mid-eighteenth century by Robert's grandfather, also named Robert Hooper, a merchant known for his "well-balanced character" and his "great energy and far-reaching sagacity." When he died in 1814, he left his heirs an estate worth over $300,000. The younger Robert did not follow his father and grandfather into business, but chose medicine instead, graduating from Harvard College in 1830 and obtaining his advanced degree in Paris at the Académie Royale de Médecine, where he trained to be an oculist (meaning an ophthalmologist). Oliver Wendell Holmes, a fellow Bostonian and a poet whose son would become a justice of the U.S. Supreme Court, was a classmate and close friend. A miniature portrait painted while Robert was studying in Paris shows a sober, perhaps bashful young man with reddish-blond hair, a narrow face, a distinctive long nose, and large, soft blue eyes.

Caroline Sturgis thought Robert too conservative, too staid, too much a man of an earlier generation, not worthy of her oldest sister. Margaret

Fuller declared Robert a bore and found it baffling that Ellen, whom she thought had been so "gifted by Nature" with beauty and intellect, had joined herself to a man "so inferior to her," once referring to Robert as that "dull man to whom [Ellen] had so unhappily bound herself." Fuller liked to pronounce on her friends' marriages, either idealizing a union, as she did initially with Nathaniel and Sophia Hawthorne, or disparaging it, as she did with the Hoopers. In any case, others had a different opinion of the Hoopers. The Reverend Peabody, who knew the couple well, thought the match "one of the happy marriages," inferring that Robert's "well-balanced and even temperament" gave support for Ellen's more "variable feelings to rest upon." Robert's caution and his more retiring nature might have seemed dull to Caroline Sturgis and Margaret Fuller but appealing to Ellen, promising ballast after a tumultuous childhood. In any case, their attachment proved powerful. Eight years after they had married, Ellen wrote this to Robert from Boston while he was traveling in Virginia: "You cannot tell how your letter made me feel—I have longed so to be with you that it seems as if I could annihilate space and time to come." Confessing that she had told her friends of her longing for him, she also reported their bemused response: "People tell me how beautiful it is and laugh at me." Clearly, Ellen adored her husband.

In the late 1830s and early 1840s, the young Sturgis-Hooper families enjoyed a close weave, living only blocks apart in the fashionable neighborhood east of the Boston Common, near Captain Sturgis's mansion at 52 Summer Street. Ellen and Robert Hooper lived at 44 Summer Street, between Washington Street and Charles Bulfinch's New South Church at Church Green; Anne and Sam Hooper lived around the corner of Church Green at 21 South Street. When James Freeman Clarke, the liberal Unitarian preacher known for his knowledge of German philosophy and his passionate commitment to social reform, organized a new congregation, the United Church of the Disciples, in 1841, he asked both Hooper families to join, an invitation they readily accepted.

Secure members of Boston's social elite, the Sturgis-Hooper families were also part of an extraordinarily fertile movement of new thinking, what Ralph Waldo Emerson called "a search for principles." Contesting the religious and social certainties of an earlier generation, the movement came to be known as Transcendentalism, a diverse collection of philosophies and attitudes about both the individual and the relationship of the individual to society that centered on the question "How should we now live?" This group of midcentury thinkers, ministers, writers, activists, and teachers coalesced into a somewhat coherent movement that claimed, in the words of one of their leaders, George Ripley, that "the truth of religion does not depend on tradition or on historical facts, but has an unerring witness in the soul." For Transcendentalists, "there is light . . . which enlighteneth every man that cometh into the world."

Although Robert Hooper sympathized with many key principles of Transcendentalism and especially advocated for social reform that would benefit those less fortunate, he never participated as directly in the intellectual and writing circles of the new movement as did his wife, Ellen, and her sisters Anne and Caroline. The Sturgis sisters were in the first group of two dozen women who joined Margaret Fuller at her weekly "Conversations," first convened in November 1839 and eventually held in the front room of Elizabeth Palmer Peabody's bookshop and subscription library at 13 West Street, a short walk from Robert and Ellen's home. What started as an experiment in women's education became increasingly popular with each successive series. Fuller had been educated to, and beyond, the standard for contemporary men of the elite, and she wanted to give women the chance to hone their abilities to think and speak clearly for themselves. Her intent for the first series of discussions, about Greek mythology, theater, and philosophy, was to foster open discussion for women, in the style of Socratic inquiry.

The appropriate role for women was much debated at this time, an outgrowth of the Transcendentalists' questioning of received religious ideas and the energy and activism of the abolitionists and other reform-minded groups. If religious practice and society needed to change, what part might women play in this transformation? Fuller's Conversations boldly engaged this issue. Once, when Fuller asked whether there was a distinction between men and women with regard to "character and mind," Ellen replied that a woman was "instinctive" and had "spontaneously what men have by study, reflection, and induction." Like her sister Caroline, whom Henry James would later describe as "light, free, somewhat intellectually perverse," Ellen was curious and unafraid of challenging questions.

But Ellen's character was not essentially rebellious. Whereas Margaret Fuller would move during her prolific career from the inner world of introspection toward the outer world of social action, a trajectory taken by many Transcendentalists, Ellen stayed within the private realm. Emerson noted in his journals that Ellen "sympathized with the Transcendental movement, but she sympathized even more with the objectors." When asked by Maria Weston Chapman, the editor of the annual gift book *The Liberty Bell,* to contribute "some writing" for the abolitionist publication, Ellen declined, replying that if she wished "to give voice to any feelings on the subject of slavery, I should prefer a different channel."

Ellen turned, instead, to poetry, where she could fully explore confidential moments and everyday feelings. She wasn't dabbling in the pastime of verse in the way that was then fashionable. Her effort was more serious. She published her poems, as did her sister Caroline, in *The Dial,* the leading journal of Transcendentalism, founded by Fuller and Emerson in 1840. Like Emily Dickinson, eighteen years her junior, Ellen tried to discover through poetic language something about inner life, about death, about the human condition. She wanted transport: "By all thou causest me to long for, oh my God / I feel how much thou hast to give." And renewal: "Open thine inner eye, thine inner ear— / A mother's low and loving under-tone / Breathes through the universe for who can hear." If hers was a poetry that searched for meaning and solace, her sensibility refused easy answers, attuned as she was to the mystery at the heart of things, what she once called a "world-old harmony." At the end of a six-stanza poem on death, her most frequent theme, she ponders the life of a "helpless babe" who "could not choose but be" and "Drinks at Creation's flow, / Then, sudden, vanisheth along / The way we do not know!" A dense, penetrating prose poem that imagines life "a wild dream full of horrors" concludes that "the children of earth groan under the experiences of a life or an age of evil and awake at last deep and safe in the beginning and heart of all—."

Ellen's reading of the Romantic poets, most likely Keats, Shelley, and Blake, inspired her choice of topics, but she made such cultural influences her own. An insistent melancholy in her poems, a trace of losses endured and losses anticipated, is balanced with a hard-won realism about the demands of life for a woman. "I slept, and dreamed that life was Beauty;

/ I woke, and found that life was Duty," is how she begins her most well-known and frequently anthologized poem. However much Ellen longed for what the educator and writer Elizabeth Palmer Peabody memorably called "a more interior revolution," she did so under the long shadow cast by a mother who had left her husband and children to somehow save herself. Rescue, Ellen knew too well, was no simple thing. She searched instead for truth and freedom not outside of but within her close domestic circle; in a word, Ellen's husband and three children were the heart of her life.

The Hoopers' eldest daughter, also named Ellen but called "Nella" or "Nellie," was born in 1838; Edward, or "Ned," was born a year afterward; and Clover followed four years later on September 13, 1843. Ellen delighted in her children, writing her husband that they "are very happy together, and so far, it could not go better for them." Robert jotted down their funny sayings, once recording how Nellie asked him to come and "sit at the parlor window and I'll count those that pass by on our sidewalk and you those that pass on the opposite one—and we'll let Clover count the dogs." But Ellen also worried about the children and took note of their strengths and weaknesses, with an eye toward their improvement. Nellie had a reputation for "a certain bravado" in her manner, as reported to Ellen by her sister, Susan Sturgis, and whenever Nellie stayed with her Hooper relatives, "their entire devotion produces in Nellie an entire self-importance." Ned was his older sister's opposite and more like his father—retiring, less skilled with people. His mother could be both pleased with and concerned about him at once: "gracious, ineffable Eddy," Ellen wrote to Susan, is "one side angel, one side simpleton as usual."

Clover, with her straight, light brown hair and round eyes, mostly escaped such sorting out in her mother's letters. The trait her mother made most note of was the young girl's boundless enthusiasm, as on her fifth birthday, when Clover became "nearly wild with delight" at the "ornamented high cake," which was topped with a white flag inscribed with her name. Ellen heaped affection on all her children, but she seemed to reserve something extra for her youngest. Once, when anxious about leaving her husband and children for a short trip to New York, Ellen implored her husband to give hugs to all the children, but gave him special instructions for Clover. "Give kisses," Ellen wrote, "on her eyes and ears and lips and the tip of her little nose."

Ellen had developed an inner strength that helped foster the growth of both her sisters and her own children, but she could not defeat her own ill health no matter how hard she tried. Several years before her marriage, Ellen had contracted consumption, at the time the more common name for tuberculosis, and she went through numerous cycles of sickness and remission. The gap between Ned's birth in 1839 and Clover's four years later indicates that her illness had flared up for a time — her first two pregnancies may have reignited a simmering tubercular infection. Her illness may also explain why she felt Clover was her "lucky" child — she probably hadn't anticipated another because of her illness. In any case, by the time Ellen was pregnant with Clover in the spring of 1843, she was in remission, writing in mid-May to her sister Caroline, who was staying for several weeks with the Emersons in Concord, that "I long since abandoned the black couch, am now restored to the usual duties of a mistress and parent and member of society . . . I am getting strong, ride, and walk."

But Ellen's letters soon enough vacillate between reporting that she's feeling better and that she's feeling worse. "Air, give me air / I am fainting here," she pleads in an undated poem.

Tuberculosis was the most potent killer in antebellum America, responsible for one-fifth of all deaths. Its symptoms were specific: fatigue, pallor, bloody cough, fever, swollen glands, and dramatic weight loss. But treatments varied greatly. If a total cure remained unlikely, remission always seemed a possibility, within reach of just one more new regimen, one more medicine. Doctors prescribed everything from iodine, mercury, nitric acid, cod liver oil, bed rest, and a bland nutritious diet to vigorous exercise, including riding horseback, which was thought to jostle and clear the lungs. Doctors also recommended a change of climate, particularly when the patient was a well-born New Englander who could afford an escape from damp air and a drafty house.

By early 1848, Ellen and her husband, desperate about the state of her health, fled Boston's forbidding weather in the hopes that the warmer climate of Savannah, Georgia, might help her condition improve. They took along their oldest children but decided that Clover, not yet five, was too young for the arduous journey and left her behind with her twenty-two-year-old Aunt Susan and grandfather Sturgis, both of whom had a special fondness for the child. After arriving in Georgia, Ellen thanked her sister Susan "for your attentions to my baby — I love to hear all she says." In April, Ellen asked her father that no one correct Clover's pronunciation — "I shall be very sorry to find her precocious in that respect when I return" — later exclaiming to him that she was "delighted to hear so good account from my Clover." In another letter, she included a note for her daughter, who was learning to read. Calling her "my precious silver grey," the color of a horse, she wrote, "I love you as much as ever. I hear you are well and good." She added, "I see your little stems of legs trotting up and down stairs."

Ellen and Robert Hooper expressed a measured hope about her health to her father. Robert wrote first, to say they had made "frequent excursions in the saddle and I think that at each successive one Ellen goes further and returns less fatigued than at the preceding. I perhaps deceive myself but if I do not, Ellen is better than when we left home." Ellen concurred: "I think I am much better." She was eager to allay the fears of her father: "I cough hardly at all," she assured him, "and I hope to throw off the remnant. But I am satisfied it was best to have come." By mid-June, however, when Ellen went with her family to Horn Pond at Woburn for a stay at her father's summer home, she was no better. Captain Sturgis worried to Caroline that Ellen "is about the same as when you saw her," saying, "I *hope* to get her in a better state by the pure air of Woburn, though I am not free from serious apprehensions about her."

At a certain point, Ellen knew she was dying. Her poems are filled alternately with the dread of leaving — "Oh no, too soon, too perfect, and too deep / Must come the sleep of Death to my young heart" — and a resolution to find strength in the inevitable: "Now I think I've stood so long / By my own cold clay, / I can back with spirit strong / And bear what for me may — ." Ellen asked that her letters be kept for her daughters, hoping her words might one day "have interest" for them, but also gave them permission to set her writing aside — "If they do not wish the trouble of looking them over, they can burn them unread." She must have been acutely aware that she was leaving her children to an unbridgeable sadness. On Friday, November 3, 1848, Ellen was at home with her husband and her sister Susan at her bedside. There is no record of who else might have been there or where the Hooper children were that day. At four-thirty in the afternoon, Ellen briefly woke and said with a weak voice: "Patience! Patience!" Robert, wishing at this point for his wife to find release after her long illness, asked, "Cannot you go to sleep?" She replied, "It is not time yet." But a half hour later, at five o'clock, Ellen died. She was thirty-six years old.

Ephraim Peabody, who had officiated at the Hoopers' wedding eleven years before and who by the time of Ellen's death had become the minister at King's Chapel, presided at her funeral. She was buried three days later next to her brother, William Junior, in Mount Auburn Cemetery in Cambridge, in the Sturgis family plot. A small marble headstone with a rounded top and the etched initials E.S.H. marks her grave. That night, Peabody recalled the events of the day: "To-day I read beside her coffin, amidst her mourning friends, the words of Christ: 'I am the resurrection and the life.'" He noted that in her last year, beset by discouragement and crushing pain, any easy religious sentiment had been burned away and she had became "almost a mystic."

Ellen's youngest sister, Susan, wrote to a close friend in the days following the funeral. "How the sunlight crinkles up the wall in the early afternoon and the nightly shadows fall so heavy on my heart because her low voice is hushed forever." She spoke of a loss for which she could find no end: "[Ellen] heard my prayers, when I was a child, and took care of me and [then] she was my baby for many years up to the hour I saw her die. She was mother and sister and home to me. She was beautiful and kind and delicate and lovely and she is dead and the world does seem very dark and empty without her and the wound deepens every day." Reverend Peabody worried about Robert Hooper, imagining that "his saddest days were yet to come" and that memories of the past would not be able to shut out a looming "loneliness of the present."

To have death settle in so close must have been terrifying to five-year-old Clover. She had neither the capacity to reason nor the comfort of an adult's religious faith, and, unlike her Aunt Sue, she had no way to make an account of her loss with words. She likely had a child's belief that wishing can bring back the dead, that magic or good behavior can find a remedy. Clover's older sister, Ellen, would mention her mother in letters, remembering the sound of her low voice and how she expressed herself. Ned later collected his mother's poetry and had eight copies of the collection privately printed as a memorial to her. By contrast, there is little record that Clover wrote or talked about her mother.

But when Clover finally started taking photographs thirty-five years after her mother's death, she often captured images of maternal figures, as if to bring her own mother back into view and back to life.

CHAPTER 2

The Hub of the Universe

IN 1847, THE YEAR before Clover's mother died, Clover's Aunt Sue had married Dr. Henry J. Bigelow, a leading surgeon at Massachusetts General Hospital. The newlyweds set up housekeeping at 2 Chauncy Place, around the corner from the Hoopers. With jet-black hair and large hooded eyes, Sue was an attractive woman and fragile, given to occasional bouts of moodiness and self-doubt. She seems to have had neither Caroline's ambition and focus nor Ellen's penchant for domestic life, but she was tender-hearted, and after her beloved sister's death, she promised to "take all the care I can here of [Ellen's] little child . . . I love Clovy. I would give a world to have her and keep her—she's just like Ellen, I do think she is." By all accounts, Aunt Sue indeed took special care, letting Clover stay at her house for extended visits. In the year after Ellen's death, she took note of Clover's play-acting, telling her sister Caroline that the young girl "dresses up like a beggar-woman and remarks plaintively that her destitute infants 'ain't dot no party-dresses.'" This vignette of a young girl, bereft of her mother, play-acting poverty and want struck the attentive aunt as both "sad and touching."

Apart from such family visits, Clover lived with her father, brother, and sister at the family home at 44 Summer Street. Ned Hooper would remember that his father's "religious feelings were strong and constant," but that he "rarely expressed them otherwise than by his personal character and conduct." Clover's father didn't go much to church, though he owned pew number 45 in King's Chapel. He never remarried, which was unusual for a man with three small children. Dr. Hooper seems to have kept his grief mostly to himself, prizing a muted toleration of catastrophe as part of genteel tradition. In the top drawer of his desk, he kept a piece of paper on which he had written in French a statement by George Sand: "good breeding meant that we hid our suffering."

Instead, when not performing his medical duties, Clover's father devoted his time to his family and to humanitarian work, bringing his "well-balanced and even temperament" to his relations with his children and recruiting from others what he couldn't provide himself. Betsey Wilder, who became a housekeeper for the Hoopers close to the time of Clover's birth, became a cherished presence in the family, often accompanying Clover during her summers away from Boston when she was separated from her father. Betsey would be Clover's most consistent mother figure, though little is known about her except for her devotion to the Hooper children. The Hoopers also depended on nearby family. In addition to Aunt Sue around the corner, Captain Sturgis lived just a few houses down the street, as did the three children of Samuel and Anne Hooper, Clover's uncle and aunt. William, Annie, and Alice Hooper were more like siblings than cousins to Nellie, Ned, and Clover, and all were close in age; William, the oldest cousin, was ten years older than Clover, who was the youngest. Their double relation gave the six children the same set of grandparents and family history. They lived in the same neighborhood, vacationed together, and, when apart, wrote letters back and forth.

From age five to twelve, Clover attended Miss Houghton's school with her sister, Nellie, and, most likely, her cousins Annie and Alice. Not much is known about Miss Houghton or her educational establishment, but the curriculum probably included reading, arithmetic, natural history, composition, American history, and languages, as well as lessons in social refinement for girls: sewing, drawing, music, and dance. At eleven, Clover proudly told Nellie that Miss Houghton had lent her a French novel, *Du Château,* to read over the summer break. Summers were spent outside the city to get away from its potent smells, stifling heat, and the threat of disease. Clover lived for months at a time with one side of her family or the other, for the first several years after her mother's death with Grandfather Sturgis at Horn Pond in Woburn and with her Aunt Eunice Hooper at Marblehead, and later in Lenox where Caroline Sturgis, whom Clover called "Aunt Cary," married since 1847 to William Aspinwell Tappan, had a summer home. Clover's father at some point would build an unpretentious second home in Beverly Farms on Boston's rocky North Shore where the family would gather for months at a time.

The young girl's summers have the atmosphere of an idyll. When just seven and staying with her Sturgis aunts at Horn Pond, Clover wrote about gathering blackberries with the women in the family: "I got a box full that is to hold a quart. I got my dress stained a great deal which I was very glad of because it looked just as if I had been berrying." When she was older, she wrote newsy letters from wherever she was ensconced, telling of tea parties with friends, theatricals, dances, hours spent playing the card game whist, and leisurely evening walks. Her summer days matched the description in the opening pages of Henry James's 1878 novel *Daisy Miller:* "a flitting hither and thither of 'stylish' young girls, a rustling of muslin flounces, a rattle of dance-music in the morning hours." She always had sewing in hand at the end of the day; one summer she announced to her sister, "I am taking painting lessons which delights both my heart and eyes." She swam and rowed and at a moment's notice would saddle her horse for a jaunt along country roads and through nearby woods.

But there were darker currents. Clover's Aunt Sue had separated from her husband, Dr. Bigelow, at some point in 1851, a development that Sue tried to write about in a letter to her sister Caroline, saying that "under the *present* circumstances I find all places where I go quite similar in one respect — i.e. — Henry is not in them — suffice it to say. He is gone and I have consented." But she could not explain further: "The personal experiences resulting from these facts are not easily narrated in a letter." As she'd said to a friend a year after her marriage, she felt she'd made a "pact with loneliness."

By the spring of 1853, the marriage was irretrievable. On June 9, while staying with her father, Captain Sturgis, at the family's summer home at

Horn Pond, Sue killed herself by drinking arsenic. The next day's papers reported her "sudden death." She was twenty-seven years old. Her only child, William Sturgis Bigelow, had just turned three that spring. Rumors circulated: that she was pregnant at the time of her death, that Dr. Bigelow had been unfaithful to her, that Clover had been staying at Horn Pond at the time and had witnessed her Aunt Sue's death. Whether or not this was the case, the loss devastated Clover, who at the time was nine years old. Her Aunt Sue had stepped in after the death of Clover's mother, caring for her and showing that she understood her, perhaps in ways that others did not.

On hearing of the calamity, Waldo Emerson, as he was known to friends, advised Clover's Aunt Cary that strength was the family's only option: "Generally, we must rely on that tough fibre, which makes the substratum of all strong individuals, — whose 'time and hour wear through the roughest day.'" Yet a young girl who had already lost her mother had no time to develop what Emerson called "a tranquility of the heart too deep to be shaken."

The next summer, 1854, Clover's sister traveled overseas for her Grand Tour of European sights. Dark-haired and petite like her mother, Nellie, age seventeen, took seriously her role as older sister — various family members would, from time to time, give her reports on Clover's behavior and mood, clearly expecting her interest. Now, in Nellie's absence, Clover feared her sister might forget her, might abandon her too. She appended an anxious note at the end of a joint family letter: "My dear Miss Hooper," Clover pleaded archly, "I write to remind you that you have a sister in existence and that sister would be grateful for any consolatory epistle that may convince her that the aforementioned lady is aware of the fact that she has a sister in America." The next month Clover admitted her jealousy on hearing that Nellie had written a friend "before me so I called you a villain and all kinds of things." Clover was joking, as was her way, but fear reverberated in her words. She hated being alone.

The following year, 1855, Clover's Aunt Cary left for an extended tour of Europe with her husband of seven years and their two young daughters, Ellen and Mary. They didn't return for five years, staying in Paris, Dresden, Rome, and Florence in the winters and summering in the Apennines and the Alps. Caroline had been far more active in the Transcendental movement than had Clover's mother. She had grown to be Margaret Fuller's closest friend and an intimate of Nathaniel Hawthorne. Waldo Emerson called Caroline, with whom he'd had an ardent erotic friendship, "my Muse." She painted, published books for young readers, and continued writing poetry, and while in Europe she would collect magnificent photographic prints by Giuseppe Ninci and Julia Margaret Cameron. Aunt Cary, who wrote to Clover from Europe and would later invite her to social gatherings, offered Clover a vital link to the lively, intellectual Sturgis side of her family, and what must have been a valued proximity to memories of her mother. Her disappearance from Clover's daily life for five years must have seemed another severed connection.

At one point during these years, Clover fought with her cousin Alice Hooper, though the exact nature of the conflict remains unclear. Clover could be sensitive about responses to her letters, and she expected a prompt and fulsome reply; she frequently urged correspondents to answer immediately and write everything they knew. Perhaps Alice hadn't answered a letter. Or maybe they disagreed over something else. In any case, Clover felt angry enough to declare in a letter, "As for Alice I can hardly bring myself to write her now. Hereafter and forever all my letters will be inscribed to Aunt Anne, Annie, and Willie, give my love to the last 3." Vacillating between needing too much and an impulse to dismissiveness, Clover pushed away those she loved when her roiling feelings became hard to manage.

By 1857, the Hooper family had moved away from their home on Summer Street, around the corner from where Aunt Sue had lived, to a distinguished brownstone at 107 Beacon Street, located in a growing neighborhood near the northwest corner of what would soon become the city's Public Garden. That same year, Boston had begun an ambitious program to fill in the Back Bay, a marshy tidal basin, and thus increase the city's landmass. Dr. Hooper may have favored the new home's more spacious proportions and its convenient location. Clover's cousins, Annie and Alice Hooper, lived up the street at 56 Beacon Street, and the neighborhood was closer to Clover and Nellie's new school in Cambridge, which the girls had started attending in the fall of 1855. But Clover's father may have also thought it time to move his young family away from the sorrows of their old neighborhood.

Something of Clover's mental and emotional state during these years might be detected in an undated scrap of her writing composed after the move to Beacon Street. Adopting the tropes and imagery of the gothic novels she was probably reading, Clover drafted a spoof of her own death, which she sent off to her cousin Annie Hooper. "The ring accompanying this note," Clover tells her recipient, "was willed to Annie M. Hooper by the owner M. Hooper [*M* for Marian, Clover's little-used given name] on the night preceding her decease. A bronze tea caddy was also included in the bequest on the night of the 6th of January 1857." As in the opening of a noir murder mystery, the victim—Clover—is brutally killed.

She passed the evening at number 56 Beacon St., her house was at 107, the same street. It was a bitter cold night and the wind howled most fearfully as the time drew near for her departure she felt a presentiment of death stealing upon her, and was loath to depart, but at last summoning up all her courage she set forth, attended only by one of the masculine tribe. She had passed in safety the three first crossings below Charles Street when arriving at the last crossing a sudden gust of wind, caught her nose—that being the most prominent feature of her body, and whirling her through the air dashed her up the frozen waters of Back Bay the servant was seized by a contrary wind and drowned in the waters of the River Charles. A milkman riding in from the country on Wednesday morning discovered her body lying upon the ice [and] on looking at the face he discovered that it was minus a nose and whilst returning in perplexity to the land he perceived a nose minus a head. A Coroner's Inquest will be held upon the body this afternoon at 3 o'clock precisely. Price of tickets 25 cents, children half price 12 cents. The tea caddy will be forked over subsequent to the inquest, enclosed in this note is a passem of blue for her funereal riggings, that color being most becoming to her style of beauty, a customary speech of hers was it's a weary world we live in, and her last speech just before reaching the 4th crossing was changed to "it's a windy world we live in." P.S. All arrangements entrusted to Miss A. M. Hooper will please be attended to promptly.

In this imaginative writing, illustrating a close acquaintance with the customs and language of funerals, Clover joined her mother and Aunt Sue in death. By making her long Hooper nose the cause of her fictional death, her satire reveals too how she hated feeling unattractive, feared being the plain-looking daughter of a mother everyone recognized as classically beautiful. The losses of Clover's childhood, its grief and uncertainties, had begun to thicken into a self-loathing she sometimes had a difficult time shaking off. Pictures of her as a young girl show her bright intense eyes, her father's long nose, reddish or dark blonde hair, and a slender face tilted ever so slightly, giving her a quizzical look. But only a few photographs of Clover as a grown woman survive, and none with a clear view of her face. Several years before her marriage, she is pictured seated on her horse at a far distance, her face mostly obscured. In photographs taken during her honeymoon, Clover bowed her head or turned away from the camera. In an undated tintype of Clover — in profile, holding one of her dogs — her face is mostly hidden. She had pulled her straw hat over it.

Education rescued Clover. The new Agassiz School in Cambridge, an academy for girls, had been organized in 1855 by Elizabeth Cary Agassiz, the second wife of Harvard's acclaimed professor of zoology and geology, Louis Agassiz, and later the first president of Radcliffe College. Just as Clover turned twelve, she and her sister, Nellie, began taking the forty-minute ride by horse-drawn omnibus every morning across the Charles River for classes held in the spacious attic rooms of the Agassiz's house at the corner of Quincy Street and Broadway, next to Harvard College. Clover's classmates included Ralph Waldo Emerson's oldest daughter, Ellen; the abolitionist Wendell Phillips's adopted daughter, Phoebe; the architect Henry Greenough's daughter, Fanny; and the Agassizes' younger daughter, Pauline, who would be one of Clover's close friends at school.

Elizabeth Agassiz believed that a young girl's education should include subjects beyond those aimed at cultural refinement, the traditional curriculum for daughters of the elite: literature, music, and foreign languages. The Agassiz curriculum added geography, natural history, biology, anthropology, and mathematics. Classes were rigorous and their content was up-to-date, as several were taught by Harvard professors. At the close of the morning sessions, Professor Agassiz himself would give his daily lecture on botany, zoology, and embryology, wanting to show, as one student remembered, "the thoughts in Nature which Science reveals." It was the best education a young girl could receive in Boston, and possibly all of America.

Clover's grandfather, Captain Sturgis, now called his favorite granddaughter "a good scholar." Academic study drew out Clover's strength and her curiosity as well as the enthusiasm her mother had noted early on. Quick and ambitious, she was gifted at languages and found the natural sciences fascinating. Clover's later passion for flowers was most likely nurtured by memorizing the classifications of plants and by Mrs. Agassiz's own fervor for botany. She filled the schoolroom with fresh flowers for the children. Clover's geography teacher, Catharine L. Howard (called Kate), only ten years older than Clover when she began teaching at the school in 1856, may have recognized something familiar in her bright, eager student, having also lost her own mother when very young. Several years after Clover had been her student, Miss Howard would ask a friend what perhaps other teachers and students wondered: "Was there ever anyone like Clover?"

Clover liked to sign her letters "Clover leaf," this name a prized gift from her mother, or with a drawing of a four-leaf clover. Above her signature, she'd sometimes write "the Hub." She was referring to Boston's moniker "the hub of the universe," a term coined in 1858 by Oliver Wendell Holmes in his monthly column in the *Atlantic Monthly*. When away from home, Ned asked Clover to "write me often giving names, dates, and further particulars from the 'Hub,'" but advised her to remember that those living in the "'Hub' don't know everything."

Clover loved being at the center of things, and how she grew had been shaped by being at the center of a city during extraordinary years of gogetting, reform, and creative achievement. The 1850 census of Boston shows the population at a bit below 140,000. The city teemed with the energies of abolitionist politics, Unitarian reform, and Transcendental individualism. There had been a "flowering"—in the literary critic Van Wyck Brooks's well-known formulation—of creative genius. Figures such as Ralph Waldo Emerson, Margaret Fuller, Nathaniel Hawthorne, James Russell Lowell, Bronson Alcott, and Henry Wadsworth Longfellow won enduring fame, to be sure, but numerous other Boston-area writers and reformers, preachers and scientists, including Elizabeth Palmer Peabody, Lydia Maria Child, Theodore Parker, James Freeman Clarke, Dorothea Dix, Oliver Wendell Holmes, Asa Gray, and Louis Agassiz, were widely influential in their day. The Boston Athenaeum's art gallery—first opened in 1827—now held shows of American and European art throughout the year. The Handel and Haydn Society, an amateur ensemble, had been started by merchants in 1815 to bring choral music to American audiences, and the Boston Academy of Music had formed a first-rate orchestra, often packing and even overflowing Odeon Hall. The Boston firm called Ticknor and Fields was transforming American publishing. A correspondent for a book trade magazine wrote in 1856 that "no other establishment in the Union issues annually a more attractive and carefully selected list of *belles lettres.*" The city was home to the country's leading literary journals, the *North American Review* and the *Atlantic Monthly;* the Boston Public Library opened its doors in 1854; bookstores dotted the city's neighborhoods. Public lectures on literature, philosophy, science, politics, reform, religion, and a host of other topics proliferated, sponsored by the Lowell Institute, men's debating associations, women's literary clubs, and numerous other organizations, churches, and colleges.

The debate about slavery, which would soon split the nation, had drawn "a line of cleavage through all Boston society," and the gathering forces of social change—industrialization, immigration, and expansion into the West—began to shake the confidence of Boston's Brahmins. Even so, when the great English novelist Charles Dickens visited Boston and nearby Cambridge in 1842, a year before Clover's birth, he observed and later recorded in his *American Notes* that "the almighty dollar sinks into something comparatively insignificant, amidst a whole Pantheon of better gods." What Dickens admired was the effort to learn, to teach, to achieve, and to build lasting institutions that fulfilled the promises of liberty. All of this striving, of course, was underwritten by generations of wealth — from trade, finance, cotton, manufacturing — which enabled Bostonians to invest not only in the city but in the rest of the country. Living in Boston meant being connected to the nation and beyond. Young men who had earlier gone off to sea and returned transformed by their travels now worked on the railroads, studied art and philosophy in Europe, and settled western towns to check the spread of slavery. They came back to the city with deepened knowledge and experience, with talents and stories.

A young privileged woman like Clover Hooper — educated, but without any clear path laid for her future, struggling with feelings that she had few ways to articulate — would live such adventures vicariously through reading, lectures, and conversation. And she would be a front-row witness to the coming war.

CHAPTER 3

Clover's War

DURING HER SIX YEARS at the Agassiz School, Clover studied hard, immersing herself in math, botany, and zoology. She read Shakespeare's plays and Tennyson's poetry, learned German, and became fluent in French. Perhaps in homage to her mother's own interest in Greek history, she developed a lifelong passion for reading and translating Latin and Greek poetry. But she was no recluse, and she engaged in the usual whirl of activities enjoyed by young girls of her social class: theater, concerts, teas and dinners at the homes of friends. If she feared closeness because it held potential for loss, she loved telling a good story or joke. Occasionally, Clover can be glimpsed in other people's diaries and letters—a quick flash of her skirt as she rounds a corner. Elizabeth Rogers Mason, a close friend of Clover's sister, Nellie, described in her diary an evening of theatricals, meaning amateur stage plays, at the North Shore home of Samuel and Eliza Cabot, Mason's future in-laws. The Cabot house, Mason wrote, was "a model one for the country home, and the little greenhouse which serves as a passage way to the theater, enchanting, full of drooping vines and beautiful flowers, and lighted by colored lanterns." Observing that the plays were "excellent," Mason also noted that the young "Clover Hooper sat in front of me."

By the time Clover graduated at age seventeen in the spring of 1861, however, her attention had turned to the news of the day. The nation was on the brink of a full-scale civil war. In January, the secession of the South had begun, with seven states withdrawing from the Union. Though Boston was far from the front lines, the city was gripped by war fever. The debate about slavery had pitted abolitionists against the manufacturing interests of Boston's commercial elite, particularly those depending on southern cotton for their textile mills. On April 17, five days after the Confederate attack on Fort Sumter, soldiers of the Massachusetts Militia (later known as the Sixth Regiment), equipped with new rifles and new gray overcoats, marched through Boston streets to board trains for Washington, D.C. There they would protect the nation's capital, which was precariously positioned between North and South. "Nobody thinks of anything but war," a neighbor of the Hoopers wrote on April 23, adding that "there is no more bunting to be bought in Boston" and "the importer was out of toy-flags."

Clover was beside herself with excitement. On May 8, she wrote a consoling letter to her cousin Annie Hooper, who was away from the city and missing all the news. "I don't wonder you are home-sick," Clover empathized on stationery with a STAND BY THE FLAG emblem in its upper left corner. "Nothing whatever would have tempted me to lose these last 3 weeks in Boston. I've had a splendid time—we literally gorge ourselves with newspapers." With her family she toured the steam frigate *Minnesota* at the Boston navy yards, with its "600 sailors and two rows of enormous dull green guns," and noticed Captain Van Brunt, whom she thought "splendid looking" in his navy uniform. She, her sister Nellie, and their friends immediately started cutting and sewing fabric to make apparel for the soldiers, and she scolded Annie: "Don't for mercy's sake make any more red flannel shirts—they have been forbidden to our troops as making them a mark for the enemy. Bluish gray is the color ordered."

Every family experienced the war in some way. Clover's father had been asked by the Massachusetts governor, John A. Andrew, earlier in the year to serve as a founding member of the Boston Educational Commission (later renamed the New England Freedmen's Aid Society), a group organized to address the immediate needs of recently freed slaves who sought protection and aid from the Union army. The organization raised money for bedding, clothes, food, and emergency health care in the early years of the war, later shifting its focus to education. Clover—like many young women—joined Boston's New England Women's Auxiliary Association (NEWAA), a soldiers' relief group of the U.S. Sanitary Commission, which, in the words of the commission's 1864 report, depended on "the never-failing fountains of woman's sympathy and aid for the sick and wounded." The group rolled bandages, knit socks, sewed blankets, collected medicines and money for the troops—tasks that gave them some tangible way to participate and contribute. Clover reported to her father that, with Alice Mason Hooper, the young wife of her cousin William Sturgis Hooper, she had been to "Dr. Howe's 'Sanitary' rooms and stamped blankets, towels, etc. from 1 o'clock till 4½. The store was cold and dark and though it was hard work, we like it."

In spite of Clover's enthusiasm for war work, she retreated from the city to the Berkshire Mountains the first summer of the conflict, taking the train 130 miles west and staying by herself for several nights at the largest hotel in Stockbridge. It was not unheard of for a young woman to travel alone, but it was not common practice either. In a letter Clover assured her father that the bed at the hotel was "very nice," the food was first-rate—"berries, salmon, good bread and butter"—and that she "shan't be lonely." Her brother, Ned, planned to arrive four days later to be her chaperone, and she visited almost daily with her Aunt Cary, who had returned with her family from their European travels the previous year.

Aunt Cary, still brilliant, increasingly complicated, often unhappy in her marriage, loved to talk and entertain—Henry James once said she was "insatiably hospitable." To her father, Clover described a typical summer day, often spent at Aunt Cary's spacious Lenox property, which had been bought in 1849 and was later known as Tanglewood. "The weather has been intensely warm here all the week so that muslins are the only wearable things," Clover reported. With family and friends, she relished sitting outdoors "since breakfast, laughing and sewing, eating New York candy and shelling peas for dinner." Aunt Cary also introduced Clover to her friends. In August 1861, Clover went along to a soiree hosted by Catharine Sedgwick, the famed author of the widely popular novels *A New England Tale* and *Hope Leslie,* published in the 1820s. Here Clover met Miss Sedgwick's close friend, the famed British-born actress Fanny Kemble. "Miss C. Sedgwick introduced me to Mrs. Kemble & sat me down by her & we talked off and on nearly an hour I should think," Clover exclaimed to her father, sounding very much like a star-struck schoolgirl. "She found I liked rowing . . . whereupon she remarked that she had a boat and would be happy to lend it to me or to have me row *her!!!!* I'm afraid I looked bland, I'm sure I felt so but I won't back down and *I'll* row her if I perish in the attempt."

But as months passed and news from the war grew more ominous, Clover's feelings about it became more ambivalent. By the early spring of 1862, it was clear the conflict wasn't going to be a ninety-day war, as some had originally predicted. Clover wrote to her cousin Annie that, though it had been "nearly a year since the war began," she couldn't quite "realize that we were ever at peace." Even so, there was also something thrilling about war: all the newspaper stories, the parades and soldiers in the streets, the occasions for real-life bravery and heroism. "What fearful times we are living in," she wrote in the summer of 1862 from Lenox, not saying where she was staying. She declared the war "nothing but disaster and excitement on all sides. I really feel ashamed to be having such a good and jolly time. Though I don't know that I can do any good by being blue."

Clover's brother, Ned, had decided not to enlist in a regular army regiment but in the spring of 1862 had instead signed up to go to South Carolina's Sea Islands with Edward Pierce, a young Boston attorney hired by Lincoln's secretary of the treasury, Salmon Chase, to prepare former slaves for — in Chase's words — "self-support by their own industry." Ned, an 1859 graduate of Harvard Law School, knew all too well he didn't have a "natural taste" for active military duty. Clover's cousin William Sturgis Hooper (called "Sturgis" by the family), the older brother of cousins Annie and Alice Hooper, enlisted that same year as a volunteer aide to General Nathanial P. Banks, a former Massachusetts congressman and governor now in charge of the Army in the Gulf, while Clover's more distant cousin Robert Gould Shaw had joined the

Second Massachusetts Infantry at the start of the war (later he would become major, then colonel, of the all-black Fifty-fourth Massachusetts Infantry).

Oliver Wendell Holmes Jr., called "Wendell," the son of Dr. Holmes and a neighbor of the Hoopers at their summer home in Beverly Farms, was commissioned with the Twentieth Massachusetts Volunteer Infantry. Wilky and Bob James, younger brothers of William and Henry James, who had grown up in Cambridge and were part of Clover's social sphere, both enlisted. Clover also met people outside her immediate circle who had joined the military. She found Henry Lee Higginson, a major in the First Massachusetts Cavalry and a charismatic music lover, later founder of the Boston Symphony Orchestra, "cozy and pleasant." She thought Higginson and his best friend, Charles Russell Lowell Jr. (by May 1863, the colonel of the newly formed Second Massachusetts Cavalry), two of the "very nicest men I know."

To keep up-to-date, Clover devoured the newspapers but also heard firsthand news from the young men among her family and friends, who told interesting and dramatic stories of the dangers of war. One of them, William Powell Mason, first caught Clover's eye while she was staying in Lenox in the summer of 1862. Perhaps his attentions accounted for some of her restlessness as well as the fact that she was "having such a good and jolly time." The two had grown up together — the Hooper and Mason families were neighbors in Beverly Farms, and Powell Mason was the brother of Elizabeth Rogers Mason, who was now married to Walter Cabot and who had long been a good friend of Clover's sister. Captain Mason, a Harvard graduate in 1856, served as an aide-de-camp with General George B. McClellan in the early years of the war. His war photograph, included in an album kept by the Hooper family, shows him tall and trim, with a dramatic mustache and wavy dark hair framing beautiful large eyes and the hint of a grin.

In early August, using boot blacking and water instead of ink, which was scarce in wartime, Clover wrote to her sister from Lenox that Captain Mason had stopped by the day before and that he was returning to his regiment the next day. Clover had been worried — "I was very much afraid that I shouldn't see him" — but quickly thereafter Powell came by and shook hands with her. "He looked older and thinner than when I last saw him," she related, going on to report breathlessly to Nellie that the next morning, after breakfast with Aunt Cary, she had come back to her hotel to find that "Powell Mason had been to call. A few minutes after I was moaning over not seeing him and combing my chestnut hair came a bang at my door and announcement of a visitor, when on pumping I found 'he looked to be a Captain.' I sprang to and was down in a wink. He stayed till dinner time and told me a great deal about McClellan."

Later that same evening, Clover and her father "spread a shawl under the elms," and Captain Mason, along with his brother-in-law, Walter Cabot, joined father and daughter, staying three hours. They talked of what had been recently in the papers — General Lee's successful defense of Richmond in what came to be known as the Seven Days Battles. Earlier in the spring General McClellan had shipped his Army of the Potomac to the tip of the Virginia Peninsula, aiming to capture Richmond from its eastern side in order to avoid Lee's troops. But McClellan miscalculated where the rebels were stationed as well as the terrain of the peninsula. Lee attacked the Union army for seven days — from June 25 until July 1, at Mechanicsville, Gaines's Mill, Savage's Station, Frayser's Farm, and Malvern Hill — and pushed McClellan back, defeating Union hopes for a quick war ending in victory.

Clover reported to her sister how Captain Mason "squatted on the shawl by my side and drew and explained the position and disposition of the army in those seven day battles." Mason told Clover that "people at home had no idea of the danger we are in," and he refused to romanticize the battlefield. "I thought he didn't speak as if there were much enjoyment in a soldier's life," Clover reported. "He said he longed for his own vine and fig tree." When he was gone, Clover noted that "his being here seems like a dream — it was like having a person come back from the dead."

If Captain Mason refused to romanticize war, Clover surely thought the tall young soldier a romantic figure, perhaps even a beau. But a romance never blossomed. By March 1863, in a long letter to her Aunt Cary complaining of a "pitiless cold and ulcerated tooth," Clover wondered aloud about how "every friend and acquaintance I have in this world has written in the last two or three months" of their upcoming marriages, decisions that had been sped up by impending service in the war. "Away they go two by two . . . What," Clover joked, "are the symptoms" of imminent marriage? "Are they toothache and cold in the head?" Was she saying that she felt herself at risk for making just such a match or that, at almost twenty years of age, she wanted one? Most likely she felt left out, and she tried to mute her disappointment about her fizzled flirtation with Captain Mason by employing her wit, her most ready tactic to fend off hurt. Now she felt differently about Captain Mason, she announced to Aunt Cary: "He will never be nice again." She scorned how he had become "too inseparable" as aide-de-camp to General McClellan and "too attached" to "a Miss Peabody," whom he eventually married later that fall. "What a dismal prospect," Clover remarked. To shore up her confidence, she decided not to settle for just any man who came along. During an evening chat by the fire with Ida Agassiz, Pauline Agassiz's older sister who had taught French and German lessons at the Agassiz School and who later that December would marry Henry Lee Higginson, Clover pledged to never lower her "standard" as she went on in life.

A "festive spree" that same March gave some respite. Pauline Agassiz, who had married the much older Quincy Adams Shaw in 1860, threw a party for several recently engaged couples and their friends at the barracks of the Massachusetts Fifty-fourth at Camp Meigs, just south of Boston. At the dinner, Clover sat next to Wilky James, a younger brother of William and Henry James and a lieutenant in the regiment, whom she liked "very much." She thought her distant cousin Rob Shaw, the commander, looked "very young and boyish," but his manner conveyed that "he knows what he is about." After a storm with "wind and hail beating on the boards overheard" and imbibing "real nectar and ambrosia," she and the other partygoers visited the various barracks and found "some soldierly looking men standing straight as ram rods" who were of "every shade of color from café au lait to ebony." Listening to them sing "John Brown's Hymn," with its message of defiance and freedom, Clover paused, remarking finally that it was a day "to be remembered."

The war was going badly. Wendell Holmes had been seriously wounded in the Battle of Antietam the previous summer, the bloodiest single day of the war. Over two thousand Union soldiers had been killed and over nine thousand wounded. Trains filled with the dead and wounded traveled from the battlefield back to Boston, where a weekly newspaper, the *Boston Pilot,* described the horror. The dead were "strewn so thickly that as you ride over the field you cannot guide your horse's steps too carefully." The debacle at Chancellorsville, in early May of 1863, cost the Union army over seventeen thousand casualties.

By midsummer, when news traveled back to Boston of the bloodshed at Gettysburg, Dr. Hooper got on the first train available so he could help tend the wounded soldiers on the battlefield. If Clover asked what he had witnessed, he would have protected her from the worst of it. That same month, on July 18, Wilky James sustained grave injuries when he was shot in the ankle and the back in the attack by the Fifty-fourth on the Confederate stronghold of Fort Wagner, near Charleston. He had been standing next to Colonel Robert Shaw, who was shot and killed instantly. Colonel Shaw was buried in a mass grave along with his fallen troops. When efforts were made to retrieve his body, his father, Frank Shaw, resisted this, saying that he could "imagine no holier place than that in which he lies, among his brave and devoted" soldiers.

The man who brought the conflict closest to Clover, though he was not immediately engaged in battle, was her brother, Ned. The two had always gotten along well. Ned was the teasing older brother who referred to Clover as "The Infant." Their natures were complementary: hers fiery, his more temperate. They confided in each other. She depended on him for company and comfort, and they shared common interests in the arts, particularly painting. At one point, Ned had wanted to be an artist, but he didn't think he had the disposition to survive the disappointments endemic to such a career. Taking after his father — gentle, kind, talented, but shy — he didn't have the outsized ambition of his grandfather Captain Sturgis, but his penchant for details and organization made him ideal for his assignment with Edward Pierce on the Sea Islands off the coast of South Carolina.

When he applied to serve there, Ned got a recommendation from James Freeman Clarke, his family's one-time preacher, who wrote in a letter to Pierce that Ned was "a young man every way suited to this work — one of rare conscience, love of usefulness, a religion's purpose." Of the 150 applicants from Boston, 35 were sent to South Carolina with Pierce, along with others from New York, for a total of 53. The group—composed of both men and women—included reformers, medical doctors, engineers, and teachers. They became known as Gideon's Band, and on March 3, 1862, they boarded the steamer *Atlantic* in New York, despite horrible weather. Six days later, they disembarked at Beaufort in Port Royal Sound to join the Union army and Treasury agents charged with overseeing what the government called "contraband," the ten thousand slaves abandoned by their white owners when they fled inland after the Union army captured Port Royal. The tasks were many: establishing a coherent rule of law; providing medical care, religious instruction, and education; harvesting cotton and protecting the fields for the next year's crop; and proving to business leaders in the North that the paid labor of freed slaves would be less expensive than the free labor of slaves.

Ned was assigned to General Pierce as his personal assistant, and he described his experiences to Clover in newsy, affectionate letters. He stayed first at the Eustis plantation on Lady's Island in Port Royal Sound, across the river from Beaufort, marveling at the lush beauty of the blooms, already flourishing in mid-March. "The Island is lovely," Ned wrote, adding details about the foliage because he knew how much his sister loved flowers. "Yellow jasmine everywhere. Roses, orange flowers in spots, etc., etc." Ned also reported on the situation of the recently freed slaves, who were desperate for rations of salt but had "nothing now except their 1 peck of corn a week to each grown person and a proportional quantity to the children. Nothing else is dealt out to them and few of them have money to buy anything else." Ned wrote respectfully of the Negroes, bringing to life and capturing the dignity of a people with whom neither he nor his sister had previously had such direct contact. He helped Clover visualize, in all its daily particulars, the great thing he was witness to—the long-awaited coming of freedom:

When we first reached his [Eustis] plantation we were received with great delight by the negroes, especially by old "Mary Ann," who at once produced her "old missus'" looking glass, which she [Mary Ann] had hidden under her gown when she saw the plunderers come. Soon afterward I saw about half a dozen negro women coming towards the house, two with mahogany tables on their heads and two with chairs and one with two large china dishes, others with andirons, etc. — all things hidden away to prevent their falling into the hands of the soldiers.

By that June, Ned was promoted to military captain on the staff of General Rufus Saxton, the commander named when responsibility for the Port Royal effort moved from the Treasury Department to the War Department. And a year later, Ned's excellent service was recognized. In a newspaper clipping dated June 13, 1863, about the work of the Freedmen's Inquiry Commission, a relief effort organized by the federal government after emancipation, Ned was cited as "diligent, intelligent, courteous, and so admirably adapted and valuable in his service as to merit this prominent mention."

Clover prized her brother's letters because she was proud of him and they connected him to her. But she also relished the front-row seat Ned gave her to what would long fascinate her: the politics and the policy-making of government.

Once the hostilities were over, Clover insisted on going to Washington, D.C., after reading in the Boston papers the announcement that a victory parade was to be held in the capital, a "grand review" of the federal armies, on May 23 and 24. "Then and there," she later wrote to her first cousin, Mary Louisa Shaw, called "Loulie" (and a first cousin to Colonel Shaw), "I vowed to myself that go I would. I begged Father to take me, but he hooted at the idea of such a thing."

Clover finally persuaded Henry Rogers, who was active in the Sanitary Commission, to take her with him to Washington, along with her sister, Nellie, and Rogers's own daughter, Annette. They first tried to make arrangements to stay with Clover and Nellie's uncle, Sam Hooper, a U.S. congressman from Massachusetts since 1861, who lived on the corner at 1501 H Street. But the newly installed president, Andrew Johnson, and his administration were then encamped at the Hooper home to give Mrs. Lincoln time to move out of the White House after her husband's assassination, so there were no available rooms except in a cramped attic. The travelers decided to stay down the street at a house near Willard's Hotel.

Early on Tuesday, May 23, Clover and Nellie made their way to seats on the congressional platform, set up along Pennsylvania Avenue across from the White House; their Uncle Sam had secured these places for them. Under the order of General Grant, the Army of the Potomac, led by General George Meade, would march on May 23, followed the next day by General Sherman's armies of the Tennessee and Georgia, which had formed the left and right wings for his victorious March to the Sea at the end of 1864. It could not have been a more thrilling insider's introduction to the capital city. Now almost twenty-two years old, Clover had no way of knowing that she would call Washington her home sometime in the future.

The weather was cool and bright. Rain the previous week had cleared the air and tamped down the dust on the city's dirt streets. "We were early and got nice seats, roofed over to keep off the sun; and eighty feet from us across the street sat the President, Generals Grant, Sherman, Howard, Hancock, Meade, and many others—Secretaries of War and Navy—diplomatic corps and ladies," Clover reported to Loulie, who was then traveling in Europe.

> The platform [was] covered with Stars and Stripes, gay flags; between the pillars, pots of flowers—azaleas, cactus, and all in full bloom; then Grant's victories in great letters laid over the flags between the pillars—Vicksburg, Shiloh, Richmond, Wilderness, Antietam, Gettysburg. Up drove Uncle Sam's carriage . . . out got the President. He [President Johnson] sat in the middle of the box, [Secretary of War Edwin] Stanton on his right—Grant on Stanton's right—Sherman in the corner on the left, opposite Grant; and then after each crack general had passed out of sight with his division, he came on foot and into the box, shaking hands all around, and then looked on with the rest . . . And so it came, this glorious old army of the Potomac, for six hours marching past, eighteen or twenty miles long, their colours telling their sad history. Some regiments with nothing but a bare pole,

a little bit of rag only, hanging a few inches, to show where their flag had been. Others that had been Stars and Stripes, with one or two stripes hanging, all the rest shot away. It was a strange feeling to be so intensely happy and triumphant, and yet to feel like crying.

That night Clover and Annette went to Ford's Theatre and visited the house across the street to see where President Lincoln had died. "The room is a small one," Clover reported. "The pillow is soaked with blood . . . it is left just as it was on that night — a painful sight, and yet we wanted to see it, as it is an historical fact and it makes it so vivid to be in the place where such a tragedy had been enacted." The drama was not lost on Clover. As she explained to Loulie, her visit to Washington had made her feel as if she'd finally had her "eyes wide open . . . and my pulse and heart going like race horses."

Two months later, Clover went with her father, Nellie, and Ned to Harvard's Commemoration, a day-long service in honor of Harvard graduates who had died in the war. Her older cousin William Sturgis Hooper had died almost two years before, from complications of an intestinal disorder, while serving with General Nathaniel P. Banks in Louisiana. Sturgis was only thirty. In the year following his death, Clover had visited his young widow, Alice Mason Hooper, and their five-year-old daughter, Isabella, hoping to bring some cheer. "I pine so much now and then for a good talk," Alice wrote to her mother-in-law, Anne Hooper. "Intimate talk with a man — it's an utterly hopeless indulgence." Clover had tried to help Alice feel better, Alice reported, "by making me laugh — by advising me to advertise for one [a conversation] for twice a week." The younger cousin had been intimate with loss and death and knew that one possible response was to laugh in the face of it.

On the morning of July 21, 1865, Dr. Hooper, Clover, her sister, and her brother met Alice, so they could travel by train together from Boston to Cambridge. Though the day was steamy, a breeze from the northwest tempered the heat. On entering Harvard Yard, visitors were greeted with streams of black bunting, large displays of flags and shields, and a twelve-foot eagle, which held in its beak a banner that read, in Latin, MAY BOTH YOU AND THE NATION HAVE PEACE AND HAPPINESS. RETURN

TO YOUR COUNTRY AND YOUR HOME. Alumni and the graduating class of 1865 gathered at Gore Hall, which housed the library, at the site where Widener Library now stands, then slowly marched, two by two, to the Unitarian Church across from the Yard. The dirge-like music kept the pace slow.

Clover, together with Nellie and Alice, crowded into the upper balconies of the church with the other women. The sanctuary, decorated with greens and bundles of flowers, was "crammed," Alice reported to her mother-in-law. "When the time arrived—heroes came in, all in uniform and of course every one clapped." The women's colorful dress made a sharp contrast to the military garb of the sober procession below. The music, beginning with a rousing version of "A Mighty Fortress Is Our God" and followed by the introit and sanctus of Cherubini's Requiem, was accompanied by a twenty-six-piece orchestra, which thrilled the crowd. The sound shook the church rafters. A young Phillips Brooks, just twenty-six at the time, offered a prayer, a supplication that many remembered (a listener recalled that "one would rather have been able to pray that prayer than to lead an army or conduct a state"), but no one, unaccountably, wrote it down. Afterward, the women dined at the Harvard Hall on salmon and lobster salad, tongue and cold chicken, ice cream, tea, and coffee, while the men gathered to swap war stories.

Ceremonies commenced again in the afternoon, with a long parade of over twelve hundred Harvard graduates marching to an enormous tented pavilion erected in the yard. The graduates sat at tables festooned with white linen and black bunting. Clover, Nellie, and Alice watched the proceedings, with all the other women in attendance, on bleachers under the pavilion. General Meade, who had led his troops to bloody victory at Gettysburg, stood up to speak to thunderous applause, followed by Ralph Waldo Emerson, who said in his brief speech that "the war gave back integrity to this erring and immoral nation." Other dignitaries followed, and the day concluded with the poet James Russell Lowell reading his long, moving ode: "We sit here in the Promised Land / That flows with Freedom's honey and milk / But 'twas they won it, sword in hand, / Making the nettle danger soft for us as silk."

Coming of age during a war, Clover had been utterly absorbed by national events, devouring newspaper reports of battles and political maneuvering, talking with high-ranking soldiers, listening with rapt attention to Ned and her father talk of their war-related work. She had access to national politics and pageantry via her Uncle Sam Hooper. She had borne witness as many close to her sacrificed their lives for a noble cause. The war had been, in many ways, her university and her most enduring education.

CHAPTER 4

Six Years

UNLIKE MANY YOUNG WOMEN in her social circle, Clover did not keep a diary—or if she did, she never mentioned doing so, nor did anyone else make reference to it. Though a talented writer, attentive to detail and pace in her compositions, she didn't enjoy writing much. She despised her handwriting and often asked the recipients of her letters to excuse her "wretched-looking scrawl." She complained at times about the drudgery of constant letter-writing and once stated to her father her hope that "pen and ink will be banished in the next world—a celestial telephone will be a great relief."

But in the years after the war, Clover began keeping another record, a visual one, to preserve her experiences and memories. Sometime during her trip to watch the Union army victory parade in the spring of 1865, Clover bought stereographic photographs made from the negatives of Mathew Brady's studio; they included images of dead soldiers on the battlefield, a panoramic view of Richmond, and a picture of the victory parade itself. Stereographs are dual side-by-side photographs that produce a 3-D visual effect when seen together through a viewer. This way of looking at photographic images had been popularized by Dr. Oliver Wendell Holmes with his 1861 invention of a handheld stereoscope; Clover may have first heard about this new viewer from Holmes. In any case, on the back of each Civil War stereograph, Clover carefully noted in her distinctive hand the date and place of her purchase of the stereographs: "May 26, 1865, Washington."

In 1866, less than a year after the Washington parade, Clover began putting together a photograph album that would create a record of the European Grand Tour it was now her turn to take. The war had not changed the fact that this overseas trip constituted a mark of social refinement for young women of her social class. Together, she and her father traveled to Paris, then to London; then they toured through England, Wales, and Scotland, and finally through Germany and Switzerland.

In an album with a gold-embossed green pressboard cover, inscribed "Clover Hooper, London, March 29, 1866," she kept track of the tourist sites she visited by purchasing professionally produced photographs and then pasting them into her album. They provide the only record of her trip. Under each of the sixty photographs, she marked the name of the view: "Louvre," "Rue de Rivoli," "Notre Dame," "St. Paul's," "Westminster Abbey," "Stonehenge," "Salisbury Cathedral," "Geneva," "Valley of Rhone," and so on. To personalize the photographs—to invest them with her memories and make them more her own—she meticulously framed each image, using gold, blue, green, yellow, and red colored pencils. Under an image of Marie Antoinette's Petit Trianon, she attached two stems of violets, her favorite flower, and a small leaf of English ivy, as if to say, "I was here, I saw this."

Clover returned home with her father in 1867 to a city transformed by the aftereffects of war. As a later historian put it, "In that Civil War the elder America perished." Boston was no longer the financial, cultural, and spiritual center of the country that it had been twenty-five years before. The cataclysm had badly shaken the already shifting foundations of Boston's elite. Big business and industrial interests in other cities, most notably New York, had become the chief drivers of the economy, and settlement of the West took up the energies of the young and adventurous. Many trends threatened the comfortable homogeneity of old Boston: increasing immigration, especially by the Irish; urban congestion; and technological developments, such as the telegraph and the ever-expanding railroads, which changed the pace of life. The cherished values of an earlier generation—self-reliance, moderation, intellectual pursuit—seemed antiquated, eclipsed by other concerns.

Much had changed in Clover's household as well. When Ned returned from the Sea Islands, he didn't come home, but rather set up housekeeping with his new bride, Fanny Chapin, whom he had married in 1864. Marriage threatened Clover's close connection to Ned, something she had dreaded. Upon hearing that Ned would marry one of her good friends—Fanny was a soft-spoken young woman with a kind manner—Clover had gone almost limp with relief. "I feel about this," she told her Aunt Cary, "as if I had gone to the dentist, had my tooth out and found it a most enchanting sensation."

More changes were afoot. Clover's sister, Nellie, who now preferred to be addressed by her given name, Ellen, announced her engagement to Ephraim Whitman Gurney and their plans to marry in the fall of 1868. Ellen and Whitman, as he was known, were well matched. Alice James, the youngest sister of William and Henry James and the same age as Ellen, would later remark that Ellen was "certainly the most *married* and the most happy woman I know." The two had met when Ellen was a student at the Agassiz School; Gurney had been her Latin tutor. He was a professor at Harvard, first teaching Latin, then philosophy, and then history, and he later served a distinguished term as the first and much-beloved dean of the faculty. Known less for his written scholarship and more for his teaching, Gurney had a remarkable "capacity for personal attachment" and a "ready sympathy." According to Ned's wife, Fanny, Clover thought it very nice "to have such a bright person come into the family." This gave Clover, as she said, a chance to "learn something."

Even so, Clover dreaded Ellen's impending nuptials. She had depended on her older sister's care and concern. Whatever the nature of their intimacy—so little of their correspondence survives—they'd shared many interests, including a love of horseback riding and an abiding passion for books and learning. In fact, Ellen would later help organize the Harvard Annex for women college students, a precursor to Radcliffe College. But Ellen, who spoke with her mother's low voice, tended to be more introspective and shy with others than was Clover. Ellen Emerson, the oldest daughter of Waldo Emerson, once watched as Ellen put on her gloves before a party, remarking that "her hair was done so beautifully that I shall never forget it." Another friend recalled her "lovely head and figure," her "beautiful hands and feet," the "exquisite way" she held herself; perhaps Clover felt some envy for her sister's beauty. In any case, as Ellen prepared for her wedding, Ellen Emerson, also unmarried, reported that Clover had been complaining about the way that "'Cupid has made dreadful ravages in Beverly life this summer.'" Too many were engaged and "'withdrawn,'" in Clover's words, "'from old pursuits.'" Clover felt left out. Why didn't Ellen and Whitman Gurney just elope, she wondered. "'It would save a great deal of fuss.'" Ellen Emerson went on: "Poor Clover does not find [the wedding] a cheerful prospect in any way, [and] it changes her lot into housekeeping and solitude." Solitude, feeling left behind — this was exactly what Clover most feared.

If fortunate in her new in-laws, Clover watched her siblings start new lives in full knowledge that her own marriage prospects were dimmed by the quandary faced by many women of her generation. The deaths of so many young men in the war had severely skewed the male-female ratio. In 1870 women outnumbered men by fifty thousand in Massachusetts, which had at that time a population of almost 1.5 million residents. Clover was not unhappy living with her father at 114 Beacon Street. (The Hooper address changed in 1862 from 107 Beacon Street to 114 Beacon Street after new homes had been built on the other side of the street.) Clover's close and intense bond with her father had given her security and a certain confidence; being the mistress of her father's house had its benefits. Unmarried women from an established family could enjoy considerable latitude, even power. Yet Clover found that the freedom and privileges of an unmarried woman could become tiresome as she "drifts towards her thirties."

Clover's uncertain situation might have devolved into symptoms of physical debility. Newspapers, women's journals, and advice manuals were filled with apprehension in the postwar years about an apparent decline in women's health. Abba Goold Woolson, a Boston columnist and poet, alarmed that many of the women she knew were "constantly ailing," argued that womanhood in America had come to be equated with debility. "To be ladylike," declared Woolson, one had to be "lifeless, inane, and dawdling," and concluded that "our fine ladies aspire to be called *invalides*." The increasingly common malady of neurasthenia, a diagnosis made first by the neurologist George Beard in 1868, located the problem in the nervous system. A patient with this problem suffered from nerves that were depleted or overly excited—either condition was said to produce a chronic illness that often proved difficult and complicated to manage. Its symptoms might include sick headaches, hopelessness, fainting, ringing in the ears, phantom limb pain, uncontrolled thoughts, chronic pelvic pain, and fears of contamination, and these various complaints might shift from day to day. Alice James, almost five years younger than Clover, suffered an emotional breakdown at age nineteen and never fully recovered; she later received several diagnoses, including hysteria and neurasthenia. In her diary she would characterize herself as "an appendage to five cushions and three shawls."

Clover escaped chronic debility, though she couldn't seem to shake an undercurrent of restlessness and discontent, which intensified during her twenties. Her father was no substitute for a mother or some other female role model who might show Clover how a young woman might craft her future. She was interested in art. She had taken up watercolors during the war, painting meticulous landscapes and portraits of friends. One such portrait depicted her childhood friend Eleanor Shattuck, daughter of the prominent Dr. George Cheyne Shattuck, a professor of medicine at Harvard. In this painting Eleanor sits primly on a dock with her spectacles carefully drawn onto her expressive face. Clover had opportunities to pursue this interest more seriously. William Morris Hunt, a student of the French artist Jean-François Millet of the Barbizon school, had begun offering, in 1868, drawing and painting classes to women in Boston. But Clover's interest in watercolor painting and collecting photographs remained a hobby, a diversion, much like needlework or knitting—something to do during leisurely afternoons and long summer evenings.

Instead, Clover kept busy with volunteer work and her round of friends. She served as assistant treasurer, with Ned as treasurer, on the board of the Industrial School for Girls in Dorchester, Massachusetts, a school started in 1853 for destitute girls between the ages of six and ten.

Together with Ellen, she was involved in the Howard Industrial School for Colored Women and Girls, which had been organized in Cambridge in 1865 for freed slaves sent north by General Charles Howard. She donated one hundred dollars and became a life member of the recently chartered Massachusetts Infant Asylum for abandoned and destitute children. And she was a founding member of the Massachusetts Society for the Prevention of Cruelty to Animals, organized in 1868 by the Boston lawyer George Angell to stop the brutal treatment of horses. Dr. Hooper would at times protest Clover's reform work, perhaps wanting her to stay close to home. He sometimes said to her, as Clover repeated to Ellen Emerson, "I hope you're not going to *that place* to-day!" But at a dinner in 1868, when Dr. Hooper made an impatient speech about his daughter's activities, Clover disregarded her father's grumbling, saying he'd been "terribly inconsistent," especially given the example of his commitment to social reform and his often-repeated refrain to "go teach the orphan boy to read, or teach the orphan girl to sew."

Clover also spent time with friends, most of whom she'd known since childhood, though the substance of these relationships is somewhat unclear — the direct record of these postwar years is sparse. Josephine Shaw Lowell, called "Effie," the sister of Colonel Shaw and the young widow of Charles Russell Lowell, would visit on occasion with her young daughter, Carlotta. One winter, Clover reported to Eleanor Shattuck that she'd spent "perfectly delightful" days with Pauline Agassiz Shaw and Quincy Adams Shaw during a bitter cold snap. With her school friend Ida Agassiz, who had married Henry Lee Higginson during the war, Clover picked up more serious studies and together they "plunged through" Theodor Mommsen's three-volume *History of Rome* in the original German. Clover's friends counted on her to be entertaining. Ellen Emerson reported how Clover was "full of funny stories" at a "perfect dinner party" hosted at the Hoopers'. And Clover could display a generous spirit to a friend in need. When she found out that Kate Howard, a favorite teacher from the Agassiz School, was struggling with ill health and had few financial resources, she hatched a plan to send her to Europe for a year, giving her five thousand dollars to cover all her travel and living expenses. "Switzerland in the summer and Italy in the winter," Clover exclaimed to Kate in the spring of 1869. "You may think me interfering, if you like, but that I consider one of the perquisites of a spinster friend."

Though Clover occupied herself with volunteer work, friends, and her father, she found herself caught between eagerness and an uneasy boredom, not knowing what to do next, counting the months as they passed, waiting for something to happen. After a while, all the teas and dinners, theater and dances added up only to a "mild drizzle of gaiety," as she told Eleanor Shattuck in the early spring of 1871. In the same letter, she hinted at a flirtation with Eleanor's brother, Frederick. At the age of twenty-seven, Clover had passed the typical age for marriage at the time. But if she hinted at romance, she also quickly countered any notion that Frederick might represent her future by portraying him as a mere child — though, at twenty-three, he was Clover's junior by only four years. "Your brother dined here today," she reported to Eleanor, "and was very silly and amusing in his accounts of his journey," adding that "he also took me to church a fortnight ago and was ever so good and only whispered once."

Clover wrote to Eleanor again several weeks later on a sunny Sunday morning. She began with a pleased confession that she had skipped church, delighting in the first signs of spring. There's a suggestion of sensual consciousness in her languid description of a "hot sun going through me":

> It seems a fitting time for a friendly chat when the gay church bells have rung the good white sheep into their respective folds, and left the naughty black ones to outer sunshine and quiet. I'm so happy sitting on the floor with my back against the window and hot sun going through me bringing a prophecy of spring and summer and green things. I'm afraid that your carnal nature craves lower topics than rhapsodies about sunshine tho' and yet nothing happens to tell you of.

Her "small sprees," as she liked to call them, were not completely without interest. At one dinner, she sat next to Charles Eliot, Harvard's president since 1869. At a soiree at her sister Ellen's, she sat between the

American historian Francis Parkman and the Reverend Phillips Brooks, the young preacher who had so impressed the attendees at Harvard's Commemoration six years before and who was now the rector of Trinity Church. She found Brooks "very unclerical and jolly and full of talk. He told me interesting things of Paris . . . and [I] think him much nicer out of the pulpit than in. I've heard him preach twice but each time neither heart nor brain got any food tho' I like his earnestness very much." But as she closed her letter to Eleanor, she undercut herself, asking that her friend not take anything she wrote too seriously. "Of all the stupid letters I've written you this surely is the most but spring sunshine has a softening effect on the brain."

Clover suspected that her most ready path to a secure future and a home of her own was through marriage and motherhood. Despite the fact that some women in her own family, such as her Aunt Cary, had flouted convention and lived more according to their own preferences, Clover recognized the powerful social realities of her class and era and her own deep desire for stability. She had many interests but none were well formed enough to serve as the foundation of her life. Her charitable concern for those less fortunate, her passion for art, her love of the outdoors, her facility with foreign languages, together with her excellent education—all these attitudes and skills made her *more* suitable for marriage, not less, and she hoped that marriage would enable her to establish herself in the world. But achieving this would require a delicate balancing act of patience and discreet pursuit.

CHAPTER 5

Henry Adams

CLOVER HOOPER FIRST met Henry Adams in the spring of 1866 at a dinner party in London while on her Grand Tour with her father. Henry was in London, working as his father's secretary at the American Legation, and noted their meeting in his social calendar. On a page dated May 16, 1866, he listed thirty-one dinner guests for that evening, including "Dr. & Miss Hooper." She left no record of the occasion or what her impressions of it might have been.

The meeting that mattered occurred nearly six years later, almost a year after Clover had written her "rhapsodies of sunshine" letter to Eleanor Shattuck. Sometime near the start of 1872, Clover, now twenty-eight, crossed paths again with Henry Adams at the Cambridge home of her sister, Ellen, and her brother-in-law Ephraim Whitman Gurney. Henry had accepted a Harvard professorship in medieval history and taken over the editorship of the *North American Review* from Gurney, who by now was the college's dean of the faculty. Though he felt he knew next to nothing about medieval history, Henry had nine hours of classes and two hundred students to teach. Lonesome after moving from Washington, D.C. (where he had been a journalist), scornful of much of Boston society, overworked by the dual demands of teaching and editing the prestigious *Review,* and with no home of his own (he lived in a few rooms at the home of his uncle Edward Everett, in Cambridge), he found refuge at the Gurney home, his "oasis in this wilderness." Clover had been coming to Cambridge with some regularity to visit with her sister and to study Greek with her brother-in-law. On meeting her again, Henry admitted to his youngest brother, Brooks, that he had "the design" to pursue Clover and had "driven it very steadily."

Whereas Clover's family had made its name through trade, shipping, and banking, Henry's family was one of the most famous in nineteenth-century America. As T. S. Eliot later observed, Henry Adams knew that "never in his life would he have to explain who he was." His great-grandfather John Adams was the central architect of the young country's government and its second president, and his grandfather John Quincy Adams, its sixth president. His father, Charles Francis Adams, served in the Massachusetts house and senate before an unsuccessful run in 1848 for vice president on the ticket of the Free Soil Party, a third party opposed to the expansion of slavery. After one term as a U.S. congressman for Massachusetts, he was named by President Lincoln to serve as minister at the Court of St. James's. When Charles Francis Adams married Abigail Brooks in 1829, his family declared that he now would not have to worry about money — Abigail's father, Peter Chardon Brooks, was reputedly one of the richest men in Boston.

Henry, born in 1838, the fourth child and third son of Charles and Abigail's seven children, inherited the name of the family's first Henry Adams, who had immigrated to Massachusetts two hundred years before, in 1638. He also inherited the weighty mantle of familial expectation woven from many strands: political prominence, intellectual brilliance, financial affluence, and an extraordinary capacity for hard work. But these were entwined too with darker elements, which Henry's father recognized when he wrote, "The history of my family is not a pleasant one to remember. It is one of great triumphs in the world but of deep groans within, one of extraordinary brilliancy and deep corroding mortification." Charles Francis Adams, Henry's father, had fared far better than many in his family. The stunning achievements of earlier generations had been followed by breakdowns and problems with alcohol. Charles Adams, the second son of John Adams, had died of alcoholism at the age of thirty in 1800. Between 1829 and 1834, John Quincy Adams's first son, George Adams, committed suicide at the age of twenty-eight, followed by the alcoholic death of Thomas Boylston Adams, John Quincy's youngest brother, followed by the death, also from drink, of John Quincy's youngest son, John Adams, at thirty-one. By 1834, four years before the birth of Henry Adams, there were no paternal uncles left; of these siblings, only Charles Francis Adams survived, "the only one," he wrote in his diary, "to keep the name and family in our branch at least from destruction."

Charles Francis Adams had found that being the son of a famed father and grandfather was daunting, confiding in his diary at the start of his political career that, "strange as it may seem, the distinction of my name and family has been the thing most in my way." His son would at times feel likewise, though he would become his generation's most well-known Adams: an accomplished historian who changed how the study of history was practiced in America and a revered public intellectual. By any measure, Henry Adams was a success. But, like his father before him, he found that his family history cast a long shadow, and he would join his immense talent to a brooding insistence on failure, which found its most profound and ironic expression in his posthumously published *The Education of Henry Adams* (1918).

Henry Adams stood no more than five foot three inches tall; it is likely that a childhood bout of scarlet fever stunted his growth. Despite this, or perhaps because of it, he held himself in a commanding way. Trim and well proportioned, he was known for his stride—he would stick out his chest and walk with markedly erect posture, which made him somehow seem taller. He had the habit of thrusting his hands into his pockets when friends approached him or when pacing in front of his students. His fine features were accented by piercing dark eyes and a voice that combined the slightest British burr with a somewhat nasal tone. Impeccably dressed, he was already, in his words, "very—very bald" by the time he got to know Clover in his early thirties. He could be moody, shy, relentlessly introspective, and pessimistic. A master with words—even his earliest letters shine with detail and interest—he thought most emotions were best left unexpressed. He had prodigious work habits and a child-like curiosity concerning just about everything. He enjoyed fine food and cigars; devoured books of every sort, finishing off three detective novels a day when traveling; hated argument for the sake of argument; relished gossip and chat; and had a flair for making fair-minded judgments, which made him his family's preferred counselor. Both his mother and father admitted at various times that Henry was their favorite child, the one they felt closest to.

Henry had grown up in both Boston and Quincy. The family lived at 57 Mount Vernon Street on Beacon Hill for most of the year; its second-floor library held a collection of over eighteen thousand books. Summers were spent ten miles south in Quincy, in a hilltop house not far from the Adams family manse. Because his father was a legal resident of Quincy and his Brooks grandfather owned the title to the Mount Vernon Street home, Henry was ineligible for attending Boston's prestigious Latin school. He went instead to a private Latin school at 20 Boylston Street, just outside the city limits. In 1854 he went on to Harvard, following his father, grandfather, and great-grandfather. After graduating in 1858 — he gave the Class Day oration, on the dangers of greed — he studied languages, principally German and French, and the law at universities in Berlin and Dresden. In the years leading up to the Civil War, Henry and his father were antislavery and staunchly pro-Union. A founding member of the new Republican Party, which had been formed in 1854 to stop the expansion of slavery into the territories, Charles Francis Adams urged a measure of caution in containing Slave Power in order to avoid the catastrophe of disunion and all-out civil war. This view stood in contrast to the firebrand antislavery rhetoric of Charles Sumner, family friend, senator from Massachusetts, and putative head of the Radical faction of the Republican Party, who urged the destruction of slavery at any cost and who dined many Sundays at the Adams table at Mount Vernon Street.

Though twenty-three when the war started, a prime age to serve, Henry did not enlist, as did so many of his classmates from Harvard and his older brother Charles, who would go on to fight at Gettysburg as captain of a cavalry unit, ascending by the end of his career to the rank of brevet brigadier general. On hearing of his brother's enlistment, Henry wrote to Charles, "One of us ought to go." If the younger brother ever felt he missed out by stepping back from the cataclysm of his generation, he rarely spoke of it.

Henry was working as a journalist until the spring of 1861, when President Lincoln appointed his father, then a U.S. congressman, as minister to England. Henry went along as his father's private secretary, and there he met various leading lights of the time: John Stuart Mill, Leslie Stephen (Virginia Woolf's father), Charles Dickens, the poets Charles Swinburne and Alfred, Lord Tennyson. For a time, he wrote an anonymous column for the *New York Times* as its London correspondent. He remembered these years in London with his father, from 1861 until 1868, as "a golden time," later musing to his closest English friend, Charles Milnes Gaskell, that sailing to England in 1861 had been, perhaps, "the biggest piece of luck I ever had." When Henry returned at the age of thirty to a much-changed America, he again worked as a journalist, writing articles for the *North American Review, The Nation,* and the *New York Evening Post,* among other publications. But his biting criticism of the rampant corruption in President Grant's administration made him some enemies and prevented him from participating more directly in politics. When Ephraim Whitman Gurney, together with Charles Eliot, president of the college, asked Henry to return to Harvard, he could hardly refuse. His father encouraged him, writing that "it is the teacher who can make the greatest mark, who will make himself all powerful."

Professor Adams was, by all accounts, a brilliant teacher — innovative, inspiring, and original. He had been hired to teach medieval history, about which he felt "utterly and grossly ignorant," as he told Gaskell. But he walked into his classrooms of a hundred or more students armed not with mere historical facts but with a completely new way of teaching — asking questions, demanding that his students think for themselves, engaging in debate with both rigor and humor. One student, Edward Channing, a future historian at Harvard, called him the "greatest teacher" he'd ever known, and another, Henry Cabot Lodge, among the first students to graduate from Harvard with a Ph.D. in history, would model his own teaching on that of his favorite professor. Lodge recalled how Henry had eschewed lecturing and preferred a more Socratic method, an approach Lodge would carry into his own teaching:

"I allotted to each man a certain number of questions on the syllabus," Lodge would remember, and "sent him to the library and had him come in with his results and lecture to me." Although Henry didn't inspire his students to divulge personal confidences — one student described Professor Adams as "a man of pure intellect" and not someone "a person in deep trouble" would confide in for "advice and sympathy" — he was surely on their side. He set up a system of putting library books on reserve for his students to use, an innovation at the time, and urged the library to arrange tables in the library where students could study.

But, like Clover, Henry was at loose ends in Boston. He found teaching exhausting and he loathed college politics. He would write letters and lectures at the back of the faculty room as he endured the tedium of lengthy meetings. Society wore him out. He despised how the Brahmin class "cultivated their genealogies," and, with his parents living nearby at 57 Mount Vernon Street in Boston, he had a complicated family situation of his own to deal with at close range.

Henry was particularly burdened by his mother's nervous fears and debility. Mrs. Adams, lively but pampered, had been a social ornament when young. What had charmed her wealthy father, P. C. Brooks, had also captivated her husband — her buoyancy, her love of conversation, her open affection. But following marriage and the birth of seven children within fifteen years (a boy, Arthur, three years younger than Henry, had died at the age of five), Mrs. Adams found little to engage her beyond her family. Simmering unhappiness had become tightly braided with chronic physical debility — crushing headaches, sleeplessness, and constant noises in her ears.

Mrs. Adams's many complaints were complicated, no doubt, by the horrifying loss of her oldest child, Louisa Catherine Adams. Sister Lou, as she was known, had been bright but discontented, sparring frequently with her exacting parents, who were often mystified by her erratic behavior — she once said that life at Mount Vernon Street "makes me so unhappy, that sometimes I feel as if I should go away and never come home." She fled Boston with her husband, Charles Kuhn, in 1864 to live in Europe, settling in Florence. In the summer of 1870, while on holiday in Bagni di Lucca, Sister Lou was in a carriage accident that left her with a badly crushed foot. Henry, who was vacationing at the time in England, rushed to her side. She died of tetanus on July 13 after suffering through several weeks of convulsions and lockjaw. As Henry wrote to a friend, her last days had been "fearfully trying." She was thirty-eight. When Henry returned to Quincy, his parents preferred not to ask him too much about Sister Lou's last days — as Mrs. Adams said to Henry, those days were "too awful to dwell on."

Fourteen months later, in mid-November 1871, Henry's father was called back into public life by President Grant, who appointed him as arbiter for a dispute between the United States and Great Britain. It involved warships, in particular the *Alabama,* which had been built in England and sent over for use by the Confederacy, a clear violation of Britain's wartime neutrality. Mr. Adams would be overseas a long time, accompanied only by Brooks, Henry's youngest brother, because Mrs. Adams refused to take the ocean voyage in her state of health. Henry was to be his mother's principal caretaker while his father was away, a role his sense of duty made difficult to resist.

In Henry's family the key partnership was not between his mother and his father, but between his father and himself. Henry's older brothers, John Quincy and Charles Francis Jr., had married and started families of their own. As the third son, and one who was unmarried and who lived nearby, Henry was more available to help out at home. His father would later admit in his diary that Henry was "one of my trusted supports," a dependency that may have become more pronounced with the increasing instability of Mrs. Adams.

By early January of 1872, Henry was living full-time at his parents' house in Boston to help his younger sister, Mary, their mother's daily attendant; he traveled to Cambridge only to teach. He tried to maintain his composure in his correspondence with his father, assuring him that the problem with his mother "is merely that her nervous system does not recover its balance readily." She had always hated being apart from her husband. Henry resisted asking for rescue and did not request that his father return, as did his older brothers and his sister, who likely feared that their mother's misery was worsening. Faced with such intense emotions, Henry didn't quite know what action to take. When Mr. Adams asked Henry whether he should come home, Henry demurred: "I don't propose to offer any opinion on the subject." Again he assured his father that "if you can't return, we will get along somehow." The next week, however, he admitted to "a very uncomfortable week. Mamma has her good days and her bad days, but her best are by no means gay and her worst are very bad." "Her difficulty," Henry explained, was that she had "nothing to occupy her mind, to counteract the influence of unpleasant ideas. Hence the merest trifle upsets her, and a wakeful night seems to her a life-long career." He also played down his mother's suffering, whatever its origins, to make it seem more bearable: "In all this there is nothing that seems to me very serious, though of course it makes life rather intolerable and has a most unfortunate effect on everyone's nerves."

In his reply, Mr. Adams told Henry what the son already knew: "I have great reliance on the calmness of your judgment and the clearness of your perceptions."

Six weeks after this tumult with his parents, in the early evening of February 27, 1872, Henry Adams proposed marriage to Clover Hooper. He found her "so far away superior to any woman I had ever met, that I did not think it worth while to resist." Announcing his engagement to Brooks, he wrote,

> I am engaged to be married. There! What do you say to that? I fancy your horror and incredulity. The fact, however, is indisputable, and you had better here lay down this letter and try to guess the person. Who do you say? Clara Gardner? No! Nanny Wharton? No. It is, however, a Bostonian. You know her, I believe, a little. You are partly responsible, too, for the thing, for I think you were the first person who ever suggested it. I remember well that in our walks last spring you discussed it. Yes! It is Clover Hooper.

Henry found Clover quick and expressive, witty, athletic, and unafraid of a challenge. It probably helped that she seemed so different from his mother. Henry chose her not despite but because of her directness and intelligence. He bragged that they were "happy as ideal lovers should be," and later observed that Clover "has a certain vein of personality which approaches excentricity [*sic*]. This is very attractive to me, but then I am absurdly in love."

Clover's family welcomed Henry into the fold. He had already spent many evenings at the Gurney home, and he would enjoy a genial connection with Dr. Hooper. But the reverse was not true. In a congratulatory note, Dr. Holmes assured his friend Mr. Adams that he had great confidence in the match, saying, "I am sure you cannot but be happy by the prospect of receiving Miss Hooper, whom we have found and you will find so worthy of love and esteem, into your family." Holmes added that "every body seems to be delighted with" the engagement. But the Adamses were not so sure. Henry's father confided in his diary how the engagement had "surprised" him, though he recognized Clover had a favorable "reputation among her friends, which could be desired at the outset." Henry's brother Charles Francis Jr. found Clover hard to understand, and Mrs. Adams would complain that Clover sat on her daybed, clutching a pillow in her lap. And from the start, Charles worried about Clover's mental balance, blurting out, when Henry had told the family of his engagement, "Heavens!—no!—they're all crazy as coots." Henry reacted little to his family's response. Perhaps their diffidence concerning Clover helped him pull away from their strong influence and their need of him.

Clover could barely contain her excitement. She had found what she'd been waiting for. Henry was brilliant, gallant, and from a family of lustrous repute. Best of all, she enjoyed his pursuit of her. She assured her childhood friend Eleanor Shattuck that their bond of friendship would not suffer because of her impending marriage, revealing how her relationship with Henry had made her feel more, not less, connected with others: "I love you more because I love Henry Adams very much."

A letter to her sister that same spring revealed, in metaphors more powerful than she may have recognized at the time, her awakening sexuality, a feeling of emerging into a world of sunshine and love and connection, a lifting of long-held sorrows. In early March, a week after announcing the engagement, Clover wrote to Ellen about a "horrid dream" she'd had for many years. In the dream, Clover and her sister sat "side by side with a high wall of ice between us & very often I tried to look thro' it I saw something in you that was so like myself that it made me cold all over." But with Ellen's marriage to Whitman, the "sun began shining on your side of the wall that it began to thaw," making it possible for Clover to have a "nice time with you." Clover, however, remained enshrined in ice. But during the winter, "the sun began to warm me," despite how she "snapped my fingers at it & I tried to ignore it," fearful of what the thaw might bring. Then, on the afternoon Henry proposed marriage, "the sun blinded me so that in real terror I put my hands up to my face to keep it away and when I took them away there sat Henry Adams holding them and the ice has melted away and I am going to sit in the Sun as long as it shines thro' as Whitman [Ellen's husband] says." Clover found it terrifying to emerge from a cold but protective shell, one that had kept other people at a safe distance, and move toward connection. "I am a 'Hooper,'" she wrote to her sister, "and if a feeling is very pleasant I feel as if it were wrong." But falling in love was also a source of hope; it was not effortful or difficult; it had happened though she and Ellen had "done nothing at all." It was Whitman and Henry who "have waked us up." Connection, love, being awake — it was what she wanted. "You tell me it grows better and peacefully *all* the time . . . I've learnt that in less than a week," Clover wrote proudly. "I always was quick at languages, when I put my whole heart into it — ." Learning the language of love was no different.

Henry too was thrilled about his choice. But he could be awkward, defensive, and sometimes of two minds about Clover, and he tried to sort out this ambivalence and confusion. His report of his engagement in a letter to Charles Milnes Gaskell, for instance, seems oddly disloyal for a man who professed to be so in love:

One of my congratulatory letters further describes my "fiancée" to me as "a charming blue." She is certainly not handsome; nor would she be quite called plain, I think. She is 28 years old. She knows her own mind uncommon well. She does not talk *very* American. Her manners are quiet. She reads German — also Latin — also, I fear, a little Greek, but very little. She talks garrulously, but on the whole pretty sensibly. She is very open to instruction. *We* shall improve her. She dresses badly. She decidedly has humor and will appreciate *our* wit.

She has enough money to be quite independent. She rules me as only American women rule men, and I cower before her. Lord! How she would lash me if she read the above description of her!

Though proud that Clover knew several languages, Henry feared that her intellectual interests and competence also made her a "charming blue," or "bluestocking," a derogatory term used for women who had ambitions beyond proper female conventions, particularly those who were thought to compensate for a lack of womanly beauty with a sur-feit of manly brains. Two months later, in another letter to Gaskell, he recorded Clover's own resistance to the nickname "blue," once more ad-miring Clover's intelligence even as he undermined it.

My young female has a very active and quick mind and has run over many things, but she really knows nothing well, and lights at the idea of being thought a blue. She commissions me to tell you that she would add a few lines to this letter, but unfortunately she is unable to spell. I think you will like her, not for beauty, for she is certainly not beautiful, and her features are much too prominent; but for her intel-ligence and sympathy, which are what hold me.

Henry would never be as talkative about Clover as he was during the days leading up to the wedding, when he was weighing his feelings and coming to terms with his choice. But the way his genuine love for her was marbled with a persistent turning away, a covert withdrawal hidden within overt approval, would persist throughout their marriage.

Clover and Henry married at noon on Thursday, June 27, 1872, at her father's summer home in Beverly Farms on the North Shore, attended by just thirteen people, mostly family. Henry's parents were not present. His father was still in Europe and his mother did not want to come without him. The brief ceremony took place on the lawn, with an easterly breeze bringing to shore the salty smell of the sea. Roast chicken and champagne were served afterward at an indoor luncheon. Henry's brother Charles found the ceremony "peculiar," but the newlyweds were quite pleased with it. Clover thanked her father, saying, "We think our wedding and the lunch went off charmingly thanks to your cheerfulness and care and we shall always remember how you did everything in your power to make our engagement and marriage smooth and pleasant." Henry concurred, writing on the back of Clover's letter, "I most heartily endorse every word Clover says on the last page, and that I cannot express warmly enough the feeling I have of your kindness and assistance."

The newlyweds stayed a week with Anne and Sam Hooper, Clover's aunt and uncle, at their summer house in Cotuit on Cape Cod. There they yachted, rowed, caught bluefish, and walked in the woods, despite an intense heat wave. Wedding gifts inundated the new couple: a pearl and diamond breast pin, silver and gilt candlesticks, Dresden coffee cups, an amber necklace. Clover wrote to Ned and Fanny, asking them to come say goodbye before she and Henry pushed off for their year-long honeymoon overseas. But they did not. Perhaps Ned dreaded the scene of parting with his younger sister on the Boston docks. On Tuesday, July 9, Clover and Henry Adams boarded the steamship *Siberia*, bound for England. After a short stay there, the couple planned to go to Geneva to visit Henry's father, who was finishing up his work on the *Alabama* claims, then on to Berlin, to Italy, and to Cairo by early December for a three-month float down the river Nile. The opening pages of their guidebook, Murray's *Handbook for Travellers of Egypt*, recommended touring between December and February to take advantage of the steady north winds, stating that the least amount of "time for seeing Egypt conveniently and satisfactorily is three months."

CHAPTER 6

Down the Nile

CLOVER AND HENRY ARRIVED at the Liverpool docks on July 20, a clear, cool Saturday night, with a full moon shining on the Mersey River, a sight Clover found "very beautiful." The eleven-day voyage across the Atlantic, traveling at 250 miles a day, hadn't been easy. Both Clover and Henry got horribly seasick, though Henry more so than Clover. They complained in alternating entries in a daily diary, which they eventually sent back to Clover's father. Only two days into their journey, Henry "cursed the sea and life in general," and the next day wrote, "Long fight with seasickness. Clover quite upset. Wishes she had staid at home. Much sleep." By day four, Henry was incredulous: "Deadly sick and a calm sea." But Clover reclaimed her humor, writing, "Cold and fog. Deck too exposed. H. and I lie and gaze at each other. Wonder if life has anything in store for us. Swallow beef tea. Think it may have."

The tedium of life on board the ship was somewhat broken up by the companionship of other passengers, who happened to be friends: John Holmes, Wendell Holmes's younger brother; Francis Parkman, a historian of American exploration; and James Russell Lowell, then a professor of modern languages at Harvard, who was taking a two-year European tour with his wife, Frances. They played shuffleboard on deck when the weather cleared, which wasn't often, and Henry gloated when he beat Lowell and Parkman at the game. Clover and Henry read and talked and read some more. As an engagement present, Henry had given Clover *Their Wedding Journey,* William Dean Howells's just-published first novel, a lightly told "gossamer-like web," as Henry called it in his review in the *North American Review,* that follows Basil and Isabel March on their honeymoon tour from Boston to New York City, Niagara Falls, and Montreal. But mostly periods of boredom alternated with queasiness, so much so that Clover resolved to "see all we want this time" because this was going to be their "last trip to Europe." By the end of their journey, she imagined her family summering in Beverly Farms and wrote to her father, "Often think of Beverly and long to hear how you are faring. Write me everything." She enclosed with her letter a quick pen sketch showing her and Henry, prone on their respective beds in stateroom 35, laid low by seasickness and heaped with blankets; Clover's hair is mussed.

Shortly after arriving in Liverpool late in the evening of July 20, they took a train eighty miles south to Much Wenlock in the county of Shropshire to stay with Charles Milnes Gaskell at the Gaskell family estate. Slight, bearded, not yet thirty, and unmarried, Gaskell had gone to the best English schools: Eton, then Trinity College at Cambridge. Born into enormous privilege, he joined his wealth and influence to a sense of social responsibility and an intense interest in the arts, literature, and politics. He had a gentleness and sense of privacy that put Henry at ease. With Gaskell, Henry could relax. In a letter to her father, Clover noted with pleasure how her new husband, together with Gaskell, would "scour" the surrounding hills on foot and "behave like young colts in a pasture." "We feel," she declared, "quite at home and welcome." The immense, ivy-covered ruins of Wenlock Priory, which formed part of the Gaskells' estate, were surrounded by gardens "full of roses, white lilies, and ferns," and she and Henry stayed in the eight-hundred-year-old Norman wing of the estate; its lancet windows and old carved furniture made her "feel as if I were a 15th-century dame and newspapers, reform, and bustle were nowhere." Gaskell gave the couple some books by Eugène Viollet-le-Duc, the French architect known for his restorations of French medieval buildings, to read on their travels.

At the end of July, Clover and Henry took a train to London, where they breakfasted with Francis Turner Palgrave, Gaskell's brother-in-law and the oldest son of Sir Francis Palgrave, a historian of early England. The younger Palgrave had distinguished himself as an art critic "too ferocious to be liked," as Henry later noted. Palgrave showed them several drawings he had collected for them to see: one by Rembrandt; one by Van Dyke, depicting the children of Charles I, which Clover found "very charming"; and one by Raphael. As a wedding present, he gave them a drawing by Blake — "Ezekiel, I think, weeping over his dead wife." But it was a particular image of Blake's mad King Nebuchadnezzar, "untrammeled by clothing," that, as Clover put it, would have made her brother Ned "gasp." She and Henry would later buy it. She was thrilled to view with her new husband the art that she'd first seen during her European tour in 1866 or that she'd read about in the several books on painting that she'd collected, including Hippolyte Taine's *Philosophy of Art,* in the original French, and Richard Redgrave's *Century of Painters of the English School.* Now she and Henry toured some of Europe's great museums, where they'd stand for hours looking at art "until brains and legs cry for mercy."

After England, they traveled to Brussels, then Antwerp, then Amsterdam, where they saw "pictures in the gallery . . . and enjoyed them much." "Holland," Clover observed, "seems like a quaint toy." From there, they went on to Bonn, where Henry learned that the books he requested would be much easier to purchase in Berlin. "They had never heard of any book Henry asked for," Clover reported.

They arrived in Geneva on August 23 to meet up with Henry's father and mother — Mrs. Adams had joined her husband in the spring, after recovering her health enough to travel. At Geneva, Clover felt illprepared for the many parties and dinners, telling her father she didn't feel she looked half as nice as she did when Betsey, Dr. Hooper's housekeeper, helped her get dressed. She also felt uneasy in the presence of her mother-in-law. At a party hosted by William Evarts, the counsel for the U.S. delegation that was settling the *Alabama* claims, Clover and Henry sat out the dancing, playing instead, as Clover wrote to her sister, Ellen, "the role of old married people." Mrs. Adams, Clover noted, was "quite disgusted with me for having given up waltzing." All the touring and socializing could be wearing. "Travelling would be quite perfect," Clover mused to her father, "if only one could go home at night."

In Dresden, where the great German Romantic painter Caspar David Friedrich had worked in the early 1800s, they went to the famed city gallery, where Clover found the pictures "so rich that I was quite distracted." She was relieved not to be let down by her first viewing of Raphael's "Madonna" — "I did not feel [disappointed] and long to see it again tomorrow," she wrote her father, exclaiming, "And such Titians and Veronese!" The two art-goers, in Berlin, had "bad luck in the matter of seeing pictures." Day after day of cold rain made it impossible to see any paintings at the gallery, which depended on sunlight for illumination. There were, of course, no electric lights to dispel the gloom of cloudy days. As the weather cooled and the days shortened, Henry and Clover began reading aloud from Friedrich Schiller's *Thirty Years' War* in the original German, which Clover found "hard" but also "good fun." She made mention of taking up George Eliot's latest novel, *Middlemarch*, which was being published in segments, though she said little about what she thought of Eliot's sprawling exploration of marriage, class, political reform, and the status of women, except to comment later that "though it's dreary, I like it."

Almost ten days of rain ruined their visit to Venice, and when they got to Florence in early November, they had little time to enjoy the clear weather or see much of the city's famed art. They were too busy and distracted getting ready for their trip to Egypt, on which they were to embark in a week's time. Preparations were extensive. They had arranged for their own guide, a dragoman, and intended to hire a boat, or *dahabeah*. Clover found herself in a flurry "to patch up my wardrobe," and their Murray guidebook recommended an extensive list of staples for the boat, including coffee, curry powder, dates, figs, flour, ham, jams, matches, night lights, pepper, pickles, salt, sardines, soap, sugar, tea, rice, vinegar, spermaceti candles, candlesticks, brooms, and water bottles made of Russian leather, which were especially good for desert travel. Fresh meat, eggs, fruit, and vegetables could be gotten at the markets along the river.

Though Clover and Henry were far from home, they stayed in contact with relatives and kept up with news. Some of it was troubling. Boston had erupted in flames on the evening of November 9, near to Summer Street, the neighborhood where Clover had grown up. Though none of the Hoopers or Adamses had been injured, nor had they lost any property, the fire had consumed over sixty acres in the commercial district, killed approximately thirty people, and left over a thousand homeless. Clover also anticipated news from Ned and Fanny, who were expecting their first baby. (Ellen Sturgis Hooper was born on November 12, and when Clover got the news almost a month later, she was greatly relieved, writing that she "rejoiced to hear of it.")

The transition to married life for the first several months had been challenging. Clover was often homesick. From Antwerp she wrote to her father, "Beverly is certainly nicer than any other place and I am always homesick for you"; from Dresden, "I miss you all the time, and miss you very much"; and from Venice, "I miss you very, very much, and think so often of your love and tenderness to me all my life." She was reassuring him, but she was also reassuring herself that her marriage would not break her bond with her father.

If she feared losing her close connection to her father, if she worried that he would be too lonely without her, she was also finding her way, thriving, in love with Henry and with the expanded world that life with him brought her. From Brindisi, their jumping-off port in southern Italy, she communicated both feelings at once: "I miss you and want to see you," Clover reminded her father, but she was careful to add, "Henry is so utterly devoted and tender." "I am sure," she concluded, "that you would wonder at my ever feeling a yearning for the old diggings, which I do very often." Henry also wrote a solicitous, if somewhat self-conscious, letter to assure Dr. Hooper of Clover's well-being. "Clover gained flesh and strength so that she was in better condition, I think, than I had ever known her to be," Henry wrote. But he didn't want to imply that Clover had severed any bond, adding, "Not that she had or has at all forgotten you, or her home, or has in the least lost her attachment to America. I have no fear that she will ever do that."

On November 21, Clover and Henry arrived at Alexandria, where they drove through "dimly lighted streets," with "ghostly figures wrapped in white stalking past us." There was, Clover noted, "a strong flavour of the Arabian Nights about us." The next day they chose their *dahabeah*, the *Isis*, which had three single cabins, a double stateroom, a dining room of twelve square feet, a bathroom, and a roomy upper deck, with a table and two sofas shaded by awnings. Because the Nile runs from the south northward, travel downriver had to be powered by rowers (with progress boosted by sail power when a steady breeze came from the north); Henry and Clover hired a crew and also a dragoman, whom Clover would later describe as "competent and faithful." The following day the couple traveled by train south to Cairo to await the start of their journey on the Nile some ten days later. Roses and jasmine scented the warm, dry air. With their *dahabeah* anchored near Cairo, Clover and Henry spent several days touring the Great Pyramids and the Sphinx, at one point meeting up with friends from Boston, the financier Samuel Gray Ward and his wife, Anna Barker Ward, who'd been a close friend of Clover's mother. "We saw them several times and enjoyed them very much," Clover wrote her father.

Though the climate was ideal—"the air bracing and soft, the sunshine almost incessant"—Clover started to feel bewildered in a place completely foreign to anything she had experienced before, and she found it hard to get her thoughts in order. On December 5, while still anchored near Cairo and busy with final preparations for their long tour down the Nile, Clover complained to her father that she had "tried to write in the past ten days but gave it up in despair . . . for a long time past I have found it impossible to get my ideas straightened out at all." After leaving Cairo on the southward journey, she found the slow travel and the sameness of the scenery disorienting: "One day is so like another so far that we do not even remember the names of the days." And she began to feel self-conscious. She told her sister-in-law, Fanny Chapin Hooper, "letter-writing is not my forte." A week later, she pleaded with her father not to "show my letters to anyone" because "they sound so silly and homesick." She felt keenly that she had not yet found a way to communicate her impressions, her feelings, what she found interesting. At times, she could appreciate aspects of the scene. She noted with delight the young girls who came down to the river's edge to fill earthen jars, "which they balance most gracefully on their heads." Beneath their only garment, "a long dark blue cotton mantel which covers their head and falls to their ankles," Clover spied their "silver bracelets" and she envied some of the girls — "they are so becoming." But she recoiled from what she called the "ugly and miserable" towns that lined the Nile valley.

By the time she arrived in Thebes in the New Year, the discomfort caused by her surroundings was turning into true self-loathing and paralysis. "I must confess," she confided to her father, "I hate the process of seeing things which I am hopelessly ignorant of, and am disgusted by my lack of curiosity." And later in the same letter, she despaired. "I have become utterly demoralized about writing . . . I cannot write except to you who are used to my stupidity and shortcomings." Two days later her senses had gone numb: "I never seem to get impressions that are worth anything, and feel as if I were blind and deaf and dumb, too."

It was as if the blinding sun of Clover's vivid dream after her engagement to Henry was now shining down on her from the Egyptian sky. She felt overwhelmed by all she was experiencing: the sights, smells, and sounds of the Nile, heightened by the heat, by confinement on the boat, and by the physical intimacy of married life. She had longed for a new life throughout the six years between finishing at the Agassiz School and meeting Henry. But she must have felt that much of what had defined her was now superfluous. Also, the anchoring love of her father must have seemed a million miles away.

Was Clover's paralysis making her markedly more withdrawn? Was it difficult for her to carry on ordinary conversations? Henry must have noticed a change, given the close quarters of the boat and their daily travels on shore. He may have felt alarmed, though he said nothing in his letters. As Clover observed some time later in the trip, "How true it is that the mind sees what it has means of seeing." Protecting Clover, protecting his marriage, protecting himself, Henry's silence wagered that whatever troubled Clover would blow past like a desert wind.

By the end of January 1873, they anchored near the tiny island of Philae. Considered the jewel of the Nile, Philae is situated near the first cataract, where the Nile widens on the border of what had been ancient Egypt and Nubia (now Sudan). Clover and Henry strolled amid ruins dating from the time of the pharaohs and the caesars. And they had company. Also anchored near the tiny island were the Wards. Thoughtful, magnetic, and extraordinarily well read, Mrs. Ward had been known for her exquisite beauty—when she was young the American sculptor Hiram Powers asked to have a cast made of her face because he deemed her an ideal American type. Emerson wrote of her in his journal, "The wind is not purer than she is." Perhaps the two women talked of old times and of everyone they knew in common: Clover's parents, the Sturgis aunts, the Hooper cousins, Catharine Sedgwick, and the rest of the social circle on Beacon Hill and in Lenox, where the Wards had a farm they called Highwood next to what would be Aunt Cary's Tanglewood estate. Mrs. Ward had tried to comfort Clover's mother during her long illness, inviting her for extended summer visits at Highwood, writing in 1848, the last summer of Ellen's life, "Dear, sweet Ellen Hooper, I want to see you," and assuring Ellen the trip from Boston to Lenox would be easy, "just a day's journey to spend a week or two with the two people who love you."

Clover knew the Wards well and had undoubtedly visited their home as a young girl during her summers with Aunt Cary. Now, on the Nile, Mrs. Ward may have given Clover a sense of how to carry herself in foreign surroundings, how to adopt a dignified yet friendly demeanor, and how to be a companion to her husband without the trappings of home. She may have comforted Clover, even helping her remember how much her mother had loved her. In any case, after a week's time in the company of Mrs. Ward, Clover seemed calmer than she'd been for several months. Her spirits lifted. "I doubt if we find any place as beautiful as this," she enthused to her father on January 24, 1873. "The scenery in every direction from this island is exquisite." She even agreed to an expedition of "shooting the rapids" in a rowboat, which she found "quite exciting" though not "half as dangerous as people pretend."

Henry had bought a photography outfit in London (camera, glass plates, chemicals, developing equipment) and was, according to Clover, "working like a beaver at photographing" at Philae and farther south, at the enormous temples of the colossi at Abu Simbel, what Clover called the "most wonderful thing we have yet seen." At one point she wrote that "we waited for an hour or two to photograph," and she may have helped with the complicated printing-out process, which required numerous steps and following detailed chemical formulas—"we have been printing photographs to pass the time," she noted later during a particularly slow stretch on the river. And one photograph of Henry sitting in their cabin may have been taken by Clover, unless Henry enlisted one of the boatmen to take it. Otherwise, at no point did she indicate she had taken any of the numerous photographs she sent to her father along with her letters. It was Henry's camera, his photographs, his vision of their trip.

In early February, they rolled up their boat's sail to prepare for the return trip to Cairo, then Europe. When they got back to Philae, they missed by just a few days the Emersons, the sixty-nine-year-old philosopher and his oldest daughter, Ellen. In Cairo, they went to gold bazaars and "bought many nice things — silk handkerchiefs . . . barbaric necklaces and earrings, Turkish slippers" until they had to make a "vow at last that we should stop."

By mid-March they were sailing again on the Mediterranean, second-class this time, on a French boat. Now Egypt and Africa seemed to Clover "like a far-off dream." "Our winter," she confidently declared to her father, "had been a great success. We feel as if we had had a great bath of sunshine and warmth and rest, and are quite made over new. The charm of the East grows on us." The fright that had gripped Clover, making it so difficult for her to concentrate and get her thoughts in order, had by this time wholly eased.

In the same week Clover wrote to her father of the "bath of sunshine," she exclaimed in a four-page letter to Mrs. Ward, "How much we have lived through this winter, we feel as if we went home with a new lease of life and happiness to begin with." And she added her thanks: "For all that you have done to make our winter pleasant we shall be grateful as long as we have any faculty of memory." The coming of spring, the imminent return to the more familiar environs of Europe, and the prospect of her arrival home to Boston and her family had restored her sense of well-being. Aided by the sensitive attention of an older woman who "was home to me," Clover made an important transition on the Nile. She had come to terms with her separation from her father and her marriage to Henry and had overcome a time of panic, finding anew her place in the world. Perhaps at twenty-nine, she had grown up.

As they approached Naples, Clover got up before dawn to see the "sun rise between the two summits of Vesuvius." "I perched on top of a pile of trunks and waited" for the sun to appear, Clover told her father, adding, "I shall never forget my first sight of the Bay of Naples, with Capri and Ischia half hidden in the early morning mist."

It was as if Clover herself had risen to a new dawn.

From spring of 1873 until their return to Boston in August, Clover and Henry retraced many of their travels through Europe, but added several new excursions: to the ruins of Pompeii, to Sorrento, to the Amalfi coast — where they traveled on ponies on a "path lying between stone walls covered with ferns and violets, with oranges and lemons hanging over our heads" — and to Rome. In the Eternal City they visited the studios of the American sculptor William Wetmore Story and the painter Elihu Vedder, also an American, with whom Clover was not impressed — there were too many "stuffs and accessories" in his pictures. The couple also went to the studio of the Spanish painter Mariano Fortuny, whom Clover thought "very clever," but who had, as she said, "tapestry on the brain." She didn't see "any soul . . . in his pictures." Clover, increasingly confident of her taste, was beginning to make discriminating judgments about art.

By April they arrived in Paris, where they stayed for two weeks at a small hotel on the corner of the rue de Rivoli and place Palais-Royal and lived "à la française . . . — early coffee and tea, then a stout midday meal, and dinner at eight at some restaurant. We each buy a paper and get behind it!" And they shopped — bronzes from Japan, linens, a china serving set, and clothes, which Clover found "very pretty here this spring." In May they were staying in the "swell part" of London, with their own servants, in a townhouse at 28 Norfolk Street, Park Lane. Gaskell's father had died earlier in the spring, and he had opened up his father's townhouse as a wedding gift to Clover and Henry. "If I were a boy," Clover declared to her father, "I should say we are having a 'bully' time; being a staid matron I can only say we are enjoying ourselves extremely." Being the daughter-in-law of Charles Francis Adams had paved the way socially for Clover — she was greeted kindly by many of his colleagues and friends. But she knew that because of her social class her experience of London was unlike that of most people: "England is charming for a few families but hopeless for most." Clover held on to her American attitudes, though she admitted it had been "an uncommonly nice thing to visit England for a few months, and I like the people and they stand American 'sass' very good-humouredly."

But by the end of July 1873, Clover declared to her father in no uncertain terms that she and Henry had "enjoyed much, but are quite ready to come home and buckle down to hard work."

PART II

"Very Much Together"

Live all you can; it's a mistake not to.
— HENRY JAMES

CHAPTER 7

A Place in the World

CLOVER AND HENRY ENJOYED mostly calm seas on their return voyage to America in mid-August of 1873, though Henry reported that Clover had a bad toothache, which "pulled her down" for a few days. They had been abroad for an entire year. Upon returning, the two spent the month of August with Clover's father in Beverly Farms, "a small Boston world" where friends and family stopped by to welcome the couple home. Her brother, Ned, noticed with relief that Clover seemed "quite unchanged in looks." For his baby daughter, Ellen, she'd brought a gift of "a silver anklet with bells from Egypt," which delighted both baby and doting aunt. After much debate about where to live, Clover and Henry decided to buy a two-story brownstone at 91 Marlborough Street, in the newer neighborhood of the Back Bay, two blocks south of Boston's Public Garden. Set on the corner at Clarendon Street, the house had sunny rooms on both floors and a library with room enough for two thousand books. An added bonus for Clover was that her father lived less than two blocks away, at 114 Beacon Street.

Clover had worried about what she'd need to set up house, at one point turning to her sister, Ellen, for advice. "I want you to send me a full list of your linen outfit," Clover requested while in Venice on her honeymoon. A motherless daughter, she admitted to feeling "utterly adrift as to how much I need." She said she had forgotten during her engagement that "things have to be bought and do not come of themselves," adding self-consciously, "Please don't let anyone see this—it is private and confidential and not quite what one is supposed to write from Italy." But back in Boston, Clover seemed more at ease with the idea of running a household. The ship carrying all they'd collected on their honeymoon—twenty-five wooden crates packed with rugs, linens, glass, china, silver, paintings, drawings, and various kitchen things—arrived in mid-October, shortly after they moved into their new home. She and Henry hung many of their watercolors in the first-floor dining room, placing a large yellow Indian rug on the floor to complement the room's yellow wallpaper. They kept a watercolor titled *The Valley of Martigny* and an early India ink drawing of an ancient ruin, both by the English master J. M. W. Turner, behind curtains to keep them from fading in the bright sunlight. Henry hung Blake's startling drawing of the mad king Nebuchadnezzar in the library where, as he joked, it "excites frantic applause." Henry admired Clover's energy and skill in setting up their home, managing servants, and decorating, telling Gaskell, "My wife is very well and seems to thrive under a tremendous amount of work."

That fall of 1873, Henry returned to Harvard College. He taught a general history of Europe for upperclassmen, an honors course on medieval institutions, and, later, a brand-new course on American colonial history. Henry's Harvard salary of $2,000 a year (roughly $38,000 in today's terms) made up only a small percentage of the couple's income. He and Clover had an array of financial resources, including trusts, investments, and generous cash gifts from Dr. Hooper. When Henry's grandfather Peter Chardon Brooks died in 1849, he left an estate of $300,000 to be divided among his heirs. Likewise, Captain Sturgis, Clover's grandfather, left a sizable estate, with trust funds for all his grandchildren, after his death in 1863. Clover and Henry were not multi-millionaires on the scale of the industrialists, acquiring riches in a manner wickedly satirized by Mark Twain and Charles Dudley Warner in their 1873 novel, *The Gilded Age*, which became a byword for this era. But they were very wealthy. Their yearlong honeymoon had posed no financial hardship. They felt little impact from the financial panic of 1873, which tipped the

American economy into a painful six-year recession—in the first two years alone, eighty-nine railroads went bankrupt, eighteen thousand businesses failed, and unemployment ran to 14 percent. Widespread misery prevailed. At that time the government did almost nothing to provide a safety net to help the unfortunate; the largesse of churches, communities, and individual philanthropy were the primary sources of aid. But, except for having to watch their spending more closely—they had lost "nearly all surplus revenue," Henry noted to Gaskell—Clover and Henry emerged unscathed.

In January 1874, Henry resumed editorship of the *North American Review*, hiring as assistant editor his star student, Henry Cabot Lodge, who would later serve thirty years as a U.S. senator from Massachusetts. The literary journal, issued four times a year, published a roster of postwar intellectuals and writers: James Russell Lowell, William Dean Howells, Henry James, Francis Parkman, Daniel Coit Gilman (the first president of Johns Hopkins University), and Sarah B. Wister (daughter of the actress Fanny Kemble and mother of Owen Wister, a future writer of westerns and other fiction). In critical notices of new books, which Henry often wrote himself, he chided writers about style, urging historians to "keep the thread of the narrative always in hand." A historian, Henry declared, "must be an artist." With good prose, Henry told Lodge at one point, "the reader ought to be as little conscious of the style as may be. It should fit the matter so closely that one should never be quite able to say that the style is above the matter,—nor below it."

Clover poured her energies and ambition into Henry's work. It gave her a chance to continue learning and to satisfy a hunger to know the world, a deep curiosity she'd always had, even as a young girl. He would read aloud to her from manuscripts submitted to the *North American Review* and, in the evening, they'd read books of literature, history, and science aloud to each other in front of the fireplace. She made sure the routines of their daily life protected Henry's time and energy, urging him on. She told one of his students how she inspired her husband by reminding him how many candles the American historian George Bancroft had burned to the quick "while writing before breakfast." Just before their first wedding anniversary, Henry acknowledged his debt, saying to Gaskell, "I have been hard worked and have deputed to my wife all that I could get her to do." Whatever Henry may have given Clover to do — grades to compile, bibliographies to check, pages to read — he didn't say. Nor did she.

The summer of 1874, Clover and Henry escaped Boston's heat to spend several months in Beverly Farms, with its sparkling light, smooth sandy beaches, and rocky cliffs. The Eastern Railroad had had a depot in Beverly Farms, midway between the larger town of Beverly to the west and Manchester to the east, since 1847. Early residents who had bought up "farm and woodland that drifted and tumbled down to the sea" composed a who's who of prominent Boston families, including numerous branches of the Lowell, Putnam, and Cabot clans, as well as other notables, such as Captain Thomas Wentworth Higginson, the Civil War hero and later an editor of Emily Dickinson's poems; Richard Henry Dana, the lawyer and author of *Two Years Before the Mast;* and Dr. Oliver Wendell Holmes. During the first summer after their honeymoon, Henry, who'd been worn out by teaching and editing, liked to walk in the afternoons "into the depths of the forest," with its dappled light, where he'd find "a sheltered spot" to "lie down on my back till dinner-time."

In 1875, Clover and Henry built a home of their own design, with a mansard roof, on a lot of more than nineteen acres in a wooded area purchased from J. Elliot Cabot, half a mile back from the coastline and a short walk southeast through the woods to Dr. Hooper's house. Pitch Pine Hill, as they called it, was no Gilded Age mansion, like many other homes along the seacoast. It was, by comparison, a relatively modest hideaway, though it accommodated at least four servants and a number of guests. The rooms had odd shapes and low ceilings, and each, including the upstairs bathroom between Clover's and Henry's separate sleeping rooms, had a fireplace. Ceramic tiles depicting medieval castles, knights, and medallions studded the entry hall floor; elegant Morris tile work lined the many fireplaces; and Clover's collection of china plates decorated with four-leaf clovers was displayed on the mantel in the dining room. The couple packed up their collection of English watercolors — by John Robert Cozens, Thomas Girtin, John Sell Cotman, John Varley, and William Clarkson Stanfield, among others — to live with them seasonally in their second home. They put Henry's large writing desk on the first floor, in a room facing the sea; it had an awning-covered porch open to the salty breezes. Clover's upstairs room had a view of the ocean above the treetops. Her garden included Spanish roses, nasturtiums, morning glories, and beds of fragrant mignonette. She also designed a small oval-shaped pond, which was rimmed with brickwork and situated at the edge of the front lawn, just before a perilous drop-off, a wooded embankment, and the sea beyond. The pool caught the glimmer of sunlight and fleeting reflections of birds and leaves overhead. Henry boasted to Gaskell that "our new house is more than all we ever hoped. We are delighted with it and all about it. I am perfectly happy here, and potter about, trimming trees, eradicating roots and rocks, opening paths and training vines, all day, with rapture unknown to poets." He added: "I could write a sonnet on the pleasures of picking up stones out of one's lawn."

Summers meant time outdoors — swimming, weeding the garden, walking along the beach, and taking long rides on horseback through the wooded countryside. The warm-weather edition of Boston's social whirl was slower paced than "the season," and Clover spent long afternoons with her family. Daughter and father often met in the afternoons for a midday dinner at half past two. Sometimes Henry would join them. Or Clover and Henry would talk later in the day over tea. Clover's sister and brother-in-law, Ellen and Whitman, often stayed at Dr. Hooper's house, as did her brother and sister-in-law, Ned and Fanny, and their young daughters. By 1879 Ned and Fanny had five girls: Ellen, Louisa, Mabel, Fanny, and Mary, who loved to scamper back and forth between Dr. Hooper's house and Pitch Pine Hill.

The nieces would long remember these summer days. Mabel Hooper recalled how "a footpath, strewn with fragrant pine-needles, and bordered with ferns and lichened rocks" led to Pitch Pine Hill. For a young girl, "it was like having a private entrance into fairyland," where her uncle and aunt "kept the keys and arranged the scenery." Henry spent the mornings at his desk, dressed in "cool white summer clothes," and "only the scratch of the pen would break the silence." In the afternoons Clover and Henry appeared and their nieces watched "almost enviously — the two figures on horseback vanishing into the flickering sunlight of the woods."

• • •

During these early years of her marriage, Clover had no need to write letters to her family—they lived in Boston or Cambridge or were together in the summers on the North Shore. She left scant record of this time. Henry, by contrast, regularly wrote to, among others, Henry Cabot Lodge, Charles Gaskell, and Sir Robert Cunliffe, Gaskell's cousin and a friend from Henry's days in London in the early 1860s. In 1875, Henry convinced Harvard's president, Charles W. Eliot, to inaugurate a graduate seminar in history, the first of its kind offered at the college. In the evening, after they dined together, Henry gathered his students before an open fire in his second-floor library on Marlborough Street to read through "German codes of the Visigoths, Burgundians, and Salian Franks" to discern how they informed Anglo-Saxon institutions, the basis of English law, and, eventually, the American legal code. He delighted in the work. "This adventure in research" made him "like a colt in tall clover," one student remembered.

The course culminated the following spring in the volume *Essays on Anglo-Saxon Law* (1876), with an introductory essay by Henry, followed by dissertations written by his seminar students, Henry Cabot Lodge, Ernest Young, and J. L. Laughlin. For their work, the students received the first doctorates awarded in history at Harvard. The professor could not have been happier, writing to Lodge on the occasion of Lodge's graduation, "Nothing since I came to Cambridge has given me so much satisfaction and so unalloyed satisfaction as the completion of our baking this batch of doctors of philosophy." He declared himself "pleased as Punch about my Ph.D's."

Henry wrote too of his pursuits with Clover: they rode horses and took long walks, they gardened and attended dinners, and they ended many days in front of the fire, reading together. They got Boojum, their first long-haired Skye terrier, in 1876, four years into their marriage, and over the years they would add Pollywog, Possum, and Marquis to their ménage of dogs. A niece remembered that their "long-haired terriers were always to be seen tumbling about their feet or trotting after them on their walks." They entertained. If Henry found Boston stultifying, once comparing the city's social scene to "isolated groups of ice-bergs," he often repeated to friends how he and his wife were "flourishing."

One extant letter by Clover, written on March 29, 1875, to Charles

Gaskell, confirms her contentment. She reports on her wide interests and is clearly independent enough to do as she pleases. Earlier that morning she had read a letter from Gaskell, and in the evening, while waiting for Henry to come home from a party she had no interest in attending, she pulled out a sheet of her creamy writing paper and her pen and inkpot. "As I've not bored you with a letter for many months, I propose to now," she began, telling Gaskell how she'd locked herself in Henry's library until his return because of a spate of robberies and murders in the neighborhood. The financial panic of the previous year had put the city on edge with a rash of crime. "Robbery," Clover explained, had gone "out of fashion because there is nothing left to steal," replaced with "cutting throats."

But Clover didn't linger long on such news. She thanked Gaskell for his letter, which reminded Henry how books by the art critic John Ruskin were going up in price — that very same day Henry had gone out to buy her all of Ruskin's leather-bound second editions and started reading to her from *Modern Painters*. She regaled her correspondent with how her husband had bought her a complete set of *Punch*, a popular British magazine renowned for its satire. "If your unmarried conscience ever rebuked you," she joked with the still-single Gaskell, "marry and gratify every whim." But remember, she cautioned, to "preface the opening of every parcel with 'my dear, I bought you a little present today.'" After trading more social gossip, she concluded, "It is very late and he cometh not." But then she heard Henry coming in the door. With relief, she added, "oh here he is — so good night," signing her letter rather formally as "Marian Adams."

If Henry James, who had known Clover since childhood, found her somewhat "toned down" by marriage from what he called her "ancient brilliance," James's younger sister, Alice, remarked in her inimitable way, both approving and cutting, that being married to Henry Adams had "had a good effect upon" Clover. Marriage had "added a charm, a feminine softness which was decidedly wanting before." Perhaps Alice James noticed (and envied) what her brother couldn't see — Clover's newfound confidence, her diminished fear, her powerful sense of having found a place in the world.

CHAPTER 8

City of Conversation

IN NOVEMBER 1877, after Clover and Henry had lived in Boston for four years, Henry announced to Charles Gaskell, "As for me and my wife, we have made a great leap in the world." They planned to live in Washington, D.C., for a year or two, hoping to lease their Marlborough Street home while they were away. At thirty-nine, Henry had been asked by Albert Rolaz Gallatin, who knew his reputation at the *North American Review* and at Harvard, to write a biography and edit the papers of his father, Albert Gallatin, Thomas Jefferson's brilliant secretary of the Treasury and later the founder of New York University. Henry had suspected his time at Harvard would be limited. Though his graduate teaching had been successful, he told Gaskell the year before, "I regard my university work as essentially done. All the influence I can exercise has been exercised." He had also given up the editorship of the influential *North American Review*. The October 1876 presidential election issue, detailing political corruption in Washington and the inability of reformers to do much about it, had angered the owner of the *Review*, James Osgood, who thought Henry had been far too partisan. Though drawn to politics by family and interest, Henry felt less and less pull to take an active part. "The more I see of official life," he said during a brief trip to the capital in 1874, "the less I am inclined to wish to enter it." But Washington offered a welcome change of scene, and publishing Gallatin's papers was a chance to do research and write full-time.

Clover had traveled to Washington after the war, and she'd accompanied Henry for a brief visit there in 1874. During their next trip, in early February of 1875, they were invited by and stayed with Clover's Uncle Sam Hooper, by now a longtime congressman from Massachusetts. Hooper was lonely because his immediate family had left for a tour of Europe, but by the time the Adamses arrived, he had also fallen dangerously ill with pneumonia. He died several days later, on February 14. With his immediate family away, Clover and Henry had to, as Henry wrote, "assume control of everything," helping coordinate a state funeral at the Capitol. There is no record of Clover's impressions of these tumultuous weeks.

But Clover surely knew, from conversation with her family and her own experience there, that living in the capital, with its foreign diplomats and politicians, scientists and writers, made it possible to meet and talk with a broad range of people. A move to Washington meant she and Henry would be entering a wider social world. If she worried about leaving her father behind in Boston for the winter months, she did not say. She could be sure that Ned and Fanny, and Ellen and Whitman Gurney, who all lived nearby in Cambridge, would take good care of him.

Henry resigned his teaching position and, in early November of 1877, he and Clover moved to Washington and leased Sam Hooper's large house at 1501 H Street, which had been purchased by William Corcoran, the art dealer and philanthropist who owned much of the real estate bordering Lafayette Square. Clover thought it a "charming old ranch," with its climbing wisteria and "superb rose trees" planted in front. On arriving, she hired three servants to get the place up to her standards. They scrubbed floors and whitewashed walls until she found the house satisfactory, declaring, once the work was finished, that she felt "as if we were millionaires." She had a knack for setting up a comfortable, pleasing home. Henry joshed with her that it was the first time he felt "like a gentleman," and he later gave her credit, telling Gaskell she had created a home that was "always amusing and interesting."

The neighborhood of the Square, next to the White House, was the city's most exclusive. Friends lived nearby. George Bancroft, the widely admired historian of the multivolume *History of the United States of America, from the Discovery of the American Continent,* and his wife, Elizabeth Bliss Bancroft, who'd taken part in Margaret Fuller's Conversations, along with Clover's mother, lived a short walk west down H Street in a generously proportioned, old-fashioned house. Emily Beale, several years younger than Clover, lived across the street in the old Decatur house with her parents, General and Mrs. Edward Beale. Emily soon became a frequent and "uncommonly lively" guest, though Clover was occasionally wary of her aggressive chattiness and sometimes kept her at a slight remove. Carl Schurz, a former senator from Missouri, now secretary of the interior under the narrowly elected Republican president Rutherford B. Hayes, often stopped by for tea on his walk home. He was one of Clover's favorite visitors. She loved to hear Schurz, a German immigrant with a kindly manner, play her piano, especially Chopin: "the instrument seems like a wonderful human voice under his hands."

The city of Washington had been transformed since the Civil War. That conflict and a rapidly growing population had strained its antiquated infrastructure. As one Cleveland newspaper writer wryly noted, it was as if "a whirlwind had picked up some great town, mixed the big houses up with the little ones, then cast the whole together in one miscellaneous mass, keeping intact only the city streets." Not long ago, midwestern politicians had agitated to move the seat of government west to St. Louis. But by the early 1870s, "Boss" Shepherd, the governor of the District of Columbia, had imposed order and transformed the capital into a more modern metropolis. Sewers were dug and canals filled in; horse-drawn streetcars and cabs provided more efficient ways to move through the city. Scores of newly planted trees shaded mile after mile of spacious new sidewalks and wide asphalt-paved streets. Horse-drawn street-cleaning machines whirred through, equipped with large brooms of stiff twigs to brush away dirt and horse manure. "What had been a most unsightly place three years ago," President Grant had declared in 1873, was "rapidly assuming the appearance of a capital of which the nation may well be proud."

Washington had always teetered, in culture and custom, between North and South. With almost 150,000 residents in the early 1870s, the capital was half the size of Boston, and African Americans comprised almost 40 percent of the population. Tens of thousands of emancipated slaves had migrated to Lincoln's capital during the war and after, joining a smaller group of long-time residents led by a coterie of black leaders who agitated for school reform, started newspapers, worked in federal jobs, and, for a time, held political office. But the dreams of postwar unity between whites and blacks were short-lived. As the aims of Reconstruction collapsed in the mid-1870s, blacks found themselves excluded from leadership roles and confronted by virulent racism; they had to live in separate communities, attend separate schools, and worship on Sunday mornings in separate churches.

Clover made little comment on such matters. She did have sharp words for the attitude of William Henry Trescot, a lawyer from South Carolina who'd been sent to Washington to represent the state's interests in Reconstruction. At a dinner party Trescot told Clover that he thought "a slaveocracy the only perfect form of human society," an idea she found appalling. When Trescot tried to garner Clover's sympathy for an upper-class southern woman who'd been reduced to baking and selling bread to feed her family, Clover wanted to tell Trescot that such poverty "serves her right." But she bit her tongue and said nothing.

Both the Adams and Hooper families had long advocated for the abolition of slavery. John Adams, a conservative Federalist, detested the institution. He thought slavery "a foul contagion in the human character." His wife, Abigail Adams, had a visceral hatred of it, saying that slavery "always seemed a most iniquitous scheme to me — to fight ourselves for what we are robbing the Negroes of, who have as good a right to freedom as we have!" John Quincy Adams, after his one term as president, worked tirelessly as a congressman, despite threats and charges of treason, to rescind a gag rule in the House of Representatives that barred abolitionist petitions from being heard in Congress. In 1845, at the age of seventy-eight, he succeeded. At one point in his career, Henry's father, Charles Francis Adams, came to be known as "the archbishop of antislavery." Once the Republican Party was founded, in 1854, the Adamses became staunch members of the party. While not as well known for activism, the Hoopers too were Republicans and strongly antislavery, donating money and doing work to support and educate freed slaves.

After the war, Clover had done work for the Howard Industrial School for Colored Women and Girls in Cambridge, which was devoted to the education of freed slaves. Yet she had little direct knowledge of African American life beyond what her brother had told her of his war work. Most of her servants in Washington were black, but their world, separate and unequal, was beyond her ken. Soon after moving to Washington, Clover did help a family living in an abandoned cabin by the Potomac River. They had "no food and no clothes," Clover explained in a letter, and to her horror, the city had "no organized system of relief." But this family, which had been reduced to abject poverty after the war, was white.

What drew Clover and Henry to Washington was its growing cosmopolitanism, a combination of politics and culture unlike that of any other city in the country. Henry declared Washington the "only place in America . . . where life offers variety." Politicians from every region gathered during the congressional term, and foreign diplomats, writers, scientists, and artists played their part in this diverse and ever-changing crosscurrent of people. Though not as large as London, Paris, or Rome, Washington was, as Henry said, surprisingly "complete." Henry James agreed and aptly called the capital a "City of Conversation," one marked by an unmatched drive and intensity.

In mid-December of 1877, a month after they arrived, Clover and Henry took a three-hour drive in an open carriage through Rock Creek Park, a short distance from the White House. The weather, almost balmy, with plenty of sun, proved enticing to the two Bostonians, accustomed as they were to the long, cold, and dark New England winters. Clover and Henry, now married five and a half years, got out of their black carriage and walked farther up the creek on "a lovely path" covered with tulip and beech trees to sit together on a tree trunk, dangling their feet over the water below. To Clover's astonishment, the December weather was "as if in summer." She enjoyed her first months in Washington so much, she wanted time itself to slow down, wishing that "Sundays wouldn't come so fast. Not because I must write a letter but because I hate to see the 'milk going out of the bowl.'" As she told her father, life promised "new possibilities for us."

• • •

Henry plunged immediately into work, going most days to the State Department to read through enormous collections of letters and documents for his project on Albert Gallatin. Clover joined him. "I've been working at the State Dept. with Henry," Clover told her father the week before Christmas. "If you want to know how we look, see Cruikshank's illustration to Old Curiosity Shop," a reference to the novel by Charles Dickens. Poring over papers at the archives, Clover and Henry looked like "Sampson and Sally Brass on opposite stools." Clover relished her tangible proximity to history. She told of reading through the correspondence between the French philosopher Voltaire and Gallatin's grandmother, who was Voltaire's neighbor. Some notes, Clover explained, had been "written on the backs of playing cards — one in which he and his housekeeper Mme. Demis wish to borrow 'twenty cups of flour.'" She went on to explain that Voltaire was then "75 years old — sick and feeble and witty," adding, "I read and counted [the cards] this morning — fifty three in all! Probably no one since the lady to whom they are written has read them till now."

She also threw herself into what she saw as her main responsibility — protecting Henry's work time by managing the house and servants and by coordinating their social life, a task not without challenges. Polite society, what Edith Wharton later called "a hieroglyphic world," required steely nerve and an exquisite ability to read subtle clues and gestures. Without such skills, one might misunderstand an invitation or accept one from somebody best avoided because of scandal; one might inadvertently offend someone who loved to gossip or become inundated with social obligations. "Politeness is power," one observer noted, yet it was also exceedingly complex. A booklet on Washington etiquette published in 1873 advised that the intricacies of Washington society required extra caution. Because social life was "composed, in so great a degree, of official personages, who represent the mechanism of the State," the writer noted, "the social obligations and customs have become about as complex as the constitutional laws." Yet at the same time polite social life had "no constitution, or defined code."

Clover recognized the dangers of social embarrassment and strove to avoid it. "In this social vortex," she noted to her father, "one has to steer gingerly." But she found many routines of polite society boring.

She described a luncheon attended by twenty-five women, most between fifty and seventy years of age, as "a discipline worthy of the Spanish inquisition." She reported repeating the mantra "this too shall pass away" until she could get up and flee. She found attending church tedious as well. When a neighbor stopped by one Sunday morning, asking her to go to services, Clover feigned weariness, later telling her father, "I think I'd best announce that I'm a Buddhist or a Mormon — the Washington females are such church goers." She had particular disdain for morning calling. She'd receive dozens of calling cards from people wanting a visit, each requiring some sort of reply. Etiquette manuals filled pages with detailed rules for how to maneuver through this sensitive arena. The stakes were high. "The 'calling' nuisance," as Clover dubbed it in a complaint to her father, "requires a cool head and imperturbable nerves to meet it squarely."

But whereas Henry sometimes wanted more peace and quiet and "sighed for his pines" at Pitch Pine Hill in Beverly Farms, Clover preferred the company of "humans." To manage, she instituted a daily five o'clock tea at their home on H Street, an open house that gave her escape from more tiresome rituals yet at the same time offered select friends a chance to stop by for some gossip, which she relished. "It's very cozy," she quickly declared. Once, Charles Nordhoff, the Washington correspondent for the *New York Herald,* stopped by alone, talking candidly with Clover and Henry about "state secrets." "I drank it in with my tea," she reported with delight.

Late in the year, Clover and Henry went to an eight o'clock tea at Mrs. Phoebe Tayloe's, widow of Benjamin Ogle Tayloe, who'd been an activist in the Whig Party, formed in the 1830s to protest the policies and politics of Manifest Destiny and Jacksonian democracy. The Tayloes had built a "charming old house" on Madison Place, which had been a celebrated salon before the Civil War. Mrs. Tayloe "looked like an old picture as she sat pouring out tea," Clover observed, "dressed in black velvet, with one big diamond on her lace stomach [a triangular panel at the front of her gown] and a soft widow's cap tied under her chin." Mrs. Tayloe, a friend of the new President Hayes and his wife, Lucy, invited Clover and Henry to pay their respects at the White House. Clover found Mrs. Hayes, with her low soft voice, "quite nice looking — dark — with smooth black hair combed low over her ears." The president seemed "amiable and respectable," but in spite of her overall sympathy with him politically, Clover couldn't resist adding that she found him rather dull— "not a ray of force or intellect in forehead, eye, or mouth."

Many evenings, Clover and Henry went to the theater, the opera, or concerts. One night they went for "a late carouse" at the Schurzes to hear the Hungarian violinist Eduard Reményi, a protégé of Franz Liszt, play privately for a few friends from eleven in the evening to one in the morning. When the violinist told Clover how much he'd enjoyed performing at a recent concert in Boston, she replied that Boston audiences had the reputation of being cold. "Cold!" Reményi exclaimed. "It was for me tropical vegetation!"

The Adamses fielded multiple requests to attend dinners and parties, but they preferred inviting friends for dinner, finding their own house "more agreeable than most others," as Henry said. In the glow of their twenty-candle chandelier, the talk was of politics and art, scandal and history. Clover, alert to the most recent fashions, took pains to dress well but not extravagantly, opting for jewel-colored gowns and French yellow suede gloves that reached to the elbow. Men vied to be her dinner companion. Her attraction was her curiosity, her shining intelligence, her wit. She was an original. General William Tecumseh Sherman often sat next to her, knowing she'd be a perfect audience for his chitchat. At one dinner, he joked with her about President Grant "being the king of 'Vulgaria.'" At another, he recalled for her his famous Civil War "march to the sea" by re-creating it "with knives and forks on the tablecloth" and concluding his story by sweeping "the rebel army off the table with a pudding knife, much to the amusement of his audience."

Henry didn't seem to mind when Clover was the center of attention. One guest remembered how he would double over at the dinner table in "uproarious laughter" after listening to one of Clover's anecdotes, "waving his napkin up and down." Another recalled that he seemed "so proud of her that he let her shine as he sat back and enjoyed listening to what she said."

Sometimes the "talk parties," as Clover called them, wore her out. She didn't like it if people talked *at* her, particularly if she found them too impressed with themselves, as was the case with William M. Evarts, the secretary of state. "Mr. Evarts came in for a long talk the other night," Clover reported in one letter. Luckily, she had stepped out of the room moments before and went immediately to bed — "I love him not — he orates too much." After an exceptionally grueling week of hosting several dinners of twenty or more people, Clover joked to her father, "For a middle aged slightly spavined Boston nag last week's pace has been too fast — last night I dropped on the track and went to bed at 7 o'clk." From time to time, she'd be slowed down with a stinging cold, an aching tooth, a sick headache. In the spring of 1876, Clover had been so sick she couldn't sleep or swallow and had difficulty breathing, frightening Henry out of his "wits for a week," as Henry confessed to Gaskell. He feared diphtheria. But this bout of illness was an exception. Clover typically didn't languish in bed for long.

What Clover enjoyed most was listening to a good story and seeing, for herself, the fascinating human scene. She often had a front-row seat. Early on in their life in Washington, she and Henry had driven by carriage out of the city to see friends, only to learn that those friends had traveled in the opposite direction to visit them at H Street. "So we came home a roundabout way," Clover explained, and at a mill east of the Capitol building they spoke to the owner, who recognized Henry's name, saying he used to know "H's grandpa very well." He took Clover and Henry to see his rose houses, which she described as a "fairyland — 6-7-8 feet high all in bloom — such roses." The man, it turned out, had once owned much of the land on Lafayette Square, from H Street to I Street, buying it for "3 and ½ cents a foot." When Clover told him that the value of their lot was $30,000, he "gasped a little." Then the man said, as Clover recounted to her father, "Well, there's other things than money in this world — that's of little count — I lost my only child last year — we couldn't save her — I've enough to keep me from want — that's all that's needed." The man insisted Clover not go home until he had covered a carriage seat with "superb roses."

On the morning of December 7, 1877, a very tired General Nelson A. Miles delighted Clover by stopping in for a visit. Miles had just returned to Washington after a long season in Idaho and Montana, chasing down the Nez Perce. A farm boy from Massachusetts, the general had been wounded four times in the Civil War. Though not a graduate of West

Point, he'd advanced rapidly through the military ranks. The previous year, commanding the Fifth Infantry, he'd fought the Sioux and Cheyenne after General George Custer's death in the Battle of Little Big Horn. When Miles walked into Clover's kitchen, she asked him if General William Tecumseh Sherman, as commanding general of the U.S. Army, had ordered Miles "to report to duty to 1501 H St." The often cantankerous general didn't catch Clover's joke, but nonetheless settled down with some hot tea to tell his rapt listener of his adventures. He'd been part of the months-long 1,700-mile pursuit of the Nez Perce, which ended with Chief Joseph's surrender on October 5 at Bear Paw in upper Montana territory. Whether Miles repeated Chief Joseph's speech—"Hear me, my chiefs! I am tired; my heart is sick and sad. From where the sun now stands, I will fight no more forever"—Clover did not say.

But the general did relay to her what he and Chief Joseph talked about while riding side by side on the tribe's long removal to Oklahoma Territory. Chief Joseph said that when "he saw the Indians about the agency hunting in small buckets for bones to gnaw he registered an oath never to become an 'agency' Indian." Clover added incisively in a letter to her father that until "Miles conquered him he never was." She noticed that General Miles did not deem the Indians mortal enemies, worthy of complete destruction, as did General Sherman, who had undoubtedly told her his views on the matter at one of their numerous shared dinners. General Miles, by contrast, spoke "very kindly and tenderly of them." The general may not have mentioned to Clover his role in preventing the Nez Perce from returning to their homeland in Oregon, but he did tell her of his frustration at not being able to secure a hearing in Congress about building a large reservation school for the Nez Perce, a plan that Clover admired. When the general left that morning, Clover requested that he bring her a "warrior's bonnet." It wasn't possible to obtain one, he explained, because the Nez Perce "never leave their bonnets behind." The general promised, however, to bring her an Indian pipe on his return visit.

Most Sunday mornings, Clover sat down with her pen and ink to tell her father of her week, sometimes alarming herself by how much she'd written. She headlined one twelve-page letter with the words "How long

Oh! Lord how long!" Her continuing claim to loathe the task of writing is hard to credit, given how her missives from Washington overflow with juicy gossip, set pieces, reports on friends and politics, quips, satire, and observations about fashion and art. "A propos to nothing," she wrote in one letter, "isn't this worthy of Mark Twain—a man the other day was describing to me how he saw a nitroglycerine explosion of Wells Fargo's Express office in San Francisco—he said 'I was standing at the hotel window opposite when the front blew out and the air was darkened with my intimate friends.'" She was a master at portraying people: the French philosopher Ernest Renan is "charming, most sympathetic, and chatty—as big as a whale, no neck, and jolly round face rising directly from his shoulders—you can think of nothing but a full harvest moon rising above a mountain;" the British physicist John Tyndall "looks like a typical Yankee 'store-keeper'—just the keen-lantern jawed brush bearded face." While visiting with a mother and daughter from New York, friends of friends, the mother asked, "'Mrs. Adams, didn't your husband marry a Miss Ogden?' 'Why, no,' I said, 'he married me.'" After they both laughed, the older woman asked Clover not to pass on her mistake to Henry, fearing he'd think her only a "silly old woman." And in early spring of 1878, Clover witnessed the birth of a new technology. She went to the weather signal bureau and talked into a telephone, conversing with a man in Virginia at the other end of "forty-three miles of wire." After she asked him several questions, she thanked him and heard him clearly say, "'Very welcome Madame.'"

Clover meant to entertain her father with these stories, of course. Her letters provided a way for him to watch her as she went about her life, just as he'd done over the years as she'd grown up. And clearly, having a way to be seen and valued through her letters, to have a home to send them to, was of almost magical importance to her. Once, after a dinner party, when Henry repaired to the billiard room with the other men to smoke their "midnight cigars," Clover retreated to her rooms to write her father. "I've a superstitious feeling," she wrote, "that I must keep my prize of a Sunday letter to you and I've only fifteen short minutes left to do it."

Dr. Hooper wrote back to Clover every Sunday, letters now lost; we get only one side of their weekly conversations. But he treasured her letters and kept every one, writing the date of each on the outside edge of its envelope and often reading portions aloud to family and friends. How could he resist? Clover's exquisite powers of observation were like those of a novelist gifted with an unerring eye for detail and character.

Sometimes her rapier wit drew a little blood, whether she intended it to or not. In a letter of December 1877 she described how a young woman "stood under a chandelier and gave a recitation—every spire of hair . . . tortured into a distinct and separate spiral in order to heighten the pathos of her recitation." At the same evening performance, another older woman recited her poetry, "'pomes' she called them—one was about magnolias and babies between whom she fancied she detected a strong resemblance." To keep from laughing, Clover stared at the mantelpiece "and tried to think of sad things." But, she cautioned her father, in the first of several warnings, "Beware how you quote me." Several Boston women had attended the party, and she didn't want her "gibes to come back and hurt any feelings."

Her worry that she might cause harm or bad feeling by what she wrote was not unfounded; she had gotten into just that kind of trouble almost immediately after moving to Washington. Early in 1878, an innocuous comment she'd made in a letter to her father found its way to Mrs. Adams, who took offense. If Henry's parents hadn't liked Clover from the start, they'd managed to keep up appearances. But now, upon hearing Clover's comment that Henry had for the first time felt "like a gentleman" after their move to Washington, Mrs. Adams reacted with rage. She wrote Clover a scathing letter, calling her a fool. "A most annoying pin 300 miles long twisted and sharpened has come in a letter from Boston," Clover told her father in late January of 1878. "If we are fools we are," she declared defiantly, and "too old to reform." Dr. Hooper blamed Henry's youngest brother, Brooks, for passing on the offending phrase, but Clover defended him, saying to her father that he did "Brooks [an] injustice—he is far too busy and loyal to nag" his parents. She instead suspected her cousin by marriage, Alice Hooper Mason, and begged her father to "never quote a word or syllable" to Alice, who'd recently divorced her second husband, Charles Sumner, and then moved back to Boston, taking up her maiden name, Mason. "Her tongue," Clover cautioned, "is a weapon which cuts right and left and I am cowardly enough to stand even at this distance in terror of it!" Clover felt relieved at having explained the family conflict. "There! That's all — and I feel better," but she added, with emphasis, "*Burn* this!"

Later that spring, Mr. Adams, in an attempt to cool tempers, made plans to meet with Clover and Henry but missed them because of a miscommunication. Then Henry went by himself to visit his parents at the old manse in Quincy to try to save the situation and explain things. But the damage was done. Mr. Adams had felt abandoned when Henry first moved to Washington, admitting in his journal, "I feel as if [Henry] was now taking a direction which will separate us from him gradually forever." To protect his relationship with his son, Mr. Adams blamed Clover for the breach in the family, writing in his journal two years later that "I have no feelings but those of affection and love for him. I pity rather than dislike his wife. But henceforth I must regard her as a marplot." Mr. and Mrs. Adams thought Clover nothing more than a high-flown meddler. From this point on, she would make few visits to the old homestead in Quincy.

Dr. Hooper, meanwhile, kept reading aloud from Clover's entertaining letters. She warned him again in late March after four months in Washington that "I am told on high authority that you disregard all my prayers and tears and threats and inflict on patient friends my weekly filial drivel." Dr. Hooper promised in a postcard that he followed her orders and hadn't passed on what she said. Clover fired back that despite his claims, she'd heard otherwise. "Your postal card," she wrote, "would be reassuring if not overborne by other testimony," and she listed names as proof: "Mrs. Adams, Miss Bigelow, Adie Bigelow, Sally Russell, Ida Higginson, Henry Higginson, Mrs. George Perkins, Nanny Wharton, E. W. Hooper, F. C. Hooper, E. Whiteside, Mrs. Parkman, etc., etc., etc." "All I can say," Clover went on, "is that you don't know how pleasant my notes *might* be if written to you only — you don't know how many spicy things I should put in if I could trust you."

The mad rush of dinners, conversation, and intrigues continued through the spring of 1878. Clover's brother, Ned, came to stay for several weeks early in the year, and her father arrived for a two-week stay in mid-April. Clover made no mention of whether her sister, Ellen, visited or declined to do so, as she would the following spring when Ellen sent Clover only "a laconic line" of regret. The sisters spent much of every summer living only a short distance from each other at Beverly Farms. They exchanged occasional letters, though very few survive. From time to time, Clover communicated with her sister through her father, asking him to pass on tidbits of gossip or requests. But it is also true that she mentioned Ned more frequently than her sister in her letters to Dr. Hooper.

That summer of 1878, Clover and Henry again stayed on the North Shore at their beloved Pitch Pine Hill, spending the months, as Henry said, "icing ourselves by the sea-side, and wondering whether Washington really exists." But on moving back to "winter quarters" the next fall, Henry wrote to Gaskell that Washington was now home, "where we find ourselves on the whole more contented than anywhere else." Clover reported to her father that they found everything in order; the dogs were "wild with joy to see us." Eighteen months after their arrival, Clover and Henry proved their "experiment," as they called it, a shining success. Theirs had become one of the most coveted invitations in the capital. They'd made good friends and, except for the hubbub with Henry's parents (which Henry didn't protest much), they'd avoided major social embarrassments. So much of it had been thrilling.

They'd lived the first years of their marriage, including these months in Washington, as Henry said, "very much together." He had told Gaskell it was one consequence of their not having children, a fact their friends and family had begun to note. Gaskell had married Lady Catherine Henrietta Wallop, daughter of the fifth earl of Portsmouth, in late 1876. When Henry heard that the Gaskells were expecting their first child, he wrote to his long-time friend, "I have myself never cared enough about children to be unhappy either at having or not having them, and if it were not that half the world will never leave the other half at peace, I should never think about the subject." But Henry did think about it. If what he said on the occasion of Gaskell's announcement was something of a dodge, a way to hide his true feelings, he was reconciled enough with the situation to forthrightly mention their childlessness. In these years, Clover probably never did this, and certainly not to her father. She liked children, took care of her five nieces every summer, and enjoyed their antics. Clover's life with Henry had an extraordinary fecundity of another sort—love, productive work, friends, wealth, lively conversation, entrée to much that was best. But she may have also felt a sense of loss and feared that she had disappointed Henry. Perhaps, at thirty-six years old, she still held out hope that motherhood might yet be in her future. Perhaps not.

"Of ourselves I can, thank Heaven, give you only pleasant news," Henry wrote to Gaskell at the end of 1878. "I have worked hard and with good effect. My wife has helped me." Henry had found his stride in his work. By the spring of 1879, he'd sent the publishers his *Life of Gallatin* and finished editing the three volumes of Gallatin's papers. When the publisher's indexer made a mess of things, he had to write his own index to those three volumes, which together numbered three thousand pages. When he finished in mid-May, Clover observed that her husband's shoulders were at last "springing back to their normal position." With Clover's help, Henry had launched his new writing career as a historian and biographer. He also had a clear idea of what his next project would be. He and Clover would need to return to Europe. Archives in London, Paris, and Madrid held documents and correspondence that would help him better understand the administrations of Presidents Thomas Jefferson and James Madison. This research and writing would turn into a massive endeavor, ultimately producing Henry's "prose masterpiece," *History of the United States During the Administrations of Thomas Jefferson and James Madison*, in nine volumes. The first two would not be published for ten years.

After taking care of "900,000,000 things," Clover and Henry left Washington on May 19, stayed a week with Dr. Hooper in Boston, and on May 28, 1879, boarded their ship, the *Gallia*, in New York. They were bound for England.

Ellen Sturgis Hooper, Clover's mother, as a young woman.

MARY BUNDY COLLECTION, STURGIS LIBRARY, BARNSTABLE VILLAGE, MASS.

Clover's aunt, Caroline Sturgis, younger sister of Ellen Sturgis Hooper.

MARY BUNDY COLLECTION, STURGIS LIBRARY, BARNSTABLE VILLAGE, MASS.

Unless otherwise indicated, illustrations are reproduced courtesy of the Massachusetts Historical Society.

Dr. Robert W. Hooper,
Clover's father.

Clover's older brother
and sister, Ned and Ellen
Hooper.

Clover at two or three. Her mother called her "Clovy" or "my blessed Clover."

Clover at eight or nine, near the time of her Aunt Susan's suicide.

RIGHT: Tintype of Clover at ease on her horse, taken in October 1869 at the Hooper summer home in Beverly Farms, Massachusetts. She had just turned twenty-six.

BELOW: Clover added this sketch to a letter to her father, depicting the newlyweds' seasickness aboard the steamship *Siberia*, on their ocean crossing to England in July 1872.

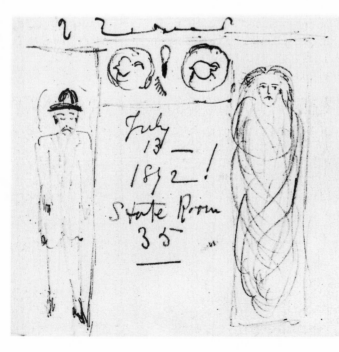

ABOVE: Henry in the stateroom of the *Isis*, the boat he and Clover leased for their honeymoon travels on the Nile in 1872. Clover may have taken the photograph.

BELOW: Clover and Henry at the Chapter House at Wenlock Priory, July 24, 1873. Left to right: Henry, Lady Eleanor Sophia Cunliffe, Charles Milnes Gaskell, Clover, Lord Pollington, Lady Pollington, Sir Robert Cunliffe. Clover's right eye is unaccountably scratched out in the photograph.

Undated tintype of Clover holding a Skye terrier that might be Possum, the dog she and Henry acquired in 1881.

LEFT: Portrait of Anne Palmer painted by the American artist Abbott Handerson Thayer in 1879, the year Anne and Clover became friends.
MEMORIAL ART GALLERY, UNIVERSITY OF ROCHESTER

BELOW: Frances Benjamin Johnston's photograph of Elizabeth Cameron, "a dangerously fascinating woman," taken several years after Clover's death.
FRANCES BENJAMIN JOHNSTON, LIBRARY OF CONGRESS

Clover wrote to Dr. Hooper on Sundays, usually in the morning. Sometimes she signed her name Clover, but most often M.A. (Marian Adams). He kept every letter she wrote, noting the date on the envelope.

Untitled bronze statue, known as "Grief," by Augustus Saint-Gaudens (1891), marking the graves of Clover and Henry in Rock Creek Cemetery, Washington, D.C.

PHOTOGRAPH BY THE AUTHOR

+

CHAPTER 9

Wandering Americans

THE OVERSEAS TRIP to England was trouble-free. Clover and Henry experienced little of the seasickness that had plagued the honeymoon voyage seven years before. On arriving in London, Clover announced to her father she agreed with the great English polymath Dr. Samuel Johnson when he wrote, "'He who is tired of London is tired of life.'" Henry reported that they dined out incessantly. Clover would later muse to her father that the "vastness of this London society strikes you more every day," but added, "We always drift into the same set here—respectable—mildly literary and political." Clover and Henry rented and settled into a large sunny house at 17 Half Moon Street, north of Buckingham Gardens. They went to concerts at nearby Westminster Abbey, scoured print shops to add to their growing art collection, and traveled through the countryside north of the London. There, Clover found the "gardens and great trees and old cottages . . . so beautiful" that seeing them exhausted her. It was as if, she joked with her husband, "this English world is a huge stage-play got up only to amuse Americans. It is obviously unreal, eccentric, and taken out of novels."

In mid-July they attended a private dinner and showing at the new Grosvenor Gallery, which had opened two years before in the fashionable shopping district on New Bond Street. Lady Blanche Lindsay, whom Clover described as "young and not pretty," hosted social gatherings at the gallery, which she and her husband, Sir Coutts Lindsay of Balcarres, had established as a "refuge of the Pre-Raphaelites" whose work had been rejected by the Royal Academy. Dinners at the gallery had become the social invitation of the summer season. Clover admired the new building's long paneled rooms lined with crimson brocade and frescoes. She was less enthusiastic, with few exceptions, about the art on display that season, which included works by George Frederic Watts, Edward Burne-Jones, John Everett Millais, and William Holman Hunt. Upon seeing James McNeill Whistler's large portrait of Connie Gilchrist, Clover thought it a "joke," agreeing with John Ruskin's view that Whistler's paintings were overly abstract and seemed somehow unfinished, as if he had flung "a pot of paint in the face of the public." The aesthetic movement, with its doctrine of "art for art's sake," didn't hold Clover's attention as much as the virtuosity of the Old Masters and the early-nineteenth-century Romantics.

Henry spent most of his days "pegging away" at the London Records Office. Sometimes Clover joined him, reading through old British newspapers. Or she found other ways to occupy her time. She often "loafed with" Anne Palmer, who'd taken an apartment just four doors away on the same street. She and Anne had met two years before through Carl Schurz's daughter, Agatha, while attending the theater together in Washington. Earlier in the year, she had invited Anne to travel along with her and Henry to the famed Niagara Falls, and while there, the two women had dared to walk across the ice bridge between Canada and the United States, jumping crevasses beneath the "sparkle and glitter" of a "warming sun." Despite an age difference of fourteen years, Clover and Anne shared a spirit of adventure, and by the time they met again in London six months later, they were friends. With Anne, Clover relaxed. Anne had grown up in New York, outside the "whispering gallery" of Boston and Washington that often made Clover behave cautiously, especially around other women. Though Clover stayed in contact with her women friends from before her marriage, including Adie Bigelow, Eleanor Shattuck (now Whiteside), and the Agassiz sisters, her friendship with Anne had a heightened intimacy. Anne, a striking, slender woman with large, dark brown eyes and wavy brown hair, shared Clover's passion for art as well as a quick sense of humor. Both had known a full measure of loss: before Anne's tenth birthday, three of her younger siblings had died, and her youngest brother, Oliver, was severely handicapped. Anne felt close to her father and brother, but not to her mother and sister, a family dynamic Clover understood. Clover could be Anne's friend and protector, providing nurture and fun. Together in London, they attended dog shows and flower exhibitions, once rowing on the Thames River to Twickenham. Whatever they did, they often found themselves laughing till all hours.

The American novelist Henry James, who had moved to London in 1876 and was living nearby, thought Clover and Henry to be "launched very happily in London life," as he wrote in a letter to his family. James was staying in a modest apartment two blocks away from the Adamses, on Bolton Street, and in the late afternoons, after he finished writing, he often stopped by for some of Clover's tea and gossip. They were the same age, and having grown up together in Boston and Cambridge, knew many of the same people. He thought Clover had "intellectual grace." She called him Harry. At thirty-six, Harry had—in the words of Cynthia Ozick—"become Henry James," the celebrated author of the bestselling *Daisy Miller*. The novelist, who cut an impressive figure, was solidly built, with a beard and receding brown hair, a strong profile, and a quiet, self-absorbed manner. One friend remembered how he "banishes all expression" from his enormous gray eyes. He was in the midst of an intensely creative period, having already written *The American*, *The Europeans*, and a biography of Nathaniel Hawthorne, among other essays and short stories. He finished *Washington Square* in the freezing winter of 1879 and laid plans for drafting, the following spring, what he called his "wine-and-water" novel, *The Portrait of a Lady*.

Did Henry James talk with Clover about what he was writing? Neither one said. But surely these two confirmed raconteurs exchanged stories, chitchat, turns of phrase—at one point James promised to bring her "plenty of anecdotes—if your store has got low." James considered Henry Adams "a trifle dry," but he found Clover "conversational, critical, ironical," with a wit distinguished by "a touch of genius." Clover thought James talked a lot, but fussed over him and fretted over his extended absence from America and his literary reputation. She couldn't comprehend what made him stay away from his own country for so long. She found James's fascination with London, which he once called "the most complete compendium of the world," perplexing, and mused, "what it is that Henry James finds so entrancing year after year we cannot understand . . . A man without a country is one to be pitied in ten years." And later, when American critics accused James in "savage notices" of giving short shrift to American culture in his biography of Nathaniel Hawthorne, Clover worried. "It is high time Harry James was ordered home by his family." While she realized the critics were "silly and over-shoot the mark in their bitterness," she also reasoned that her friend "had better not hang around Europe much longer if he wants to make a lasting literary reputation."

But if these two Bostonians had a close friendship, and they did, a kind of coolness defined its center, with each observing the other, each taking notes. James's attention flattered and entertained Clover, but nothing more. She resisted the magnetic pull of his all-consuming imagination. Her self-containment demanded little from him. They both managed life by deflection — she with her fierce humor, he with a distancing charm — a tactic each must have understood in the other. "He comes in every day at dusk and sits chatting by the fire," Clover wrote her father, but added that she thought him "a frivolous being" for dining out as much as he did. After reading *A Portrait of a Lady,* which James would later send to her, she wrote to her father, "It's very nice, and [there are] charming things in it, but I'm aging faster and prefer what Sir Walter [Scott] called the 'big bow-wow style.'" It wasn't that her friend "bites off more than he can chaw," she concluded, "but he chaws more than he bites off."

Clover reported to her father that Henry James, on hearing that she and Henry planned to spend the next months in Paris, felt "half dis-posed to go with us." Whether they all traveled together, no one said, but the three turned up around the same time in mid-September of 1879 in the City of Light.

"The second act of *Innocents Abroad* is now beginning," Clover reported upon arriving in France. She thought Paris less welcoming than London and would later call it little more than "a huge shop and restaurant." But early in the fall of 1879, the city shone under luminous skies, its seductions in full view. While driving in her carriage through its most stylish park, the Bois de Boulogne, Clover found everything better than in London: "better horses, better liveries, and of course the women immeasurably better dressed." Henry planned to work on his research into Jefferson and Madison in the archives, but these institutions were closed until October 1, so Clover and Henry had some leisurely days together — "We have quiet mornings to study, noon breakfasts, and Bohemian dinners." She already knew French from her lessons at the Agassiz School and had started learning Spanish in preparation for travels in Spain. Henry James came by every day at six-thirty, after which they dined out and attended the theater several times a week. On September 13, for her thirty-sixth birthday, they went to the Louvre, where they feasted on the Old Masters; Clover discovered that "every time one comes back to the good pictures they seem better." Afterward, they met with James for dinner at an open-air café and went to the Paris circus, followed by ice cream on the wide boulevard of the Champs-Élysées.

The three revelers were joined that same evening by Isabella Stewart Gardner and her husband, Jack. Clover had known "Mrs. Jack," as everyone called her, since her marriage in 1860. The two women, only three years apart in age, had much in common, inhabiting similar social circles both in Boston and on the North Shore, where the Gardners had a summer home in Beverly. They had met in Washington when Mrs. Jack traveled to the capital, and again in London, where they attended a party at the Grosvenor Gallery and critiqued English fashion for "twenty minutes side by side in the vestibule waiting for our respective broughams." In Paris, Mrs. Jack introduced Clover to her dressmaker, the renowned designer Charles Frederick Worth, famous for his couture and his use of sumptuous materials; he suggested that Clover order a dark green merino dress trimmed in dark blue, similar to a dress he'd designed for the duchess of Würtemberg.

Mrs. Jack's toughness, her refusal to adhere to social convention, and her sense of style and élan had earned her acclaim in the papers — a local reporter called her "one of the seven wonders of Boston." A friend remembered her "gliding walk, like a proud ship under full sail." She had already begun amassing the art that would one day fill her magnificent Boston palazzo. Clover was fully aware of Mrs. Jack's reputation, may have even envied it a little. She also knew that the "breeziest woman in Boston," as a New York gossip magazine would later dub Mrs. Jack, expected obeisance. Once, while at her desk writing to her father, Clover put down her pen and went outside, walking over to Mrs. Jack and another woman "who were smiling and bowing" at her from across the street. She explained to her father, "We have asked them to dine on Wednesday and as Mrs. Jack wants to see diplomats I've sent for the German minister — the Turkish ditto — and Count de Suzamet (French). Three diplomats and terrapin ought to make them happy." Henry James treated Mrs. Jack as she wanted to be treated, as a queen. One gets the sense that Clover found this harder to do.

If Paris was the second act of their trip, Spain was its third. After Henry figured out he wouldn't be able to gain access to the archives he needed without more negotiation, the Adamses had decided to leave Paris, planning a return visit nearer to Christmas, and arrived in Madrid by overnight train on October 19. Henry found the city "without exception the ugliest and most unredeemable capital I ever saw." But they were besotted with "a sky so blue that one can scoop it out with a spoon." Clover raved, "The sun seems to drive out the damp and cold of London and Paris and the air is delicious." The Prado Museum was a feast of art. "Day after day we stroll into the gallery and gorge ourselves with Titian, Tintoretto, Veronese, and Velásquez," Clover exclaimed, adding that a Titian oil of "seventy babies with small turquoise wings" seemed as if it had been painted with "powdered jewels soaked in sunshine." When they traveled to southern Spain at the beginning of November, Granada left "nothing to wish for — sky, trees, flowers, air are simply perfect." She and Henry stayed at an inn on a hill under the fourteenth-century Moorish castle the Alhambra, less than a mile from the city, under towering elms and golden poplars that seemed "like enormous lighted candles." They lived "out of doors" with a wood fire in the evening, reading aloud in Spanish from *Don Quixote*. Spending a day in nearby Córdoba, they "poked about for hours in the winding little streets, peeking into house after house, with their marble vestibules as clean as a Shaker could wish; a door of iron lacework in quaint Moorish patterns, and behind a cool patio or open court round which the house is built, with orange trees, roses, blue jasmine, heliotrope, and other gay flowers in masses of colour — it was the *Arabian Nights* come to life again."

They took a steamer ship across the Strait of Gibraltar to Ceuta at the northernmost tip of Morocco, where Clover wrote, "We are having a beautiful time." From there, they embarked on an all-day trip by donkey caravan to Tetuán, like Ceuta, a city governed by Spain. They left early in the morning, together with the postman, several guides, and a rabbi with an enormous white beard, and traveled south along the Mediterranean coast, over long sandy beaches, and then across "plains of heather in bloom" and low palmetto trees. Henry wrote that the "ride was almost the most beautiful thing I ever saw." Clover gushed that it was the "most enchanting road all the way for nine hours," feeling proud that she was the first American woman ever to visit the ancient city. She proved her mettle when the donkey she was riding spooked at an imagined snake and fled, with her astride, into nearby bushes, bringing her into "abrupt contact with the soil of Africa," which, she added, "did me no harm."

Clover and Henry returned north in late November, in a rush to get to the archives in Seville, where Henry wanted to study diplomatic dispatches made by the Spanish minister in Washington during President Jefferson's administration. During a train trip to Córdoba, Clover had talked, in her novice but effective Spanish, with a woman whose husband knew someone in Granada who could introduce Henry to the archivist. Once in Seville, Clover took charge, convincing officials to open the archives despite a four-day celebration of the marriage of King Alphonso XII, for which all city offices had closed. During the three hours that Henry combed through bundles of documents, Clover talked with the tottering archivist, who had "one lonely tooth" and proudly showed her the papal bull given to Christopher Columbus, "allowing him to go in search of America." In playing such a significant part in advancing Henry's research, she couldn't have been happier: "It's a great satisfaction."

The joys of sunny Spain ended with the couple's mid-December return to Paris. They traveled by train for forty hours during the fiercest cold snap on record, with temperatures reaching far below zero. "Bitterly cold," Clover reported on arriving in Paris, with "streets piled with eight days' snow . . . yellow fog like cheese." The newspapers told how officials set open-air fires to help people keep warm while walking in the streets. Paris remained frozen for most of their six-week stay; the sun hung "like a white frost-bitten ball in the sky." More than the weather had changed. Henry left every morning for the Musée National de la Marine, not returning to their hotel on the rue de Rivoli until dark. Henry told Henry Cabot Lodge that he was working hard, but progress was slow: "Manuscripts are clumsy things to read, and there are few slower occupations than taking notes." After reading "hard all the evening," Henry returned in the morning to his "blessed archives," as Clover now called them. She was lonely and the acute cold made things worse. There was little for her to do except hover by the fire and read. Even the Louvre stayed closed. By Christmas week, Clover's unhappiness spilled over in her letters. "I hate Paris more and more," she complained. "It grieves me to think of the cakes and ale we are missing in Washington, — sun, saddle horses, dogs, friends, politics." All she could think about was their travels in Spain and Morocco, "a full feast," not only because of the Mediterranean sun and sky but because she and Henry had been together, side by side, and the memory filled her with "so much pleasure."

Three weeks later, Clover and Henry arrived back in London, where the dense fog and smoke made it seem as if they walked "under a big yellow gray umbrella." Henry James resumed his afternoon teas at Clover's fire, reporting to Isabella Stewart Gardner that "the Adamses are here, and have taken a charming house." Twenty-two Queen Anne's Gate was located in central London just south of Bird Cage Walk, not far from where they'd lived the previous summer on Half Moon Street. The house, with "every detail charming," had been pursued, as Clover reported, by the poet laureate Lord Tennyson, but the Adamses had gotten there first. With old mantelpieces, a cozy kitchen that would "make a picture for one of Caldecott's books," and an expert cook-housekeeper and under butler arranged for by Henry James, the household made Clover feel as if she and her husband had "lighted on our feet like two old cats." She looked forward, as she said, to "six months of peace and plenty."

Henry put himself on a strict work schedule; a month before, from Paris, he had written that he faced a "mountain of papers and books" to read through before summer and felt as if he hadn't "an hour to lose."

Many mornings he went to the British Museum to work. When not accompanying Henry, Clover spent time with her old friend Adie Bigelow, who was in town with her family, as was the gossip-prone Alice Mason, with her twenty-year-old daughter, Isabella. Clover had tea with her one-time idol, the famed English actress and abolitionist Fanny Kemble, now approaching seventy, who lived in the fourth-floor apartment of a nearby Queen Anne mansion. The meeting had been set up by Henry James, who'd first met Kemble in 1873 and thought her a woman of rare insight — she had "no organized surface at all," James wrote his mother, but was "like a straight deep cistern without a cover." Perhaps Clover reminisced with Kemble about the time Caroline Sturgis Tappan had introduced them at the Sedgwick estate in Lenox, Massachusetts, almost twenty years before. In any case, Clover found Kemble "gracious and agreeable" and hoped for a return visit.

There were other diversions. On a "lovely spring day" in early February of 1880, she and Henry went to watch Queen Victoria open Parliament, "a pretty show" she wished her nieces could see: "lots of gilt coaches with horses weighed down by brass trimmings and coachman and footman," and the last coach, drawn by eight bay horses "nearly smothered in brass," carrying the queen. She was dressed all in white, with an ermine cloak, and wore as a brooch the enormous Koh-i-Noor diamond, which had been given to her when she was pronounced the empress of India in 1877. The queen, Clover wrote, was "fat and red faced and ducked her old head incessantly from side to side." When a "Mrs. Houkey" invited Clover to watch a debate in the House of Commons, she couldn't refuse. The two women sat "as if in a harem," looking through "a lattice screen from the ladies Gallery" and listening to the speaker, Henry Brand, with his long robes and "hornet's nest wig." During the numerous long prayers that opened the proceedings, the "Tory side bow their heads while advanced liberals show impatience." The sight made Clover laugh.

Clover and Henry steered through London's "social rapids." Dinner invitations often stacked up three and four deep per night — "one misses a large proportion of them," Clover sighed, at the start of the season. But there were high points. At one dinner, she sat between the British physicist John Tyndall and the French philosopher Ernest Renan, with the poet Robert Browning sitting across from her. She was most disappointed in Browning, telling her father he had the "intellectual apathy in his face of a chronic diner," but forgave him, given the beauty of his verse. She thought the social Darwinist Herbert Spencer looked "like a complacent crimson owl in spectacles with an assumption of his own science in his manner." She spied his arrogance: "You are let to imagine that his very first principle of all is belief in himself." At another dinner, she defended the right of George Eliot, whose *Middlemarch* Clover had read on her honeymoon, to marry John Cross, a man twenty years her junior. Cross, a banker for an American investment company, was somehow acquainted with Ellen and Whitman Gurney. The news of Eliot's late-life marriage had "burst like a bomb shell" at an evening party where only Clover, Henry, and the poet Matthew Arnold knew of John Cross, and so they were "beset with enquiries." "We declare," Clover declaimed to her father, "that a woman of genius is above criticism." In mid-July she and Henry escaped to a manor house, Loseley Park, south of the city, along with the politician Sir Robert Cunliffe, whom Henry had always thought was "what a gentleman ought to be." They met Henry James and his older brother, William James, who was visiting England that summer. Together they took a walk through "fields of wheat and poppies — quaint little byroads with old red tiled cottages half smothered in roses," followed by tea, a lively dinner, and an evening by the fire, where the entertainment was what Clover enjoyed most: "a spring-tide of anecdotes and stories."

But Clover also wearied of the endless round of dinners out, saying "one dinner in six" was worth attending. Most were "sloughs of despond." Dr. Hooper asked her if she was homesick and wanted to come back home. But she didn't want to hear it. "Of course, we're 'homesick,'" she replied, defending their decision not to return to Beverly for the summer and early fall, as had been their habit. Discipline was in order. Feeling homesick, Clover explained, was "no reason for going home until the object which brought Henry over is accomplished." And she insisted their six months in London had been a success, reassuring her father: "We've had a good deal of pleasure — made many new acquaintances — and stuffed our little minds with new impressions."

Henry finished everything he needed to do by the end of July 1880, having collected much of the primary source material for the history of early America, which was now taking clearer shape in his mind. He'd closely studied English politics from 1801 to 1815 and gotten a vast store of French and Spanish papers in order, determining it would take him six volumes to tell the story of the period adequately. "If it proves a dull story," he wrote to Henry Cabot Lodge, "I'll condense, but it's wildly interesting, at least to me."

Scotland would replace Beverly Farms as a supplier of fresh air and breezes, and the couple left for the north as soon as they closed up the London house. At Matlock Bath, near the Peak District in northern England, Clover gloried in the change of scene, with "air like champagne after London." She had always wanted to visit the nearby medieval manor house Haddon Hall, and when the keeper said that no one could tour it on Sunday, Clover convinced him to make an exception by pleading they'd "come all the way from America" and offering a half crown to the keeper's young daughters for the favor. Though "not done up or patched" since 1699, the house was "enchanting." In one room hung an enormous tapestry picturing Aesop's fables, which Clover explained to their young tour guides. They left the next day by train for Edinburgh, then north via Perth for the hill country surrounding Dunkeld, where they stayed with friends of Ellen and Whitman Gurney. From there, they traveled fifty miles across the Grampian Hills and Spittal of Glenshee on a "sunny blue day" that Clover would long remember, with its "wild heather covered hills with white sheep and patient collies." The "crimson moors and blue hills" of the Scottish Highlands, which she found intensely romantic, were "reeking with history and legends." Henry put it another way in a letter to Gaskell: "My wife is flourishing and delighted with Scotland."

Clover and Henry were coming to the close of their trip. The "wandering Americans," in Clover's words, were finally going home. In early September of 1880, they arrived in Paris via London to shop for clothes and furnishings in preparation for their return to Washington and the new house they'd leased on H Street. Clover ordered a new wardrobe, including eight gowns by Mr. Worth. She found the task tedious but capitulated to Henry's dictum of the previous fall: "People who study Greek must take pains with their dress." Her husband was vain about appearances and continued to dress immaculately. He wanted his wife to look a certain way: "15,361 gowns and other articles of dress have thus far been delivered," Henry joked to Gaskell, "and there remain only 29,743 to come." They'd also collected a trove of paintings and drawings during the previous months: the "wee little early Turner" watercolor Clover gave Henry and Henry's reciprocal gift of a Johann Zoffany portrait to celebrate their seventh anniversary; several works by William Mulready, Copley Fielding, and David Cox; an enormous Moorish cabinet; embroideries from Salamanca, Spain; and much more.

During their eighteen months abroad, Clover and Henry had established "a wide acquaintance ranging from Tetuán in Morocco to Drum Castle in the Highlands," which had the paradoxical effect of making "the world seem larger and smaller, too." Clover had experienced no recurrence of feeling lost, as had happened on the honeymoon journey on the Nile. In Europe she knew exactly who she was. Her experiences had expanded her, deepened her, confirmed in her a keen appreciation for being an American. She had written from Spain that the "more we travel, the more profoundly impressed we are with the surpassing-solid comfort of the average American household and its freedom from sham. They beat us on churches and pictures in the Old World, but in food, clothing, furniture, manners, and morals, it seems to us we have the 'inside track.'" What distinguished America from Europe was more than comfort—it had something to do with attitude and spirit. "Our land," she said, "is gayer-lighter-quicker and more full of life." Henry James would miss his "good American *confidents*." They'd had many "inveterate discussions and comparing of notes." Though James thought Clover and Henry were both sometimes "too critical," he knew he'd miss their company. "One sees many 'cultivated Americans,'" James wrote to a friend, "who prefer living abroad that it is a great refreshment to encounter two specimens of this class who find the charms of their native land so much greater than those of Europe."

It would be the last time Clover would travel overseas, and somehow she sensed this, having written her father the previous winter, "As I don't expect to come abroad again, I want to make the most of this." Europe was a "pleasant story," she said, that "began well and ended happily," but it was one she did not "care to read over again." In conclusion she said, "I'd rather read a new one which may not end so well but still is new."

CHAPTER 10

Intimates Gone

ON HEARING THAT Jerome Bonaparte, the great-nephew of Napoleon I, would be wintering in Washington with his wife and two young children, Clover hoped the city would not become "too fashionable," although she added facetiously that she'd "rather winter in a first class American coffin" than any place she'd stayed during the previous months in Europe. She and Henry signed a six-year lease at two hundred dollars a month for another three-story mansion owned by William Corcoran, this time the "little white house" at 1607 H Street on the northern edge of Lafayette Square, nearer to Sixteenth Street, still known as the Slidell house after the bellicose Louisiana senator who had lived there briefly in the early 1860s. But they had to stay almost two months at the crowded Wormley's Hotel while workmen finished renovations, including new mantelpieces, built-in bookshelves, a large detached kitchen in back, fresh coats of paint inside and out, and a brand-new stable for their horses, Prince and Daisy. Henry continued to defer to Clover's skills in such matters. She had by now in their marriage set up or made over four homes, not including several temporary houses in London and Paris. As Henry wrote to Charles Gaskell, "My wife is fairly weary of house-furnishing." To all of this, she brought a mix of energy and exasperation, acknowledging at one point that the contractor "didn't realize when he undertook to put the house in perfect order that he would have two driving New Englanders at his heels." By the first week of December, after hiring servants and the delivery of fifteen wagon loads of black walnut and cherry furniture from Boston, she could finally announce "We are really in." She was pleased to be home, and Henry's contentment complemented her own — she reported how he thought "his house charming," saying virtually the same thing three months later: "Henry hard at work, gloating hourly over his comfortable quarters."

They were quickly caught up in the social events of the capital. "The town is filling fast and we expect an interesting winter," Clover wrote in mid-November. Dinner guests included James Lowndes, a lawyer and former colonel for the Confederacy; Aristarchi Bey, the Turkish minister; Secretary of the Interior Carl Schurz, still a favorite of Clover; neighbor Emily Beale; the Bonapartes; Jushie Yoshida Kiyonari, the Japanese minister, and his wife. Clover found General Ambrose Burnside, a senator from Rhode Island, a "nice old fellow and his dinner[s] very funny and informal . . . ; everyone stretches across the table and all talk at once."

There was much to discuss late in 1880 in Washington, principally the shifting political scene after November's election. John Hay thought no one since John Quincy Adams had entered office more qualified than President-Elect James Garfield, a Republican from Ohio with eighteen years' experience in Congress who'd won a slim victory over his Democratic rival, General Winfield Hancock, the hero of Gettysburg. The transition of power brought with it a turnover in the staffing of important posts, a process Clover followed with avid interest, writing her father that the "air is full of rumours of the coming Cabinet."

Clover paid particular attention to gossip about James D. Blaine, a senator from Maine, former Speaker of the House, and leader of the so-called Half-Breeds, a faction of the Republican Party that advocated civil service reform. The Half-Breed opposition to the Stalwart faction of the GOP, which had supported a third term for President Grant, had split the party, making room for Garfield to capture the nomination. Upon his election, Garfield named the shrewd, smooth-talking Blaine — Clover called him a "pretentious blatherskite" — as his secretary of state, though Blaine had been damaged earlier by never-proven accusations of receiving financial kickbacks from the railroad companies. On hearing of Blaine's appointment, Clover remarked that "it's a gross insult to the moral sense of the community, and a beginning which makes even friends and supporters of Garfield shake their heads and say, 'Who's next?'" Henry called the selection a "thunder-clap." Blaine's taint of corruption, his double dealing in regards to reform, and his antipathy toward their friend Carl Schurz were enough to poison Clover and Henry's opinion of him. They had refused to recognize Blaine and his wife socially. Now, with Blaine in the Garfield administration, Clover found herself in a difficult position: "For us it will be most awkward; never having called on them before, it will simply be impossible to make up to them now, and as we are on terms of great intimacy with several of the head officials in the State Department the position is not easy." Two weeks later, when a comment Clover made at a large dinner hosted by the Beales was repeated in the *Boston Herald,* the incident reminded her that on such occasions "one must always be on . . . guard."

Clover and Henry found refuge from Washington's ever-present "whispering gallery" with a small group of friends — John Hay, his wife, Clara, and Clarence King — with whom they could talk freely. For a brief time during the winter of 1880–81, all five of the "Five of Hearts," as they came to be known, lived in the same place at the same time and got in the habit of seeing one another almost every day. Though the origin of this group moniker remains unknown, it captured the immense pleasure they took in one another's company.

John Hay, born the same year as Henry, had grown up in Illinois, attended Brown University, and studied law at his uncle's law firm, located next door to Abraham Lincoln's practice in Springfield. At twenty-two, after working as a campaign aide in the 1860 election, Hay followed the new president to Washington as his assistant secretary, living in a corner room upstairs in the White House. He would recount those years with Lincoln in a massive ten-volume biography cowritten with John Nicolay. Hay's subsequent career as a diplomat took him to Paris, Madrid, and Vienna, followed by six years as an editor at the *New York Tribune.* By

1874, his marriage to Clara Stone, the daughter of the Cleveland industrialist Amasa Stone, had made Hay independently wealthy. Hay first
met Henry Adams in 1861 when both were in Washington, but their close
friendship, which would provide ballast for both men, began in the late
1870s, when Hay went back to Washington to serve as assistant secretary
of state under William Evarts in the Hayes administration.

Clara Hay, deeply religious and the most conventional of the group
(in Clover's words, "a handsome woman — very"), rarely said a word.
Not that she had much of a chance. Hay liked to chat "for two," as Clover
noted. Henry later wrote that Hay's table talk, impossible to capture on
the page, was "frivolous and solemn, quick and unaffected, unconscious,
witty, and altogether unlike the commonplace." Teddy Roosevelt, under
whom Hay later served as secretary of state, agreed, observing that Hay
"really did say things which every one of us would like to say but never
think of until after the opportunity for saying them is passed." Hay was
fastidious, affectionate, somewhat shy, generous, sidelined at times by
waves of self-doubt and undefined illnesses. His talent was tempered,
as one Washington journalist recalled, by "a touch of sadness." When
asked later in life to write his autobiography, he replied, "I am inclined
to think that my life is an oughtnottobiography." For all his good humor,
his manner had a distinct formality. "No matter how intimate you were or
how merry the occasion," one friend remembered, "nobody ever slapped
John Hay on the back."

The group's "fifth heart" was the rugged, handsome, peripatetic Clarence King, the one everyone thought most likely to succeed at anything
he decided to do. A Yale graduate in chemistry, he became, at the age of
twenty-five, the U.S. Geologist in charge of the U.S. Geological Exploration of the Fortieth Parallel and spent six years exploring and mapping
vast reaches of the American West. King was also an enigma, a keeper
of secrets. He later fathered five children with Ada Copeland, an African
American woman in New York whom he married, posing as a black man
with the alias James Todd. But King didn't inspire suspicion among his
friends — only envy and worry. They fretted about his whereabouts, his
health, and his ever-shaky finances, which he blamed on his never-ending
duty to a dependent and demanding mother.

What his friends knew of King was what he showed them: his considerable personal talents. Henry had known King since the summer of 1871, the year before his marriage to Clover, when they'd camped together in the Uinta mountain range in Utah Territory. Finding a new friend as winning and gifted as King was "a miracle," Henry wrote. King, who'd been leading the fortieth parallel survey from the Sierras to eastern Wyoming since 1867, knew "America, especially west of the hundredth meridian, better than anyone." Hay, who'd become friends with King earlier over drinks and cigars in New York, said King "resembled no one else whom we have ever known." Hay marveled at King's humor, his grasp of art and literature, and his "intelligent sympathy which saw the good and the amusing in the most unpromising subjects." King had, according to Hay, "an astonishing power of diffusing happiness wherever he went." Clover joked at Hay's tendency to effuse, especially about King, saying at one point that, for Hay, the younger man was "like the sun in heaven." She added dryly, "I never imagined such frantic adoration could exist in this practical age." But Clover herself was not immune to King's considerable charms. They shared a passion for art and exchanged letters about current women's fashion, and whenever he returned to H Street after a western tour, he brought her something, once giving her "a basket made by the sister of a [Paiute] Indian chief," Clover reported, "who was buried in Mr. King's dress coat."

With these friends, Clover felt recognized, known, seen, and able to lay aside the filigreed screen of elite social life. She called Clarence King "our prop and stay." John Hay, who would remain Henry's closest friend, called Clover the "first heart," a gesture of affection she cherished. His ease and warmth were what she craved, and perhaps his own struggles with self-doubt helped him recognize what wasn't so obvious about Clover — her sharp wit often covered a deep craving for reassurance and tenderness.

With an office next door to the White House in the State, War, and Navy Building (currently known as the Old Executive Office Building), Hay would stroll through Lafayette Park to join Clover and Henry for five o'clock tea. Hay's wife, Clara, often came along as well , though at times she had to return to Cleveland to tend the Hay children and her parents. Already the author of two highly respected books, *Mountain-*

eering the Sierra Nevada in 1872 and *Systematic Geology* in 1878, King now came by H Street after he finished his work as first director of the U.S. Geological Survey, which mapped and investigated geological and mineral resources. Tea at Clover's small round table turned into dinner, which turned into late-night conversations, as the Five of Hearts gathered around the fireplace in low-slung red leather chairs. It was always "a good deal of good talk," as Clover told her father.

But fear and runaway sorrow intruded on Clover's idyllic domestic scene. Her sister-in-law, Fanny Hooper, was sick with a gasping cough she couldn't shake. "Is there disease in either lung or is it merely an obstinate cough such as we all struggle with at times," Clover had asked nervously from London the previous spring, clearly haunted by the memory of her own mother's fatal cough thirty-two years before. She speculated with her father that the physical strain of bearing five children in seven years had been "too much" for Fanny, fearing she'd contracted the dreaded scourge of tuberculosis, a possibility that the doctors later confirmed. What was to happen to Ned's five little girls who, at the time, ranged in age from two to nine? But by August, Clover had written with relief, "It's nice to hear of Fanny as riding and getting stronger," a sentiment she echoed in a missive the following week: "It's nice to have such good news of Fanny."

Now, in late February of 1881, Clover's father wrote to her about Fanny's "increased suffering," and Clover announced she wanted to go to Cambridge to help. She waited for her father to give her a cue as to what she should do. "Write or telegraph me if we can be of any earthly use either to Fanny, Ned, or the children or to help lighten Ellen's care," Clover pleaded on a Wednesday. "I will be nurse or read story books all day long or play games or anything to fill any gaps. Henry and Mr. King will do nicely together and I can leave at two hours' notice. If we were in trouble Ned would find fifty ways of helping us, and we feel like two brutes to keep five hundred miles off and do nothing."

The following Sunday morning, February 27, Clover wondered why she hadn't heard word from her father and worried about how the unfolding family tragedy might be affecting her sister, Ellen, who lived in Cambridge next door to Ned and Fanny: "I've been half expecting a summons from you by mail or telegraph in answer to my note of Tuesday," Clover queried. "I should think Ellen needed reinforcement by this time; the continued strain of responsibility and sympathy must be very wearing." That same morning, several hours later, two telegrams arrived, from Dr. Hooper and Ned. Her family had kept from her the news that Fanny had died two days before. Clover missed Fanny's death and would be unable to attend her funeral, which had been planned for later that same Sunday afternoon.

Her family's decision to exclude her in this way, to reject her offer of help, must have been intensely painful. Perhaps Clover worried that she had failed somehow by not returning from Europe the previous spring and summer, when first told of Fanny's illness. There was no real explanation.

On hearing the horrible news, Clover wrote back immediately, but protected herself: "I want to go on and see all of you but after turning it over and over have decided to wait at least a few days. Henry flatly refuses to let me go alone and I am not willing to pull him up from his work. If you had sent us a telegram Friday night we should have gone on, now we think we should be a bore." On Saturday, March 6, Clover asked to hear "how Ned's babies get on and who is to take charge" and explained her absence again with the excuse that Henry would not let her go to Cambridge by herself: "I have not the heart to drag him off from his work, in which he is much absorbed." She adopted an even more distant tone five days later. "Unless I am really needed I don't fancy the idea of going north in March," she wrote dully, adding, "I shouldn't pull well in single harness after so many years' practice in double."

How to explain this extraordinary family scene of suffering, rejection, and self-protection? Was it Henry who prevented Clover from seeing her family after Fanny's death, as she seemed to claim? His letters during these weeks explained how he'd immersed himself in writing — "deep in history," as he put it — and nowhere does he mention Fanny, Ned, or Clover's concerns. And surely he loathed deathbed scenes, writing at one point that "of all the experiences of life, there are none whose accumulations are so heavy in their weight on the mind, as the death-beds one has to watch." Yet if Henry didn't insist they both go to be with Ned and his girls, he also apparently didn't actively stop Clover from traveling to see her family during the crisis.

Instead, what may have been some reluctance on Henry's part and what can only be seen as the Hoopers' misguided protection of Clover's emotions gave her a way to dodge her own roiling feelings. She tried to escape sorrow by declaring the priorities of her life with Henry, as if Fanny's death threatened to engulf her and take these responsibilities away from her. Perhaps what she most wished to avoid were the faces of Ned and Fanny's young daughters, now bereft of their mother, because in them she would have seen again her own young face. Did Ned, Ellen, and Dr. Hooper intuitively understand her dread of this and, in order to spare Clover (and themselves), thereby neglect to send a telegram on the day of Fanny's death, knowing their delay would prevent Clover from attending the funeral? Impossible to know. In any case, Clover turned away from them, a withdrawal that may have divided her from her family in a way that was new. As spring approached, her cheerful mood of the previous fall and early winter had darkened.

Overtly restless and bored, Clover directed her attention to her garden, a "patch" measuring seventy-five by fifty feet behind the house; she hired George Bancroft's expert gardener to plant chrysanthemums, lilies of the valley, and roses to border a lawn with a red maple at its center. She spent many afternoons on horseback, sometimes riding again after five o'clock tea. She kept up with her Greek lessons and decided to read Edward Gibbon's six-volume *The Decline and Fall of the Roman Empire*, "a bone which will take months to gnaw." She was always reading something, telling her father what he might enjoy: Anatole France, William Dean Howells, Goethe. But that spring of 1881 her heart wasn't really in it, and by May she complained, "It's read, read, read, till I loathe the very sight of a book."

After President Garfield took office in March, John and Clara Hay decided to leave for Cleveland, and Clarence King resigned his post as director of the U.S. Geological Survey and headed for the silver mines of Mexico. The Five of Hearts stayed connected, visiting frequently and writing letters to one another on stationery Hay designed, with a five-of-hearts playing card reproduced on the upper left-hand corner. Even so, Clover dreaded the breakup of the group. "In this ever-shifting panorama of course we shall find new combinations, but we shall hardly have the same intimate cozy set that we did," Clover mourned as her friends left the city. She noted King's departure to her father at the end of March, only a month after Fanny's death: "One by one our intimates are gone."

+

CHAPTER 11

"Recesses of Her Own Heart"

ONLY MONTHS EARLIER, in the less bereft days of late 1880, Clover had written wryly to her father, "I am much amused but not surprised at your suspecting me of having written *Democracy*." She was referring to Henry's first novel. He had started the manuscript during the late fall of 1878, sending it off to the publisher Henry Holt just before he and Clover left for their European travels in May 1879. Since its anonymous publication earlier in 1880, while the Adamses were safely away in Europe, the scathing satire of Washington politics had caused a sensation, selling out nine printings in its first year alone. A favorite game in Washington parlors and beyond was guessing the novel's author and the inspiration for each of its thinly disguised characters. Clover was amused to find herself on a "black list" of possible authors, along with "Clarence King and John Hay!" Only Holt, E. L. Godkin (the founder and editor of *The Nation*, later editor-in-chief of the *New York Evening Post*), and the rest of the Five of Hearts were in on the ruse.

When the book was released two years later in England, Hay would write Henry from there that people talked about nothing "except the authorship of D." He told Henry how, while he had been strolling through Kensington Park with Clarence King, Henry James, and William Dean

Howells, all in London at the same time, Howells suddenly blurted out to the group that he and Charles Warner (Twain's co-author of *The Gilded Age*) had solved the mystery. The Connecticut writer John William De Forest had to be author of *Democracy*. "We were astonished we had not thought of it before," said Howells, in Hay's report. In his reply, Henry would ascribe authorship to Hay, musing with mock sympathy, "Much as I disapprove of the spirit of your book . . . I can see that in English reflection it must become somehow more terrible to its creator than to anyone else." It was a charade the friends conducted back and forth for years.

Democracy was Henry's first novel, a satiric roman à clef that took as its subject national values dimmed by President Grant's corrupt administration and a spoils system that defied reform — a narrative unwinding of the myriad ways by which politics undoes governing. The central character, Madeleine Lee, is in flight from New York to Washington after the catastrophic deaths of her husband and her baby, but "bent upon getting to the heart of the great American mystery of democracy and government." Madeleine is accompanied in her search by John Carrington, a genial lawyer from Virginia. His rival for her affection is Senator Silas P. Ratcliffe from Illinois, a thinly disguised portrait of Senator James G. Blaine, who personifies all the failings of Gilded Age politicians. Other minor characters include Baron Jacobi, a Bulgarian minister, whose "witty, cynical" banter mimicked the humor of the Turkish minister Aristarchi Bey, and the "mischief maker" Victoria Dare, who "babbled like the winds and streams" while passing on social gossip; she was inspired by Clover's young neighbor Emily Beale. (Emily recognized herself in the novel's pages and called the novel "a horrid, nasty, vulgar book, written by a newspaper man not in good society.") As Madeleine searches for democracy's first principles, her two suitors — the honest, dull Carrington and the corrupt Ratcliffe — continue their pursuit of her. Finally, on the brink of marriage to Ratcliffe, his acceptance of a $100,000 bribe is revealed. Madeleine is saved from a loveless union, but no closer to understanding democracy or anything else, except her own vulnerability.

Although the final confrontation between Ratcliffe and Madeleine has a spark of vital feeling, most of the characters are not much more than types: a corrupt politician, a southern lawyer, a cynical diplomat, a Boston Brahmin, a president from the Midwest (a blend of both Hayes and Grant) buffaloed by forces he doesn't understand. Henry James thought the novel "good enough to make it a pity it isn't better." But Teddy Roosevelt's assessment savaged its bitterness and pessimism, its suffocating sense of defeat. *Democracy* had a "superficial and rotten cleverness," Roosevelt wrote to Henry Cabot Lodge, not knowing that his good friend Henry Adams had been its author and dismissing the romp as "essentially false, essentially mean and base."

The only character that resonates is Madeleine Lee, but perhaps not in the way Henry intended. Madeleine is a projection of the author in several respects. Her determination to understand democracy and her tendency to scrutinize her feelings and doubt their authenticity recall her creator's traits. But Madeleine also has a resemblance to Clover. Like Clover, Madeleine presided over her Lafayette Square home with a flair that made it "a favorite haunt of certain men and women." Like Clover, she was an American "to the tips of her fingers" who resisted "admitting social superiority in anyone." She scorned religious piety, doubting its capacity to answer big questions. She said attending church "gave her unchristian feelings." This sounds so much like something Clover would say that it's no wonder Dr. Hooper thought his daughter wrote such a quip.

But there is a more evocative echo between Madeleine and Clover. Ratcliffe had not appealed to Madeleine's "religious sentiment, to ambition or to affection." Instead, he had seduced her by making her feel that her self-sacrifice in marrying a man she did not love would result in making her important, powerful, of "use in the world." Sensing how she "atoned for want of devotion to God, by devotion to man," he appealed to her "tendency towards asceticism, self-extinction, self-abnegation," which had the effect of blinding her to her own self. She had, in the words of the novel, "not known the recesses of her own heart." Madeleine escaped a loveless marriage to Ratcliffe with a return to her own principles, but her experiment in Washington was over and her future promised little more than flight and drift. Her attempt to "escape from the torture of watching other women with full lives and satisfied instincts, while her own life was hungry and sad," had come to nothing.

Many specifics of Madeleine's story differ, of course, from Clover's life. Yet Henry's explanation of Madeleine's predicament as a woman without family and without focus for her considerable curiosity and intelligence limned aspects of Clover's own increasing restlessness and solitude. As a woman without children of her own or a focus for her talents, Clover surely asked the central questions posed in the novel: "Was the family all that life had to offer? Could she find no interest outside the household?"

The author of *Democracy* was doubtful a woman could find such satisfaction.

From June through September of 1881, Clover and Henry lived again in Beverly Farms. From the Harvard library Henry requested access to the university's collection of American newspapers, asking that material dated 1800 to 1809 be boxed and shipped to him there: "A weekly instalment [*sic*] of six or seven volumes would be all I could manage." He was drafting the first two of what he now projected would be nine volumes about the administrations of Jefferson and Madison; the opening six sections, or books, would present, as he put it, "the social and economical condition of the country in 1800." He had also accepted a request from John T. Morse, editor of the American Statesmen series at Houghton, Mifflin and Company, for a short biography of the Virginian John Randolph, a leading proponent of states' rights and the southern cause who'd been an enemy of both Adams presidents. Henry finished a first draft in little more than a month, working ten-hour days. He wrote to Charles Gaskell, at one point, that "my eyes ache and my hand aches."

Clover planned to start reading Plato's *Republic* in Greek as well as Virgil's *Eclogues* that summer. She was also busy with Ned's five daughters, who were staying at Dr. Hooper's nearby summer home. The girls were coping with the recent loss of their mother as best they could. In a note to Anne Palmer, Clover mentioned that her nieces had taken her "to their doll cemetery yesterday—it was 'Decoration Day'—six mangled noses—arms and legless dolls lay in peaces [*sic*]—'Sawdust to dust' with chunks of white marble at their heads—pasteboard crosses and names to mark them and flowers ad libitum." Though the eerie scene in the woods impressed itself upon Clover strongly enough that she described it to Anne, she didn't note whether she grasped that the girls might have been reenacting the loss of their mother in their play, as she herself had done at her Aunt Sue's house so many years before. Nor did Clover report in her letters to Anne news of how Ned was coping without his wife. She mentioned her sister, Ellen, but only in passing.

That fall, Clover and Henry stopped for several days in New York on their way back to Washington from Beverly Farms. They met Anne Palmer and joined John and Clara Hay and Clarence King for a night at the theater, dining together at the famous Delmonico's restaurant before curtain time. But Clover was relieved to return home in October, writing to Anne, "We found the house as clean as soap and water and brooms can make an old trap ready—fires burning—nice driver, ecstatic dogs—placid horses—blooming roses in garden and gorgeous maples in front and behind—I feel like a field lily." Politics was once again at the forefront since President Garfield's shocking death in September 1881 after an assassin's bullet. Clover approved of the cabinet choices of the new president, Chester Arthur, whom she thought was on the "road to Damascus" regarding civil service reform. Helpful to Henry was the fact that James Blaine was out as secretary of state. Henry had refused to work at the State Department archives while Blaine was in charge there, but with the appointment of his friend Frederick Frelinghuysen as the next secretary, he now felt he could resume that research.

Clover resolved on New Year's Day 1882, perhaps with the tragedy of Fanny's death less than a year earlier close in her thoughts, to "make all one can out of life and live up to one's fingers' ends." With the social season in full flower, requiring attendance at countless teas and dinner parties, Clover wrote her father at the end of January that "life is like a prolonged circus here now." Henry's youngest brother, Brooks, was their houseguest for several weeks, and Henry James, also in town, was a frequent dinner guest. She asked her father to write her a postcard with the following prescription: "My dear child: Let me beg of you not to make calls and as few new acquaintances as possible. I know better than you the delicacy of your constitution. Ride on horseback daily but avoid visiting and evening parties. Medicus."

But she didn't take her own advice and on one occasion had to explain to her father why she hadn't had the chance to write her usual Sunday missive: "I really was so driven yesterday by people that not one blessed moment could I get even for a note." Her father warned her to "beware of 'partisan' politics" after she'd sent several long letters detailing how Blaine had become the subject of a congressional inquiry regarding his Latin American diplomatic practices. She managed to elude the omnipresent Oscar Wilde, in town in early 1882; she shared the opinion of Henry James regarding this colorful character: "a fatuous fool," as Clover noted. But she also described with considerable relish how she'd seen him while on a stroll on Pennsylvania Avenue: "long hair, dressed in stockings and tights, a brown plush tunic, a big yellow sunflower pinned above his heart, a queer cap on his head." When Clover turned to look at Wilde as he passed by, she saw "a large blue card on his back, 'Oscar Wilde on a wild toot.'"

Collecting art was for the Adamses an antidote to the "prolonged circus" of social life. When their dealer, Thomas Woolner, the Pre-Raphaelite sculptor and poet, sent from London a second small painting by the English Romantic artist Richard Bonington as a gift, Clover proudly noted that her collection of Boningtons now numbered four — "we shall at this rate leave fine pickings for our heirs." To her delight, she received at the end of January a note written anonymously but in "a lady's handwriting" that said, "'If you will go to 1905 F Street before January 25 . . . you will see . . . two portraits by Sir Joshua Reynolds which will be sold at reasonable prices.'" Almost ten years before, while on her honeymoon in 1873, Clover had reported her assessment of several paintings by Reynolds: "Sir Joshua's pretty women and children [are] enough to make your hair stand on end with envy."

Several days later, Clover took Agatha Schurz, daughter of Carl Schurz, and Henry along to the run-down stucco house, where servants showed Clover photographs of the two portraits. After discussing the matter with the head librarian at the Library of Congress, Theodore Dwight, Clover bought the portraits, a matched pair of a husband and a wife, for $150 each. "They are not *first*-rate; are very dirty, no varnish, and badly cracked," she wrote her father. "The lady, snub-nosed and pale, in pink satin with blue gauze scarf and pearl ornaments, hair drawn up over a cushion; Mr. Grover, stout and handsome, in powdered wig, gray brocade coat, and white neckerchief." She added that she preferred "the woman; Henry the man, though he wished neither and 'hates portraits,'" preferring to have landscapes on his walls. Clover satirized the difference between them with a rhyme: "Jack Sprat dislikes portraits, / His wife dislikes paysages, / And so betwixt them both / The choice is very large."

After buying the portraits, Clover wrote to Thomas Woolner in an effort to confirm their authenticity and provenance. He replied in early April that the portraits were of Mr. and Mrs. Groves (not Grover), who had sat for Reynolds in 1755. But before she got Woolner's answer, Clover had already confirmed that the portraits were "genuine Sir Joshuas," having been owned for five generations by the Galloway family in Maryland. "Eureka! Eureka!" she exclaimed to her father: "I am their first purchaser!" She hung the two portraits between the library windows, "side by side," as she told her father. Henry, Clover decided, could "look the other way." It was the first time she recorded any kind of difference with or defiance of Henry's tastes and wishes.

As much as Clover enjoyed her adventures in purchasing art, she found herself feeling drained. In March, Secretary Frelinghuysen asked Henry to serve as foreign minister to Central America in Guatemala City. Clover was given the unpleasant task of communicating her husband's refusal of the unexpected offer—Henry hated doing such things—and she told the secretary it would be "an unwise appointment." Yet she had regret, telling her father, "I wish we wanted it, it would be so new and fresh." That same day she wrote to Anne Palmer that most of their friends no longer resided in the capital. Carl Schurz had moved to New York City, John Hay was in Cleveland, Clarence King "had nearly died," as Henry reported, from a rupture of an old injury. Melodramatically quoting Shakespeare, she wrote how she and Henry sat "in these 'bare ruined choirs' where they so lately sang—and try to warm ourselves by burnt out fires." By May, after unusually cold and wet weather, she told her father, "Every fool becomes a philosopher after ten days of rain, so I spare you the inside view of my heart."

Summer proved equally trying. Clover had under her care at Pitch Pine Hill, as she reported to Anne Palmer, two of her youngest nieces "during the months when colic and unripe fruit prevail—so that if I cannot boast of maternal joys I can of ditto cares." She was plagued by a "nightly toothache." Otherwise, she told Anne, "It's quieter here than any average grave." Henry, absorbed in his writing, wrote to Charles

Gaskell in June that "nothing . . . disturbs history. I grind on, slowly covering vast piles of paper with legible writing, but without even thinking of the day when it will be read by others." By the fall, on returning to Washington, he admitted that they'd been "bored by our summer," though it proved "a good time for hard work." Clover was sick in bed off and on, with an infected tooth, a bad cold, a roaring noise ("like Boston") in her ears. She concluded a November letter to her father, saying, "Nerve dead, tooth finished; shall begin tinkering with Eustachian [tube in the middle ear] this week. This drivel will weary and disgust you—never mind."

She spent the holiday season of 1882 immersed in George Sand's *Histoire de Ma Vie*, written in 1855. The sprawling twenty-volume autobiography of Amandine Aurore Lucile Dupin, which was Sand's birth name, covers a span of years from her turbulent childhood to the 1848 revolution, a narrative that refrains from, as Henry James wrote in 1884, "an explicit account of the more momentous incidents of the author's maturity . . . In other words, she talks no scandal." On Christmas Eve, Clover wrote her father that she felt "glad you're reading *Histoire de Ma Vie*," explaining she found it "pleasant to be enjoying the same book. I'm in the fifteenth volume and think the interest increases." She spent Christmas Day in bed with a bad headache, but kept reading. By New Year's Eve, she had raced through another three volumes in the original French, reminding her father of his days in Paris as a young man studying medicine and imagining that he must have passed by the great bohemian woman of French literature. "How are you getting on with George Sand? To me it grows more and more interesting; volume eighteen is charming and I'm sorry it ends with volume twenty. She must have jostled you daily in the Latin Quarter in 1832 in men's clothes, dining in cheap restaurants."

Did the prolific Sand, who grew up motherless, who left her marriage, and, in the words of Margaret Fuller, "bravely acted out her nature," embody for Clover something entirely forbidden but desired: a woman's liberation? Clover did not say. But Sand's unruly life, as she told it in her *Histoire*, was certainly the literary work Clover commented on most in her entire correspondence. Nothing else quite captured her attention as much as the cross-dressing Sand, with her freedom and courage to be, as

Henry James observed, "open to *all* experience, all emotions, all convictions."

At almost forty, what Clover had found thrilling as the young wife of Henry Adams—fascinating conversations, proximity to political power, access to the most prominent figures of the day—had lost some of its luster ten years later. If Henry's desire that she stay at his side reassured her she was wanted, his demands also might have inhibited her. She began to think of herself as yoked in a double harness of togetherness and confinement. Her salon was becoming a gilded cage, which "left out on the whole, more people than it took in," as Henry James described it in his short story "Pandora," which includes a fictionalized portrait of 1607 H Street.

She continued to host her usual five o'clock teas and to attend dinner parties and the theater, but, like the fictional Madeleine Lee of Henry's *Democracy,* she couldn't figure out how to be more useful. She knew she'd always be on the sidelines when it came to politics. She didn't join any women's organization that might have offered a forum for action, in spite of her experience with reform work in the years after the Civil War and prior to her marriage. She considered women activists dreary and their luncheons worse. As much as she found tending to her wardrobe tedious, when she reminded herself of the drab appearance of two leading Boston activists in the woman suffrage movement, Abby May and Ednah Cheney, she felt inspired to place another order to Mr. Worth's workroom. Though Clover's lack of interest in the issue of suffrage would shift somewhat over the coming years, she kept her thoughts and feelings about it mostly to herself. She had built around herself a carapace that had its protections but also foreclosed wider arenas for action and feeling, exactly what she longed for and what she'd found so compelling in George Sand's *Histoire.*

Henry's temperament was cooler, more inward than Clover's. He wrote eloquent, sometimes moving letters, and his published history remains distinctive for breaking away from dry historical fact to capture the drama and emotion that underlay the founding of the country. But he had a spiky Adams manner—John Hay playfully called him "Porcupinus Angelicus." His habit of pulling away to look, examine, and understand from a measured distance made him see people as types more than as individuals, no less in life than in his novels. He said one should treat heavy things lightly and light things with gravity, which became a handy witticism, a deflection from strong feeling. As Henry's writerly ambitions increased, he turned his formidable focus ever more inward, and his detached posture became notable for its thoroughgoing irony. The burden for making the marriage work had largely fallen upon his wife. He depended on Clover's outgoing liveliness to moderate his own reserve, but when he found her discouraged, when her state of mind turned dark, his gift for irony may not have had enough light and freedom in it to brighten her mood.

By early 1883, the contentment Clover had shared with Henry three years before on their European travels seemed at a far remove. Her restlessness grew. Most painfully, Clover had begun to doubt whether she was any longer Henry's "first heart."

CHAPTER 12

The Sixth Heart

HENRY ADAMS ALWAYS had an alert eye for female beauty. To Charles Gaskell he once wrote, "I make it a rule to be friends with all the prettiest girls, and they like me much better than they did five-and-twenty years ago, and talk more confidentially of their doings." He called such young women the "Birds of Paradise." His shows of gallantry probably threw off more light than heat, but even so, Clover must have found her husband's attentions to younger women unnerving. She had never ceased to feel self-conscious about her appearance, particularly her long Hooper nose. Just as she did not seek to be photographed, Clover never had her portrait painted, though it was almost de rigueur for women in her social class and she could have engaged any of the leading portraitists of her day, including John Singer Sargent.

Clover never openly admitted to jealousy — maybe it was too hard to voice or too dangerous to leave evidence of such an emotion for someone to discover later. She did, however, make an oblique reference to what was troubling her by early 1883. In a long letter to her friend Anne Palmer, Clover reminisced about her romantic trip with Henry through Europe in 1879–80, recalling in particular a carriage ride on a clear, warm August day through the rolling Scottish countryside near Dunkeld.

While Henry drove, as Clover remembered it to Anne, she read aloud a Shakespeare sonnet (Sonnet 90), and the two memorized it during the ride:

> Then hate me when thou wilt, if ever, now,
> Now while the world is bent my deeds to cross,
> Join with the spite of fortune, make me bow,
> And do not drop in for an after-loss.
> Ah do not, when my heart hath 'scaped this sorrow,
> Come in the rearward of a conquered woe;
> Give not a windy night a rainy morrow,
> To linger out a purposed overthrow.
> If thou wilt leave me, do not leave me last,
> When other petty griefs have done their spite,
> But in the onset come; so shall I taste
> At first the very worst of fortune's might,
>   And other strains of woe, which now seem woe,
>   Compared with loss of thee will not seem so.

What Clover so enjoyed about being with Henry was exactly this: a shared love of both literary expression and landscape. Shakespeare's heightened language, read aloud in the haunting beauty of Scotland—she described it to Anne as "interlined with purple hills and rushing streams and heather and weather"—exemplified this perfectly. But Clover's backward glance to this moment almost three years in the past was tinged with sadness. The sonnet speaks of injured love as something expected, perhaps unavoidable. Was she preparing herself for this sort of rejection?

Then, in the same letter, Clover broke away from her reverie and announced to Anne that she empathized with the Greek figure Clytemnestra. Clover had continued studying ancient Greek, working her way through the plays of Aeschylus in the original language. She had started with the first play in the Oresteia trilogy, *Agamemnon,* wherein the great king returns from battle to his wife, Clytemnestra, accompanied by the lovely and conspicuously younger Cassandra, who sits alongside him in his carriage. "The result of a month's wrestling with Agamemnon has brought me to feel great sympathy with Clytemnestra," Clover announced to Anne. "Put yourself in her place—suppose your husband undertook to go after a pre-historic Mrs. Langtry taking in all the nicest men in town." Mrs. Lillie Langtry, a former mistress of the Prince of Wales who scandalized New York during her acting debut in 1882 and whose behavior Henry thought revolting, posed no threat to Clover.

But Elizabeth Cameron probably did.

Elizabeth Sherman Cameron, the niece of General William Tecumseh Sherman, was—like Lillie Langtry—a celebrated beauty. Lizzie, as everyone called her, had "a strong face, a pointed chin, small mouth, lovely hazel eyes of an almond shape that was typical of the Shermans." She was so attractive, one relative remembered, that she made "most women look like 35 cents" by comparison. Photographs taken of her by Frances Benjamin Johnston capture her abundant curls, along with her impossibly slender waist and a come-hither look directed boldly at the camera. A British noblewoman once called her "a dangerously fascinating woman."

Lizzie had first come to Washington from Ohio in early 1878 when she was just twenty. She had been sent to the capital by her family, who hoped to avert her from marrying a young man at home whom they deemed unsuitable. In Washington she was to stay under the watchful eye of another uncle, John Sherman, who was by then secretary of the Treasury in the Hayes administration. General Sherman noted her arrival to the social scene at once, saying in a letter to his wife, "Lizzie is here and she is as fresh and beautiful as ever."

Lizzie's father, Charles, the eldest Sherman brother, had never made enough money to suit her mother, Eliza, who had social ambitions for her children. To remedy this, the Sherman brothers stepped in to arrange a more advantageous marriage for Lizzie, to James Donald Cameron, a millionaire widower with six children. Cameron (his intimates called him "Don") was a newly elected senator from Pennsylvania, a replacement for his father, Simon Cameron, the Pennsylvania senator who had served as secretary of war under Lincoln until he was forced out of the cabinet because of mismanagement and corruption. The fact that Senator Cameron was also twenty-four years older than his prospective bride seemed not to bother the Sherman family, though newspapers took note, one calling the match "Beauty and the Beast."

The couple had had a lavish wedding in May 1878, and they then moved to Scott Circle, several blocks north of the Adamses, on a street that was connected to Lafayette Park by Sixteenth Street. The marriage was disastrous from the start. Don Cameron, tall and thin, sporting an enormous mustache, had interest in politics, poker, and little else. Taciturn, brusque, and stained by the reputation of his powerful father, who still controlled his career, the senator sank into alcoholism, which got neither worse nor appreciably better.

To escape, Lizzie Cameron, age twenty-three, started going to the Adamses for tea and conversation in early 1881, befriending both Clover and Henry. She'd meet Emily Beale, who was three years older, and together they'd stroll across the street to 1607 H Street, the Beales' family dog in tow (once, to Clover's delight, the dog arrived all on his own to her tea table at the usual time). They'd rap their umbrellas on Henry's first-floor study window to be let in for a visit, telling Clover it was better than ringing the doorbell because Henry couldn't make the excuse that he was busy. "Miss Beale and Mrs. Don Cameron come to tea every day and are great fun; the latter is very pretty," Clover reported early in their acquaintance.

But though Clover and Lizzie became friends, Henry's connection to Lizzie grew deeper and more powerful. On a lonely day in early March 1883, missing Hay, King, and other friends, Henry wrote to Hay, "If it were not for dear Mrs. Don I should be sad." The next month, he wrote about Lizzie to Hay again, saying, "I adore her, and respect the way she has kept herself out of scandal and mud, and done her duty by the lump of clay she promised to love and respect." When Lizzie and her husband were preparing for a European tour, Henry eagerly tried to smooth the path for her, even as he kept a careful distance from her husband. Henry explained to Hay that he didn't want to "saddle his friends" by giving formal social introductions for the Camerons, but he urged Hay, who was traveling in England, to "tell our friends to show *her* kindness." Henry asked Charles Gaskell to look out for "my dear little friend Mrs. Don Cameron," and to James Russell Lowell, who was in London at the time, Henry gave special instructions. "She is still very young," Henry confided, but she was also "most sympathetic and American" and because of her husband's "pretty poor" character, he worried she would be lonely. Henry asked Lowell to "take Mrs. Don to some big entertainment and point out to her the people she wants to see or know," then confided, "You will fall in love with her, as I have." Henry and Clover missed meeting Lizzie at the train station for her send-off, but Henry's explanation did not clarify much: "Our feelings overcame us. Will you forgive?"

Henry needed no forgiveness from Lizzie. The strain was on his wife. Clover and Lizzie liked each other, enjoyed each other's company, wrote letters, and exchanged gossip. Once Clover wrote to her father how Lizzie and Emily Beale came to "tea every day and are great fun." There's no such direct record of Lizzie's feelings for Clover, though she must have been grateful for Clover's welcome and offer of friendship. Even so, Clover was too astute not to notice the growing attraction and bond between her husband and Lizzie. Noticing inspired worry, and Clover's worst fear—loss—arose as a possibility. As was her habit, she escaped fear by turning to a different subject and exercising her knack for mockery. In mid-March, Clover wrote to her father about "a somewhat ghastly tea at ex-Secretary McCulloch's—Calvinist divines sleek and smug with their wives, Indiana friends of the hostess, newspaper feminine correspondents whom I've been carefully dodging for six winters." Two weeks later, another typical sign of Clover's darker moods surfaced: boredom and restlessness. She wrote, "We've had no gaiety this last week; only one or two things offered, which did not tempt me."

What may have troubled her most was the vanishing possibility that she and Henry would ever have a child. Eleanor Shattuck Whiteside, Clover's childhood friend from Boston, actually mused that their childlessness may have been "a greater grief" for Henry than for Clover. In Henry's family, marriage equaled children, and he was worried enough about their childlessness to obtain a copy of the 1873 edition of *Clinical Notes on Uterine Surgery with Special Reference to the Management of Sterile Conditions,* by J. Marion Sims, M.D. If within her own family Clover was protected from feeling too anomalous by the fact that her sister and brother-in-law also had no children, she must have worried that she disappointed Henry, most likely blaming herself for their childlessness, regardless of the actual medical reasons that might have explained it. Clover managed her feelings about such things in a way she'd learned as a child: by turning away. In a chatty letter to her father in the spring of 1883, Clover requested he send along newspaper clippings on the doings of Boston society, but with a caveat: "So give me a marriage and death column, weekly—births, I'm not interested in especially."

The highlight of the spring of 1883 for Clover turned out to be an out-of-town visit with Anne Palmer, who had stayed in Washington earlier in February. After Anne's departure, Clover remarked in a letter to her friend that she'd "not laughed since you went—it seems 5000 years since our week of giggling and sunshine." Anne reciprocated, inviting Clover for a midweek visit to New York City to stay with her and her parents, Susan and Oliver Palmer. At first Clover demurred, claiming she didn't want to miss out on the blooming wildflowers, that she was busy with the arrival of another puppy, their fourth Skye terrier, "and so on & so on." But in the next breath, she admitted a restlessness that a trip to New York might cure: "On the other hand, I've not seen a locomotive since October and I want a lark . . . I shall stay two days and come back Thursday so if you're bored it won't be for long. I've no shopping to do, [and] I've trimmed my bonnet myself." She added an afterthought: "H & I have not been separated for eleven years and I want to test his affection."

Together she and Anne had a wonderful time. They went to Barnum's Circus, where Clover especially enjoyed the races, and they met with Anne's parents and mutual friends for various dinners and teas. They spent most of their time, however, looking at art. Anne shared Clover's passionate interest in the visual arts, and her friends in New York were "various artists and out-of-the-usual-line people." Their first stop was the sixth annual exhibition by the Society of American Artists, a progressive group that had broken away from the National Academy of Art. Though Clover found the exhibit "very poor," one painting, in particular, caught her eye: a "very striking full-length portrait of a Miss Burkhardt by John Sargent." She had met John Singer Sargent once before on the trip to Spain with Henry, but when she saw his *Lady with the Rose* (1882), she confidently declared him "a promising Philadelphia artist."

They also stopped by the studio of Augustus Saint-Gaudens, an Irish-born American sculptor and a friend of Anne's. Saint-Gaudens was already at work on his bronze memorial to Clover's cousin, Colonel Robert Gould Shaw, a magnificent bas-relief that would take the sculptor fourteen years to complete. Anne had viewed a maquette for the memorial and wanted Clover to see it, but, unfortunately for them, Saint-Gaudens was not at his studio when the two women stopped by. They did meet the artist of *Reading the Story of Oenone* (1882), a painting of "five pretty Greek girls" that the *New York Times* commended as "one of the centres of attention" at the society's exhibit. Francis Davis Millet, born in Massachusetts and Harvard-educated, welcomed them into his studio to look at more of his canvases, and they met his wife, Elizabeth, or "Lil," who was both "pretty and nice," sitting as her husband's model with white garments draped about her, in what Clover called an "Eden-like costume."

Back in Washington, Henry missed his wife, sending her mournful lines from their empty house on H Street: "The dogs are well / So are the horses / So am I / We were very lonely last night / And sat up late working." After Clover returned home, she reported to her father that "Henry says he's glad I enjoyed *my* week, but that it's *his* last alone." She repeated Henry's reaction to Anne, taking pains to quote his exact words: "my husband was glad I enjoyed my visit as it would not '*happen again.*'" She appears both pleased that he missed her and annoyed that he deemed she not travel again on her own. Her trip to New York had been exactly what she craved—immersion in another place, away from Henry and his needs and concerns.

This brief release from her marriage thrilled Clover. Now she wrote to her father about being full of enthusiasm for spring and feeling happier: "A blessed rain is soaking the roots of trees and grass today . . . magnolia, japonica, and forsythia make a fine show opposite our windows and the rides are getting better every day." To Anne, she exclaimed, "It has taken me one week to unpack my mental trunk and set my new ideas in order—how I did enjoy my outing!" Though Clover never elaborated on what her "new ideas" might have been, her trip to New York appears to have sparked her interest in photography. Anne was already an avid amateur photographer. Already the previous year, Clover had written to Anne, "I long to see your photos." Now, less than three weeks after her trip to New York, on Sunday morning, May 6, 1883, Clover picked up her newly purchased camera and took her first photographs. In the coming months, she would begin to explore through this form of art what her mother had explored in her poetry—a wrestling with loss and a love of beauty woven together with queries about life's meaning and a woman's place. And, like her mother, Clover would try to convey what she herself was thinking and feeling — not with words, but with expressive, life-packed images.

Henry, meanwhile, grew restless and unsettled. In a letter to Lizzie Cameron that summer he would write that his wife now did "nothing but photography."

✦

PART III

Clover's Camera

Isn't it odd how much more one sees
in a photograph than in real life?
— VIRGINIA WOOLF

CHAPTER 13

Something New

"WE'VE BEEN RIDING far and hard this last week," Clover wrote to her father soon after her return to Washington. One day she and Henry rode out twenty miles to Rockville, Maryland, then back home through Bladensburg, "a picturesque old town," then nine more miles to return home. She organized a three-day excursion to the Luray Cave in Virginia's Shenandoah Valley, planning to bring along friends, including Lucy Frelinghuysen, the youngest daughter of the secretary of state; Captain von Eisendecker, the new German minister, and his young wife; and the charming southern lawyer James Lowndes. To her father she admitted some nervousness about it: "How I wish you were going with us, I know you would enjoy the company and all; it's my invention, too, so I feel responsible." She need not have worried. The tour turned out to be a "great success from first to last" and the landscape delighted her: "The Shenandoah River is the most picturesque, the banks lined with flowers, while dogwood and red-bud trees fill all the middle distance." The next month, Clover observed that the capital continued to attract the most talented people—writers, diplomats, scientists. The tales of western adventure told by Raphael Pumpelly fueled her fascination with the West. Pumpelly, soon to be named director of the New England branch of the

U.S. Geological Survey, was currently at work on the Northern Trans-continental Survey for the Northern Pacific Railway. "Mr. Pumpelly to tea and stayed on to dine, was charming as ever," she told her father. "His account of the Great Northwest on the line of the Northern Pacific is like a fairy tale."

But photography held Clover's attention most. Her most successful day in the early weeks of picture taking was also her first, May 6, 1883, when she had some beginner's luck. Of the six glass-plate negatives she exposed that day, she made prints from all six, crossing out three as failures in her notebook. The two prints she saved depict subjects she found closest at hand: Henry; Marian Langdon, the nineteen-year-old daughter of a family friend; and two of her dogs, Toto and Marquis. In the first exposure, Henry sits rather stiffly in profile on the back-porch stairs of their home at 1607 H Street, his right hand holding the paws of Marquis, who couldn't keep his head still. Henry, in his tweeds, trimmed beard, and straw hat, is a vision of the leisured class. The pale leather gloves he cradles in his left hand are for fashion, not to protect his hands from calluses. In the next exposure, Marian Langdon sits on the same stairs, holding Marquis; the other dog, Toto, is a blur of movement. Though Clover's camera is moved back a bit for this shot, in other ways the composition reflects the photograph of Henry; taken together, the two compose an initial sketch of sorts, a first try at picturing a man and a woman of leisure.

The next week Clover was not so lucky. She took two exposures of her garden wall, and both were failures. Her portraits of Aristarchi Bey, taken the following Saturday, were equally disappointing. Bey, the Turkish foreign minister who had been the model for the amusingly cynical Bulgarian minister in Henry's *Democracy*, had stopped by at 1607 H Street for lunch to say goodbye after being recalled from service. Clover told her father that "politics is at the bottom of it." He'd been a guest for tea and dinner many times and was another of Clover's favorites. She took two exposures of the foreign minister holding her dog Boojum, one exposure for two seconds, the second for four. She pictured him, as she said, "as a 'dude'—small hat on his head." Clover was intent, it seems, on creating her own characterization of Bey. But each exposure failed and "will not print." The next evening she loaded up Henry, their three dogs, and their driver, John Brent, for a carriage ride to Rock Creek Park in order to try out, as she wrote to her father, her "new machine." Clover carefully made two related entries in her notebook, as if conducting a science experiment: "Waterfall at Rock Creek, 2 seconds, smallest lens" and "3 seconds, next smallest lens." But she did not make prints from these exposures either. Picture taking was a far more complicated process before George Eastman's point-and-shoot camera, which would be introduced on the market in five years. Clover had to learn which lenses to use and how to gauge the sunlight and exposure times, as well as how to mix the exact chemical solutions needed for developing. The learning curve was steep.

But Clover had made a start doing what would distract and absorb her in the coming summer days—she had begun to picture her world.

Photography itself had become much more popular with amateurs after dry-plate negatives became commercially available in the late 1870s. Instead of drenching a sheet of glass with a mixture of light-sensitive chemicals that stained clothes and hands, then putting the wet plate immediately into the back of the camera to take the picture, Clover could purchase glass negatives that had been treated with a light-sensitive gelatine-bromide coating. This eliminated the need for the dangerous chemicals and cumbersome darkrooms that previous photographers had had to carry with them. Clover still needed to develop the negative and print the photograph on paper treated both before and after the "printing out" process with complicated chemical baths. But with the advent of dry-plate negatives, picture taking was, without doubt, less daunting.

The new technology made photography more accessible to women, though they had never been wholly excluded from it. Since the beginning, with the invention of the daguerreotype in 1839, women had worked in photographic salons and as camera operators. *Outing: An Illustrated Monthly Magazine of Recreation* noted that women "have always been employed in some important capacity in the photographic establishments." But by the early 1880s, amateur photography manuals and guidebooks touted the newer, lighter camera outfits—camera, glass-negative holder, tripod, carrying case — as just right for women. One could make multiple exposures, keep the negatives in a small holder that kept out light, and develop the images later, at one's leisure. In 1882 Henry Clay Price, in his book *How to Make Pictures: Easy Lessons for the Amateur Photographer,* declared that "amateur photography is destined to be taken up by ladies of refinement and quick artistic perception."

The record created by a photograph — what was made visible in the image itself — seemed to defeat distances between people and to make time stand still. Dr. Oliver Wendell Holmes, a long-time friend of Clover's father, observed that because of photography, "those whom we love no longer leave us in dying, as they did of old. They remain with us just as they appeared in life." Photography was deemed an appropriate activity for women precisely because of its emotional power, its ability to tie the viewer to "absent loved ones," claimed *The Young Lady's Book: A Manual of Amusements, Exercises, Studies, and Pursuits.* A photograph registered what people looked like both individually and in relation to one another, making visible the connection between spouses and the heritage passed on from parents to children to grandchildren. Women were expected to bind together relationships in the family, and photography, despite its highly technical aspect, was ideally suited to bolster this emotion-charged responsibility.

The status of photography in relation to the fine arts also made it more accessible to women. The British art critic John Ruskin argued that a woman's familial and social duties included cultivating taste, refinement, and beauty, and that she must be educated to enable her to "assist in the ordering, in the comforting, and in the beautiful adornment" of society. This relation between the arts and a woman's duty encouraged more women to attend art school to learn painting, even sculpture, in the 1870s and 1880s. But a line was drawn. A woman's primary relation to the fine arts remained that of a viewer. She could visit art museums, be trained in the arts, and even make beautiful objects, but true art and the social identity of being an artist belonged principally to men.

At the same time, photography itself was not yet considered a fine art. Though critics had made a compelling case for its aesthetic and graphic power, photography would not be recognized as meriting such distinction until the early twentieth century. It would take Alfred Stieglitz, with his journal *Camera Work* and his New York gallery, known as 291, to change how the medium was viewed, so that it could emerge as a legitimate form of fine art, to be collected by and displayed in museums.

Until then, photography was deemed inferior to painting. Its dependency on chemical potions and mechanical contraptions made it seem closer to a science than an art, and it was often linked to the decorative arts, with their emphasis on beauty rather than deeply personal artistic expression. In fact, photography met Ruskin's standards as an appropriate way for a woman to make pictures precisely because of its multiple failures as a fine art. "There has been some discussion whether photography can be called one of the arts," *The Photographic Times* noted in 1883, "but there can be no question, we think, that it can be made a recreation."

If Clover found photography daunting in that first month, she kept up her courage. She purchased up-to-date equipment and set aside a room in her house where she could develop her negatives and make her own prints. She sought guidance from Clifford Richardson, a chemist at the U.S. Department of Agriculture who was also interested in photography, and she and Anne Palmer kept in contact, exchanging their photographic prints. Clover's camera was, as she told Anne Palmer, "a new and small machine," made of fine-grained mahogany, an ideal wood to keep out moisture; it had brass hinges, closures, and other fittings around the camera lens. At that time, photographs were made like contact prints. The glass negative was placed directly on photographic paper, and then both were exposed to bright sunlight for an allotted amount of time. Clover's camera used five-by-eight-inch dry-plate glass negatives, and her prints, almost without exception, measured likewise.

In large letters, Clover wrote "Photography" at the top of the first page of a small lined notebook she had bought for other purposes but now appropriated for her new passion. In its pages she noted the date and time of day of each exposure, listing the numbered exposures in neat rows. When she developed the negative, she used another color of ink to cross through the number, putting an X through entries that proved unsuccessful. The photography manual she chose for advice was Captain Abney's *A Treatise on Photography* (1878), which emphasized the scientific aspect of picture taking: chemical reactions and optics. She carefully copied out in the back pages of her notebook recipes for developing solutions, which looked like a kind of chemical poem:

Pyrogallic acid 6 grains to 2 oz water

Ammonia— 1 oz

Brom Potass 3 oz in graduate

Water for 5 x 8 negative

Hypo—5 oz to 20 of water—or

1 L. to 4—water—Alum saturate solution—ten minutes for negative

The literary critic Edward Mendelson observes that "as soon as the self commits itself to someone or something, the fragments converge; they become purposive and whole; you become yourself." This is what happened with Clover. Restless in the previous months, increasingly uneasy about her marriage, Clover found with photography a polestar around which to focus her considerable energies and interests. She was a superb writer, but her marriage had room for only one author. Photography was a wholly different activity, more active and more social. And it drew on Clover's natural abilities: her keen eye, her acute powers of observation, and her attuned sense of the distinct features of an individual's personality. Also, something surfaced in her photographs that was not readily apparent in her witty, sometimes barbed letters, and certainly not in Henry's rather acid fictional portraits: a richness and subtlety of feeling.

CHAPTER 14

At Sea

CLOVER PUT HER CAMERA down for most of the month of June 1883. She told her father that much of the city had cleared out for the summer, including Lizzie Cameron, who had gone for a two-year tour of Europe. "No society this week," Clover wrote, sounding a note of loneliness. "We see none of the people who used to drop in to tea." In early June, her horse Daisy tore her leg so badly she could no longer be used as a saddle horse. Clover bought a thoroughbred horse in Baltimore she named Powhatan, after the father of Pocahontas. He was, she proudly bragged, "beautiful and swift, brave and gentle." Henry, four years into the project, was steadily at work on his *History*, rewriting a draft for a private printing; this he would use to solicit comments and give to others for safekeeping. His brother Charles, John Hay, George Bancroft, Carl Schurz, and Abram Hewitt, then a U.S. congressman from New York, were selected as recipients. As Henry wrote to a friend, "You can never tell what you want to do, till you see what you have done." He also complained about Washington's beastly hot weather — "the thermometer outside is about 90" — and he was relieved to be going once again to the quiet and cooler weather of Pitch Pine Hill.

The annual packing up for the summer's escape usually took a few weeks. Clover and Henry had to make arrangements with servants for both homes, ship by train their horses, and gather up their collection of beloved English watercolors. They didn't like to live without their art. They left Washington on June 18, arriving at Beverly Farms via Albany. Once there, Clover wrote to Anne Palmer about an exploit in a nearby marsh, as she rode Powhatan and Henry rode his horse, Prince:

> On Friday — in Harding a marsh — slimy green above — he [Powhatan] balked — got in too deep — became terrified — dashed into a tree — which swept me from my saddle — he leapt over me and the young tree — & dashed away — through bog and bush — I in my brand new habit — that unpleasant — he fled to Henry on the far side of the bog and put his bridle into his hands — then I had to wade to him and we led those two beasts thro' a mile and more of thick woods — through the "Pole Marsh" on planks — Prince slipping and I slipping and he treading on my toes and I on his — Henry and Powhatan in front — my saddle too muddy to mount — & my safety stirrup going — we got home at dusk . . .

She also described the routine of their midsummer days: "Our days go swiftly riding — Greek o' evenings — history writing from 9 to 5 — breakfast at 12 — no dinner — tea at 8." Perhaps keeping her rival close, she wrote the same story and noted the same routine to Lizzie Cameron, joking that her "husband is working like a belated beaver from 9 to 5 every day in gambling the history of his native land as run by antediluvian bosses — called Thomas Jefferson and James Monroe." She also promised Lizzie she'd send along a photograph of Henry and the dogs, Marquis and Possum, sitting in the window of the children's playhouse she'd built for the Hooper girls two summers before. After a short time away from her camera due to moving house, she had picked it up again and found herself completely engaged. She wrote to Clara Hay, "I've gone in for photography and find it very absorbing."

Clover's pictures that summer focused on those closest at hand: Henry, her father, her nieces, her dogs, her new horse, visitors. When Clover photographed Pitch Pine Hill, she did so from the drive at a distance below the house, which emphasized its hilltop location and gave the image an almost gothic quality. The modest house becomes castle-like, in keeping with the medieval medallions in the red-cement floor of its foyer. In picturing the bucolic scene, Clover aspired to the popular French Barbizon style, a genre of early impressionism she had encountered on her visits to Doll and Richards, Boston's influential art gallery. The leading promoter of the style, the painter Jean-François Millet, invested rural life with a noble, almost sacred, grandeur. Postwar Boston audiences, troubled by an erratic economy and crowded streets, found such scenes hugely appealing. Clover's photographs of lazy Holstein cows pasturing near ancient stone fences at her neighbor's farm were infused with nostalgia, recalling the colonial past.

She spent a late afternoon photographing three of her older nieces, dressed in matching summery white frocks and straw hats, as they perched on large rocks at the seashore. Nine-year-old Louisa, called Loulie, stands to the right of the frame, gazing soberly at her aunt's camera and holding a small bucket in her right hand. The other two girls, Ellen and Mabel (Polly), are seated nearby and carefully posed in profile, looking out to the water. Clover didn't like their expressions in the first exposure, but concerning the second exposure she wrote in her notebook "very nice." The image links the sisters through their similar clothing, yet each appears to be a distinct individual; the composition, with its inward focus, calls to mind John Singer Sargent's *Daughters of Edward Boit*, painted the previous year and shown in Paris, though Clover would not have had the occasion to see it.

When people stopped for a visit, Clover gave them food and drink and put them in front of her lens. Francis Parkman, the American historian well known for his 1849 book, *Oregon Trail: Sketches of Prairie and Rocky-Mountain Life*, and his multivolume *France and England in North America*, turned up on July 29, and that afternoon he sat for Clover's camera in a rattan chair against a backdrop evoking his western travels: boulders rising from the ground behind him, sun-dappled branches. The vigorous-looking sixty-year-old sat cross-legged, with his shiny black boots catching the light and a fashionable white-felt derby perched on his head. Clover took two exposures, trying out different compositions and exposure times. She developed the negatives and made prints from both, placing them one after another in her album.

Parkman was an outspoken opponent of woman suffrage, and Clover couldn't help but comment on his marked prejudice, an attitude she was beginning to find wearisome. To her father she had mentioned that the Confederate general Richard Taylor "disbelieves in democracy and universal suffrage as firmly as Mr. Frank Parkman." She also joked that the long-widowed Parkman would never find his "ideal woman" in America and that if she had to talk "much with him, I should take the stump for female suffrage in a short time." At no point, interestingly, did she mention that Henry and Parkman were closely allied in their views on ideal womanhood. In any case, her photographs of Parkman capture his intelligence and élan as well as his Brahmin pose of casual superiority.

When Clover and Henry went to Quincy for a visit at the Adams family's Old Manse the next day, she took her camera with her. One can only imagine her in-laws' comments. She photographed Henry's youngest brother, Brooks Adams, standing next to his horse, Snowden; the horse's tail is a blur of movement against the stable's brick wall. But the most compelling image of her Quincy visit is her portrait of Mr. and Mrs. Adams. The two are seated on the porch of the manse, on either side of the front door, which is open. Mr. Adams is on the left and Mrs. Adams on the right. The darkened doorway between them admits neither visual nor emotional access. The viewer stays on the porch. Clover heightened this feeling of exclusion by how the two are posed, each facing three-quarters toward the middle, with Mr. Adams's leg and Mrs. Adams's cane angled toward each other, to form a strong V-shape. This gives energy and stability to the image even as it emphasizes what the darkened door already communicates: "no entrance." She increased this effect by positioning her camera just below eye level so that Mr. and Mrs. Adams are doing in the photograph exactly what she knew they did in life: looking down at her with impassive disdain.

Clover made a factual comment in her notebook: "no—1. Old house in Quincy Mass. / C.F. Adams & Mrs. Adams / on piazza—Monday p.m. / July 30th 1883—longest stop 4 sec." Most of her early entries in her small leather-bound notebook are spare and concerned with the technicalities of taking pictures. But she was learning and gaining confidence. By the end of the summer, her observations became more fluid and conversational. She frequently made note of her failures: on July 12, "Parlor

Bev. Farms — 9 minutes — failed"; on July 15, the second exposure of a catboat "spoiled by not putting in a slide"; on July 25, two exposures of Powhatan were "undertimed." She also mentioned the mechanical and aesthetic aspects of the picture-making process. She wrote in her notebook that her lenses were manufactured by Dollmayer and that she bought her supply of dry-plate glass negatives from Allan & Rowell, a Boston photography studio and supplier on Beacon Hill since 1874. Her photograph of Lucy Frelinghuysen was a "very good photo — expression not good!" Likewise, her portrait of Grace Minot, in a basket chair on the lawn, is a "good photo — not pleasing likeness." She took note of backgrounds that were "too dim" and commented on how the camera could make flesh look "dead white," especially if the plate was overexposed.

Clover's photographs were not like the snapshots Kodak would later popularize. The size of her camera and extended exposure times didn't allow her to sneak a picture. Most of her images are highly formal and composed. She experimented with tone and style, but nonetheless each photograph required careful forethought and decision making concerning camera placement, the relationship of foreground to background, exposure times, and the processes for developing the prints. Portraits are in a sense collaborations — they record something, always, of the working relationship between subject and photographer. Clover's portraits reflect what she saw, what she found interesting, compelling, and worthy of a picture, but also something more elusive: her feelings.

This is particularly true of a series of photographs Clover took on August 8 near Beverly Farms. The first two exposures are of Mrs. James Scott at Manchester Beach (which is now called Singing Beach). Mrs. Scott's identity remains obscure — Clover made no mention of her in letters, nor did she give the woman's first name in her notebook. Presumably, Mrs. Scott was either a neighbor or a friend of a neighbor who had come along for the day at the beach. In any case, Clover's photographs of her capture the woman's direct, candid demeanor. In the first, Mrs. Scott, dressed in cool white vacation clothes, with her dark hair a striking contrast to her white cap, sits low to the ground. She is turned slightly away from the shore, looks directly into Clover's camera, and clasps her hands easily together, with her parasol to her right and Boojum lying at her feet to her left. A large boulder directly to her right emphasizes the stability of her pose. The next exposure has a subtly different effect. Mrs. Scott is standing this time, with her body turned to the shore and leaning against the large boulder. Boojum is out of the picture, but the parasol leans at a diagonal across her leg. Again, she looks directly at Clover's camera.

These are somewhat conventional images of the seashore. Clover borrowed the painterly convention of filling one side of her image, the left in this instance, with sand, rock, and plants, with the other side opening up to sea and sky. Mrs. Scott is seated on rocks, with the beach's most distinctive and identifying feature — Eagle Head, a rocky promontory that juts out to the sea on the eastern end of the beach — directly in the background. This view of the beach, looking east to Eagle Head, had been painted numerous times in the 1860s and 1870s by several American painters, including Winslow Homer, and Clover, of course, would have known this.

The next two exposures, however, have a significant difference. Clover and her friends move from Singing Beach west to a granite headland, Smith's Point. In the first photograph, Helen Choate Bell, the widow of the Boston lawyer Joshua Bell, sits by herself on a rock surrounded by sea grasses and brush, with Singing Beach barely visible off in the distance. She's not on the beach but placed above it, overlooking the sea. The scene is as calm as a sleepy summer afternoon, its tranquility complicated only by the way Mrs. Bell's shoulders seem to slump, as if she's ill at ease on her rocky perch. Clover positioned Mrs. Bell with her back three-quarters to the camera, a placement that invites the viewer to identify with the figure as she gazes at the sea. Yet the viewer is prevented from seeing what a photograph of a person usually provides: the subject's face. Mrs. Bell seems to have no visual link to any other person — not to Clover taking the picture nor to viewers of the image. Mrs. Bell becomes, in effect, a woman at sea, or a woman lost at sea.

Clover's photograph of Mrs. Bell is strikingly similar in composition and mood to *Woman on the Beach of Rügen* (1818) by Caspar David Friedrich, whose work embodies much of what is associated with German Romanticism — a love of nature, an emphasis on individual feeling, and what E.T.A. Hoffman has called an "infinite longing." In fact, the way Clover positions her figures within the landscape is evocative of

Friedrich's Romantic trope of *Rückenfiguren*, translated as "turned-away figures." Though Clover never stated in her letters that she had seen a painting by Friedrich, she was, undoubtedly, familiar with the painter's work.

If the photograph of Mrs. Bell was a borrowing of Romantic imagery, the next image turns Friedrich's Romanticism in a new direction. It is an artfully composed photograph of two women and a young girl on the rocks at Smith's Point, with the seashore in the background. Clover identifies her subjects in her notebook — "Mrs. Ellston Pratt — Mrs. George D. Howe & Alice Pratt — on rock." Mrs. Ellston Pratt was Miriam Choate Pratt, the younger sister of Helen Bell, the subject of Clover's previous photograph, and both were daughters of the powerful Boston lawyer and former Massachusetts senator Rufus Choate. Noted for their charm, the Choate sisters were well ensconced in Beacon Hill society. The second woman, Alice Greenwood Howe, was a friend of the sisters, and all three were close friends with the author Sarah Orne Jewett — who would, in fact, dedicate her novel *The Country of Pointed Firs* to Alice Greenwood Howe. The third name in Clover's list, Alice Pratt, was Miriam Pratt's young daughter.

What kind of friendship did Clover have with the women she photographed on that August day? She made mention of Helen Bell and her sister, Miriam Pratt, several times in her letters, always complimentary, on one occasion telling her father that their visit to Washington was socially successful: "It was charming to see Mrs. Bell and Mrs. Pratt . . . It's well that folks here should see that Bostonians can be decent and well-bred." Alice Howe, older than Clover by half a generation, was prominent in Boston society — one of the founders of the Boston Symphony Orchestra and a member of the Museum of Fine Arts and the Humane Society. She and her husband, George D. Howe, the wealthy owner of a cotton mill, had a summer estate on Lobster Cove, near Smith's Point. Even so, Clover and Alice Howe were more like neighborly acquaintances than close friends.

Certainly, Clover's photograph of Mrs. Pratt, Mrs. Howe, and Alice Pratt on Smith's Point is not a straightforward portrait intended simply to capture the likenesses of three specific women. Instead, Clover carefully stage-managed the composition, creating a mood not of friendship and connection, but of lost possibility. Alice Pratt sits near the bottom right of the frame, her summery white dress suggesting a life of leisure infused with optimism. Her body faces the camera, her hands fold easily on her lap, and her young face—open and faintly smiling—is caught turning a bit to her right. Next to her sits Alice Howe, dressed all in black and turned in the other direction, with her back to the camera, her right earring glimmering above her high collar, her hair just visible through the netting that obscures her face. She is more ghost than living woman. Miriam Pratt stands in the middle of the frame in a three-quarter position, with her elaborate bustle clearly visible. Her strong posture anchors the image, but her head is downcast and her hands are held almost too deliberately in front of her. The figures of the two older women are turned away, yet their stance differs from that of Romantic *Rückenfiguren*. The women are connected neither to one another nor to the sea, which might otherwise open up their visual world, and their turned-away position shuts out the viewer.

Clover was a month away from her fortieth birthday. While she had seldom shown an inclination in her letters or conversation to critique her social position, there is evidence she had grown into a clearer understanding of the strictures that limited a woman's horizons. And if, in the process of making photographs, Clover transformed herself from a passive woman to an active one—she was both composer and viewer—this image nonetheless evokes an undeniable feeling of isolation, loss, and constraint. It pictures exactly what the photographer did not have: a mother figure and a daughter, women from the previous generation and the succeeding one, who might have otherwise accompanied Clover.

CHAPTER 15

Esther

IN MID-AUGUST of 1883 Clover took her camera to her father's home in Beverly Farms. She photographed Betsey, her father's housekeeper, wearing a lace cap and doing handwork on the front porch, as the dog, Doudy, lay at her feet. Clover next took two exposures of her father sitting in his open buggy, holding the reins of his horse, Kitty, harnessed and ready for a ride. She paired a print from one of these exposures with her photograph of Betsey, to form a kind of parental portrait in the album—these were the two people who had most directly raised her. The character of her father is further emphasized in the print that follows. In this second image, Dr. Hooper stands upright, directly in front of a tree. His white hair and mustache frame a distinguished visage; his long legs and slender frame echo the slender trunk of the tree. Still a vigorous man, he anchors the composition, twinned with an equally stabilizing element, the tree. In her portrait of him, Clover made clear what she relied on—her father's quiet strength.

That August, Clover also took a series of photographs of Henry. In May she had captured his image on the back stairs of their Washington home on the very first day she tried out her camera. Later in the summer, she took two exposures of him holding their dogs Marquis and Possum in the window of the playhouse built for her nieces behind Pitch Pine Hill. She listed these photographs in her notebook and sent copies to Lizzie Cameron but never included them in her albums. Clover's most well-known portraits of her husband were taken six days later, on the morning of August 19, 1883. She seated Henry at his desk, where he directs his gaze downward to the paper he's writing on. Light pours in through French doors that faced south and opened out to the front yard. The neatly stacked papers to his left are most likely manuscript pages of the first volumes of his *History*. In her notebook Clover stated that Henry's face was "good" in the first exposure, but she didn't like his black coat. So in the next exposure, Henry now wears a lighter tweed coat, which she likes much "better." The last exposure of the morning was a self-portrait. She wrote in her notebook that it was a "hideous but good photo"; she hated the way she looked. It is unlikely she made a print from its glass negative, and if she did, she didn't include a copy in her album.

The portraits of Henry are rather conventionally composed. But Clover chose to display them in an unconventional way. When it came time to put the portraits of Henry in her album, she didn't place the two prints on facing pages, as she had done with her two exposures of Francis Parkman, or even in sequence, as she had done with her father's portraits. Nor did she mount her self-portrait next to his, as might be expected. Instead, Clover chose to put Henry's portraits next to prints of a lone umbrella pine tree clinging to a rocky bank at Smith's Point, which she had photographed later in August. And she did this not once, but twice, in the album. By pairing her husband with a desolate tree, Clover perhaps portrayed him as holding on to the rocky cliffs of his intellectual pursuits—alone, brave, a survivor in the face of implacable nature. But the doubling also amplifies what's already apparent in the portraits: the solitude demanded by Henry's work was of a piece with a pervasive solitariness in his personality.

Clover seems to have understood this aspect of Henry. She didn't rebel against it in the way that Mrs. Adams had pounded on the closed gates of Charles Francis Adams's fastidious nature, nor did Clover echo the frustrated complaints her mother-in-law hurled at her father-in-law: "You judge me by yourself, you might not—we feel things so utterly unlike"; "You can't understand my feelings." At the same time, Clover made clear that loneliness permeated her life with Henry. She took pictures of him, alone, while she remained behind the camera, and in her album, her image never appears alongside his. Even while alive, Clover made herself a missing presence beside her husband.

Henry found Clover's continuing absorption in photography unsettling, unnerving. As Clover refined her skills, he began a second novel, *Esther*, which would be published in March 1884, with a title character, an amateur painter, who "was audacious only by starts" and who had "not the patience to be thorough." Esther's struggle to develop her own visual vocabulary, her wanting to know if she could be something more than an amateur painter, matched Clover's own efforts. Part of what Henry did in the novel was to try to sort out what all this might mean. As with Madeleine Lee in *Democracy*, only more so this time, Henry borrowed from Clover for his eponymous Esther, beginning with Esther's looks and comportment. His description of his lead character carries startling similarities to his undermining description of Clover in his letter to Charles Gaskell reporting his engagement, more than ten years before:

> She is too slight, too thin; she looks fragile, willowy as the cheap novels call it, as though you could break her in halves like a switch. She dresses to suit her figure and sometimes overdoes it. Her features are imperfect. Except her ears, her voice, and her eyes which have a sort of brown depth like a trout brook, she has no very good points. . . . Her mind is as irregular as her face, and both have the same peculiarity.

But the resemblance went further. Both women had adoring fathers; both had lost their mothers early on; both were strong-minded, with a quick wit and an interest in and talent for the fine arts; and both relished nature, finding more purpose and meaning there than in conventional religious belief. Esther's lament—that she could not "hold my tongue or pretend to be pious"—was Clover's own. Clarence King thought the resemblance between Esther and Clover so complete that he speculated to John Hay that Henry harbored "regret at having exposed" his wife, particularly her "religious experiences."

As Henry drafted the manuscript in the late summer and early fall of 1883, he in effect composed his side of the coded conversation that he and

Clover carried on inside their marriage. He told no one he was writing a second novel—in fact, his authorship would not be publicly confirmed until much later. But Clover knew. While she was making photographic portraits of Henry that made oblique comment on their marriage, he was doing the literary equivalent. These two exchanged few letters over the course of their years together because they were so infrequently separated. But in her photographs and in his novel, each created a portrait of the other, showing each other their thoughts and feelings in eloquent, troubling form.

Esther Dudley is a privileged young woman of New York City, the only child of William Dudley, a widower rich enough from a family inheritance that he can afford to ignore his law practice. Ill with a weak heart, he worries that his daughter, now twenty-five, is not yet married and is pursuing her interest in art and painting instead of seeking an appropriate match. "Poor Esther!" exclaims her father. "If things go wrong she will rebel, and a woman who rebels is lost." The novel begins in the fall of 1880 at the newly built Saint John's Cathedral on Fifth Avenue, its decoration as yet unfinished by an artist identified only as Wharton. Esther and her cousin George Strong, a geologist, attend the church's opening service, interested more in Wharton's art than the high-minded sermon delivered by the renowned preacher, the Reverend Stephen Hazard, who intones: "You were and are and ever will be only part of the supreme I AM, of which the church is the emblem." When the impressionable Catherine Brooke arrives in the city from Colorado, she is everything Esther is not: a younger, beautifully composed child of nature, "fresh as a summer's morning." As the narrator enthuses, "No one could resist her hazel eyes or the curve of her neck, or her pure complexion which had the transparency of a Colorado sunrise."

As he had done in *Democracy,* Henry closely fashioned his characters after his intimates: Esther is Clover; Mr. Dudley is Dr. Hooper; Catherine Brooke is Lizzie Cameron; George Strong is Clarence King. Stephen Hazard at Saint John's is Phillips Brooks of Boston's Trinity Church, while Wharton's battles with Hazard mirror the frequent conversations John La Farge, the muralist of Trinity Church, had with Brooks. But the overarching theme of the novel—the clashing and competing assertions of artistic expression, Darwinian science, and religious faith—obscures the characters, too often making them stand-ins for abstract ideas. As one early critic noted, the characters talk like "embodied doctrines."

The plot revolves around the romance between Esther and Stephen Hazard, who are introduced by the geologist, George Strong. They begin as friends, talking of art and science, politics and faith. When her father dies of heart failure midway through the narrative, Esther feels "languid, weary, listless. She could not sleep . . . She could not get back to her usual interests." Her friends and family fear a breakdown. In mourning, she sees only one person besides the members of her family: Stephen, who takes charge and, shortly thereafter, proposes marriage. Esther accepts, now "saturated with the elixir of love." But conflicts arise almost immediately. Though Esther genuinely loves Stephen, she does not share his religious beliefs. She discovers she is unable to do the one thing that faith, and her marriage, would require of her: submit. "Some people are made with faith. I am made without it," she laments. The harder Stephen tries to convince her to accept his love, the more she resists, fearing marriage would force him to choose between the woman he loves and the church he serves, and she knows who would win such a contest. Stephen and his profession "are one" and she is honest enough with herself to know that to be "half-married must be the worst torture."

This conflict between love and religious faith, very much at the center of the novel, was not what most preoccupied its author. Henry was not troubled by Clover's aversion to Christianity, but by her increasingly obvious artistic ambitions. Like Clover, Esther is stirred by art, while religious faith leaves her feeling at sea, "in mid-ocean." Though she wants to love and be loved, she also wants to paint. This is the conflict Henry revealed, discussing it most overtly at the start of the novel, but then shunting it off to the plot's periphery.

When Catherine, just arrived from Colorado and in need of someone to look after her, begins visiting Esther in her art studio, Esther paints her portrait. It proves good enough for Wharton to ask Esther to paint Catherine again, this time as Saint Cecelia, for one of the undecorated transepts at Saint John's. On completing this second portrait, Esther becomes "a little depressed"—she doesn't want the experiment to end. She likes the company of the other workmen, the conversations, the work, and "above all, the sense of purpose." She complains of what she calls a "feminine want of motive in life," explaining to Wharton that he couldn't "know what it is to work without an object." But she knows her options. "Men can do so many things that women can't," she demurred. And when she critiques her finished Saint Cecelia, she agrees with Wharton's judgment—she has failed. Wharton had earlier declared "she is only a second-rate amateur and will never be any thing more." Now she exclaims in sheer frustration, "I am going home to burn my brushes and break my palette. What is the use of trying to go forward when one feels iron bars across one's face?"

The novel never answers Esther's plaintive question. Instead, it closes at the dramatic setting of Niagara Falls, where Esther flees for refuge after breaking off her engagement to Hazard, telling him, "I am almost the last person in the world you ought to marry." Esther escapes to the West, to nineteenth-century Americans the most resonant symbol of Nature. Here she finds an absolute claim that soothes her hurt and restless spirit. Henry, who had many times witnessed Clover recover her spirits when on horseback and who remembered their own trip to Niagara in midwinter four years before, brought a sharp intimacy to his description of Esther sitting in her rooms, with a full view through her window of the roaring Niagara Falls:

> The sea is capricious, fickle, angry, fawning, violent, savage and wanton; it caresses and raves in a breath, and has its moods of silence, but Esther's huge playmate rambled on with its story, in the same steady voice, never shrill or angry, never silent or degraded by a sign of human failings, and yet so frank and sympathetic that she had no choice but to like it . . . She fell in love with the cataract and turned to it as a confidant, not because of its beauty or power, but because it seemed to tell her a story which she longed to understand . . . She felt tears roll down her face as she listened to the voice of the waters and knew that they were telling her a different secret from any that Hazard could ever hear.

Grand, implacable Nature gave Esther — and Clover — spiritual solace. Nature and art were all she wanted of submission and worship.

If Nature calms Esther, the narrative never resolves her quandary. Her future as a painter is impossible, foreclosed by Wharton's judgment and her own — she will be never more than a "second-rate amateur." And by refusing to submit to a religious faith that would violate her sense of integrity, Esther loses the chance of sharing life with a man she loved. She learns (as the novel's readers are intended to) that a woman — as imagined by Henry Adams — cannot both enjoy love and be truly herself in her creative ambition or beliefs. The opinion of Esther's Aunt Sarah is practical but deeply pessimistic: "Women must take their chance. It is what they are for. Marriage makes no real difference in their lot. All the contented women are fools, and all the discontented ones want to be men." The novel concludes with both Esther and Hazard isolated and alone. When Esther rejects Stephen's attempts to convince her to stay with him, he cries out, "Do you know how solitary I am?" Esther too faces an unknown future, finding herself unmoored and "in mid-ocean" with "plenty of rough weather coming." Their mutual love proves no match for the relentless isolation deeply buried in the novel and its origins.

In early September of 1883, Clover wrote to Clara Hay from Pitch Pine Hill that the weather had been unusually cool — "we being chilly folks keep fires going in parlor, study and bed rooms." Two days later, Henry characterized their summer to Charles Gaskell as the "remotest of existences," reporting that he wrote "history five hours a day." Though he didn't tell Gaskell of his novel, he reported he and Clover had been reading aloud the "dolorous letters" of the wife of Thomas Carlyle. The two-volume *Letters and Memorials of Jane Walsh Carlyle,* published earlier in 1883, unveiled the complicated, uncomprehending marriage between the Scottish writer, famous for his three-volume history, *The French Revolution,* and the brilliant Jane Walsh Carlyle, a woman who with great resentment enabled her husband's career through her dedication to his domestic ease, vigilantly protecting him from noise and unwanted visitors. Now Clover had begun adopting Jane Carlyle's sobriquet for Thomas Carlyle, addressing her own husband as a "man of genius," as Henry told Gaskell, "after the example of that painfully droll couple." Perhaps Clover saw something of herself in the self-sacrificing wife whose own abilities deferred to the ambitions of a "man of genius." Perhaps she'd been inspired to do so upon reading the manuscript pages of Henry's *Esther*.

Henry wrote the novel quickly, and within months, page proofs were already on his desk. He told no one except Clover — not even his closest friends — what he was working on. But in a note to John Hay, he revealed something of what he may have aspired to when he quipped that William Dean Howells "cannot deal with gentlemen or ladies; he always slips up. [Henry] James knows almost nothing of women but the mere outside; he never had a wife." But though Henry Adams wanted his own portrait of a lady to be more authentic, he also wanted to avoid publicity, once again feeling ambivalent about exposing his authorship. He used the feminine pseudonym Frances Snow Compton, asking his publisher, Henry Holt, to print an initial run of a thousand copies and to send the novel into the world without advertising or reviews, as an experiment to see how the reading public might react. Only *Publishers Weekly* announced the book with a paragraph summary of the plot. Not surprisingly, the book sold just 514 copies in the first year.

Clarence King would later write to John Hay that "of course . . . *Esther* is by Henry," saying he thought it "far more compact and vivid" than *Democracy*. King also explained how he'd told Henry he should have "made Esther jump" into the Niagara Falls, "as that was what she would have done," to which Henry replied, "Certainly she would, but I could not suggest it." Henry had transformed what was preoccupying him into literary form, in particular the anticipated death of a beloved father, the emotional risks of artistic ambition, and the failure of love. But he stopped short of fully imagining what may have troubled him most and what must have been unspeakable between him and his wife — some sort of creeping fear that Clover might one day destroy herself. No wonder Henry would admit to John Hay a few years later that he'd written the novel with his own "heart's blood."

Clover had always been one of Henry's first readers, and she usually told her father about what her husband was writing. Not this time. Unlike her frequent references to *Democracy*, it seems she mentioned the novel to no one. What were her thoughts and feelings upon reading Henry's searing portrait of her? Was she in part flattered? After all, Esther is a woman of enormous emotional and intellectual honesty. What about his luscious descriptions of Catherine, so recognizably Lizzie Cameron, with her translucent complexion and her need to be taken care of? Did Clover see the failed love affair between Esther and Stephen as Henry's comment on her and their marriage? Did she recognize herself in Esther, with her dependence on a beloved father, and if so, did the vision of Esther's collapse after his death frighten her? Or did she see it as Henry's warning to her, his way of saying what he didn't communicate directly? Perhaps these passages about the experience of grief, which would become a prophetic insight, somehow assured Clover that her husband understood her after all.

In any case, Clover said nothing. It seems certain, though, that given Clover's fascination with photography and her pleasure in her many successes, it must have disheartened her to read that her fictional counterpart would never be more than a "second-rate amateur." Perhaps she read the novel as Henry's caution to her that she had better not put too much into her photography. Whatever she felt, discouragement most likely lay behind Clover's refusal, later that winter, to publish one of her finest photographs.

CHAPTER 16

Iron Bars

IN MID-OCTOBER, CLOVER and Henry packed up to move back to Washington from Beverly Farms, but before heading home, they visited John and Clara Hay in Cleveland, whom they'd not seen for some time. The Hays had returned from Europe the previous May to horrible news — Clara's father, Amasa Stone, had committed suicide. He had never recovered after being held responsible for the collapse of the Ashtabula railroad bridge in 1876 in northeastern Ohio. A jury had determined that Stone, chief engineer of the iron truss bridge, was at fault for the disaster, which killed ninety-two people and injured sixty-four. Though the Hays were "most cordial," they were also still in "very deep mourning," so Clover and Henry saw "no society" while in Cleveland.

Clover, however, had brought along her camera. The Hays' new two-story stone mansion was "very large" and not much to her liking. "John Hay in his expensive house," Clover told her father, "has no fireplace in the large elaborately filled up dining room and unsightly steam heaters in every room." Her photograph of the dining room captures its glittering but somewhat chilly ambiance. She also took pictures of the Hay children. She photographed the youngest, Alice Hay, on her velocipede (a mechanical hobbyhorse), and the two older children, Del and Helen, dressed in Scotch jackets and flanking a tree trunk. To take their portrait, Clover knelt, so that her lens was even with and close up to the children's delighted faces, putting them on an unexpected equal footing with the photographer and capturing something of their relaxed grace.

Upon returning home to Washington, Clover continued with her photography. She joined a local camera club that had formed in early 1883. This group of twelve amateur photographers, both men and women, met every Monday evening at seven P.M. at the National Museum to discuss new techniques and show one another their photographs. They went on field trips when the weather was clear, so that members could take "views," as the *Photographic Times* reported, and they displayed their work in local shows. This was a significant commitment for Clover. Since her marriage she had shied away from joining groups of any kind. But she felt pride in her work. Though she never mentioned the camera club in her letters to her father, when the *Washington Post* reported on a show in mid-November, Clover clipped its short review, proudly sending praise of her work to her father: "Mrs. Henry Adams is also very skilful." She also told her father that after "two good morning hours to develop photographs two or three of my Cleveland [photographs] will be good." She sent copies of her images of the Hay children to their father, who wrote back, "The children are puffed up with majestical pride over their photographs."

On November 26, 1883, the Hays returned to Washington for a quick two-day visit. Clover's salon quickly filled up: Lucy Frelinghuysen and the southern lawyer James Lowndes "came to dine Monday evening and many people to 5 o'clock tea." Clover also convinced John Hay to sit in front of her camera, and she took two exposures. In the first, he sits in a chair, holding a copy of the French translation of Henry's novel *Democracy*, still a frequent topic of conversation among the friends. Clover was making a visual joke, playing on the misconception that Hay had been the novel's author. In the second exposure, Hay sits at Henry's office desk, with folding panels placed behind him to hide bookshelves that would have made the image too cluttered. Clover liked her portraits to showcase the person. What she captured best, especially in the second portrait, was John Hay's kindness. His expression is warm and direct, and the way he slightly leans toward his photographer communicates something of his fondness for Clover. He had always called her "our First Heart." Clover declared the first exposure "good" and the second "very good." Hay was pleased as well, writing a month later to Henry to say that "I sit all day after our photographs a half-Narcissus."

The day after their visit with the Hays, Clover and Henry went for tea to their near neighbors George and Elizabeth Bancroft, and Clover brought along her camera. She seated the revered American historian where he most truly belonged—behind his writing desk, with the rattan back of his chair visible just beyond his right shoulder. His books lie open all around him; his left hand holds pages while he takes notes with his right. His white hair and beard glow against the darkened background. He embodies, like Dr. Samuel Gross in Thomas Eakins's *The Gross Clinic* (1875), the enlightened mind.

Clover liked the print she made from the negative. She wrote to her father that the portrait of "Mr. Bancroft is very good sitting at his library table writing history a profile view. His hair and beard came out silvery and soft in the print." John Hay was also impressed, recommending it to Richard W. Gilder, the editor of the *Century,* urging that he get a copy of it to put on the cover of the magazine: "Mrs. Henry Adams has made a remarkable photograph of George Bancroft in his study. He is now eighty-three, and one of these days will be gone. I suggest that you get a copy of it and put it in the hand of your engraver—in time." Gilder agreed, and Hay wrote to Henry five days later, sending along Gilder's request that Henry write a short biographical essay about Bancroft to accompany Clover's photograph. Hay asked Henry not to tell Clover about his role—"Please give this [Gilder's letter of request] to Our Lady of Lafayette Square—and if she be angered at my blabbing of her Bancroft, tell her I did not do it, or some such fiction. I hope you will both think it worth while to comply with Gilder's prayer."

Shortly thereafter, on November 6, 1884, Clover told her father of Gilder's invitation, telling him she "was amused" to read Gilder's letter "asking if I would let him have a photo of Mr. Bancroft. Someone had spoken to him of it 'with a view to its reproduction in the magazine' and wishing Henry to write an article on papa Bancroft of 7 or 8 pages to go with it." Clover was clearly glad to be asked, pleased that her reputation with her camera had reached as far as the respected Gilder.

But then, in the same letter, Clover quickly backed away. She mentioned how William Dean Howells and Henry James had been accused, in the English press the year before, of forming an American "Mutual Admiration Society" after Howells enthused in print too fervently that James was the principal author now "shaping and directing American fiction." She informed her father that "I've just written to decline and telling him 'Mr. Adams does not fancy the prevailing vivisection' the way in which Howells butters Henry James . . . The mutual admiration game is about played out and ought to be." That same day, Henry spoke for them both in a letter to Hay. "We have declined Mr. Gilder's pleasing offer," he explained. "You know our modesty . . . As for flaunting our photographs in the *Century,* we should expect to experience the curses of all our un-photographed friends. I admit also to a shudder at the ghastly fate of Harry James and Howells. The mutual admiration business is not booming just now."

But this excuse was also a fig leaf, a way for Henry to change the subject. He dismissed Clover's opportunity to gain public notice for her work by emphasizing his hesitation to applaud Bancroft in print. Henry did, in fact, think Bancroft's prose dull. He didn't particularly want to pretend he thought otherwise. Also, publishing Clover's photograph along with his essay might have had an effect he dreaded: it could have drawn a popular audience to him. As a descendant of a famous family, Henry both wanted attention and denied wanting it; he both invited and evaded it, as he did in the way he published *Democracy* anonymously and *Esther* under a pseudonym. In rejecting Gilder's offer, Henry tangled Clover in his own ambivalence toward publicity and the public.

Henry also specifically didn't want public attention drawn to his wife. He preferred convention. He had a conservative notion of equality between men and women, dependent not on legal rights, but rather on a relationship of mutual respect. He thought the suffragists incomprehensible, "a vile gang," and saw little reason for a woman to have the right to vote. If a man loved his wife sufficiently, Henry surmised, he would seek a kind of equality with her. His only public lecture, given in 1876 at Boston's prestigious Lowell Institute, presented an investigation of the role of women in primitive society, which he later published as "The Primitive Rights of Women." Drawing on a wide range of sources — Native

American tradition, Egyptian stories and myths, early Christian history — Henry asserted that women in the primitive past were not slaves of their powerful male relatives, but rather enjoyed, by virtue of their fecundity and motherhood, a lofty social position. He countered a long-held claim that Christianity had rescued women from a brutalized past by elevating them to equality in the eyes of Christ. Instead, he argued, the early church had degraded the status of women by relying on rigidly hierarchal power structures to regulate social life. Women and children lost rights under patriarchy, a process espoused and justified by emerging church doctrine.

Though Henry imagined that women in the primitive past were powerful, he also held that women were utterly different from men — the opposite sex indeed. Equality was based not on what was shared but on profound differences, and could be achieved only by affirming a woman's essential nature and her role within a separate domestic sphere. In thinking this, he differed little from most members of his generation. Henry failed to recognize that a woman might want a share in what he himself needed — satisfying work to do, social esteem, and the possibility for self-reliance balanced with friendship and love. Henry idealized the qualities of sentiment and spontaneity; he found them in his wife and thought them essential to a woman's character. Yet he also disparaged these qualities, as he did in a long letter to one of Clover's nieces: "The woman's difficulty is that she is fooled by her instincts and her sentiments which are at the same time her only advantages over the man." Henry's view of women put actual women at a distance, just beyond his reach.

On Christmas Eve, 1883, Clover scolded her friend Anne Palmer, also a photographer, insisting that she "send me photos." She also learned about the platinotype, a new printing process prized for how it produced stunning blacks and grays that did not fade with time. She spent three hours on the morning of December 30 in the "photograph rooms" at the National Museum in order to learn the "wonderful process" from the person who owned the patent. To her delight, her photography friend Cliff Richardson, who still worked as a chemist for the city, had "very kindly smuggled me in as the only woman."

In the back of her photography notebook, she folded a sheet of directions published by Willis & Clements of Philadelphia, the primary proprietors of the platinotype process. The list of four steps for developing photographs — sensitizing the paper, exposing it to light, developing the image, and clearing and washing the final photograph — confirmed what Clover told her father: photography was "science pure and simple." This appealed to her. Photography helped fulfill Clover's desire to carefully catalog what she saw with her own eyes. She had, in a long letter to her father on Washington politics, asserted something of this when she claimed: "My facts are facts, too."

In addition to its interesting technical aspects and its ability to record detail and capture nuance, photography allowed Clover to deepen her passion for art. For her compositions and her choice of subjects, she drew from the rich visual world of nineteenth-century painters: both Europeans, such as Caspar David Friedrich and the painters of the Barbizon school, and Americans, such as F. D. Millet, John Singer Sargent, and Winslow Homer. By trying on ideas that were in wide circulation, she let her private feelings and memories be poured, like clay slip, into the mold of high art. Like her mother a generation before, who had crafted poetry to explore the connections between her private world and wider realms of human expression and experience, Clover had begun reaching for what artists reach for.

But with Henry's help, Clover circumscribed her ambition. She had internalized his standards for feminine self-restraint, which her culture emphasized. She didn't dare stretch these limits in any way that would risk Henry's disapproval. According to him, a woman's mind — "thin, wiry, one-stringed" — was not improvable. Or, as Clover's fictional counterpart, Esther, exclaims, "What is the use of trying to go forward when one feels iron bars across one's face?"

CHAPTER 17

A New Home

IN MID-DECEMBER of 1883, Clover wrote her father her usual newsy Sunday letter, this time announcing she had sold her thoroughbred horse Powhatan to Anne Bayard, the young daughter of the Delaware senator Thomas Bayard. The horse had become "unmanageable," particularly for Henry, who had neither Clover's confidence nor skill with horses. Watching Henry get thrown off Powhatan at Beverly Farms was one thing, Clover decided, but "fighting a balking horse on the slippery asphalt pavements" was too dangerous for "both horse and rider." She reported happily that Anne would be "a good mistress" for the "handsome beast" because the young girl had decided to buy him even though he had already run away with her, such that she had to "jump from his back to save her head from a tree trunk." Clover also told how Possum, their Skye terrier, whom she called "our ewe lamb," had been struck by a carriage on Pennsylvania Avenue earlier in the week. "He was brought home in a wagon in extremis," Clover reported, and when she and Henry came home, they found him on his back. "He wagged his tail faintly and gasped out 'I see them beckoning to me.' I said 'Possum the angels never take dogs who can wag their tails.'"

But Clover put the real news of the day in a postscript. She and Henry had decided to build a new house on Lafayette Square. "[John] Hay has bought the vacant lot next to us," Clover explained, "the whole lot is 98½ feet east to west by 131¼ north to south." Hay planned to build on the corner, at Sixteenth and H Streets, and she and Henry would build on land between his corner lot and their current house on H Street. The scheme had originated earlier in the fall. The Hays were interested in moving back to Washington, and when they stayed with the Adamses in November, they'd gone real estate shopping, wanting a house close by their two hearts. When it became clear that the corner lot was for sale, Hay gave Henry the go-ahead to purchase the whole lot on his behalf. Hay then turned around and sold to Henry — on Henry's suggestion — a forty-four-foot portion of the lot for "⅓ the price of the whole tract." The sale was completed on December 11 for "approximately $73,800" for both lots, with the Adamses paying $25,500 for their portion.

Clover wrote to Anne Palmer with the news that they wanted to "put up a modest mansion — 44 feet wide — 43 high." The building plan was an enormous relief to Clover. The land had been bought previously by a developer who wanted to put up a seven-and-a-half-story apartment building, which would have made the back of the Adamses' current house "dark and untenable." She had been dreading losing three large trees that would have been felled to make room for construction. The real estate deal with John Hay had resolved these issues in one stroke, though Clover still wanted approval from her father and brother. "We hope," Clover admitted, "that you and Ned will not think us unwise." She talked finances, saying Henry could borrow what funds they needed and reminding her father she still had roughly $27,000 in her trust (in today's terms more than $600,000). By Christmas week, she announced that she wanted "no more jewelry or bric-à-brac" because all attention had turned now to "drains, plumbing, and bricks." Three days later she wrote again to her father to thank him for his very generous Christmas gift, telling him she intended to put the money toward "one definite part of the house," such as "iron wrought grills for the entresol windows on the street." Henry had already "drawn to scale" the interior rooms, and she promised to photograph their initial plans so her father and Ned could make "suggestions and improvements."

No other architect but Henry Hobson Richardson, America's most influential, was mentioned as a possibility for the Adams house. Frank Lloyd Wright, who would be inspired by Richardson's profound sensitivity to the relation of buildings to physical space, would later write of him, "Richardson was the grand exteriorist." Richardson's Romanesque style, with its rounded arches, thick walls, and clearly articulated parts, a style later described as "quiet and monumental," was most perfectly expressed in Boston's Trinity Church, dedicated in February 1877. Clover and Henry likely attended the dedication ceremony.

Richardson's prodigious talents were matched by his voracious appetite for food, art, conversation, and music. On weekends, he liked to hire chamber orchestras to play at his Brookline offices outside Boston (which he rented from Clover's brother, Ned Hooper), inviting clients, neighbors, and friends for a two-day musical salon. When Clover's father wrote to her about one of these soirees, she replied, "How I wish I could hear Richardson's concerts!" Richardson suffered most of his adult life from Bright's disease, which radically elevated his appetite, but even chronic ill health couldn't dampen his energy and optimism. He had a gift for friendship. To Henry, he scrawled in his large rolling script, "Tomorrow your lamp and two little red jars go to Washington addressed to you. I wish you and Mrs. Adams to accept the jar with plenty of love and my best wishes." An upstate New York state senator, who observed Richardson's machinations in getting more funding approved for his completion of the senate chamber in the New York State Capitol at Albany, said of him, "He would charm a bird out of a bush."

Though the two Henrys couldn't have been more different in temperament and physical stature, they had enjoyed a long friendship. They were born the same year, and Richardson, a native of Louisiana, graduated from Harvard a year after Henry, in 1859, with Ned Hooper's class. Henry said he met no one at Harvard whom he "valued" later in life "so much as Richardson." The two became close friends—not at Harvard, but in Paris, when Richardson was studying at the prestigious École des Beaux-Arts in the 1860s, the first American to do so. Henry would sneak away from his duties at the British Legation in London for a weekend in Paris, and the two young men would walk the neighborhoods, dine at the Palais Royal, and talk history and art.

Clover also enjoyed Richardson's company and often commented on his high spirits, once telling her father after a dinner engagement that Richardson "can say truly 'I am my own music,' for he carries off any dinner more or less gaily." And she thought his architecture was extraordinary. She and Henry had traveled to Albany to see Richardson's State Capitol, and she reported to Lizzie Cameron that the senate chamber, with its red mahogany furniture, wainscoting made of "great slabs of Mexican onyx," and upper walls of gold leather, was "the handsomest room I ever saw." But it was Richardson's commission for General Nicholas Longworth Anderson's new home at Sixteenth and K Streets that gave Clover and Henry a front-row view of Richardson's construction methods.

Even before the Andersons moved in, Henry decided that "Nick Anderson's new house [is] . . . the handsomest and most ultimate house in America in my opinion, and the only one I'd like to own." On November 12, 1883, Clover brought her camera and tripod over to the Andersons' house and, from across the street, on the northwest corner at the intersection of Sixteenth and K Streets, she took its portrait; horse manure is clearly visible on the dusty city street. She also took a close-up exposure of the mansion's elaborate ironwork door leading to the carriage driveway. She put both prints in the opening pages of her second album, as if to acquaint its viewer with the highlights of her neighborhood; she also sent prints to General Anderson, who forwarded one to his son. Clover, a confirmed fireplace devotee, told her father after a quiet dinner with the Andersons that she didn't like how the house was "excessively furnace heated" despite the presence of Richardson's "handsome open fireplaces," but she found their new house "charming" nonetheless.

Clover and Henry wanted their own house to be smaller and more quietly grand, what Henry would call later a "Spartan little box." Clover didn't want a parlor, but a sunny library instead — she said she could "sit all day in the library." Henry's study would be next door. The dining room would be located near the back of the house, with steps leading into the garden. Just as she had once before, at Beverly Farms, Clover aspired to infuse her new home with a New England coziness, though of a high-toned sort, with fireplaces in every room set off with warm-colored marble mantels and subtle decoration.

Clover also planned a large photography studio of several rooms in the back of the house on the third floor. She wanted an overhead skylight, several sinks, an elaborate ventilation system, shelving for chemicals, and a darkroom. The studio's large five-foot window would face north to take advantage of consistent daylight, a siting sought by painters of portraits.

After the New Year, Clover wrote an impatient note to Richardson to "hurry him up," as Henry reported to John Hay, and by early spring the architect stayed with Clover and Henry in Washington to talk over his ideas and drawings. Clover wanted the best of everything—plumbing, furnace, fixtures, wainscoting, and floor-to-ceiling bookcases. But she resisted extras. There would be "no stained glass—no carving," for she wanted not a "fine house," but an "unusual one." Sometimes Richardson pushed back, writing on one drawing that showed his plans for a carved abutment: "These I shall put back again at whatever the cost." But Clover could not have been more pleased with the eventual plans, writing to her father that Richardson had "worked up something very satisfactory to all of us." She particularly liked how he managed the scale of the outside windows, saying he "dealt with it like a master." On hearing of the Adamses' approval, Richardson wrote to Henry to say "I am glad you are pleased with the drawings," noting he would be "very glad indeed" to see the "photographs your wife has taken of the elevations."

The first photograph Clover took in 1884 was of H. H. Richardson, who sat for his portrait on January 18 at 11:15 A.M. at Henry's desk in his study. Her notebook reads: "Jan 18—H. H. Richardson—11.15—/in H. A's study—large stop—/10 seconds/good." Ten seconds was a long time for someone like Richardson to sit still. Holding an architect's drafting T-square in his right hand, with drawing plans in front of him, he can't quite repress a smile, which makes his eyes squint. Clover captured his vivacity and his companionable good nature. As a gesture to his simmering fatal disease and a counterpoint to his energy and push, she situated Richardson in front of Jean-Baptiste Oudry's *Dying Lion,* a mournful black-and-white chalk drawing that hung on the study's back wall. Clover knew that's what Richardson was—a dying lion.

CHAPTER 18

Portraits

CLOVER BEGAN 1884 engrossed in election-year politics, closely following accounts of heated debate in newspapers and the *Congressional Record*. Congress was in an uproar over high tariffs on imports, which were
largely favored by industrialists but despised in other sectors because the
policy inflated prices and created an unwieldy surplus in the federal bud-
get. Clover told her father to alert Ned to "expect some very lively tariff
discussions in a week or two," explaining the situation with her usual
journalistic brio: "New Jersey in hysterics over its silk, and Ohio split
as to wool and Congress with $150,000,000 surplus, a standing tempta-
tion to robbery and corruption, each party afraid to touch the matter just
before a presidential election and equally afraid not to." She cheerfully
added, "It never was more interesting here than this winter and growing
more so every day."

She happily reported that Anne Palmer, by now clearly her closest friend, intended to move from New York City to Washington for a
season, plans that would "add much to us." She also enjoyed the company of a new friend, Rebecca Dodge, who lived nearby in the neighborhood. The two women had met the previous autumn when Clover
noticed the much younger Rebecca walking by on H Street and asked a

mutual acquaintance about her. Rebecca would remember, years later, how Clover's "generosity knew no bounds," particularly if she really liked someone. There were other diversions that winter. Passionate as ever about her Skye terriers Boojum, Possum, and Marquis, Clover decided to enter Marquis in a local dog show. After the papers reported he was a contender for a top award, she pledged to donate the prize money to the Massachusetts Society for the Prevention of Cruelty to Animals, an organization she'd supported since its founding after the Civil War. And she found herself surprised by her continued excitement over house plans. As she'd explained to Lizzie Cameron at the beginning of the year, she had "always been utterly opposed to building" but was now the "one who jumped first," adding, "I like to change my mind all of a sudden."

This season, though, Clover had been determined to limit her involvement in Washington's endless and demanding social obligations. Some occasions were, however, a pleasure; there'd been several enjoyable dinners. At one she sat next to General Philip Sheridan, who gave her "a long account of his experience as eye witness the day after Sedan, where Napoleon 3rd surrendered to Bismarck." Sheridan answered her many questions about the Franco-Prussian War, which President Grant had ordered Sheridan to observe; he talked with Clover throughout most of the dinner, a conversation she enjoyed "extremely." But Clover wrote to her father that the "society rabble" wasted her time, that "hardly a day passes that someone doesn't bring a letter of introduction and that means a dinner time taken and a call at least." She struck an imperious pose as a defense, explaining that "pushing people who almost force their way in to your house have to be adroitly met—no one is admitted now by my majestic orders if they ask if I 'receive' and so only those who walk in without asking come at all." She also resolved to make the many teas and receptions only "a small part of our existence." After a week of "quiet evenings and gray days," despite being invited to innumerable parties, she concluded that the "only way of existing at all is to keep out of it."

Clover had something else to occupy her attention and fill her time—photography. She took a remarkable number of exposures—over fifty—that winter and spring of 1884, the best of which she developed, printed, and carefully pasted into her second red-leather album. She had opened her first album, dated on the inside cover "May 1883," with a quintessential summer image of catboats becalmed in Manchester Harbor, near Beverly Farms. The following forty-six photographs, most made during the summer and fall, included those of family, friends at the seashore, Henry at his summer writing desk, farm places, the parlor at Pitch Pine Hill, and the view of the treetops from Clover's upstairs porch. This was Clover's summer life. The second album is more somber than the first, beginning with a winter scene of Lafayette Square, dusted in snow, followed by the two prints of General Anderson's new house on the corner of Sixteenth and K Streets. Many of the forty-seven photographs in the second album are figure studies or portraits.

In the late months of 1883, Clover had experimented with posing her women friends in various ways as she learned about exposure times and how best to use light to highlight features and expressions. In mid-September, she achieved a notable success, taking two exposures of the famous singer Lillie de Hegermann-Lindencrone, formerly Lillie Greenough, a childhood acquaintance from Cambridge and now the wife of a Danish diplomat. With its plain folding screen and two large potted ferns on either side, the setting replicates something of Madame de Hegermann-Lindencrone's theatrical milieu, as does her head covering, a shawl of fine black lace, and the pale rose pinned to her bodice, which complements the open fan held in her hand. Madame de Hegermann-Lindencrone's daughter, Nina Moulton (Lillie had formerly been married to the banker Charles Moulton), is posed in much the same way as her mother, but more simply, with the white rose in her hand, drawing the eye to her wasp waist. Under entries in her notebook about exposure times, Clover wrote simply: "all good."

Clover continued learning, borrowing here and there from the visual vocabulary of past and contemporary fine art painting. For instance, one winter afternoon, Rebecca Dodge stopped by for a visit, bringing along her banjo. Using a new Dallmeyer wide-angle lens, Clover positioned Rebecca in the corner of a room near a window, holding her banjo as if she were playing. A soft northern light casts a flattering glow on Rebecca's face, which is turned toward the window and tilted slightly downward. Clover exposed the negative for a full fifteen seconds. Rebecca's ease in front of the camera is obvious in the relaxed way she holds her banjo and in her slight smile, creating a charming image of feminine leisure that is not easy to categorize: it is not quite a genre image of everyday life and not quite a portrait. Clover experimented further with Rebecca, taking another exposure of her, this time wearing lace around her head and a rose at her shoulder. For this shot, Clover tried a rapid lens. But she didn't like the glass negative enough to make a print. Nor did she develop a self-portrait from an exposure she took that afternoon, with a Dallmeyer lens held open for a full twenty-five seconds. She jotted down the reason in her notebook: "Marian, expression not good." But Clover declared in her notebook the first exposure of Rebecca with her banjo "very good" and sent a copy to her father, telling him proudly that Rebecca's mother had been "enchanted with it, and thinks it perfect."

In February 1884, Rebecca Dodge came back for another day of photography, this time joined by Elizabeth, wife of the American painter and illustrator F. D. Millet. The Millets, whom Clover had met on her trip to New York to visit Anne Palmer the previous year, had traveled to Washington because the artist was testifying about art tariffs before the congressional Ways and Means Committee.

The three women spent a rainy afternoon experimenting with Clover's camera. Clover positioned Rebecca and Elizabeth in "different poses as statuary," draping them in free-flowing garments that they'd found in the art trunk Millet took with him when he traveled. The images look more like a classical fantasy than traditional portraiture. The style of drapery, which Clover had called an "Eden-like costume" in her description of her visit to Millet's studio the previous spring, and the poses themselves reflect those of Millet's work, including his *Reading the Story of Oenone* (1882), which she had seen at the Society of Artists show in New York. In that painting, five women gather on a low bench to listen to the story of Oenone, the first wife of the warrior Paris, whom he abandoned for the fabled Helen of Troy; the tableau conveys a strong sense of solidarity among the young women, as they listen to the legend of a man betraying a woman. Clover, by contrast, pictured her own classically dressed figures alone, each to inhabit her own visual frame. Unlike Millet's highly decorative work, she included little detail other than the elaborate drapery, and her images evoke none of the emotional closeness present in Millet's piece, which had garnered excellent reviews.

Because of the dreary, dim February weather, an extended exposure time was needed for each image, and two of the four photographs Clover printed are blurry with movement because the women couldn't remain still long enough. Even so, Clover declared in her notebook that some of her experiments were "very nice." Shortly thereafter, she announced to her father she intended to buy a camera specifically for portraits, once she had decided "which one I want." Her current camera was made for "out of doors work," and she wanted to keep taking photographs when cold or rainy weather drove her indoors.

As Clover's skill improved, her reputation grew, and she began fielding requests for what she began calling her "photographic work." Madame Bonaparte stopped in one morning with her young son and daughter, wanting Clover to photograph her children for prints to send to the duchesse de Mouchy. Clover kept for her own album a clear print of Jerome Bonaparte IV, age six, proudly sitting "astride a chair blowing a trumpet." She posed the "little brown-eyed boy" in profile to better suggest the imperious features of his "dim ancestors in Corsica of 100 years ago." She didn't make for herself a print of her portrait of the younger sister, though she hoped the family would find her photographs "worth keeping."

In the winter of 1884, after she had printed "photos for nearly two hours," Clover and Henry traveled to C Street near the Capitol to the offices of their friend the Mississippi senator L.Q.C. Lamar, a former Confederate envoy to Russia, who was a frequent dinner guest and, according to Henry, one of the "most genial and sympathetic of all Senators." Lamar wanted Clover to take his photograph. She placed him on a plain chair against a blank wall, seated in profile and facing to the right of the frame, with the masthead of the newspaper the *Daily Democrat* clearly visible in his right hand. Shot from a low angle, Senator Lamar looms large in the photograph. He had wanted to "brush his long hair to the regulation smoothness," but Clover refused to take his picture "until he had rumpled it all up." She was right to insist. What shines in her portrait is the senator's notable geniality, his remarkably even temperament, which would serve him well in his later duties as secretary of the interior and eventually as a justice of the Supreme Court.

That same day, she took a companion portrait of Lamar's colleague

J. B. Gordon, a former senator of Georgia and one of Robert E. Lee's prized generals, who'd been badly wounded at Antietam, surviving numerous bullets, including one that went through his left cheek and jaw. Clover positioned Gordon so as to display his left profile, showing the scar from the bullet wound to its best advantage. This gift for finding just such a detail—one that would reveal character or allude to a personal story—had long been nurtured by Clover. In her letters to her father she created many vivid portraits-in-words, and she now imported this skill into the visual realm of photography.

In thanks for his portrait, Senator Lamar gave Clover an ideal gift—a photographic print depicting the ship *Proteus* a few minutes before sinking off the Arctic coast while on a relief expedition to find the explorer Adolphus Washington Greely and his lost men. "It is dim and technically not good," Clover enthused to her father, "but is very curious and interesting."

Though Clover adopted the conventions of portraiture she was familiar with—women holding flowers or an opened letter, men holding a newspaper or sitting at a desk, children playing with a toy—she also allowed the artifice involved in picture making to appear in her work. For instance, she hung a white sheet, with its fold marks clearly visible, behind the bearded Spanish minister Señor Don Enrique Dupuy de Lôme, who grasps in his left hand a copy of the *Congressional Record*. This touch of domestic improvisation imbues the image with a jaunty, unfussy feeling and contrasts with the elaborate backgrounds often used in contemporary portraiture. Clover thought de Lôme a "funny, dark-haired copy of Clarence King," and she captured this jovial quality in his portrait. she found the minister's wife, Adela, equally charming, asking her to come by three times a week to read aloud from Spanish novels— "a rare chance," Clover told her father, "as she is very intelligent and has a most bewitching accent." Clover's portrait of Señora de Lôme records her new friend's lively spirit and intellect; again, the backdrop of the wrinkled white sheet appears, this time showcasing the woman's lace shawl and the open fan in her right hand. For indoor portraits like these, she carefully considered how light and shadow could together bring out the distinct features of a face: the focal point of a portrait.

Clover was also interested in portraying modern life and sometimes borrowed aesthetic ideas from the contemporary painters who challenged conventions. Using a plain backdrop for a portrait is one instance of such experimentation. Her two portraits of Oliver Wendell Holmes Jr., the future chief justice of the Supreme Court, also lean toward the future in their complete lack of decoration and their meticulous composition; they even suggest comparison with James Whistler's *Arrangement in Grey and Black: The Artist's Mother* (1871), which Clover had seen on her honeymoon in 1872. If Clover thought Whistler's painting technique "mad," she'd nonetheless been influenced by his spare, modern principles of composition.

And sometimes Clover reached for an evocation of deeply held values and unnamed longing, as she did in her portraits of two older women, Eliza Field and Elizabeth Bancroft. Eliza Field, wife of the industrialist John Field from Philadelphia, had had her portrait painted by some of the leading artists of her day, including Thomas Sully in 1841, when she was twenty-one, and John Singer Sargent in 1882, in a joint portrait with her husband. The Fields had started frequenting Clover's tea table since moving to Washington in 1883, and Clover probably saw for herself the Sully and Sargent portraits when she paid the Fields a visit at their newly built home. Sully had emphasized the feminine qualities of the beautiful young Eliza, showing off her long graceful neck and her black hair sharply parted down the middle in the antebellum fashion. Forty years later, Sargent drew attention to the intimacy of her marriage, posing the Fields so that they almost faced each other, their arms entangled and their affection obvious. Clover places Mrs. Field, still striking at sixty-four years, in front of a painted screen and seated on a wooden chair, which points a bit to the right; her black cloak and flattering hat are flooded with light. She wears her dark hair just as she had in her youth—parted in the middle, drawn down over her ears, then back on either side. But Mrs. Field looks to her left, as if noticing that someone had just appeared through a door. This position puts her face in a three-quarter profile and gives the image an immediacy and energy absent in the Sully or Sargent portraits. Clover's portrait emphasizes neither Mrs. Field's beauty nor her marriage but rather the older woman's keen intelligence and engagement with life.

Clover's longtime H Street neighbor Elizabeth Bliss Bancroft, born in

1803, was a woman of large experience and subtle intellect. Henry was to give Mrs. Bancroft a copy of the first volumes of his *History* to critique, once commenting that she was "by long odds the most intelligent woman in Washington." Mrs. Bancroft had known Clover all of her life, meeting up with her in Boston and Egypt and Washington too, ever since the Adamses' early days there. In the spring of 1884, Clover reported to her father, "Mrs. Bancroft looks very frail and has been in her room for six months but reads and discusses everything from Henry's history to the Supreme Court decisions." Clover admired Mrs. Bancroft's attitude toward life and death and captured it brilliantly in a portrait she made that spring of 1884. Sitting upright, Mrs. Bancroft gazes directly into Clover's camera, a bright light shining on one side of her face, casting the other into almost complete darkness, a compelling chiaroscuro. Mrs. Bancroft is wrapped in a fine patterned blanket and a white lace shawl, accouterments of a privileged old age, and her gray hair is carefully combed. Clover had written to her father about this woman's compelling ability to endure all: "Her will bids fair to keep her alive as long as she chooses, unless death catches her in a nap, and that I believe she is on her guard against by dozing with one eye open." To underscore such determination, Clover put Mrs. Bancroft's portrait in her album next to a photograph of an ancient pine tree growing beside Tenleytown Road, north of Washington. But to balance this quality with necessary knowledge of mortality, she placed on the following page a platinum print copy of an exposure she'd taken the previous autumn of Arlington National Cemetery. Strength, life, and death — Clover linked these themes in her portrayal of her mother's old friend and the photograph's visual companions in the album.

Despite all the activity of 1884 — election-year politics, house planning, photography — the creeping sense of isolation that had begun to encroach on Clover's marriage had become more palpable. Clover wondered aloud to Lizzie Cameron "how any man or woman dares to take the plunge" into marriage. In February, Henry complained to Charles Gaskell that high society in Washington, with its endless round of dinners and rituals, had become "a mob almost as uninteresting and quite as crowded as in any other city." While Clover was busy photographing her friends, Henry said they'd been "rather more solitary now than at any other season."

As Clover looked ahead to another summer at Beverly Farms, she wanted to make sure she wouldn't be lonely. She wrote to Anne Palmer, asking her to come for a two-week stay at Pitch Pine Hill. Clover spent an enormous amount of time alone, admitting to Anne that Henry James had told her recently she "spelled solitude with a large S." Though Clover called her picture making "photographic work," she knew full well it was more like a pastime, something for her to do with her day. Her retreat from Gilder's offer to publish her portrait of George Bancroft in *Century* magazine had avoided direct conflict with Henry, but it had also robbed her of the chance to garner a wider appreciation for her photography. She would never be recognized as an artist in her own right.

All of this was complicated by Lizzie Cameron's unexpected return to Washington in May 1884 from her European tour. Clover had reported receiving a dreary letter from Lizzie earlier in the year: "Poor little Mrs. Cameron is very homesick and bored in Europe," Clover told her father. Evidently, things were not going well between Lizzie and her husband. As Clover dryly observed, "I wish Don would get well or something, but I fear he's not wanted above." Clover had answered Lizzie, wanting to cheer her up. She described her excitement about Richardson's design for the new house, but she also provided what a forlorn woman might need to hear most. Addressing Lizzie affectionately as "Perdita, perdita," after the abandoned baby girl in Shakespeare's *A Winter's Tale,* Clover tried to console her by telling her, "We miss you, miss you, miss you" and that Washington was "always pleasant" but "pleasanter when you're around."

Henry thought so too. From the beginning, Henry's connection to Lizzie was something different from his habitual admiration for pretty young women who, as he wrote to Charles Gaskell, "chatter" and "smile on my gray beard." Lizzie flattered Henry, looked up to him, and found him fascinating. Her youth and beauty gave her a social power almost equal to his, and this intensified their mutual attraction. But he concealed his feelings in the guise of an acceptable sympathy for a young woman in a terrible marriage. He could assure himself, and anyone else who might have noticed, that his attentions to her were chivalrous, honorable.

Clover noted Lizzie's premature return to Washington in a letter to her father. Retelling the previous day's events, of guests coming and going, she included that Lizzie had stopped by "all in white muslin and blue ribbons, looking very young and pretty, just back from 1 year of Europe and enchanted to get back." Henry meanwhile wrote to John Hay with relief that "Mrs. Don has come home, which consoles me for much. The society of this village is charming with the mercury at 90°." But even with the blistering heat, Henry was "loath to go off to the sea-side." He didn't want to leave Washington so soon after Lizzie had returned home.

How could Clover not have been unnerved as she saw Henry's eager attentions move away from her and toward a much younger woman? In *Esther,* Clover's fictional doppelganger frets that the younger Catherine, modeled after Lizzie, has taken "a fancy" to the artist Wharton, one of several fictional disguises Henry adopted for himself in the novel. Wharton comes to see Catherine "or sends for her every day," Esther worries. Feeling helpless, she asks, "What can I do about it?" Henry would write much later that a woman goes "shipwreck" because "when she loves, when she hates, when she is jealous, she does not know it until someone tells her, and then she is furiously angry at being told, and won't believe it." Perhaps he was remembering a moment when he pointed out to Clover her jealousy of Lizzie, and Clover flared up in anger to deny it.

For all the times Lizzie came over for tea, for dinner, or for a horseback ride, Clover never once took her photograph. There were other missing portraits. Anne Palmer never sat for Clover's camera, though Anne too was a photographer. Henry James had portrayed Clover as Mrs. Bonnycastle in his 1884 short story "Pandora" as a gracious, savvy woman who grasped the Washington social game, but Clover never photographed her friend Harry. Many others eluded Clover's lens — Clarence King, Clara Hay, Clover's brother Ned Hooper, and her sister and brother-in-law, Ellen and Whitman Gurney. Yet one of Clover's photographs is strongly suggestive of Lizzie, albeit in a disguised, hieroglyphic way. In a photograph taken on October 9, 1883, which Clover placed in her first red-leather album, a beautiful young woman, Grace Minot, sits at Henry's desk at Pitch Pine Hill, reading page proofs. Clover's entry in her notebook reads: "Miss Minot as 'Muse of American History' — in

H's study/reading proof—time 1.30 p.m.—/16—or 17 seconds—/ very charming—little over timed/making neck & hands dead white & not enough modeling." Either at that time or later, Henry labeled the image on the lower left-hand corner of the album page as "Miss Minot in study at Beverly Farms." But Clover added her own title on the right-hand corner, the title she also used in her notebook: "Muse of American History." If Clover never fashioned herself as Henry's muse, it must have been unnerving for her to see attentions exchanged between Mr. American History and his bevy of young female admirers—most especially Lizzie Cameron.

In August 1884, during a long summer at Beverly Farms, Henry announced to John Hay, "My wife and I are becoming green with mould. We are bored to death with ourselves, and see no one else. At long intervals we chirp feebly to each other; then sleep and dream sad dreams." Clover mentioned photography less and less, and by then, she'd stopped keeping track of her photographic work in her notebook. She wrote to Anne Palmer of the quiet summer days, with Henry working at his desk until "riding time" as she studied Greek. They had few visitors. Henry and Clover's routine changed little when they returned to H Street later that fall. Henry wrote to a friend, "I never feel a wish to wander, and for eight months at a time never even enter a railway train. My wife is worse than I am. Nothing will induce her to contemplate any change except final cremation, which has a certain interest of new experience." Perhaps what was becoming hardest of all was something Henry had already described in *Esther* the year before—"the worst part of their depression was that each was determined to hide it from the other." These two had lost their way of finding each other at the end of the day.

In December, Henry wrote to Lizzie with a flirtatious flourish: "I shall dedicate my next poem to you. I shall have you carved over the arch of my stone door-way. I shall publish your volume of extracts with your portrait on the title-page. I am miserable to think that none of these methods can fully express the extent to which I am Yours, Henry Adams."

PART IV

Mysteries of the Heart

Nothing is much worth saying between man and woman except the
single phrase that concentrates the whole relation in three words.
— HENRY ADAMS TO ANNE PALMER, DECEMBER 5, 1886

CHAPTER 19

Turning Away

BY EARLY JANUARY of 1885, Henry had finished his manuscript on the second administration of Thomas Jefferson (eventually volume four of his *History*) and had the pages typeset. The past five years had been extraordinarily productive. He had not only reached the midway point in his *History*, but he had also finished biographies of Albert Gallatin and the Virginian states' rights advocate John Randolph, as well as his two novels, *Democracy* and *Esther*. Even so, Henry felt a pervading sense of depletion and ennui. In a note to George Bancroft, he wrote appreciatively of Bancroft's revision of his own monumental American history. "In you," Henry observed, "I detect no sign of the weariness and languor which mark the close of other men's histories, and which, I regret to say, have descended on the middle of mine." He also admitted to his publisher, Henry Holt, that his experiment with *Esther* had been a failure, which "is disappointing" — as far as he could tell "not a man, woman or child has ever read or heard of *Esther*."

When John La Farge, the American painter and master designer of stained glass windows, came for a visit in mid-February, Clover took his picture as he sat in a leather chair. In one hand he held a book, which he was reading; in the other, a lit cigar. Shelves of books lined the walls in the background. The balance of the composition and La Farge's casual demeanor emphasize his even-tempered nature, and the photograph was for Henry, as he would write later, "the only portrait" of La Farge "as he showed himself always to me."

In late winter, Clover reported on the inauguration of Grover Cleveland, the first Democrat to reach the White House in over twenty years. She had followed the 1884 election with keen interest, at one point apologizing to her father at the end of a long letter, "Excuse so much politics but it absorbs our minds." She and Henry were appalled by the machine politics of the Republican Party and how the party of Lincoln had been damaged by politicos and a corrupt patronage system. Rejecting the Republican candidate, James G. Blaine, Henry voted for Cleveland, as did other so-called Mugwumps — those who had bolted from the party and demanded large-scale reform of the civil service and government finance. At one point, Henry described himself to friends as a "free-trade Democrat." As Clover explained to her father, there had been "no alternative" for those "independents and Republicans who have any decency but to bolt" when the party nominated Blaine, a politician — in her words — "tattooed with corruption." She hoped that after defeat, the "rotten old soulless party may be laid in its grave."

Writing on March 5, a Thursday instead of her usual Sunday morning, Clover began a letter to her father announcing that "Grover Cleveland is safely installed over the way." Two decades before, she had described in close detail General Grant's victory parade through the streets of Washington. Now, with reporting skills considerably more acute, she gave a full account, knowing how much her father would enjoy witnessing the inaugural parade and celebrations through his daughter's eyes.

Yesterday we took our breakfast at eleven, and at twelve mounted Prince and Daisy and started out to see the show . . . First we went down to the State Dept. and up Penn. Avenue past the grand stand — the dense crowd opening for us — then up F. St. till we could tap the Avenue again at 11th St. and cross it so as to get over to the Smithsonian grounds — as we squeezed thro' and stood in the middle of the Avenue. It was a sight worth seeing from the Treasury to the Capitol one great black sea — we rode fast to the south side of the

Capitol under the hill—suddenly the cannon gave the signal that the speech was over—we pressed up to the great square east and caught the whole picture—wound our way in and out among the regiments waiting to start and finally got into a little triangle about 15 feet or less from the line of March just as they turned the slope from the Capitol. There must have been from 25 to 35,000 troops . . . one band would pass playing "Dixie" and the next playing "The Union Forever, Hurrah! Boys, Hurrah" and marching thro' "Georgia" and every one looked gay and happy as if they thought it was a big country and they owned it. We sat and watched it for about an hour and a half and the big drums banged under the horses' noses and the fifes screamed in their ears—but like the crushed tragedian they "rather like it" . . . We did not go to the ball—contented ourselves with a fine display of fireworks which being just south of the White House were nearly as good from my bedroom windows as from there.

Three days later, Clover wrote her father again, opening with a reminder that she had sent him an "'extra' on Thursday as part of my office duty being your special Washington correspondent." She regaled him, as usual, with snippets of what she found amusing. "Last Sunday evening," she reported, her friend the southern lawyer Mr. Lowndes had "dropped in and chatted in company with General [James H.] Wilson," commander of the Union troops that captured Columbus, Georgia, on April 16, 1865, nearly the last battle of the war. When Wilson left, Lowndes turned to Clover and asked who he was, to which she replied, "'The man who captured Jeff Davies.' 'Oh,' said Lowndes, 'he captured me in North Carolina once.'"

Despite this jocular tone, Clover ended the same letter with an anxious request: "Take care of yourself." Dr. Hooper's health was starting to fail from heart disease. He was in his mid-seventies and had suffered from severe angina for some time, but his condition over the past few months had worsened precipitously. Ned Hooper had built a new home in Cambridge, on Fayerweather Street, right next to Ellen and her husband, Whitman Gurney. The two older siblings moved their father from his Beacon Hill residence to the Gurney home so they could all tend him more closely.

By March 7, Henry wrote an anxious note to John Hay: "Bunged up by the nastiest cold I have had for years, I write in double straits because my wife may have to go to Boston next week, and possibly I may go with her, or for her." Six days later, Henry and Clover left Washington for New York, with Clover going on alone to Cambridge to be with her father. Henry met with John Hay, Clarence King, H. H. Richardson, John La Farge, and Augustus Saint-Gaudens, who were all in New York at the same time. Henry soon after traveled back to Washington with Hay to oversee house building and to avoid what he dreaded most: deathbed vigils. During the next six weeks, Henry visited Cambridge only twice. He said he was eager not to get in the way. Sometimes he felt sorry for himself. At one point, at loose ends and alone in Washington, he complained to Rebecca Dodge that "nobody wants me in either place. They won't take me for a nurse, and I can't live all alone in a big, solitary house when it rains and I can't ride."

In Cambridge, Clover stayed with Ned and his five daughters, and every morning she walked next door to the Gurneys' to be at her father's bedside. Dr. Hooper refused to employ trained nurses, so his children took turns day and night, coordinating his feeding and bathing—all the tasks of attending the dying. Once, to break the fear-drenched monotony, Clover arranged for one of Henry's nephews studying at Harvard to come for a party so that Ned's five motherless daughters could learn to dance. But other than that exception to routine, Clover stayed at her father's bedside. Did she reminisce with him? Did she read aloud from her mother's poems? When Clover's mother faced her own death she had written, "So methinks do the children of earth groan under / the experiences of a life or an age of evil and awake at / last deep and safe in the beginning and heart of all." Did this comfort Clover and her family? For six weeks the daughter's world contracted to the size of her father's sickroom.

Henry sent letters almost daily, and Clover did likewise, though her side of the correspondence is missing. He talked of social gossip, of gas pipes and hammering workmen, of the horrid late-winter weather, of friends stopping by to ask after the Hooper family. He reported on Edith Newbold Jones's engagement to Teddy Wharton and that Lizzie Cameron was "in despair because Don has decided to take her with him to California. I fancy she will be gone before you return." On a Saturday evening in late March, Henry asked Clover to imagine him "seated by the library fire, writing this on my knee while Boojum snores at my feet." He admitted to feeling "low in mind" and finding it hard to work, and that one bad day was saved when H. H. Richardson walked in. "I was mighty glad to see him," Henry wrote with relief. But Henry didn't tell his wife he missed her. Instead, the weather or the dogs were miserable: "The day is gloomy with rain. The dogs and I try to be gay, but Possum is in very low spirits."

Henry's weaving of daily gossip provided distraction, normalcy. It had been their habit as a couple to treat light things seriously and serious things lightly. But beneath the banter, Henry worried about Clover's reaction to losing her father. He had already imagined the circumstance in *Esther*—midway through the novel, Esther's father dies of heart problems, and in her grief, Esther cannot sleep, feels disoriented and unspeakably "weary," and eventually slips into "days of vacancy, with no appetite for work and no chance for amusement." Henry's worry made him awkward, ill at ease. He addressed Clover affectionately: "Dear Mistress," "Dear Angel," and once, "Dear Aspasia," a reference to Pericles' beautiful mistress. After six weeks, he wished "for his wife again," asking, "How did I ever hit on the only woman in the world who fits my cravings and never sounds hollow anywhere?" But he wrote to her in the third person, not addressing her with the more intimate "you." When Clover's father was dying, Henry did not give what she needed most: reassurance of his love and his confidence that she was strong enough to bear her loss and would be all right. Lost in his own fear, he did not or could not see her as she was.

By early April of 1885, Dr. Hooper could no longer digest food. On April 13, he lost consciousness and died, with his family surrounding him. He had been "unselfish and brave and full of fun" until his death, Clover later said, never having lost his "humor and courage." It was these two qualities—humor and courage—that Clover so prized. He was buried alongside his wife, Ellen, who had died thirty-seven years before, in Mount Auburn Cemetery in Cambridge.

Clover had felt enormously proud of her father. He'd been a trustee of venerable Boston institutions, including the Public Library, the Athenaeum, and the Museum of Fine Arts. After he donated Washington Allston's *Saint Peter and the Angel in Prison* to the Worcester Asylum, the institution commended his "kind heart and generous hand" in the local newspaper. But most of all, Dr. Hooper had been a good father. When Clover's brother, Ned, wrote to his father from his post in South Carolina during the Civil War, asking him to take care of his fiancée, Fanny, living nearby in Brookline, Ned revealed his debt: "You must take good care of her for me—as good as you have always taken of me." Shortly before leaving for her honeymoon in June 1872, Clover said to her father, "It seems to me more than I deserve to go from the care of such a kind father to a good husband and I am very grateful." And all her weekly letters in the years after were a testament to her devotion and their close bond. In her father's later years, Clover protected him more, knowing he fretted about her. She hadn't told him about her and Henry's trip to Niagara Falls in 1879 until she got there, knowing that he was "of an anxious make." But if he worried about Clover, he had not intruded on her life. In fact, Henry marveled at one point that Clover's father interfered "as little in his children's affairs as I can conceive possible."

Clover seemed at ease in her letters to him. She may have concealed her darker moods and feelings; she may have felt an obligation to take care of him, to ensure he wasn't lonely. But if she chafed or rebelled against their closeness, she registered this neither in her letters nor in her photographs. When she lost her mother, her father stayed close by; he had secured for her much of what had been good in her life. More than that, he had always held his younger daughter steadily in his gaze: he was clearly proud of her, and he occasionally urged her to live by the highest standards, warning her, for instance, that she was sometimes too judgmental. And it was all of this, this safe harbor, this easy back-and-forth intimacy, that she now lost.

Clover didn't articulate her grief in this way. Instead, she did what she'd learned to do when faced with incomprehensible loss—she shrank back and turned away. As she told Anne Palmer in the days following her father's funeral, "No one fills any part of his place to me but Henry so that my connection with New England is fairly severed." On the surface, this seems contrary to fact: she still had many friends and family members, including her sister and brother-in-law, her brother, and his five daughters living in and near Boston. Yet her statement tells the truth of an emotion: to lose both parents, at any age, is to be orphaned, to feel at least in part like an abandoned child. This, to Clover, was an overwhelming and dangerous feeling.

CHAPTER 20

"Lost in the Woods"

AFTER RETURNING TO Washington, Clover felt "tired out in mind and body." Her usual escape from the hot weather, Boston's North Shore, no longer held much appeal. Too many memories crowded in of the leisurely afternoons she'd spent there with her father in Beverly Farms, only a short walk through the woods from Pitch Pine Hill. A tour of Europe would be a distraction but was out of the question. Clover had decided long ago that she no longer enjoyed overseas travel. She was curious, however, to see for herself the American West. She'd enjoyed many descriptions of its landscape and stories of its native people in her conversations with Clarence King, who would often bring her mementos from his various western tours: an antler's head, a woven Paiute basket—and, once, an oversize glass-plate negative from one of his surveyor's giant cameras.

Now, in the wake of her grief, Clover wanted an adventure, something out of the ordinary, a chance to do what she so enjoyed—spending the day outdoors, on horseback. She and Henry planned to stay in Washington until mid-June and then, when the weather warmed, to take a train west for a six-week excursion through the Rockies and Yellowstone National Park, which had become a popular destination for wealthy easterners since its opening in 1872. As she reported to Anne Palmer, they hoped to "camp out" in the Rocky Mountains, "taking our own outfit—horses, tents, etc." More than anything, she was determined to move forward. Her husband, observing her resolve, told John Hay with obvious relief that Clover seemed "in better condition than I feared."

Yet Clover's forward-looking posture was just that: a posture. Anger simmered just beneath her grief. She'd long had a habit of teasing and making jokes; for her it was a way to make light of hard things. This sense of humor was part of her charm and made her a delightful companion at dinner parties. But, as her father had warned her, this tendency could harden into sarcasm and push people away. After her father's death, Clover's wit soured, and Anne Palmer, her closest friend, became an early casualty.

Clover and Anne had enjoyed a steady friendship for six years, since 1879. They shared a love of art, flowers, and social gossip, and a similar sense of humor, trading puns and anecdotes in their letters. Clover never had to compete with a husband and children for her friend's attention, and Anne's obvious motherly qualities—her kindness and patience, her careful attention to others' needs—had been a boon to Clover.

Now all of this seemed at risk. In the early spring, Anne had announced her engagement and upcoming marriage to an Englishman, Edward Nelson Fell. Clover had had no time to reply promptly because just then she had been taking care of her dying father. But at the end of April, she at last responded to her friend's happy news. She began by saying she was "very glad" to hear of Anne's engagement, and was confident that her friend would not have agreed to marry "anyone if you could possibly have helped it." At twenty-eight, Anne was the same age Clover had been when she had married thirteen years before, and Clover knew too well that "the freedom of an American spinster becomes wearing as she drifts towards her thirties." She joked that Anne's wedding announcement gave her "a weapon for all time." Perhaps Clover was masking her vulnerability, her fear of more change and loss coming so soon after her father's death, in this clever banter.

Then Clover's humor took exactly the sort of turn that her father had warned against. She began to wield her own "weapon" by mocking the English. "I like Englishmen," she intoned to her friend, "when they are

not lords and not affected and have not their money or their county position on their minds. What my friend Sir John Clark calls 'the insolence
of the British aristocracy' irritates me." Then Clover's mockery grew
more pointed. "I have a yearning in my heart that Mr. Fell shall turn out
to be a widow with four plain daughters — to see you bossing a brood of
pious little English girls, wrestling with their catechism and hereditary
traits would give me lifelong joy." She added, "I also assume that your
new charge is poor because rich Englishmen marry only heiresses." As
Anne moved toward a new life of her own, Clover conjured up a poison-
ous scenario of motherless, plain-looking girls, a ghostly copy of her own
childhood. In the haunted weeks of late April 1885, all she could see and
feel was that Anne's impending marriage would be for her yet another
unbearable loss. Anne's response to Clover's letter is not known. Perhaps
she took it in stride, perhaps not. In either case, Clover never again wrote
Anne a letter.

Losing her father had deeply unsettled Clover. Fatigue and fear began
to develop into something that simple rest could not remedy. Henry was
watchful and patient, though distant. He did what he could to contain his
wife's sorrow, hoping her grief would blow past like a strong wind, as
had her confusion on the Nile. But he was also worried about Clover. By
early June, he postponed their western trip until August, telling a friend
that it was "on account of the flies and gnats" that infested the western
mountains in midsummer. His excuse gave discreet cover to the fact that
Clover was not recovering.

Instead, Clover and Henry spent the early part of the summer of 1885
exploring the Virginia countryside and taking the water cure, a therapy
popular since the middle of the nineteenth century, which emphasized
moderate exercise, healthy foods, time spent outdoors, and numerous
baths in mineral waters. On June 11, with their two saddle horses packed
into a railroad car, Clover and Henry traveled southwest by train 250
miles to White Sulphur Springs, West Virginia, the historic summer spa
for antebellum plantation owners and their families, located on the eastern edge of the Allegheny Mountains. The sloping valley was ringed
by misty, low mountains, with high oaks and lush vegetation. It was, as
Henry remarked, "a country less known to Bostonians than could be
found in Europe." They bathed in the mineral pool, long famed for its

curative powers, and they rode out by horseback to take in the views, particularly the riot of early-summer flowers. The "flaming yellow, orange, and red azalea" and "masses of white and pink laurel," Henry remarked to a friend, made the landscape seem "like the most beautiful Appenines." Henry's language — his descriptions of flowering plants — echoes Clover's in her many letters to her father.

The accommodations, however, were "so ideally bad" that four days later they rode seventeen miles farther south to another prominent resort, Old Sweet Springs, located in Monroe Country on the Virginia border. "Old Sweet" was a vast improvement. There the Adamses rented a small white wooden cabin, with a front porch the length of the house, that was comfortably shaded by a giant oak tree. When the southern heat became unbearable, they hiked over to the nearby bathing pool, which was kept a relatively cool seventy-six degrees. They spent their days swimming, reading, riding, and going for meals at the large red-brick hotel reputedly designed by Thomas Jefferson. Clover's recovery was their primary aim. Though the resort had few visitors so early in the season, Clover and Henry had company: shortly after their arrival, their Washington friend Rebecca Dodge and her cousin, Cliff Richardson, the photographer who had introduced Clover to the newest developing processes at the National Museum eighteen months before, came by the early-morning train to stay with them.

Clover had taken along her camera and equipment, and after a season of not taking any photographs, she again turned her surroundings into pictures. Eight photographs from the Virginia trip are included in Clover's third and last photograph album, which contains eighteen images. The first three photographs depict Henry, Rebecca Dodge, and Richardson, lounging on the front porch of their white clapboard cottage, the heat of the southern sun all but palpable in the grainy images. The first print includes all three figures, while the next two portray only Henry and Cliff Richardson. The figures take up different positions — in the first, all are seated; in the second, one is seated, one is standing; and in the third, two are seated. Though Henry is identifiable, in his usual light-colored summer suit, no one's face is clearly visible because Clover put her camera at a farther remove than was typical for her. At this point, she seems less interested in portraits than in context. The giant oak tree hovering over the porch, the surrounding vegetation, the way the house sat on the land—Clover was paying attention to all of this. She captured the details of the Virginia countryside, a landscape that still bore the marks of battle and dislocation twenty years after the end of the Civil War.

Old Sweet Springs lies on the border between West Virginia and Virginia, between the Alleghenies to the west and the Shenandoah Valley to the east. Two years before, in the spring of 1883, Clover had arranged her horseback tour of the Shenandoah Valley, what had been the breadbasket of the Confederacy, with Henry and others, including Lucy Frelinghuysen, James Lowndes, and the von Eisendeckers. She had written to her father that the sight of "the ruins of a stone house or mill remind us that we were among the old battle fields and in the valley which Sheridan ploughed so deeply." Clover was referring to General Philip Sheridan's scorched-earth campaign of September 1864, which rendered the fertile farmland useless to the Confederates. Of course, other key battles of the war had taken place in this area and the surrounding region: Stonewall Jackson's outsmarting of the Union army in the spring of 1862, which allowed him to retake the valley; the brutal Wilderness Campaign of May 1864, in central Virginia; and the climactic battle of Cedar Creek in October 1864. During the war almost no other region sustained as much damage—to plantations, crops, houses, railroads, schools, mills, and businesses—as did Virginia. Twenty years after the Confederate surrender at Appomattox, Virginia's economy was still struggling.

Clover knew this history well. She had lived through it as a young woman, obsessively following Union troop movements and battle reports in Boston and New York newspapers, and she had lost several friends in the war, including her cousin Robert Shaw at Fort Wagner near Charleston and Charley Lowell at Cedar Creek. Clover and Henry also had entertained many of the central participants of the war at their table, Union and Confederate generals alike.

Now, with her camera in hand, Clover recorded a landscape still haunted by the effects of war, focusing specifically on one Virginia farm and the man and wife who lived there. She took her first image at a distance, in order to get into frame the entire battered log structure, which combined living quarters on one side and a barn on the other. Chickens peck at feed in the yard, and a woman stands in the doorway of the house, with a crude apron tied around her waist. The downstairs window has a curtain across it, but the upstairs window has been boarded over with rough-cut lumber. The old man, his white hair clearly visible, stands in the large doorway leading to the barn, leaning on a piece of farm equipment. Both stare intently and directly into Clover's camera. The next photograph is similar, only this time the man and woman stand close together in the doorway of the house. The woman is barely visible behind her straight-standing husband, who holds one arm cocked on his hip. Though the image evokes the defeat of the South, it is also a vision of unbowed determination and self-sufficiency in the face of poverty, not unlike Dorothea Lange's much later documentation of the refugees of the Great Depression.

It's not clear when Clover developed these negatives, made the prints, and pasted them into her third red-leather album. By the summer of 1885, she was, of course, no longer writing letters to her father; much of what is known about her practice of photography was recorded in the pages that she had penned every week, until now. Nor did she leave any notes about making these prints. The sequence of images, so carefully considered in the two prior albums, is more haphazard in the third. There are several empty pages, and a number of close-up portraits made at an earlier time, including her portrait of John La Farge. Also, the third album differs from the previous two in that Clover didn't write her name in the frontispiece or provide captions for the prints. Instead, at the time or perhaps much later, Henry carefully wrote captions for most of the images in his meticulous handwriting, something he'd done only rarely in Clover's previous albums. "Old Sweet Springs, Virginia, June 1885, Rebecca Dodge, Cliff Richardson, H. A.," Henry wrote, and "Virginia farm-house, Old Sweet Springs, June, 1885."

But disjointed as it is, with its gaps and silences, the third album nonetheless suggests a narrative, a theme: youthful promise fallen into irreparable decline. It opens not with the trip to Old Sweet Springs, but with photographs taken earlier of Falmouth, Virginia, just north of Fredericksburg, near the Spotsylvania battleground. A young girl, "Miss Hayward," stands in front of a towering field of corn, dressed fashionably, wearing a straw bonnet and holding in her arms a small striped kitten. She is full of promise. But the mood quickly changes. In the next image, also taken at Falmouth, a young boy and his dog can't stand still in front of Clover's camera. They are a blur of movement, but behind them looms an old brick windmill, its severely damaged white wooden sails clearly visible. The windmill, in its uselessness and disrepair, is the focal point of the image, not the boy and his dog.

Following this are four photographs of broken-down houses near Bladensburg, Maryland, a town seven miles from Washington, where the Army of the Potomac had once bivouacked. Clover and Henry liked to ride there on horseback often, following military lanes and crosscuts marked out on an old army map that a retired Union general had given them. At some point, though she didn't indicate when, Clover must have taken her camera along. Placed after these earlier Bladensburg images, showing abandoned Confederate homes with broken panes of glass and overgrown vines, are the later vacation photographs of Old Sweet Springs as well as two images of Rebecca Dodge standing alone in a field of tall grass, in profile and looking down, a sequence that creates a pervading tone of gloom. A broken-down windmill, abandoned houses, a vacation cabin dwarfed by surrounding vegetation, a solitary woman, and an ancient overgrown farm—all these images, though formally rigorous like her earlier photographs, are also sadder, a signal of defeat, and full of wreckage.

During their six-week sojourn in the South, Clover and Henry took long horseback rides in the countryside, following old trails and mountain turnpikes. Henry hoped that this form of recreation, a favorite of Clover's, amid gorgeous scenery, would be enough to revive her. It had always done so in the past. But he began to suspect that this time it wouldn't be enough, that he couldn't do enough, that a separation had grown between him and Clover that was becoming darker, more sinister. A bleak feeling began to enter his letters. Once, while near White Sulphur Springs, as Henry described to Charles Gaskell, "we got a long way into the wild mountains by a rough path; and the groves of huge rhododendron were so gloomy and seemed to shake their dark fingers so threateningly over our heads, that we turned about and fled for fear night should catch us, and we should never be seen any more by our dear enemies who would like to have us lost in the woods."

Clover and Henry were, of course, already lost in the woods.

CHAPTER 21

A Dark Room

IN MID-JULY of 1885, Henry Adams received a worried note from John Hay, asking, "Whither have you vanished? I shoot this inquiry into the vague of space?" Henry replied on July 17 from Beverly Farms. They'd had "a month of rambling," he explained, and currently "various domestic necessities have forced us to return home and abandon our Yellowstone adventure." Henry resisted spelling out their circumstances more clearly to Hay, one of his and Clover's closest friends. He didn't mention his wife; he didn't say that she was by now slipping into a dangerous depression. At the end of July, Clover received a long letter from her cousin Sturgis Bigelow, Susan Sturgis Bigelow's only child, who'd been living in Japan since 1882. He confided to Clover that his "private opinion" was that "you and Henry have not got enough enterprise" and, not knowing how serious her condition had become, asked her, "Why in the—never mind what—did you not come out here this summer?" He brightly insisted that she "just do it next year, without fail."

Though Clover had dreaded going to their summer home, thinking it would be, as Henry told Charles Gaskell, "a gloomy spot," she now secluded herself at Pitch Pine Hill. Her family surrounded her: Ned

Hooper was on the North Shore with his five lively daughters for much of the summer, as were Ellen and Whitman Gurney. Most crucially, Beverly Farms provided much-longed-for privacy. It was a far better option than what Clover must have feared most—the humiliation of being hospitalized at McLean Asylum near Boston, in Somerville.

Clover did not delve much into the subject of madness. At times, she could be solicitous toward those afflicted by mental suffering. She was desperately worried about her childhood friend Adie Bigelow when, in 1882, she broke down. In a series of letters to her father, Clover explained that she knew from Adie's "own lips her horror of insane persons, and of those who have been sent to asylums," begging him to urge the family to send her instead for recovery to a "softer, milder climate," adding, "You can do much with that family. They will take your advice." When she heard of Adie's admission to McLean Asylum a week later, she lamented, "I cannot bear to think that what we feared most has come to pass."

Regarding other cases, Clover kept up on the gossip and sometimes, in her father's opinion, displayed a "taste for horrors," an unbecoming *schadenfreude*, an almost gleeful interest in the illnesses and mental breakdowns of others. She looked upon insanity with a kind of spooked curiosity combined with eagerness to stay away from it, as if protecting herself from something that might be contagious. "The insane asylum," she mused to her father, "seems to be the goal of every good and conscientious Bostonian—babies and insanity the two leading topics of interest—Mrs. so and so has a baby—she becomes insane and goes to Somerville—baby grows up and promptly returns to Somerville—it's all nonsense." Uneasy dread lay at the heart of this humorous dismissal of the subject. Now, in the summer of 1885, Clover was in the midst of the very thing she had feared, and bluster no longer protected her.

There is little record of what Clover did from late July through mid-October of 1885. She tried to keep up a semblance of her usual routine, and one can imagine her walking in the nearby woods to find flowers, going for a horseback ride at the seashore, and swimming in the sea. Perhaps she felt as she had while on the Nile—"blind and deaf and dumb." But whatever she did, nothing seemed capable of easing her mind—not Henry, her family, her friends, her garden, her dogs, her horses. At one point, she managed to reach out to Rebecca Dodge, who was dutifully taking care of an ill mother. "Dearest Rebecca," Clover wrote, "you seem to have heavy burdens to bear but you are so sweet and brave and strong that you never seem to lose courage." As she felt herself slipping farther and farther out of reach, Clover admired Rebecca's courage the way a person who is drowning envies a strong swimmer capable of reaching shore.

Clover's depression was unrelenting. She lost her appetite and could not sleep. Whitman Gurney told E. L. Godkin that his sister-in-law was suffering "in the gloomiest state of mind, and the gloom has not yet lifted." Gurney surmised that "time seems the only remedy," adding that Clover's "general depression has been accompanied by the greatest sweetness towards us." Ellen agreed, telling a friend how her sister had apologized repeatedly to her family for "every reckless word or act — wholly forgotten by all save her." Few had suspected that beneath her wit and quickness, Clover had, over the years, carefully preserved a guilty tally of all her misdemeanors. Shame alternated with a descending fog of unreality. Robbed of her protective humor, she grew disoriented, pleading with her sister again and again, "Ellen, I'm not real — Oh make me real — you are all of you real!"

There were treatments Clover might have tried. Dr. George Beard, who made the first diagnosis of neurasthenia in 1869, had had success in curing depression with electrotherapy. Dr. S. Weir Mitchell was renowned for his ability to make well "all the dilapidated Bostonians," according to Phillips Brooks, rector of Trinity Church, and prescribed with some success his rest cure, a strict regimen of bed rest, fatty foods, and retreat from everyday activities. Clover had met Dr. Mitchell when the famous nerve doctor had stopped in at H Street for tea the year before, and she'd found him fascinating, "very bright and full of talk." She had access to the very best physicians in both Boston and Washington. Even so, if she or Henry or any other member of the family consulted with a doctor about what was happening to her during these months, they left no evidence of having done so. Nervous troubles and mental instability were often a source of enormous shame and could be damaging socially. It was often thought that such difficulties pointed to moral lapses or a family's bad stock, and mental illness surely fed the gossip mill. For those surrounding Clover, the safest route was to wait out Clover's despondency, with the hope that a modified version of rest and seclusion would eventually bring her back to life.

In the darkening days of mid-October, Clover and Henry left Beverly Farms for Washington, where she retreated into almost complete isolation at 1607 H Street, leaving her upstairs rooms only for an occasional carriage ride with Rebecca Dodge through the familiar streets of Washington, a city Clover used to relish in the autumn weather. But not this year. Rebecca remembered that during these outings, Clover would talk for a while, then stop abruptly, rubbing her forehead as if she had forgotten something, as if she was trying to put her thoughts back in order.

Henry, meanwhile, was a mix of nervousness and detachment. He did what he knew how to do — he read and researched what was happening to his wife. He owned the recently published *Body and Will, Being an Essay Concerning Will in Its Metaphysical, Physiological, and Pathological Aspects* (1884) by Henry Maudsley, a treatise on the brain-mind connection in which the well-known British mind doctor explored depressive illness. Henry penciled exclamation points in the book's margins next to specific passages. One passage clearly resonated for him:

It is a common event in one sort of mental disorder especially at the beginning of it, for the person to complain that he is completely and painfully changed; that he is not longer himself, but feels himself unutterably strange; and that things around him, though wearing their usual aspect, yet somehow seem quite different. I am so changed that I feel as if I were not myself but another person; although I know it is an illusion, it is an illusion which I cannot shake off; all things appear strange to me and I cannot properly apprehend them even though they are really familiar; they look a long way off and more like the figures in a dream . . . it seems as if an eternity of time and an infinity of space were interposed; the suffering that I endure is indescribable: such is the kind of language by which these persons endeavor to express the profound change in themselves which they feel only too painfully but cannot describe adequately.

Did Henry talk with Clover about any of this? They had at one point shared so much of their reading, sometimes reciting aloud whole books to each other. Perhaps he wouldn't have wanted to frighten Clover any further, and he had to cope with his own fear about what was happening. His mother's chronic health complaints had tyrannized him, and this legacy may have made it all the more difficult for Henry to cope with Clover's suffering. The thing he desperately wanted at this point, besides his wife's recovery, was to guard their privacy. He never disclosed to his family the seriousness of the situation, merely telling them that Clover wasn't feeling well. When Henry's publisher raised the possibility of republishing *Esther*, whose title character so resembled Clover, Henry pleaded against it. "I am peculiarly anxious not to wake up the critics just now ... I never had so many reasons for wishing to be left in peace, as now." On November 4, he admitted to Theodore Dwight, his private secretary, that Clover "goes nowhere," and four days later, he wrote to Charles Gaskell that "my wife is unwell; we are in mourning." But despite mentioning, at least briefly, the troubling situation to these friends, he wrote several letters that same month to John Hay that discuss the building and design of the new house while revealing nothing about Clover. He stated only that she sent her "best love" and that he saw "no one" because "my doors are tight shut."

By early November, friends started to exchange anxious letters, commenting on Clover's marked decline. John Field, who along with his wife, Eliza — the subject of one of Clover's finest portraits — had grown particularly fond of both Clover and Henry, revealed his growing alarm in a series of letters to Theodore Dwight, who was traveling in New York at the time. On November 7, Field wrote that Clover was "very low in mind, and shows it." Even so, he held out hope that "horseback and fresh air will bring her up before long." Field's optimism was short-lived. He had convinced Henry to talk more frankly about Clover, and four days later Field wrote Dwight again. "I saw the Adamses yesterday. She sags — she is very low ... Adams spoke truly to me, and he seems sad."

Then, in late November, Clover seemed to revive. H. H. Richardson arrived just before Thanksgiving, with more architectural drawings for the new house, most likely for interior designs and embellishments. He stayed two days with the Adamses and found Clover "much improved." She had started to sleep again and she showed something of her earlier strength, engaging in conversation about the almost-finished house and acting more like herself.

Weeks before, Lizzie Cameron had come back to town. She was having trouble with her marriage and her health. Two months pregnant, she was confined to bed. On a warm evening in early December, Clover, alone, went to see Lizzie to cheer her up, bringing along a large bouquet of yellow Maréchal Niel roses for Lizzie's bedside table. In the language of flowers, popular at the time, yellow roses signified "I'm yours, heart and soul." Was Clover's gesture a kind of reproach, a concession that very soon she would be stepping aside, leaving Henry, "heart and soul," to Lizzie Cameron?

Clover's reprieve of calm, which others had interpreted as newfound energy, had come with her resolve to kill herself. The next morning, Sunday, December 6, began hazy, and colder. Henry left the house for a walk and a quick visit to his dentist about a bothersome tooth. Sunday mornings had previously been the time of the week that Clover set aside to write to her father. She liked to sit at her desk beneath the upstairs windows as she wrote, looking south across H Street to Lafayette Square and to the White House beyond, its roofline visible just beyond the trees. Now there was no letter to write; it was as if the floor of her life had fallen away. At some point she wrote a note to her sister, Ellen, in which she insisted that Henry had been "more patient and loving than words can express." She tried to protect him from what others might think, protesting that he was "beyond all words tenderer and better than all of you even." If there was also a note for Henry, she told no one, and neither, ever, did he.

Instead, Clover aimed all the blame at herself. "If I had one single point of character or goodness," she lamented to her sister, "I would stand on that and grow back to life." She found instead only grief, hopelessness, and a self-loathing that had turned into something lethal. Completely alone, she cast off the world with all its interests and the love of those closest to her and the profound hurt she could not end any other way. She got a vial of potassium cyanide from the shelf of chemicals she kept on hand to develop her photographs, opened it, and took a swallow. Her tongue and throat burned. The poison cut off her body's ability to process oxygen, making her choke and gasp for air, in all likelihood triggering convulsions. She lost consciousness and would have died within the half hour.

When Henry returned, he found her sprawled in front of a chair near an upstairs fireplace. In a rush to revive her, he carried her to a nearby sofa. The bitter smell of cyanide permeated the room. It was, of course, too late. He immediately had telegrams sent to his brothers and to Clover's brother and sister, Ned and Ellen, but he could not bear to see or talk to anyone. On that Sunday night he wrote a note and had it delivered to Rebecca Dodge: "Wait till I have recovered my mind. I can see no one now. Tomorrow I must be myself; and I can't think yet. Don't let any one come near me." Taking on the mantle of loneliness that had shrouded Clover in the preceding months, Henry sat vigil all day and all night, alone in the house with his wife's body. Neighbors reported seeing him at an upstairs window, staring out to the street below.

By the time the Hooper siblings arrived the next day, Henry had regained some of his composure. "God only knows how he kept his reason those hours," Ellen wrote to a mutual friend, noting that when they arrived on Monday, Henry "was as steady and sweet and thoughtful of us as possible—almost like a child in his touching dependence."

The family stayed with Henry until the funeral the following Wednesday. It was small and private, held in the H Street house. The Boston clergyman Edward Hall officiated at the brief service, of which there is no record. That afternoon, in a procession of five black carriages, the family drove Clover's casket north from Lafayette Square to Rock Creek Cemetery, next to the oldest church in the city. The weather was wretched. Rain poured down so hard, they had to postpone the interment for three days because the ground was too saturated for a burial. On December 12, Clover was buried in a slope of a hill near the graves of Revolutionary War soldiers—it was a place, her sister noted hopefully, where "spring comes early."

• • •

The mood resonant in so many of Clover's photographs reflects what the British poet and critic A. Alvarez called, in another context, "a terminal inner loneliness." The people in her images are often separate from each other, they rarely look directly at the camera, and they are often disconnected from or turned away from the viewer. And though Clover transformed what saddened her into something beautiful and something she could share, this transformation of loss — the early loss of her mother, of her Aunt Susan, the absence of children, the fading closeness with Henry, and finally, the loss of her father — did not and could not save her. In the end, she seemed no more than a ghost.

Creativity can be compensatory, redemptive, a release, a reach toward freedom and hope. But this is not always the case. Artistic expression is not always consolation for emotional pain. Things can sometimes go the other way. Creativity also undoes, overwhelms, gives power to hidden undertows. What's brought forward in expression is exposed and becomes irrefutable. Perhaps this also happened with Clover. On July 26, 1883, just shy of her fortieth birthday, knowing full well that her chances of ever having a child were behind her, Clover wrote to Lizzie Cameron, who was then traveling in Europe. She asked her to "go to the Louvre" and "in the middle of a long gallery find a portrait of a lady in black, young child standing by her, by Van Dyck and tell her how she haunts me." It was unusual for Clover to use the word *haunt*. It is more revealing than she usually chose to be. Less than two weeks later, Clover echoed Van Dyck's masterwork of confident Dutch maternity in a photograph of her friend, Mimi Lyman, and her son, Ted. This picture registers, as do other images in her collection, what she rarely wrote down: what haunted her, what was missing, what was beyond her reach. And as she expressed in her photographs something of her inner life — her sense of loneliness, of being separate and disconnected — she also exposed it to herself.

It's no wonder, then, that the chemical that allowed Clover to bring to light in photographs what was too dangerous to put into words was the same one she used to kill herself.

Clover's Photographs

ABOVE: Henry with Marquis on the back stairs of the Adams house at 1607 H Street, Washington, D.C., May 6, 1883. Clover listed this image on the first page of the notebook in which she kept a detailed record of her photographs.

BELOW: Pitch Pine Hill, the summer home in Beverly Farms that Clover and Henry designed, was finished in 1876. It was, according to Henry, "more than all we ever hoped."

All photographs by Clover Adams reproduced courtesy of the Massachusetts Historical Society.

ABOVE: Henry's parents, Charles Francis Adams and Abigail Brooks Adams, July 30, 1883.

RIGHT: Clover left little doubt about her loving feelings for her father in this portrait of him, taken on August 12, 1883.

ABOVE: "Ellen, Loulie, & Polly on rocks, very nice—time good, 2nd stop, 1 sec." So wrote Clover of this portrait of three of the five daughters of her brother, Ned Hooper, taken on August 21, 1883.

BELOW: Del and Helen Hay, children of John and Clara Hay, October 24, 1883.

ABOVE: Henry reading a manuscript at his summer desk at Pitch Pine Hill, August 19, 1883. Clover thought his "face good," but his "dark coat bad."

BELOW: Clover paired Henry with a photograph of an umbrella tree at Smith's Point near Beverly Farms not once but twice in her album.

ABOVE: Possum, Marquis, and Boojum, the Adamses' Skye terriers, at tea.

LEFT: The American architect H. H. Richardson, a man who could say, as Clover remarked, "I am my own music."

A view of snowy Lafayette Square across the street from the Adamses' home at 1607 H Street.

ABOVE: John Hay thought Clover's photograph of George Bancroft, the leading historian of America, worthy of the cover of *Century* magazine.

LEFT: John Hay, November 27, 1883.

ABOVE: Elizabeth Bliss Bancroft, wife of George Bancroft. Henry wrote that she was "by long odds the most intelligent woman in Washington."

BELOW: Clover labeled her photograph of Grace Minot, one of the young women who frequented the Adamses' home, with the words "Muse of American History."

ABOVE: Clover's haunting image of Miriam Choate Pratt, Alice Greenwood Howe, and Alice Pratt at Smith's Point on Boston's North Shore.

BELOW: Virginia farm couple, summer 1885. This is one of the final photographs Clover took on the trip south, which Henry hoped would restore her to health.

CHAPTER 22

"That Bright, Intrepid Spirit"

THOUGH FEW FRIENDS attended the funeral, two of the "Five of Hearts" wrote Henry immediately in a rush of sympathy and a desire to share his burden. Clarence King sent a note from New York as soon as he heard: "I think of you all the time and lament that such great sorrow as yours cannot be more evidently and practically shared by those who love you. But I know too well the indivisibility of grief." John Hay, also in New York, sent a message to Henry the day of the funeral. "I can neither talk nor keep silent," Hay wrote, saying that Clover's death was a loss to him as well. "The darkness in which you walk has its shadow for me also. You and your wife were more to me than any other two. I came to Washington because you were there. And now this goodly fellowship is broken up forever." He closed with a tribute to Clover. "Is it any consolation," he asked, "to remember her as she was? That bright, intrepid spirit, that keen intellect, that lofty scorn of all that was mean, that social charm which made your house such a one as Washington never knew before, and made hundreds of people love her as much as they admired her?"

In the days and weeks after the funeral, Henry immersed himself in the tragedies of Shakespeare, sometimes reciting passages aloud to friends. He saddled up for long horseback rides alone, following the same paths through city streets and wooded trails that he and Clover had so prized. He recalled in a letter to Anna Barker Ward her great kindness to Clover those many years ago on the Nile, saying how much Clover had admired the older woman—the "peace that you have reached in this world was a delight to her." He reminded Mrs. Ward that she'd been "closely associated with the heaviest trials and keenest pleasures of our life," an acknowledgment of what seemed now the all-too-clear link between Clover's troubles on the Nile and her last months of misery. Though the "great calamities in life leave one speechless," as Henry admitted to Mrs. Ward, he tried to ease his burden by connecting his experience to the wider human scene. After receiving many "messages from men and women whose own hearts were aching," he was learning that he "did not stand alone in my extremity of suffering." When the wife of Thomas Bayard, then secretary of state under President Cleveland, died suddenly of a heart attack, Henry reached out to him. Admitting his doubts about whether to say anything at first, he decided to do so because, as he told Bayard, "sympathy has been a relief to me; and in all the world I doubt whether another person exists, beyond your family, who sympathizes with you more keenly than I do." To Henry Holt, he wrote simply, "What a vast fraternity it is,—that of 'Hearts that Ache.'"

Though Henry assured John Hay three days after Clover's death, the day of the funeral, that he would "come out all right from this," Henry's friends worried about him. Henry James told E. L. Godkin, since 1883 the editor in chief of the *New York Evening Post*, that he was "more sorry for poor Henry than I can say," adding that he was "too sorry, almost, to think of him." John Hay told Henry that "we are anxious about you. Tell us, when you can, how it is with you." Then, in an effort to build up his friend's courage, Hay observed: "You have a great sorrow, but no man should bear sorrow better than you." By mid-December Hay wrote again, saying, "You are never out of my mind but I do not write, for lack of language to express my sorrow and sympathy. If I came to you I could only sit with you in silence, like the friends of Job."

What Henry wanted most of all, as Whitman Gurney recounted, was to set "his face steadily towards the future." On December 30, Henry fled from the house he had shared with Clover into his new Richardson-designed house next door, at 1603 H Street, where he spent weeks sorting books and hanging pictures. If Clover had lived only weeks longer, she and Henry would have moved into their new home together. Now, in the wake of her death, Henry promised Lizzie Cameron he would live "henceforward on what I can save from the wreck of her life."

But Clover's suicide, with its poison of despair, cleaved Henry's life into two parts, before and after, and like the biblical wife of Lot fleeing destruction, he couldn't resist the backward glance. On January 8, 1886, a bitterly cold Saturday, Henry wrote a searching letter to Clover's closest friend, Anne Palmer Fell, now living with her husband in Florida. In it, he confessed that "I should have written to you before, but have put it off from day to day as a thing that could better wait till I had found out what had happened to me, and where I was." He found himself confused, disoriented, waiting for Clover to somehow return. "Even now," Henry wrote, "I cannot quite get rid of the feeling that Clover must, sooner or later, come back, and that I had better wait for her to decide everything for me." The sensation was "growing weaker" each day, but "the wrench has left me like a child, amusing myself from day to day, without a plan or an interest that grown people commonly affect to have."

Though Henry often changed the topic — to a land deal in Florida, rattlesnakes, and lemons — he kept turning back to memories of Clover, revealing to Anne how his grief had cracked him wide open. He was determined to reclaim his happiness with Clover, at least in memory.

The only moments of the past that I regret are those when I was not actively happy. As one cannot be always actively blissful, one must be contented with passive content, but it is a poor substitute at best, and makes no impression on the memory. My only wonder is whether I would have managed to get more out of twelve years than we got; and if we really succeeded in being as happy as was possible. I have no more to say. The world may come and the world may go; but no power yet known in earth or heaven can annihilate the happiness that is past. I commend this moral to your careful consideration. As you once said, the worm does not turn when he is trodden on hard enough. I am one of those worms. I don't turn. I don't complain. I don't tear round. But I had my twelve years, and have them still.

Clover and Henry had been married thirteen years at the time of her death. He did not include in his count their last year together, the year he lost her to a grief and depression he could not assuage.

Suicide is "the impossible subject." It defies explanation even as it obligates survivors to try to find possible causes. Like a rock dropping in a still pond, the consequences of Clover's suicide would ripple out in widening circles of anguish, bewilderment, loss, curiosity, and a sense of mystery.

Initially, Henry James offered what would become, by and large, the most widely accepted interpretation of what happened. In a letter to a friend, James stated simply that Clover had "succumbed to hereditary melancholia." It was well known that Clover's grandmother, Elizabeth Sturgis, had abandoned her husband and five daughters after her son's accidental drowning, and the subsequent suicide of Clover's Aunt Susan only confirmed the family's reputation. Henry's brother, Charles, had long thought Susan Bigelow's death had left a particularly "dangerous impression" on Clover; believing the rumors that Clover had been present at the Bigelow house when her Aunt Susan died, Charles had warned Henry against marrying her. Clover's final self-destruction, Charles concluded, was clearly due to the fact that she had "inherited a latent tendency to suicidal mania. It was in the Sturgis blood."

The *Washington Critic* stated in its report that Clover "had been suffering from mental depression." Whitman Gurney, who saw Clover frequently during her last summer, assessed her condition likewise as "general depression," employing a diagnosis that had entered the lexicon in midcentury and was used almost interchangeably with older terms, *melancholy* and *melancholia*.

Others weren't so certain. Eighty years after Clover's death, her niece Louisa Hooper Thoron, by then ninety-one years old, still searched for clues as to what had engulfed her Aunt Clover. On a printed copy of a sermon entitled "When the Well Runs Dry," given at Boston's Trinity Church on February 7, 1965, Louisa jotted down her family history of debilitating depressions. One of her sisters had had "a bad nervous break-down in 1906 at 31 years old," Louisa began, careful to confine her comments to the sermon's margins. Comparing her sister's story with her

Aunt Clover's a generation before, Louisa wrote that her sister's break-down "was handled by . . . taking her . . . to Switzerland where she was fed up and rested from the set of responsibilities and the kind of daily life that had broken her down. In her case and era Europe was [more] suc-cessful in doing this for her than America [in] 1885 for Aunt Clover."

And yet the "curious impregnability of so many suicides," accord-ing to A. Alvarez, is the person's "imperviousness to solace." This aptly describes Clover. All her wealth and advantages — none of it at the end could comfort or save her. "Like sleep-walkers," in Alvarez's evocative phrase, her life was "elsewhere . . . , controlled by some dark and unrec-ognized centre."

In early June, six months after Clover's death, Ellen Gurney wrote to E. L. Godkin about Henry. She explained that the "stoic aspect" to Hen-ry's behavior was only a "thin glaze" and that "the worm never dies — he is restless — hates to be alone." To escape his gloom, his sense of "being smashed about," Henry embarked on a train trip west, leaving for San Francisco with a traveling companion, John La Farge. He found the jour-ney "a glorious success," relishing the chance to see the countryside, La Farge's company ("who never complains or loses his temper"), and the plush accommodations arranged by his brother, Charles, president of the Union Pacific Railroad since 1884. On June 12, he and La Farge sailed on the SS *City of Sidney* for Japan. Nikko, with its waterfalls and seventeenth-century temples to the Shoguns, dazzled Henry. To John Hay he wrote that the mountain town was surely "one of the sights of the world." For six weeks Henry rested, roamed, and spent time contem-plating the principles of Buddhist thought, with its balm for restlessness, its call to rise above suffering and self. Tours of Kyoto, Nara, and Yoko-hama, where he collected bronzes, porcelains, Hokusai drawings, and kimonos, were followed by a trip west of Tokyo to Mount Fuji, which Henry sketched in his notebook. By the time he and La Farge boarded the ship for their voyage home in October 1886, Henry told Theodore Dwight he felt "as ready to come home as I ever shall be."

But Henry returned to Washington to a cascade of bad news. Ephraim Whitman Gurney, his brother-in-law, had died of pernicious anemia on September 12, 1886. For Henry, Gurney "stood in the full centre of active interests," particularly in the family. Having no children of his own, Gurney had been particularly attached to the five Hooper nieces, as is evident in a letter, dated July 1883, that he wrote to them in Cambridge when he and his wife, Ellen Gurney, were vacationing in Lenox: "I hope you have all been very well and happy and that you will be half so glad to see us as we shall be to see and kiss you." His death left his wife, Ellen, utterly bereft. Within the past eighteen months, Ellen had buried her father, sister, and husband. Henry, worried about Ellen, observed in a letter to his old friend Charles Gaskell, "When I married in 1872, my wife's family consisted of seven persons, myself included. Only three of us are left, and if I survive either of the other two, I shall have to accept some pretty serious responsibilities and cares." Henry was obliquely referring to his Hooper nieces, who in 1886 were age fourteen, twelve, eleven, nine, and seven.

In mid-November, Henry told Lizzie Cameron he hoped his "harvest of thorns is now gathered in," but two days later, on November 21, his father, Charles Francis Adams, died at the age of seventy-nine, after a long decline into dementia. To Gaskell, Henry remarked, "If the moon were to wander off to another planet, I should no longer be surprised." On December 5, the day before the first anniversary of Clover's death, Henry wrote to Anne Palmer Fell. "During the last eighteen months," he began, "I have not had the good luck to attend my own funeral, but with that exception have buried pretty nearly everything I lived for." He was grateful for Anne's news that she'd given her new baby daughter Clover's birth name, Marian. He assured her he could "manage to keep steady now, within as well as without," but admitted that her letter "gave me a wrench. I am more than grateful to you for your loyalty to Clover, and I shall love the fresh Marian dearly." When imagining what he might say to Marian twenty years hence, he concluded that "nothing is much worth saying between man and woman except the single phrase that concentrates the whole relation in three words."

The bad news continued in 1887. On a rainy Saturday night that November, Ellen Gurney wandered out of her Cambridge home to a nearby railroad track and stood in front of an oncoming freight train. She was found severely injured by the side of the tracks and died the following morning, November 20, at Massachusetts General Hospital. Ned Hooper broke down two weeks later. Incapacitated by grief and hopelessness, he stayed in bed for six weeks, unable to go to Harvard, where he'd worked as college treasurer since 1876, or to care for his five daughters. Ned recovered but struggled, haunted always by the destruction of his family.

On a Sunday in May 1888, Henry sat alone in his large library. The art he and Clover had collected on their honeymoon hung above generous shelves of books. Washington was blooming and passersby strolled beneath his open window, crossing the street to the leafy green of Lafayette Square—spring had always been Clover's favorite time of year. His mood was out of tune with the beautiful weather. He had been rereading his old diaries, which he'd kept since a boy, tearing out pages to burn in the oversized fireplace rimmed with polished pink stone. In pages that would somehow escape destruction, he cried out, "I have been sad, sad, sad. Three years!"

CHAPTER 23

"Let Fate Have Its Way"

FOR CHRISTMAS, 1885, only three weeks after Clover's death, Henry gave Lizzie Cameron a piece of Clover's jewelry, saying, "This little trinket which I send you was a favorite of my wife's. Will you keep it and sometime wear it to remind you of her?" In the months that followed, Lizzie Cameron seemed quickly to replace Clover in key ways. She and Henry could be seen riding on horseback on the same pathways in Washington he'd taken with Clover. Henry refused to return to Pitch Pine Hill in Beverly Farms, the summer home he and Clover had designed together, but he had the house opened and ready for the Hooper family and for friends to use. Lizzie took him up on his offer for her to stay, residing there for several late-summer months in 1886 and again the next summer, writing Henry long letters while looking out to the Atlantic through the upstairs windows of Clover's bedroom, where Clover had spent many despairing hours not so long before. Lizzie would return to Pitch Pine Hill numerous times. She would even try to learn photography in the 1890s, telling Henry about the process and using the third-floor darkroom, designed by Clover, at 1603 H Street.

But it was the birth of Lizzie's only child, Martha, on June 25, 1886, less than seven months after Clover's death, that accelerated rumors about Henry's fierce and growing attachment to Lizzie. Henry became completely besotted with the child, having her over for daily visits, getting specially designed toys made for her, making the knee-hole under his enormous desk a secret playroom for her, with a sign in red ink that read MME. MARTHA, MODISTE. The fact that Lizzie had a child at all was surprising, given the deteriorated state of her marriage to Don Cameron, who already had six adult children. Henry's attachment to the child only amplified speculation that Martha Cameron was actually Henry Adams's child. Later, even Henry's biographer, the Pulitzer Prize–winning Ernest Samuels, would fuel suspicion. Samuels, who got very little wrong in his three-volume biography of Henry, unaccountably puts Martha's birth year as 1887, though he corrected the mistake later in his single-volume edition of the biography.

Yet ample evidence suggests otherwise. Henry and Lizzie had almost no chance to meet alone when Clover was alive, given how seldom Clover and Henry were physically separated. Henry was a puritan in many respects. Despite his strong feelings, strict social decorum seems to have governed the conduct of his relationship with Lizzie while Clover was alive. Finally, Lizzie and Henry were not in the same place at the time of Martha's conception. During August and September of 1885, Clover and Henry were at Beverly Farms while Lizzie was in California, traveling with her husband. The Camerons and Shermans apparently did not doubt that Don Cameron was, indeed, the father. Cameron may have hidden his surprise but not his pleasure in having a child in his fifties. Finally, although Henry may have wanted to have Lizzie "carved over the arch of my stone doorway," Lizzie seems to have been interested in much less. A longtime friend remembered that though Lizzie "liked to flirt and tease, to kiss and cajole, she never went all the way."

By early 1890, though, something had shifted between Henry and Lizzie. What had started ten years before as a diverting flirtation and then a more serious infatuation had turned into something more profound, something Henry couldn't and didn't want to shake off. He had fallen irretrievably in love. In August 1890, after putting the final polish on the proofs of the last three volumes of his monumental *History,* Henry embarked on a fourteen-month sojourn in the South Seas. He and his traveling companion, John La Farge, traveled from San Francisco to Hawaii, then to Samoa, Tahiti, and Fiji; they also visited Australia, Batavia, and Singapore. From Ceylon (current-day Sri Lanka), they crossed the Indian Ocean by steamer, proceeded across the Red Sea and through the Suez Canal into the Mediterranean, and landed finally in Marseille, France. The trip was a retreat from his Washington life and an attempt to distract himself from his deepening feelings for Lizzie, to whom he wrote sonnets and lengthy missives throughout his travels. He and Lizzie planned to meet in Paris sometime in mid-October of 1891. From Samoa he wrote, "I read your letters over and over"; from Papeete on the island of Tahiti, "I need not tell you how much I wish I could have been with you at Christmas"; and upon leaving the island in early June 1891, "My only source of energy is that I am actually starting on a ten-thousand-mile journey to see — you!" Lizzie wrote in mid-August, confirming her plans to be in Paris in two months, promising, "I shall see you — and shall take you home." Sailing to Ceylon, Henry wrote with increasing excitement, "In another week or ten days, if you have kept your plans exactly as I have, you may expect to see me walking into your parlor," concluding with a flourish, "In a week, look out!" When he finally arrived in Paris on October 10, he breathlessly announced to Lizzie in a note delivered by messenger that he would "wait only to know at what hour one may convenablement pay one's respects to you. The bearer waits an answer."

On November 5, less than three weeks later and once again separated from Lizzie, Henry wrote to her in a much-altered mood. "A long, lowering, melancholy November day," his letter begins. Henry's time with Lizzie in the City of Light was over, and things had not gone well. He presumably had hoped for time alone, a tête-à-tête during which he could declare his feelings for her and learn — at last — what was really in her heart. But their days were taken up by distractions and other people, including Lizzie's daughter, Martha, and her step-daughter, Rachel Cameron. As Henry would later rather ruefully admit to Rebecca Dodge, "Mrs. Cameron and Martha were a great comfort to me as long as they stayed, though I saw much more of the two Miss Camerons than of Mrs. Cameron." Apparently, Lizzie had again eluded him.

After Henry, Lizzie, and the two Cameron daughters traveled from

Paris to London, Lizzie sailed for America and Henry traveled to stay with his friend Charles Gaskell at Wenlock Abbey. It was from there that he started writing Lizzie on that "melancholy November day" a letter that took him a week to finish as he sorted out his feelings. He was miserable, spending afternoons riding "over sodden fields, in the heavy air, talking with Gaskell in our middle-aged way about old people, mostly dead." He felt haunted by his days in Paris with Lizzie and their awkward parting in London, reminding her that she "saw and said that my Paris experiment was not so successful as you had meant it to be." He doubted himself: "Perhaps I should have done better not to have tried it, for the result of my six months desperate chase to obey your bidding has not been wholly happy." A part of him wanted to apologize for inflicting his feelings on her: "I ought to spare you the doubtful joy of sharing my pleasures in this form." A larger part wanted her to share in his misery, which he justified: "But you, being a woman and quick to see everything that men hide, probably know my thoughts better than I do myself and would trust me the less if I concealed them."

Henry tried all kinds of tactics but got surer of his feelings as he wrote, even as he hurled himself at their mutual impasse. "No matter how much I may efface myself or how little I may ask, I must always make more demand on you than you can gratify, and you must always have the consciousness that, whatever I may profess, I want more than I can have. Sooner or later the end of such a situation is estrangement, with more or less disappointment and bitterness." That was the central conundrum — Henry wanted more of Lizzie than she wanted to offer, and he could find no path through. "I am not old enough to be a tame cat," he declared, but "you are too old to accept me in any other character." He felt self-conscious about their dilemma, admitting as much when he gave Lizzie permission to "laugh at all this, and think it one of my morbid ideas." But he also didn't care to pose: "So it is; all my ideas are morbid, and that is going to be your worst trouble, as I have always told you." What he wished for was one chance to "look clear down to the bottom of your mind and understand the whole of it."

Henry concluded his long missive to Lizzie with some of the most gorgeous sentences of his entire canon — they are direct and emotionally transparent. At fifty-three, he finally found a voice for the desiring heart and dropped his guise of irony and self-defeat. As he had learned in the years following Clover's death, to hold back and not speak of his feelings was far worse than being seen as a fool.

> I lie for hours wondering whether you, out on the dark ocean, in sur-roundings which are certainly less cheerful than mine, sometimes think of me and divine or suspect that you have undertaken a task too hard for you; whether you feel that the last month has proved to be — not wholly a success, and that the fault is mine for wanting more than I had a right to expect; whether you are almost on the verge of re-gretting a little that you tried the experiment; whether you are puzzled to know how an indefinite future of such months is to be managed; whether you are fretting, as I am, over what you can and what you cannot do; whether you are not already a little impatient with me for not being satisfied, and for not accepting in secret, as I do accept in pretence, whatever is given me, as more than enough for any deserts or claims of mine; and whether in your most serious thoughts, you have an idea what to do with me when I am again on your hands. I would not distress you with these questions while you were fretted, worried and excited by your last days here; but now that you are toss-ing on the ocean, you have time to see the apocalyptic Never which has become yours as well as mine. I have dragged you face to face with it, and cannot now help your seeing it. French novels are not the only possible dramas. One may be innocent as the angels, yet as unhappy as the wicked; and I, who would lie down and die rather than give you a day's pain, am going to pain you the more, the more I love.

Henry felt uncertain as to whether he should send the letter, but then decided to do so. "To the last moment I doubt the wisdom of sending this letter; but Kismet! Let fate have its way."

Henry's chaste romance with Lizzie would in some ways prove a trap, insofar as it deepened his emotional withdrawal and isolation. It kept tidal feelings of loss awfully close — he wanted more than Lizzie could give. When she urged him to move on and marry again, he foreclosed the suggestion with the clearest declaration: "Marry I will not." When Henry had fallen most deeply in love with her, Lizzie backed off, and if she didn't exactly turn away from him, she imposed discipline. She was in an impossible corner—separated from her husband most of the time, raising Martha alone, she loathed letting go of Henry's attention and friendship. But she kept in mind the price paid for indiscretion in a world—to borrow Edith Wharton's phrase—"without forgiveness." Lizzie was, above all, practical. She had sacrificed much for her social position and likely knew the consequences of losing it. She knew too that her unavailability made Henry's worshipful longing only more romantic for them both, and if she was never fully his, he could also never really leave her.

After almost thirty thousand miles of traveling, Henry returned to Washington on February 11, 1892. He quickly set off for Rock Creek Cemetery to see, for the first time, the somber bronze statue of a seated figure that now marked Clover's grave. It had been more than five years since her death. He visited the gravesite again the next month with Clover's brother, Ned, and her cousin Sturgis Bigelow, the only son of Susan Sturgis Bigelow. Afterward Henry wrote that he'd given the memorial his "final approval," adding that his "old life" was now "closed around me."

Henry had commissioned America's leading sculptor, Augustus Saint-Gaudens, to create the memorial. Using John La Farge as intermediary, Henry instructed the artist to be inspired by only two sources: Michelangelo's frescoes of the five seated Sibyls in the Sistine Chapel and photographs of Buddhas, in particular Kwannon—he'd been fascinated by statues of the Buddhist goddess of mercy during his travels in Japan. In a burst of inspiration, Saint-Gaudens wrote a list in his notebook: "Buhda [*sic*]—Mental repose—Calm reflection in contrast with the violence or force in nature." But not much happened until two years later, when Saint-Gaudens began sketching on paper and experimenting with clay; he employed both men and women as studio models. Wanting to capture nirvana or a "philosophic calm," he intended the statue to somehow rise "beyond pain, beyond joy."

A massive hooded figure, measuring just over six feet in height, sits on a rough-hewn granite rock, deep in contemplation, with downcast eyes; a heavy cloak drapes everything but the face. The right hand is lifted, hovering near the face. Framing the figure is a large slab of polished red

marble, capped by a classical cornice, which forms one side of a hexago-
nal plot designed by Stanford White, an associate of H. H. Richardson.
A spacious three-sided marble bench is positioned at a distance from the
statue, with loose pebbles covering the space between and a grove of
holly trees providing shade and sanctuary.

An idealized portrait of Clover? A requiem of grief? A dream of
peace? John Hay was among the first of Henry's close friends to see the
statue after it was installed in March 1891. "The work is indescribably
noble and imposing," Hay assured Henry. "It is, to my mind, St. Gaudens' masterpiece. It is full of poetry and suggestion. Infinite wisdom; a
past without beginning and a future without end; a repose, after limitless
experience in this austere and beautiful face and form." The memorial,
both nuanced and extraordinarily self-assured, inspired many responses.
Henry was immensely pleased, going often to sit on the benches in front
of the statue. He once called it "The Peace of God," but he placed no
identifying plaque or nameplate on the grave. He wanted nothing to get
between the viewer and the statue. Once, in response to a letter asking
what the statue meant, he explained that everyone "is his own artist before a work of art"; he expanded on this position later when he wrote,
"The interest of the figure was not in its meaning, but in the response
of the observer . . . Like all great artists, St. Gaudens held up the mirror
and no more." Perhaps Henry had done with the memorial what Clover
had done with her photographs — turned personal loss into something
haunting but beautiful. In this way he paid tribute, however belatedly, to
his wife's artistic longing.

In 1905 Henry James finally went to see the hooded figure. He was
staying in Washington with his old friend but knew Henry didn't like
to talk about Clover. A mutual friend understood James's hesitation to
ask Adams to accompany him to Rock Creek Cemetery and offered to
go with him instead. Henry James had always appreciated Clover — her
sharp mind and enigmatic surfaces, her deflecting humor, and what he'd
once called her "intellectual grace." They had shared the habits of close
observers and were both, in their own way, portraitists. But if James had
found the ecstasy of full expression and artistic freedom, Clover had not.
When he finally arrived at her grave, he stood still for a long time under

dreary skies, holding his hat in his hand, his boots dusted with a January snow.

Almost thirty-five years after Clover's death, Eleanor Roosevelt, herself in her early forties, would make her way to Rock Creek Cemetery, where she sat for several hours on the curved marble bench in front of the statue she called by its more common name: "Grief." She had recently discovered her husband's affair with Lucy Mercer. Beset with loss and unsure of what to do next, she felt a kinship with Clover, a Washington woman from the previous generation who'd also found herself unmoored in her marriage. Roosevelt recalled to a friend that when she felt "very unhappy and sorry for myself . . . I'd come here, alone, and sit and look at that woman. And I'd always come away somehow feeling better. And stronger."

In later years, when people in Washington and Boston recognized Clover Adams's name or sat in silence in front of her grave, they knew little about her except that she'd been the wife of Henry Adams and she had killed herself. She would remain as mysterious as the statue erected in her memory, her photographs unseen.

+

EPILOGUE

IN THE SPRING OF 1901, after several months of erratic behavior, agitated conversation, and a consuming self-hatred, Ned Hooper, Clover's only surviving sibling, either jumped or fell from the third-floor window of his home at 49 Beacon Street. The only thing that saved him was a clothesline, which lessened the impact of his fall. Admitted to McLean Asylum, he stopped eating and died on June 25 from pneumonia. He was sixty-two years old.

When William James heard of Ned Hooper's catastrophe, he was staying at Lamb House in Rye, England, with his brother Henry, preparing to give the first of his Gifford Lectures (which would become the basis of his influential book *Varieties of Religious Experience*). James tried to stanch the terror and confusion he knew had besieged the Hooper girls; to Ned's oldest daughter, Ellen, he wrote, "I find it hard to express the sorrow I feel . . . He was such a model of soundness and balance, that this was the last thing I ever dreamed of as possible in his life." Then, with a distinctive equipoise both in his sentences and thought, James went on.

But anything and everything is possible for every mother's child of us — we are all in the same box, and not only death but all forms of decay knock at our gate and summon us to go out into their wilderness, and yet every ideal we dream of is realized in the same life of which these things are part, and we must house it and suffer it and take whatever it brings for the sake of the ends that are certainly being fulfilled by its means, behind the screen. The abruptness of your father's case shows well how purely extraneous and disconnected with the patient's general character these cerebral troubles may be. Probably an internally generated poison in the blood which "science" any day may learn how to eliminate or neutralize, and so make of all these afflictions so many nightmares of the past.

Henry Adams was in Paris when he received a cable with the news of Ned's death. Devastated, remembering his wife's affection for her brother, he wrote to Charles Gaskell, "For thirty years he has been the most valuably essential friend I have had . . . He was one of those central supports without which a house or household goes to pieces. Another limb is lopped off of me by his death, and if I were a centipede I should soon stop walking, I have already lost so many."

And yet in a life of enormous loss, Henry Adams had managed somehow to stay steady, an example of endurance and courage. He turned his attention to the next generation, and the five Hooper nieces adored him. His letters to them were frequent. He avoided their weddings because he avoided all weddings, yet he never lost contact with them and sought out their company, even taking all five sisters with him to Paris in 1897 for the summer. For Mabel Hooper, he was part of the "trinity of fathers"—along with her own father, Ned, and Clover's cousin Sturgis Bigelow—who "brought us up and educated us." Several nieces took up semi-permanent residence at 1603 H Street, presiding over daily breakfasts, served always at twelve-thirty, to which guests invited themselves. He remained devoted to Anne Palmer Fell's daughter, Marian, Clover's namesake, and he surrounded himself with young people of no familial relation who nonetheless called him "Uncle Henry"—nieces and nephews "in-wish," he called them. In this way, Henry was flattered, taken care of, diverted.

Lizzie Cameron held a higher rank. Aileen Tone, herself a niece in-wish who took care of Henry in the last years of his life, remembered that no one ever heard Henry calling Lizzie by any name other than "Mrs. Cameron."

Henry never again so openly expressed his romantic longing for Lizzie as he did in the long letter written after their failed rendezvous in 1891. In his later letters to her, readers can sense a lump in his throat, a holding back, a self-denial demanded by decorum, which he both despised and obeyed. He had worried aloud that such renunciation would someday rot into resentment and alienation, and yet the remarkable thing is that he and Lizzie somehow managed to maintain their friendship. Lizzie would fall in love with someone else, to Henry's unending annoyance, but she took pains not to hide this from him, and he somehow forgave her. They spent many hours together in Washington, going back and forth between each other's houses; they rode horseback together, and years after the failed rendezvous they accompanied each other to dinners and social engagements while both were in Paris. Henry liked to read aloud to Lizzie from the manuscript he was then working on, which would be published in 1913 as *Mont-Saint-Michel and Chartres*.

And they wrote many letters back and forth, no matter where they were living or what was occupying their days. From Paris in 1915, Lizzie remembered the years of their long friendship, telling him, "I kept every scrap you have ever written me." In all, Henry wrote over nine hundred letters to her. The two would be ballast for each other against much that had gone wrong in each one's marriage, and in a real way she would prove to be his lifeline. When he needed her most, she was there, reminding him again and again— "you're not dead, but very alive,—a living presence by my side." Their love for each other, troubled, baffling, fraught with social complications, and marked by a resounding "no" at its very center, endured for thirty-five years, and at a key moment in the dark days of 1885, it had, like Ariadne's red thread, given Henry a way back from the dark onrush of death.

For the rest of his life, Henry held to his conclusion that "life is grim." Pessimistic, at times self-pitying, vain, and self-absorbed, he often felt trapped by a sense that life had passed him by. But he was also bracingly honest, someone people could trust. His insistent search for truth, his deep curiosity about the world, and his capacity for friendship would sustain him and fuel his literary masterpieces: the completion of his nine-volume *History, Mont-Saint-Michel and Chartres,* and finally *The Education of Henry Adams,* which won a posthumous Pulitzer Prize in 1919. His work would win him a legion of admirers and readers, as Elizabeth Cameron noted to Louisa Hooper Thoron in a 1934 letter: "I often wonder how Henry would feel if he could know the immense appreciation of him and his works, which he used to say no one would read if he published them. So he didn't and wouldn't, then suddenly he was known — and has become the greatest of the Adams family, full of recognition and appreciation."

Every year on December 6, Rebecca Dodge laid a bouquet of white violets, Clover's favorite flower, on Clover's grave at Rock Creek Cemetery, and when Henry was home in Washington, she sent him white violets for his desk. In 1896, with Clover eleven years gone, Henry at last thanked Rebecca, saying, "I think that now you and I are the only ones who remember." He had written to Anne Palmer Fell in the years after Clover's death that "wisdom is silence," and, as a rule, he'd remained silent about his wife, most famously in his autobiography, *The Education of Henry Adams,* where he cut the years of their marriage out of the center of the narrative. No matter how many years had passed, Clover's death remained simply too painful for words.

In his eightieth year, in the spring of 1917, with World War I raging and summer renters hesitant to live on the North Shore because of concern about attacks from the sea, Henry told Aileen Tone that he wanted "to go back to the old Beverly Farms place." It was his first return to Pitch Pine Hill since vowing in 1885 never to stay there again. Now, instead of traveling by train for part of the journey, then by horse and buggy for the rest, as Henry and Clover had done years before, Henry and Aileen "dashed off in a motor to Beverly." After a thirty-two-year absence, Henry returned home to the summer place, still in use by the family, he and Clover had designed together, with its low ceilings, many fireplaces, cozy rooms, and a wide view to the shimmering sea. Again, he walked in the lush gardens and went down to the rocky shore. He wrote to Lizzie Cameron that "I wander every morning through the woods in search of something I formerly knew." Later in the summer, he attended a party with all the old Beverly regulars at Smith's Point, and he saw Alice Greenwood Howe, the woman who thirty-four years before had posed for Clover's camera on the rocks at the seashore.

Soon after that summer, when the two were visiting Clover's grave at Rock Creek Cemetery, Aileen Tone got up the courage to ask Henry about Clover. Henry looked at Aileen and said quietly, "My child, you have broken a silence of thirty years." Going back to Beverly Farms had unleashed memories and emotions long held in check. He would talk of Clover frequently then, showing her photographs and albums to Aileen and remembering their life together with "evident pleasure," referring to her always as "your Aunt Clover." After all those years, Henry finally spoke about his life with Clover, what he had called in the weeks after her death "the happiness that is past."

Henry Adams died of a stroke the next spring, in the early morning of Wednesday, March 27, 1918. Going through his things later that day, Aileen found a half-empty vial of potassium cyanide in the top drawer of his writing desk — Henry had always kept nearby the means of Clover's death. In a commonplace book, he had copied out two couplets, one by Matthew Arnold and one by Swinburne, which together expressed his personal creed: "Silent while years engrave the brow / Silent — the best are silent now"; and "For words divide and rend / But silence is most noble till the end." In a favorite book of Swinburne's poetry, *Poems and Ballads: Second Series,* he had marked out these lines from the poem "The Forsaken Garden": "The thorns he spares when the rose is taken; / The rocks are left when he wastes the plain. / The wind that wanders, the weeds wind-shaken, / These remain."

On the Saturday before Easter, a small funeral service was held at the corner house on H Street, presided over by the Reverend Roland Cotton Smith, the rector at nearby Saint John's Episcopal Church. That afternoon, Henry was buried at Rock Creek Cemetery alongside Clover. Together, they lie beneath the statue that is — like so many people in Clover's photographs — a figure alone.

The Sturgis-Hooper Family

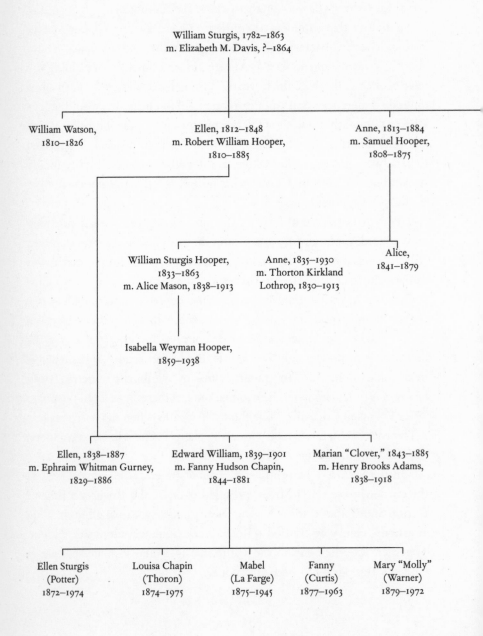

William Sturgis, 1782–1863
m. Elizabeth M. Davis, ?–1864

William Watson,
1810–1826

Ellen, 1812–1848
m. Robert William Hooper,
1810–1885

Anne, 1813–1884
m. Samuel Hooper,
1808–1875

William Sturgis Hooper,
1833–1863
m. Alice Mason, 1838–1913

Anne, 1835–1930
m. Thorton Kirkland
Lothrop, 1830–1913

Alice,
1841–1879

Isabella Weyman Hooper,
1859–1938

Ellen, 1838–1887
m. Ephraim Whitman Gurney,
1829–1886

Edward William, 1839–1901
m. Fanny Hudson Chapin,
1844–1881

Marian "Clover," 1843–1885
m. Henry Brooks Adams,
1838–1918

Ellen Sturgis
(Potter)
1872–1974

Louisa Chapin
(Thoron)
1874–1975

Mabel
(La Farge)
1875–1945

Fanny
(Curtis)
1877–1963

Mary "Molly"
(Warner)
1879–1972

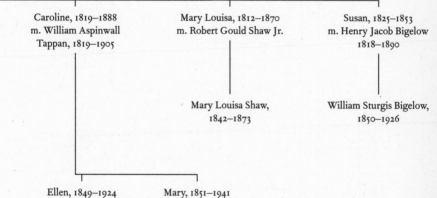

Caroline, 1819–1888
m. William Aspinwall
Tappan, 1819–1905

Mary Louisa, 1812–1870
m. Robert Gould Shaw Jr.

Susan, 1825–1853
m. Henry Jacob Bigelow
1818–1890

Mary Louisa Shaw,
1842–1873

William Sturgis Bigelow,
1850–1926

Ellen, 1849–1924
m. Richard Cowell
Dixey, 1844–1915

Mary, 1851–1941

The Adams Family

John Adams, 1735–1826
m. Abigail Smith, 1744–1818

Abigail "Nabby," 1765–1813
m. William Stevens Smith,
1755–1816

John Quincy Adams, 1767–1848
m. Louisa Catherine Johnson,
1775–1852

Susanna Boylston,
1768–1770

Charles, 1770–1800
m. Sally Smith, 1769–1828

Thomas Boylston, 1772–1832
m. Ann "Nancy" Harrod,
1774–1845

George Washington,
1801–1829

John, 1803–1834
m. Mary Catherine Hellen,
1806–1870

Charles Francis Adams, 1807–1886
m. Abigail Brooks, 1808–1889

Louisa Catherine,
1811–1812

Louisa Catherine,
1831–1870
m. Charles Kuhn,
1821–1899

John Quincy II,
1833–1894
m. Fanny Cadwallader
Crowninshield,
1840–1911

Charles Francis Jr.,
1835–1915
m. Mary Hone
Ogden, 1843–1935

Henry Brooks Adams,
1838–1918
m. Marian "Clover"
Hooper, 1843–1885

Arthur,
1841–1846

Mary, 1845–1928
m. Henry Parker
Quincy, 1838–1899

Brooks, 1848–1927
m. Evelyn "Daisy"
Davis, 1853–1926

This genealogy is limited to the direct ancestors of Henry Adams and his siblings.

✦

ACKNOWLEDGMENTS

Seeing the past in Clover's photograph albums is—as the past often is—utterly strange and deeply familiar. I would never have been able to make sense of what I saw or to tell Clover's story without the guidance and friendship of many people who helped me find my way.

There's no better place to do archival work than at the Massachusetts Historical Society, which generously gave me support with two summer research grants. Over the years, Peter Drummey, Conrad Wright, Brenda Lawson, Ondine Le Blanc, Anna Cook, and Elaine Grublin have answered my many questions and taught me how to navigate the archives. I'm proud to be an MHS Fellow. Research for this book was also funded by a Schlesinger Library research grant and a National Endowment for the Humanities Long-Term Fellowship. Hope College provided numerous summer research grants as well as several leaves of absence, for which I'm very grateful. For all their assistance, I want to thank Lucy Loomis at the Sturgis Library in Barnstable, Massachusetts, and Hope Mayo, Caroline Duroselle-Melish, and Emily Walhout at Harvard's Houghton Library. Mary Clare Altenhofen at Harvard's Fine Arts Library at the Fogg Museum gathered a stack of nineteenth-century exhibition catalogs for me to look through, sources that proved especially useful. My research was also aided by materials at the New York Historical Society, the Beverly Historical Society, the Boston Public Library, and the Library of Congress. For permission to quote from their manuscript collections, I am grateful to the Massachusetts Historical Society, the Sophia Smith Collection at Smith College, the Sturgis Library, the Countway Library of Medicine at Harvard University, and the Boston Public Library.

I'm indebted to Kathleen Lawrence for her generous insights into the Sturgis family, to Nancy Scott for her acumen about art, and to Robert D. Richardson for a brief exchange that guided me in writing about families. Clifford M. Nelson kindly spent an afternoon walking with me through Clover and Henry's neighborhood in Washington, D.C., teaching me its history, and Wanda Corn spent another afternoon talking with me about photography and fine art painting. For reading early drafts of chapters, I'd like to thank Sharon O'Brien, Melissa Banta, Sarah Chace, and Carol Bundy. Helen Sheumaker encouraged me in my early curiosity about Clover, and Leslie Tuttle responded to a penultimate draft of the manuscript in a way that made finishing it seem a possibility. John Hanson helped me see Clover's photographs anew, and Jeanne Petit read every version of the story from early grant proposals to final drafts — a steadying friendship. Shawn Michelle Smith early on told me I should write this book, and Megan Marshall did a great deal to make that happen. I owe her more than I can say. Harrison Smithwick and his mother, Frances, gave me a tour of Clover and Henry's Beverly Farms home, and I give a special thank-you to a descendant of one of Clover's nieces, who entrusted me with private papers and her family's history.

Eric Sandeen told me to write stories twenty years ago; Lewis Dabney showed me the world of biography writing; Ann Schofield introduced me to women's history; and Barry Shank taught me to pay attention to what moved my heart — great teachers all. I have many colleagues at Hope College to thank, in particular Peter Schakel, David Klooster, John Cox, Kathleen Verduin, Stephen Hemenway, Jacqueline Bartley, Elizabeth Trembley, Heather Sellers, Sarah Baar, Curtis and Lezlie Gruenler, Jeff Tyler, Jane Currie, Fred Johnson, Janis Gibbs, Julia Randel, William Reynolds, Lannette Zylman-TenHave, and the late Jennifer Young Tait. William Pannapacker early on sold me his six-volume collection of Henry Adams's published letters, saying, "You'll need these more than

I do." James Boelkins kept the faith that I could do this and provided generous support, and Priscilla Atkins responded with humor and skill to countless research questions. I've been very fortunate to have had a cadre of student assistants to whom I'm very grateful, most especially Rebecca Fry, Paxton Wiers, Gray Emerson, and Matt Vermaire; several former students have become dear friends, in particular Dana VanderLugt and Kate Paarlberg.

I'm enormously grateful to all those at Houghton Mifflin Harcourt for their rousing support for this book. Deanne Urmy's exquisite taste as an editor and her tough-minded encouragement made my work with her a joy and an education. She sharpened every page. Her assistant, Nicole Angeloro, answered my queries with remarkable speed. I'm indebted to Patrick Barry for a beautiful cover, to Susanna Brougham for her manuscript editing prowess, and to Larry Cooper, Megan Wilson, and Ayesha Mirza for their innumerable skills.

I'm more grateful than I can say to many friends, in particular Paul Karsten and Julia de Jonge, Nadine Requardt, Uta Walter, Jack and Julie Ridl, and Dick and Ruth Stravers, who have blessed my life with conversation, kindness, and a shelter from the storm. The Dutch Masters Swim Team reminded me to keep moving through the water, no matter what. Many thanks also to Jonathan Earle, Cotton Seiler, Norman Yetman, David Katzman, Kimberly Hamlin, Marni Sandweiss, Cynthia Mills, Jean Veenema-Birky, Anna Raphael, Del and Sally Michel, Jack and Lois Lamb, Wilson and Chris Lowry, Tim Gerhold, and Annie Thompson.

My father, Loren Dykstra, filled our home with music, and to this day, I never write without a tune playing in the background. My brother Greg Dykstra and his wife, Sabina, many times gave wise counsel, and my brother Stuart Dykstra insisted I not waste time. My sister-in-law Ellen Dykstra picked up her camera in the same years I started writing a book about another woman picking up her camera — our many conversations about picture-taking have guided my thoughts, and I thank her for her friendship and my author photograph. To my sister Ellen Stahl, her husband, Don, as well as my many nieces and nephews, I'm grateful for their forbearance and good humor. I want to thank my nephew Benjamin Dykstra, who saved my computer from destruction, and my niece

Sarah Dykstra, whose wit always brings light. Carol Bundy invited me into her Boston world when I needed her invitation and insight most, and Mary Bundy, Tom George, Chris Bundy, and the rest of the family kindly welcomed me into the fold as the family's newest member.

My husband, Michael Bundy, always believed I could write this book, made many nuanced suggestions, and never once complained, though he's not known me or married life without it. His gentleness, confidence in the future, and abiding love have changed my life.

This book is dedicated to the memory of my mom, Harriett M. Dykstra, whose fierce love is with us still. She loved books almost as much as she loved her children. I owe to her much that is good in my life, including a fascination with stories of the past.

+

SOURCES

Clover Adams's letters to her father, Dr. Hooper, especially those after her marriage to Henry Adams, are an essential source for understanding the shape of her life. Many of these were first published in 1936 as *The Letters of Mrs. Henry Adams*, edited by her niece, Louisa Hooper Thoron, and Louisa's husband, Ward Thoron. The originals of the published letters, dating from June 1872 to July 1873, June 1879 to December 1879, October 1880 to May 1881, October 1881 to June 1882, and October 1882 to May 1883, can be found in the Hooper-Adams Papers, Massachusetts Historical Society (MHS). Clover's unpublished letters to her family, including her father, written as a child and before her marriage, are archived in the Adams-Thoron Papers, MHS. Unpublished letters she wrote to her father after her marriage, the last of which is dated March 8, 1885, a month before his death, are archived in the Adams Family Papers, MHS. I quote directly from Clover's published letters, keeping the editors' minor changes to words and punctuation. My own transcriptions of her unpublished letters follow her writing style more exactly, changing punctuation only when really needed to make her meaning clear.

Clover enjoyed a close bond with her father, revealing in her letters to him her quick humor, her interests, and the rhythm of her married life.

But she also kept things from him, shielding him from her uncertainties and darker moods. What's more, the other side of their correspondence is missing; none of Dr. Hooper's weekly letters to his daughter are extant. Missing too are any letters to Clover from her sister, Ellen, and most from her brother, Ned. The Houghton Library at Harvard University does have a collection of letters Ned wrote to his family, including Clover, during the Civil War. Theodore F. Dwight, Henry's private secretary, preserved some correspondence sent to Clover and Henry, which can be found in Dwight's papers at the MHS. But most letters to Clover were not saved. The reason why is hard to discern, though Clover may have offered a clue in a statement to John Hay in her letter of June 13, 1882: "I do not keep letters."

Clover wrote to her cherished friend Anne Palmer with somewhat more candor than she showed in most of her letters to Dr. Hooper. There are twenty-seven unpublished letters to Anne, written between 1879 and 1885, archived in the Hooper-Adams Papers, MHS. In this collection, letters addressed to Anne were placed in one folder next to another one marked "Mrs. Philippa." In reading both files together, coordinating dates and matters discussed, I realized that "Mrs. Philippa" was a secret name Clover used for Anne, a discovery that unveiled a far richer, more complete record of an important friendship. This find was complemented by a trove of thirteen letters, recently given to the MHS, written by Henry Adams to Anne in the months and years after Clover's death.

My understanding of Clover was further transformed when I met a granddaughter of one of Clover's nieces, who graciously invited me to her home to look through a collection of family letters, many of which were written by Clover's mother, Ellen Sturgis Hooper. I am grateful for and honored by her trust with this private collection of family papers, much of it unpublished, and for her many remarkable family stories, which brought so much to life.

Henry Adams's correspondence is published in six thick volumes, edited by J. C. Levenson, Ernest Samuels, Charles Vandersee, and Viola Hopkins Winner. Secondary sources on Henry and the Adams family fill shelves, but I turned again and again to Ernest Samuels's three-volume biography of Henry, finished in 1964, awarded the Pulitzer Prize in 1965, and a model of biographical imagination and judgment. Patricia O'Toole's *The Five of Hearts: An Intimate Portrait of Henry Adams and His Friends, 1880–1918* (1990) captures the extraordinary friendships enjoyed by Clover and Henry and their social world in Washington, D.C. I want to acknowledge two previous biographies of Clover, Otto Friedrich's *Clover* (1979) and Eugenia Kaledin's *The Education of Mrs. Henry Adams* (1981), both of which were a great help to me. My enormous debt to a wide array of scholars and writers becomes clear in the acknowledgments and notes, but I want to make special mention of Jean Strouse's *Alice James* (1980). Strouse accomplishes the impossible—she makes an invalid's life extraordinarily vivid and active, retrieving Alice's story from obscurity caused in part by the glaring fame of her brilliant brothers William and Henry James. Clover and Alice knew each other, but they were not intimate friends. Nonetheless, Strouse's biography of Alice helped me write Clover's.

The most evocative source for Clover's story is her collection of photographs, which she carefully pasted into three red-leather albums, one image per page, with captions in the bottom corner listing a date or the name of a person or place. By closely reading her small notebook, where she kept track of each image, together with her albums, I discovered Clover put many, if not all, of her photographs in deliberate sequences, as if to tell what she could not or did not say in her letters. Clover never kept a diary. But her albums suggest deeply held feelings and a distinctive point of view, providing evidence for a previously undocumented time in her life that is potent, in no small measure, because it contains clues to the mystery of her death.

Clover's notebook is archived in the Hooper-Adams Papers, MHS, and her photographs are archived as Marian Hooper Adams Photographs, Photograph Collection 50, MHS. Those photographs that I specifically discuss will be listed in the notes by date (if available), album number, and photograph number (which is proceeded by the collection number, 50). Clover's albums, numbered #7, #8, and #9, were originally archived at the MHS in the wrong order; in other words, Clover put together album #8 first, followed by albums #7 and #9.

+

NOTES

Abbreviations

The abbreviations below are used for frequently cited personal names, libraries, archives, manuscript collections, photograph collections, and published sources.

Names

CFA: Charles Francis Adams
HA: Henry Adams
MHA: Marian "Clover" Hooper Adams
SSB: Susan Sturgis Bigelow
EC: Elizabeth "Lizzie" Cameron
CMG: Charles Milnes Gaskell
EHG: Ellen Hooper Gurney
JH: John Hay
EWH: Edward William Hooper
ESH: Ellen Sturgis Hooper
RWH: Robert William Hooper
HJ: Henry James
CK: Clarence King
APF: Anne Palmer [Fell] (Clover knew Anne before her 1885 marriage to Nelson Fell.)
WS: William Sturgis
CST: Caroline Sturgis Tappan

Libraries and Archives
Houghton: Houghton Library, Harvard University, Cambridge, Massachusetts.
MHS: Massachusetts Historical Society, Boston.

Manuscript Collections
Adams: Adams Family Papers, MHS, Boston.
EWH Letters: Edward William Hooper Letters, MS Am1969, Houghton.
HA-CK Papers: Henry Adams–Clarence King Papers, MHS, Boston.
S-T Papers: Sturgis-Tappan Papers, Sophia Smith Collection, Smith College, Northampton, Massachusetts.
Swann: Swann Family Collection, family papers held in private hands by descendants of the Hooper family.
WS Papers: William Sturgis Papers, Sturgis Library, Barnstable, Massachusetts.

Published Sources
Democracy: Henry Adams, *Democracy: An American Novel* (New York: Penguin Books, 2008).
Esther: Henry Adams, *Esther: A Novel,* ed. and with an introduction by Lisa MacFarlane (New York: Penguin Books, 1999).
Five of Hearts: Patricia O'Toole, *The Five of Hearts: An Intimate Portrait of Henry Adams and His Friends, 1880–1918* (New York: Simon & Schuster, 1990; reprinted 2006).
HJ Letters: Henry James Letters, ed. Leon Edel (Cambridge, MA: Belknap Press, 1975), 4 vols.
LMHA: The Letters of Mrs. Henry Adams, 1865–1883, ed. Ward Thoron (Boston: Little, Brown and Company, 1936).
Letters: The Letters of Henry Adams, ed. J. C. Levenson et al. (Cambridge, MA: Belknap Press, 1982–88), 6 vols.
Middle Years: Ernest Samuels, *Henry Adams: The Middle Years* (Cambridge, MA: Belknap Press, 1958).
Mrs. Henry Adams: Eugenia Kaledin, *The Education of Mrs. Henry Adams,* 2nd ed. (Amherst: University of Massachusetts Press, 1994).

PROLOGUE
xi "smiling landscape": MHA to RWH, April 24, 1881, *LMHA,* 285.
xii "solid old pile": MHA to RWH, October 31, 1880, *LMHA,* 229.
"coziness in the New England sense": MHA to RWH, December 2, 1883, Adams. An eclectic mix: Commonplace book of Theodore F. Dwight, Adams-Thoron Papers, MHS.
"My dear": MHA to RWH, January 25, *LMHA,* 321. Clover pursued a type of beauty in the home that balanced discretion with distinctive taste, following the

advice found in Charles L. Eastlake's influential *Hints on Household Taste in Furniture, Upholstery, and Other Details*, a domestic guide that Clover had kept on her bookshelf since before her marriage. Clover had bought the 1869 edition, signing it "Clover Hooper, 1870." Eastlake, *Hints on Household Taste in Furniture, Upholstery, and Other Details,* 2nd ed. rev. (London: Longmans, Green and Co., 1869).

"undemonstrative New Englander": MHA to RWH, October 20, 1872, *LMHA,* 50.

"This part of life": HA to CMG, January 29, 1882, *Letters,* vol. 2, 448.

"who brought people to their house": HA-CK Papers.

xiii "a perfect Voltaire": HJ to Grace Norton, September 20, 1880, in *HJ Letters,* vol. 2, 307.

"hebdomadal drivel": MHA to RWH, March 24, 1878, Adams.

"Life is such a jumble": MHA to RWH, November 5, 1872, *LMHA,* 56.

"our days go by quietly": MHA to RWH, November 4, 1883, Adams.

xiv She draped a bed sheet: MHA, November 5, 1883, album #8, 50.93.

"Nov 5—1 P.M.—Boojum": This and all subsequent references to and quotes from Clover's notebook refer to the single unpaginated lined notebook she kept of her photographic experiments from May 6, 1883, until January 22, 1884. The notebook is archived with the Hooper-Adams Papers, MHS.

"Pomeranian blonde": MHA to RWH, February 18, 1883, *LMHA,* 424.

"some crass idiocy": MHA to RWH, November 11, 1883, Adams.

xv haunting landscape: MHA, November 5, 1883, album #8, 50.94.

The complicated process: In the back of her notebook Clover kept a sheet of instructions published by Scovill Amateur View Albums, which described "methods of mounting Photographs, so that they will not warp or cockle." For information on how George Eastman marketed his new camera to women, see Nancy West, *Kodak and the Lens of Nostalgia* (Charlottesville: University Press of Virginia, 2000).

"Ich gehe durch": Translation by Louis MacNiece in *The Norton Anthology of World Masterpieces,* 5th ed., vol. 2, gen. ed. Maynard Mack (New York: W. W. Norton and Company, 1985), 550. I thank Uta Walter for identifying this passage from the first act of Goethe's *Faust.*

she recorded her world: The archives are filled with all kinds of photograph albums, donated by individuals and families to historical societies, university research libraries, and state and local archives. Such albums are neither art nor literature, neither diary nor document. Yet they nonetheless express, often in extraordinary ways, individual lives as well as social practices. I looked through hundreds of photograph albums dated from 1870 to 1890 at the New York Historical Society, the Massachusetts Historical Society, the Library of Congress, and the Beverly Historical Society; and, at Harvard University, the Fogg Museum Library, the Houghton Library, and the Schlesinger Library. For discussions of photograph albums, see Elizabeth Siegel, *Galleries of Friendship and Fame: A History of Nineteenth-Century Photograph Albums* (New Haven, CT: Yale University

Press, 2010); Amy Kotkin, "The Family Photo Album as a Form of Folklore," *Exposure*, vol. 16 (March 1978): 4–8; Marilyn Motz, "Visual Autobiography: Photograph Albums of Turn-of-the-Century Midwestern Women," *American Quarterly*, vol. 41, no. 1 (March 1989): 63–92; Philip Stokes, "The Family Photograph Albums: So Great a Cloud of Witnesses," in *The Portrait in Photography*, ed. Graham Clarke (Seattle: University of Washington Press, 1992), 193–205; Martha Langford, *Suspended Conversations: The Afterlife of Memory in Photographic Albums* (Montreal: McGill-Queen's University Press, 2001); Patricia Holland, "'Sweet It Is to Scan . . . ': Personal Photographs and Popular Photographs," in *Photography: A Critical Introduction*, ed. Liz Wells, 2nd ed. (London: Routledge Press, 2000).

xvi "pulled down": John W. Field to Theodore Dwight, November 9, 1885, Field Family Letters, MHS.

"The Peace of God": HA to Richard Watson Gilder, October 14, 1896, *Letters*, vol. 4, 430.

"Clover's death": Eleanor Shattuck Whiteside to Mrs. George C. Shattuck [1885], George Cheyne Shattuck Papers, MHS. This letter is undated but was most likely written shortly after Clover's death. Eleanor concluded her letter to her mother as follows: "Dr. Hooper's death and Clover's make a large hole in early associations and memories. By and by I will write to Ellen Gurney. Not now. If you learn anything more I should like to hear."

Part I: A New World

CHAPTER 1. "She Was Home to Me"

3 "stick out one finger": ESH to SSB, n.d., Swann.

"Clover is inestimable": ESH to SSB, n.d., Swann.

"I don't want to tend her": ESH to SSB, n.d., Swann.

"wit, her sense of the ridiculous" . . . "same as she did in company": Ephraim Peabody to William W. Swain, Boston, November 6, 1848, unpublished letter privately printed by EWH, Swann.

A lithographic portrait: The portrait of Ellen Sturgis Hooper was given to the Sturgis Library in Barnstable, Massachusetts, by Mary Lothrop Bundy, a direct descendant of Clover's first cousin, Anne M. Hooper Lothrop.

4 "full of genius" . . . "refined": Margaret Fuller to Arthur B. Fuller, January 20, 1849, *The Letters of Margaret Fuller*, vol. 5, 1848–1849, ed. Robert N. Hudspeth (Ithaca, NY: Cornell University Press, 1988), 186.

"whose character seemed" . . . "to her character": Ephraim Peabody to William W. Swain, Boston, November 6, 1848, privately printed by EWH, Swann.

"Cape-Cod boy" . . . "the sea": William Sturgis, as quoted in Charles G. Loring, *Memoir of the Hon. William Sturgis*, as prepared by resolution of the Massachusetts Historical Society (Boston: Press of John Wilson and Son, 1864), 6.

extraordinarily capable seaman: For a description of Sturgis's successful com-

mand of his first trading ship, the *Caroline,* see Loring, *Memoir,* 8–10. For more
on Sturgis, see also *Edward Sturgis of Yarmouth Massachusetts, 1613–1695, and
His Descendants,* ed. Robert Faxton Sturgis (Boston: Stanhope Press, 1914), esp.
41–42; for more family background, see Francis B. Dedmond, "The Letters of
Caroline Sturgis to Margaret Fuller," in *Studies in the American Renaissance,* ed.
Joel Myerson (Charlottesville: University of Virginia Press, 1988), 201–3.

boarding school run by two sisters: My thanks to Anna Cook at the MHS for finding information on the boarding school run by the Cushing sisters in Hingham.
Francis H. Lincoln, in *History of the Town of Hingham, Massachusetts* (Hingham,
MA: 1983), 143. Ellen's access to education was not unusual for a young woman
of her social standing. According to Mary Kelley, between 1790 and 1830 "182
academies and at least 14 seminaries were established exclusively for women in
the North and the South." Though education for a young woman was understood
as equipping her for her future role as a helpmate to her husband, the curriculum
had begun shifting from an entire emphasis on social refinements — music, dancing, reciting poetry — to subjects studied at schools for boys. See Kelley, *Learning to Stand and Speak: Women, Education, and Public Life in America's Republic*
(Chapel Hill: University of North Carolina Press, 2006), 67, 71. While at school
in Hingham, Ellen wrote to her parents: "We are studying about the war between
the Thebans and the Spartans at the time when Thebes was contending for the
empire of Greece. I want the Thebans to beat." As quoted in Otto Friedrich,
Clover (New York: Simon and Schuster, 1979), 43.

5   Ellen was particularly close: ESH to William Swain, September 1, 1844, S-T Papers. Ellen wrote to Swain, a family friend, to thank him for sending a copy of
writing by his son, Robert Swain, who had died some months before. On reading
it, Ellen was reminded of her own brother, William: "[Robert's] letters and journal remind me of my brother William in their simplicity and boyish fun as well as
in the earnestness and feeling which weaves through them. I did not know how
lovely and affectionate Robert was till I saw it here — his manliness and upright-
ness I had seen." She also revealed something of how she understood the loss of
her brother, saying that the brevity of Robert's life "seems to me not so much a
broken hope as a beautiful whole, a harmony of simple and select notes."

"very much" . . . "450 lines of Virgil": Ezra Goodwin to WS, September 21,
1810, WS Papers. On the back of this same letter, William's uncle, the Reverend
Goodwin, told Captain Sturgis that William's teacher had been "astonished" by
the young student's "first recitation of Virgil." He assured the father that he and
his wife, Ellen, who was Mrs. Sturgis's oldest sister, "shall be glad" for William
to stay as long as necessary: "He is a child by whom we set great store, and find
that the older he grows, the more valuable he becomes."

Her behavior over time: In a letter following the death of a child of a family
friend, Elizabeth Sturgis wrote to her husband, "I am shocked and grieved at
the trying event which you communicate — a solemn event which again forcibly
reminds us of the uncertain tenure of our present state of being 'in the midst of life

we are in death,' and every day's experience convinces us of this truth, darkness and shadows would rest on our condition here; so much of suffering and sorrow; so few gleams of sunshine mid renewing storms; and thro the dark vista the tomb only in prospect; but blessed be the God and father our Lord Jesus Christ, who thro him has revealed life and immortality — 'he is the way, the truth, & the life'; & 'no man cometh unto the Father but by him' 'he is the resurrection and the life' and believing as I do most entirely that there is 'no other name given among men by which we may saved' it is my earnest desire and constant prayer for me and mine that we may all be brought into the 'fold of the good Shepard [sic]' and 'that believing we may have life.' — you know I seldom mention these subjects, I feel that I am not one privileged, or worthy to descant on Him, yet the peace & joy which I am permitted to in believing, has been an 'answer sure and steadfast,' thro a trial which would have prostrated my whole nature probably, and certainly my mind; if it had not rested on the 'rock of ages.' I realize that one of my treasures is in heaven, and it is my heart's desire and prayer that we may be prepared to rejoin him; 'oh thou with what an angel smile of gladness, he will welcome me.' I feel these inflictions are salutary, and requisite, we are under a Father's administration; he both gives, and takes away and 'blessed be his holy name.'" Elizabeth Davis Sturgis to WS, July 27, 1828, WS Papers.

"walking up and down": CST to Margaret Fuller, December 1844, as quoted by Eleanor M. Tilton in her introduction to *The Letters of Ralph Waldo Emerson*, vol. 7 (New York: Columbia University Press, 1990), 31. Five years before, twenty-year-old Caroline worried about her mother, regretting her summer plans for an extended stay on the island of Naushon off Cape Cod. On arriving on the island, she urged Ellen, who had stayed in Boston, to "write me something about mother," explaining that she was not "comfortable away from home, when I know she is staying there in such a dolorous manner." CST to ESH, July 9, 1839, Swann.

Practicality and a personal toughness: The oldest of five siblings and the only boy, William Sturgis had had to support his mother after his father died at sea, which had left the family in dire financial straits. For more about Sturgis's youth, see *The Journal of William Sturgis*, ed. S. W. Jackson (Victoria, BC: Sono Nis Press, 1978).

6 His motto: In a letter to Caroline about her faulty furnace, William Sturgis wrote he would "leave you to take of yourselves. Young people must learn to take care of themselves." WS to CST, June 17, 1848, S-T Papers. Elizabeth Palmer Peabody quotes Ellen making a comment at one of Margaret Fuller's Conversations that may also reveal how much William Sturgis valued self-reliance: "Ellen Hooper asked if she did not think that it was the duty of a man in the first place to support himself — if he ought not to be impressed with the idea from the beginning that he must make for himself a place, so far at least as not to be dependent — If this independence on outward support with respect to his physical being was not es-

sential to our idea of a man?" Nancy Craig Simmons, "Margaret Fuller's Boston Conversations: 1839–1840 Series," *Studies in American Renaissance 1994* (Charlottesville: University Press of Virginia), 217.

he bought a large summer house: Caroline Sturgis describes the house at Horn Pond in a December 1844 letter to Margaret Fuller: "The front of the house is quite beautiful with the pond stretched out in front & no houses in sight. There is a lovely wooded walk between the canal & pond, an island in the center & pine woods all around." In the same letter, Caroline tells of accompanying her father to Woburn to look at the property. They spent the day together "wandering over a mountain in the most babe-in-the-woods manner." As quoted in Tilton, *Letters of Ralph Waldo Emerson,* vol. 7, 31. Captain Sturgis, for all his austerity, could be good, even fun-loving company.

"Do take the trouble": ESH to Elizabeth Davis Sturgis, n.d., Swann.

"I have not seen her": ESH to SSB, n.d., Swann.

"a mystery of sorrow": ESH to CST, n.d., Swann.

"moment I have" . . . "one minute loving": CST to Margaret Fuller, July 21, 1842, in Dedmond, "The Letters of Caroline Sturgis to Margaret Fuller," 224. Caroline wrote in the same letter that "Ellen is moping and melancholy, Annie is conscientious and hesitating, Sue rude & frivolous & not very funny, & I feel like an icicle." Though these characterizations of her sisters and herself reveal Caroline's painful efforts to sort herself out in relation to her family, they also expose something of the emotional upheaval in the Sturgis family.

7   "well-balanced character" . . . $300,000: Charles Henry Pope and Thomas Hooper, *Hooper Genealogy* (Boston: privately printed, 1908), 115.

A miniature portrait: Robert's likeness was painted by Pierre D'Aubigny in the early 1830s. I want to thank Elle Shushan for providing the identification of this portrait, which is in private hands.

8   "gifted by Nature": *The Transcendentalists: An Anthology,* ed. Perry Miller (Cambridge, MA: Harvard University Press, 1950), 402; "so inferior to her": Margaret Fuller to Arthur B. Fuller, January 20, 1849, in Hudspeth, *The Letters of Margaret Fuller,* vol. 5, 186; "dull man": Margaret Fuller to Sarah Ann Clarke, January 18, 1849, in Hudspeth, *The Letters of Margaret Fuller,* vol. 5, 172.

Fuller liked to pronounce: I am indebted to Megan Marshall for her insight on Fuller. Charles Capper, in his two-volume biography of Margaret Fuller, implies that the Hooper marriage had been a failure in his more general discussion of Fuller's reactions to her friends' marriages. But this reflected Fuller's—and no other—point of view. Conversation, Charles Capper, April 9, 2010. See also Charles Capper, *Margaret Fuller: An American Romantic Life, Vol. 2: The Public Years* (New York: Oxford University Press, 2007), 171.

"one of the happy marriages" . . . "to rest upon": Ephraim Peabody to William W. Swain, Boston, November 6, 1848, unpublished letter privately printed by EWH, Swann.

"You cannot tell": ESH to RWH, July 27, no year, Swann. Though the postmark does not indicate the year, it is most likely the summer of 1845, when Dr. Hooper was traveling in the South.

James Freeman Clarke, the liberal: *American National Biography,* ed. John A. Garrity and Mark C. Carnes, vol. 11 (New York: Oxford University Press, 1999), 140–41.

"a search for principles": Ralph Waldo Emerson, quoted in Philip F. Gura, *American Transcendentalism: A History* (New York: Hill and Wang, 2007), xii.

9   "the truth of religion" . . . "into the world": George Ripley, as quoted in Gura, *American Transcendentalism,* 142. Perry Miller defines the Transcendentalists as "children of the Puritan past who, having been emancipated by Unitarianism from New England's original Calvinism, found a new religious expression in forms derived from Romantic literature and from the philosophical idealism of Germany." Perry Miller, *The American Transcendentalists: Their Prose and Poetry* (Baltimore: Johns Hopkins University Press, 1957), ix. Robert D. Richardson states: "For better or worse, American transcendentalism was uncohesive, preferring to unravel rather than compromise its belief in the sovereign worth of each separate strand of yarn." Richardson, *Emerson: The Mind on Fire* (Berkeley: University of California Press, 1995), 250.

Although Robert Hooper sympathized: Robert Hooper was a long-time trustee of the Worcester Lunatic Asylum, the first hospital of its kind in Massachusetts. Wanting to provide more humane forms of treatment, Hooper urged the board to convert space in the hospital into workrooms so that patients could do something productive with their time. He may have gotten some of his ideas for improved treatments for the insane from his training in Paris. RWH to Edward Jarvis, September 24, 1862, BMS c11.2, Boston Medical Library, Francis A. Countway Library of Medicine, Harvard University.

The Sturgis sisters: The sisters joined a group of women that included Lydia Maria Child, already a well-known author; Elizabeth Bliss Bancroft, an abolitionist and the new wife of the historian George Bancroft; and Sophia Willard Dana, who would later found the utopian Brook Farm with her husband, George Ripley. Simmons, "Margaret Fuller's Boston Conversations: 1839–1840 Series," esp. 195–202. According to Phyllis Cole, Fuller's Conversations occupied the "intersection of liberal religion and feminist reform," incorporating an ethos of individualism that marbled Transcendental thought. Social, political, and personal transformation would occur through the education and development of every individual woman's potential. Cole, "Stanton, Fuller, and the Grammar of Romanticism," *The New England Quarterly,* vol. 70, no. 4 (2000): 546. At Elizabeth Palmer Peabody's bookshop, which was located in the downstairs parlor of a two-story brick townhouse, patrons could buy or borrow books published overseas that were not easily found in American bookstores. Peabody's shelves were lined with books by the German idealists Kant and Hegel, the novels of Victor Hugo and George Sand in French, the works of Wordsworth and Coleridge, and a set of Goethe's writings in German that ran to fifty volumes. Her shop became a central meeting place to discuss ideas, "a gathering place for . . . intellectual companions, a locus of conversations both organized and informal." Marshall, *The Peabody Sisters: Three Women Who Ignited American Romanticism*, 391–98; for more information on Peabody's bookshop, see Gura, *American Transcendentalism*, 123–27.

"character and mind" . . . "induction": ESH, quoted in Joel Myerson, *Fuller in Her Own Time: A Biographical Chronicle of Her Life, Drawn from Recollections, Interviews, and Memoirs by Family, Friends, and Associates*. Writers in Their Own Time series. (Iowa City: University of Iowa Press, 2008), 43. This is what Ellen said, according to Elizabeth Palmer Peabody, who took careful notes of comments at Fuller's Conversations. See also Kathleen Lawrence, "The 'Dry-Lighted Soul' Ignites: Emerson and His Soul-Mate Caroline Sturgis as Seen in Her Houghton Manuscripts," *Harvard Library Bulletin*, vol. 16, no. 3 (Fall 2005): 37–68. Lawrence's article is the single best source on Caroline Sturgis, her complicated relationship with Emerson, and her involvement in the Transcendental movement.

"light, free, somewhat": Henry James, *Notes of a Son and Brother* (New York: Charles Scribner's Sons, 1914), 213.

10   "sympathized with": *The Journals and Miscellaneous Notebooks of Ralph Waldo Emerson*, vol. 9, 1843–1847, ed. Ralph H. Orth and Alfred R. Ferguson (Cambridge, MA: The Belknap Press of Harvard University Press, 1971), 111.

"some writing" . . . "different channel": ESH to Maria Weston Chapman, October 14, no year, Ms. A.9.2, vol. 24, no. 38, Boston Public Library.

Ellen turned, instead, to poetry: All subsequent quotes from Ellen Sturgis Hooper's poetry are taken from a folio collection of her poetry, privately printed in 1871 by EWH, given to the author by a descendant of the family. A copy of the Hooper folio can be found at the Houghton Library.

11   "a more interior revolution": Elizabeth Palmer Peabody, as quoted in Marshall, *The Peabody Sisters*, 183.

"very happy together": ESH to RWH, n.d., Swann.

"sit at the parlor window": RWH to unknown addressee, n.d., Swann.

"a certain bravado" . . . "simpleton as usual": ESH to SSB, n.d., Swann.

"nearly wild with delight": ESH to CST, n.d., Caroline Sturgis Tappan Papers, MS Am 1221 (180), Houghton.

12   Give kisses on her eyes": ESH to RWH, n.d., Adams-Thoron Papers, MHS.

"I long since abandoned": ESH to CST, May 19, 1843, Swann. The letter was sent to Caroline in care of Ralph Waldo Emerson in Concord.

Doctors prescribed everything: Sheila Rothman, *Living in the Shadow of Death: Tuberculosis and the Social Experience of Illness in American History* (Baltimore: Johns Hopkins University Press, 1995), 13–25; William H. Burt, *Therapeutics of Tuberculosis: Or, Pulmonary Consumption* (New York: Boericke and Tafel, 1876), esp. 9–14; Richardson, *Emerson*, 91–92.

13   "for your attentions": ESH to SSB, n.d., Swann. Ellen also sent along a small charcoal drawing she made of a young slave girl in South Carolina. Lousia

Hooper Thoron, Clover's niece, later identified the place correctly on the back of the drawing, but not its date, listing it as 1849. Robert and Ellen were in the South a year earlier, in the spring of 1848.

"I shall be very sorry": ESH to WS, March 15, 1848, Swann; "delighted to hear so good": ESH to WS, April 19, 1848, Swann.

"my precious silver grey": RWH and ESH to WS, April 6, 1868, Adams-Thoron Papers, MHS.

"frequent excursions" . . . "to have come": RWH and ESH to WS, April 6, 1848, Adams-Thoron Papers, MHS.

"is about the same as when": WS to CST, June 17, 1848, S-T Papers.

"have interest" . . . "burn them unread": Half-sheet titled "Directions," 1847, Swann. Ellen's letters were preserved by the family, and though there is no direct evidence her children read through her papers, it is also hard to imagine that they did not.

14   "Patience! Patience!": Ephraim Peabody to William W. Swain, Boston, November 6, 1848, unpublished letter privately printed by EWH, Swann.

A small marble headstone: William W. Sturgis Jr. was reburied in Mount Auburn Cemetery on October 25, 1834, after Captain Sturgis bought one of the first of one hundred lots in the new cemetery. Sturgis paid sixty dollars for a three-hundred-square-foot lot, number 310, on Catalpa Path. *Circular*, Mount Auburn Cemetery, Historical Collections, Mount Auburn Cemetery, Cambridge, MA.

"To-day I read beside": Ephraim Peabody to William W. Swain, Boston, November 6, 1848, unpublished letter privately printed by EWH, Swann. To those who knew her, Ellen became after death a kind of "Transcendental angel," according to Miller, *The American Transcendentalists: Their Prose and Poetry*, 272. Wendell Phillips, the rabble-rousing abolitionist speaker and activist for women's rights, liked to copy out Ellen's most well-known poem next to his own signature in the autograph books of his Lyceum audience members. Carlos Martyn, *Wendell Phillips: The Agitator*, rev. ed. (New York: Funk and Wagnalls Company, 1890), 446.

"How the sunlight crinkles up": SSB to Mary Eliot Dwight Parkman, n.d., Parkman Family Papers, MS Am 2120 (57-69b), Houghton. The rest of the letter reads: "How shall I bear the long lonely summer days—she will never come to me again. Oh, shall I ever go to her?"

"his saddest days": Ephraim Peabody to William W. Swain, November 6, 1848, privately printed by EWH, Swann.

15   Clover's older sister, Ellen: Ellen also cherished her mother's poetry. In later years, she wrote to Alice Howe James, the wife of William James, "I send also my mothers poems. She died at 36. It is some of it—like the few strokes in a portfolio of drawings—that it is hardly fair to show—but others have I think great beauty." EHG to Alice Howe (Gibbens) James, n.d., William James Papers, MS 1092.9–1092.12 (4305), Houghton.

CHAPTER 2. The Hub of the Universe

16   "take all the care I can": SSB to Mary Eliot Dwight Parkman, n.d., Parkman Family Papers, MS Am 2120 (57–69b), Houghton.

"dresses up" . . . "sad and touching": SSB to CST, n.d., 1849, S-T Papers.

17   "religious feelings": *Harvard University Memoirs, 1830* (Boston: Press of Rockwell and Churchill, 1886), 143–44.

pew number 45: Henry Wilder Foote, *Annals of King's Chapel from the Puritan Age of New England to the Present Day,* vol. 1 (Boston: Little, Brown, 1881).

"good breeding": Clover found the scrap of paper, with the excerpt of George Sand copied in French, in her father's desk. Sand is quoting her own grandmother's account of married life. The entire quotation reads, in translation, "It's that we knew how to live, back then; we didn't have important infirmities. If one had gout, one walked anyway and without grimacing; good breeding meant that we hid our suffering." George Sand Fragment, Hooper-Adams Papers, MHS.

"well-balanced and even": Ephraim Peabody to William W. Swain, Boston, November 6, 1848, unpublished letter privately printed by EWH, Swann.

Betsey Wilder, who became: Even as a grown woman, Clover frequently asked her father to give her greetings to Betsey, saying she often missed Betsey's "good care." MHA to RWH, July 26, 1872, *LMHA,* 20. Clover and Clover's mother, Ellen, spelled Betsey's name differently at different times, not always including the second *e.*

Not much is known: Though little information can be found on Miss Houghton's school, many schools for girls were run out of individual homes. For an example of the courses offered at different grade levels, see *Circular and Catalogue, Albany Female Academy* (Albany, NY: Munsell and Rowland, 1860), 4–6.

At eleven, Clover: MHA to Ellen Hooper, July 5, 1854, Adams-Thoron Papers, MHS.

18   "I got a box full": MHA to Eunice Hooper, July 29, 1851, Adams-Thoron Papers, MHS.

"a flitting hither and thither": Henry James, *Selected Stories,* ed. John Lyon (New York: Penguin Classics, 2001), 26.

"I am taking painting lessons": MHA to EHG, August 19, 1862, Adams-Thoron Papers, MHS.

"under the *present* circumstances": SSB to CST, 1851, Caroline Sturgis Tappan Papers, MS 1221 10, Houghton. This letter to Caroline, in more detail, reads, "And yet I find it difficult to take up the thread which has been for one year kept united between us by written communications. I want to see you and your last baby and your first baby and I think I should like to see how you live and what you have about you. . . . However, I am 'picking up' so they say, which is better than being 'picked up' by Barnum for promiscuous exhibition. I couldn't think for one minute dear child of leaving my baby and certainly not for ½ a minute of bringing him, therefore my dear girl I can't come, which deduction clearly evolves itself from the statements just made. I hope to some time or other. I fear lest we shall not know one another when we do meet. We certainly cannot recognize our mutual infants. My baby does everything cunning, patty cakes, puts people bye bye, smacks his lips like Grandfather, clucks to the horses, imitates pussy cat by a prolonged squeak, kisses by bunting his head about indefinitely, tells where Mama's eye is by nearly eradicating it with his forefingers. He is very bright, has a great variety of expressions, a very wild eye, bow mouth and a particularly good nose, high broad forehead and is the image of Henry. Father and he are very confidential and happy together and I really regret to leave this calm nest, which I am to do on Monday next for Anne Hooper's. However I think it will be very pleasant there and under the *present* circumstances I find all places where I go quite similar in one respect — i.e. — Henry is not in them — suffice it to say. He is gone and I have consented. The personal experiences resulting from these facts are not easily narrated in a letter. May you never have to try it dear Cary."

"pact with loneliness": SSB to Mary Eliot Dwight Parkman, n.d., 1848, MS Am 2120 (69a–b), Houghton.

19 her "sudden death": Susan's obituary in the June 10, 1853, edition of the *Boston Daily Evening Transcript* read as follows: "Sudden death. We regret to learn that Mrs. Bigelow, wife of Dr. Henry J. Bigelow, of this city, died very suddenly last evening at the country residence of her father, the Hon. William Sturgis, in Woburn."

"Generally, we must rely on" . . . "to be shaken": Ralph Waldo Emerson to CST, July 4, 1853, in Tilton, *Letters of Ralph Waldo Emerson*, vol. 8, 371.

various family members: In the joint family letter, Eunice Hooper, Dr. Hooper's oldest sister, with whom Clover was staying, told Nellie that Clover had been "very bright and happy since she has been here and not so desirous of a change as she is sometimes when she is with us." Eunice Hooper to EHG, August 1854, Adams-Thoron Papers, MHS.

"My dear Miss Hooper": MHA to EHG, August 1854, Adams-Thoron Papers, MHS.

"before me so I": MHA to EHG, September 10, 1854, Adams-Thoron Papers, MHS.

extended tour of Europe: For a description of Caroline's European travels, see Cornelia Brooke Gilder and Julia Conklin Peters, *Hawthorne's Lenox* (Charleston, SC: The History Press, 2008), 38–39. See also George Dimock, *Caroline Sturgis Tappan and the Grand Tour: A Collection of 19th-Century Photographs* (Lenox, MA: Lenox Library Association, 1882), 61–69.

20 erotic friendship, "my Muse": Ralph Waldo Emerson to CST, May 10, 1845, in Tilton, *Letters of Ralph Waldo Emerson*, vol. 8, 27.

severed connection: Aunt Cary's flight to Europe expressed a need to get away from family, an action that may have led to Clover's subsequent detachment from her aunt. Years later, on hearing others "rave" about the "depth and freshness of her [Aunt Cary's] mind," Clover would remark that her impressions of her aunt were "dim" and that "she must be more amiable and patient than I remember her." MHA to RWH, December 3, 1882, *LMHA*, 404.

Clover could be sensitive: Clover even threatened her father once when his return letters hadn't arrived as soon as anticipated: "Write me immediately a very long letter or I won't write you another word." MHA to RWH, August 1, 1861, Adams-Thoron Papers, MHS.

"As for Alice I can": This letter is undated and incomplete, and there is no opening salutation indicating the recipient. But a letter in a nearby file, written with similar stationery and ink, has the line "I shall be 16 in September," which would make the year 1859. Adams-Thoron Papers, MHS.

21   "The ring accompanying": MHA to unidentified recipient, presumably Annie M. Hooper, n.d., Adams-Thoron Papers, MHS.

"passem of blue": This phrase in Clover's satire likely means "a scrap" or "an example." It could also be that she meant to write *passim*, meaning "here and there."

23   "the thoughts in Nature": Lucy Allen Paton, *Elizabeth Cary Agassiz: A Biography* (Boston: Houghton Mifflin, 1919), 399.

It was the best education: For descriptions of the Agassiz School and who attended, see Paton, *Elizabeth Cary Agassiz*, 45–51, 394–401; and Louise Hall Tharp, *Adventurous Alliance: The Story of the Agassiz Family of Boston* (Boston: Little, Brown and Company, 1959), 137–44.

"a good scholar": WS to unknown recipient, December 26, 1859, quoted in *Mrs. Henry Adams*, 38.

"Was there ever anyone": Catharine Lathrop Howard, *Memorials and Letters of Catharine L. Howard*, compiled by Sophia W. Howard (Springfield, MA: Springfield Printing and Binding Co., 189?), 448.

"the hub of the universe": Oliver Wendell Holmes's original phrase was actually "hub of the solar system." It became more commonly cited as "hub of the universe," keeping the Holmes attribution. See Oliver Wendell Holmes, "Every Man His Own Boswell," The Autocrat of the Breakfast-Table, *Atlantic Monthly* (April 1858): 734; Annie Fields, *Authors and Friends* (Cambridge, MA: The Riverside Press, 1897), 135.

"write me often": EWH to MHA, February 15, 1863, EWH Letters, MS Am 1969 (3), Houghton.

24   "no other establishment": as quoted in Michael Winship, *American Literary Publishing in the Mid-Nineteenth Century: The Business of Ticknor and Fields* (Cambridge, UK: Cambridge University Press, 1995), 21.

"a line of cleavage": Dale Baum, quoted in Carol Bundy's *The Nature of Sacrifice: A Biography of Charles Russell Lowell Jr., 1835–64* (New York: Farrar, Straus and Giroux, 2005), 78.

"the almighty dollar": Charles Dickens, *American Notes and Pictures from Italy* (London: Oxford University Press, 1957, first published in 1842), 27.

CHAPTER 3. Clover's War

26 "a model one": *More Than Common Powers of Perception: The Diary of Elizabeth Rogers Mason Cabot*, ed. P.A.M. Taylor (Boston: Beacon Press, 1991), 182.

27 "Nobody thinks of anything": Mary Warren Dwight to "Annie," April 23, 1861, Dwight-Warren Family Papers, MHS.
"I don't wonder" . . . "color ordered": MHA to Annie Hooper, May 8, 1861, Adams-Thoron Papers, MHS.

28 "the never-failing fountains": *The Sanitary Commission of the United States Army: A Succinct Narrative of Its Works and Purposes* (New York: Published for the Benefit of the United States Sanitary Commission, 1864), 12. The report states the commission's objective in this way: "to bring to bear upon the health, comfort, and *morale* of our troops, the fullest and ripest teachings of Sanitary Science in its application to military life" (5). Activities of the NEWAA, headed by Abigail Williams May, included caring for wounded soldiers and organizing the collection and delivery of a wide range of supplies to the Union army, such as uniforms, bandages, sheets, medicine, soap, preserves, pickles, tea, coffee, crackers, and bread. See also Judith Ann Giesberg, *Civil War Sisterhood: The U.S. Sanitary Commission and Women's Politics in Transition* (Boston: Northeastern University Press, 2000); and Nina Silber, *Daughters of the Union: Northern Women Fight the Civil War* (Cambridge, MA: Harvard University Press, 2005).
"Dr. Howe's 'Sanitary' rooms": MHA to RWH, December 5, no year (most likely 1862). Adams-Thoron Papers, MHS. Dr. Samuel Gridley Howe was one of the founding members of the U.S. Sanitary Commission and a friend of Dr. Hooper. See *Letters and Journals of Samuel Gridley Howe*, ed. Laura E. Richards (Boston: Dana Estes & Company, 1909), 479–507.
"very nice" . . . "shan't be lonely": MHA to RWH, August 1, 1861, Adams-Thoron Papers, MHS.
"insatiably hospitable": James, *Notes of a Son and Brother*, 213.
"The weather has been intensely": MHA to RWH, August 1, 1861, Adams-Thoron Papers, MHS.

29 "Miss C. Sedgwick introduced me": MHA to RWH, August 7, 1861, Adams-Thoron Papers, MHS.
"nearly a year since": MHA to Annie Hooper, April 1, 1862, Adams-Thoron Papers, MHS.
"What fearful times" . . . "by being blue": MHA to unknown addressee, August 13, 1862, Adams-Thoron Papers, MHS. It's not entirely clear where Clover stayed during the summer of 1862. Her likely host would have been her Aunt Cary, but Clover doesn't clearly indicate one way or the other. She mentions, however, that she spent the day or went to dinner at Aunt Cary's, which implies that she slept somewhere else as she'd done the previous summer.
"self-support by their own": Frederick J. Blue, *Salmon P. Chase: A Life in Politics* (Kent, OH: Kent State University Press, 1987), 184.

"natural taste": EWH to MHA, January 25, 1863, EWH Letters, MS Am 1969 (3), Houghton.

while Clover's more distant cousin: Clover's mother's younger sister, Mary Louisa Sturgis, married Robert Gould Shaw Jr. in 1841. He was the brother of Francis G. Shaw, who was the father of Colonel Robert Gould Shaw. Colonel Shaw's mother was Sarah Blake Sturgis, a descendant of the large Russell Sturgis branch of the family.

30 "very nicest men": MHA to CST, March 1863, Adams-Thoron Papers, MHS.

"having such a good": MHA to EHG, August 13, 1862, Adams-Thoron Papers, MHS.

His war photograph: A family album of mostly Hooper siblings and cousins also includes Mason's photograph, indicating his closeness with the family, and perhaps his attentions toward Clover. Swann.

"I was very much afraid" ...

31 "come back from the dead": MHA to EHG, August 5, 1862, Adams-Thoron Papers, MHS.

"pitiless cold" ... "standard": MHA to CST, March 1863, Adams-Thoron Papers, MHS. William Powell Mason Jr. (1835–1901), a graduate of Harvard College and Harvard Law School, married Fanny Peabody on November 25, 1863.

32 "festive spree" ... "to be remembered": MHA to CST, March 1863, Adams-Thoron Papers, MHS. Quincy Adams Shaw, born in 1825, was the younger brother of Clover's uncle Robert Gould Shaw Jr.

33 "strewn so thickly": quoted in Thomas O'Connor, *Civil War Boston: Homefront and Battlefield* (Boston: Northeastern University Press, 1997), 105–6.

bloodshed at Gettysburg: EWH to EHG, July 19, 1863, EWH Letters, MS Am 1969 (5), Houghton.

"imagine no holier": Frank Shaw, as quoted in Lorien Foote, *Seeking the One Great Remedy: Francis George Shaw and Nineteenth-Century Reform* (Athens, OH: Ohio University Press, 2003), 1.

The man who: Ned Hooper wrote fifteen letters to Clover between March 11, 1862, and October 26, 1863. MS Am 1969 (3), Houghton.

Ned had wanted to be an artist: Interview with descendant, June 27, 2008.

Taking after his father: Ned Hooper settled on a career that suited his talents and temperament; he would serve as Harvard's treasurer from 1876 to 1898.

"a young man": James Freeman Clarke to Edward L. Pierce, February 14, 1862, EWH Letters, MS Am 1969 (1).

34 "The Island is lovely": EWH to MHA, March 11, 1862, EWH Letters, MS Am 1969 (3), Houghton.

"nothing now except": EWH to MHA, March 26, 1862, EWH Letters, MS 1969 (3), Houghton.

"When we first": EWH to MHA, March 11, 1862, MS Am 1969 (3), Houghton.

35 "diligent, intelligent": Only the date, July 13, 1863, was preserved on the newspaper clipping. On a postcard, Colonel Robert Gould Shaw wrote that Ned was

held in "the highest opinion" by everyone. The comment by Shaw was copied many years later by his niece Louisa Jay in a letter to Louisa Ward Thoron. Louisa Jay wrote, "In looking thro some Civil war letters the other day I came across the following from my Uncle R. G. Shaw. It was written to his mother from St. Simon's Island and was dated June 18, 1863. 'Ned Hooper at Beaufort is the head of the whole contraband department. Every one has the highest opinion of him. I should like to have remained where I could see him every day.'" Newspaper clipping and letter, Louisa Jay to Louisa Ward Thoron, May 13, 1955, EWH Letters, MS Am 1969 (11), Houghton.

prized her brother's letters: Clover's return letters to Ned are missing.

"Then and there" . . . "going like race horses": MHA to Mary Louisa "Loulie" Shaw, May 23 and 24, 1865, *LMHA*, 3–10. Loulie, a year younger than Clover, was her first cousin, the only child of Mary Louisa Sturgis and Robert Gould Shaw Jr., the paternal uncle of Colonel Robert Gould Shaw. Clover was also distantly related to Colonel Shaw through Shaw's mother, Sarah Blake Sturgis. See *LMHA*, 465–67.

37 "I pine so" . . . "twice a week": Alice Mason Hooper to Anne Sturgis Hooper, October 17, 1864, Adams-Thoron Papers, MHS. For information on William Sturgis Hooper, see Thomas Wentworth Higginson, *Harvard Memorial Biographies*, vol. 1 (Cambridge, MA: Sever and Francis, 1866), 189–203. Later, in December 1864, Alice passed on Clover's news that a recent dinner party, hosted by Caroline Sturgis Tappan to give people the chance to meet Ralph Waldo Emerson after his Sunday evening lectures, had been "very successful." Alice M. Hooper to Anne Sturgis Hooper, December 19, 1864, Adams-Thoron Papers, MHS.

38 "crammed" . . . "everyone clapped": Alice Mason Hooper to Anne Sturgis Hooper, August 6, 1865, Adams-Thoron Papers, MHS.

"one would rather": Quoted in Hamilton Vaughan Bail, "Harvard's Commemoration Day, July 21, 1865," *The New England Quarterly*, vol. 15, no. 2 (June 1942): 266.

Other dignitaries followed: *New York Times*, July 25, 1865. The coverage of the memorial service that day took up the entire front page of the New York paper. The Hooper family had already left by the time of Lowell's reading. As Alice Mason Hooper wrote to her mother-in-law, "We had to go away before it was over—because as usual Uncle Will [Clover's father] got fidgety about their train so we left an hour before it was necessary." To have missed anything of that dramatic day must have grieved Clover.

CHAPTER 4. Six Years

40 "wretched-looking scrawl": MHA to Fanny Chapin, September 15, 1862, Adams-Thoron Papers, MHS.

"pen and ink will be banished": MHA to RWH, January 27, 1878, Adams.

41 each Civil War stereograph: War Views, Adams-Thoron Photographs, Photo. Coll. 42, MHS.

The war had not changed: See William W. Stowe, *Going Abroad: European Travel in Nineteenth-Century American Culture* (Princeton, NJ: Princeton University Press, 1994).

album with a gold-embossed: Henry Adams Photograph Collection, Photo. Coll. 40, Album 5, MHS.

"In that Civil War": Barrett Wendell, *A Literary History of America* (New York: Charles Scribner's Sons, 1900), 478. Wendell was a professor of literature at Harvard College from 1880 to 1917.

The cataclysm had badly shaken: For a vivid description of the city's transformation, see *Middle Years*, 7. Charles Dickens wrote to his friend Charles Sumner, the long-time Massachusetts senator, on his return visit to Boston in 1867 for a reading tour of *A Christmas Carol* and *The Pickwick Papers*, that his twenty-five-year absence seemed "but so many months" except for the city's "sweeping changes." Quoted in Stephen Puleo, *A City So Grand: The Rise of an American Metropolis, Boston, 1850–1900* (Boston: Beacon Press, 2010), 154. Henry Adams would fear becoming what Bostonians became mocked for. "I care a great deal," he wrote to Henry Cabot Lodge in 1875, "to prevent myself from becoming what of all things I despise, a Boston prig (the intellectual prig is the most odious of all)." HA to Henry Cabot Lodge, May 26, 1875, *Letters*, vol. 2, 227–28.

42   "I feel about this": MHA to CST, August 31, 1863, Unprocessed Thoron papers, *93M–35 (b), Houghton.

"certainly the most *married*": Alice James to Anne Ashburner, February 13, 1875, in Rayburn S. Moore, "The Letters of Alice James to Anne Ashburner, 1873–78: The Joy of Engagement (Part 2)," *Resources for American Literary Study*, vol. 27, no. 2 (2001): 198.

"capacity for personal attachment": *Proceedings of the American Academy of Arts and Science*, vol. 22, no. 14 (1887), 527. Ida Agassiz Higginson, older sister of Clover's friend Pauline Agassiz, remarked on Gurney's capacity to "look all around things." Quoted in Edward Waldo Emerson, *The Early Years of the Saturday Club: 1855–1870* (Boston: Houghton Mifflin Company, 1918), 444.

"to have such a bright person": Fanny Hooper to Lillian Clarke, June 1868, Swann.

43   "her hair": Ellen Tucker Emerson to Edith Emerson, January 8, 1858, in *The Letters of Ellen Tucker Emerson*, ed. Edith E. W. Gregg; foreword by Gay Wilson Allen, vol. 1 (Kent, OH: Kent State University Press, 1982), 139.

"lovely head": Bliss Perry, *Life and Letters of Henry Lee Higginson*, vol. 2 (Boston: The Atlantic Monthly Press, 1921), 373.

"'Cupid has made'" . . . "housekeeping and solitude": Ellen Tucker Emerson to unknown addressee, n.d., Gregg, *The Letters of Ellen Tucker Emerson*, vol. 1, 501.

women outnumbered men: The 1870 census records the Massachusetts population as 1,457,351 residents. U.S. Bureau of the Census, *Historical Statistics of the United States: Colonial Times to 1957* (Washington, DC: GPO, 1960), 13.

114 Beacon Street: *The Boston Directory, Embracing the City Record, General Directory of the Citizens, and a Business Directory for the Year* (Boston: Adams, Sampson,

& Company, 1862). See also www.bosarchitecture.com/backbay/beacon/114 .html.

"drifts towards her thirties": MHA to APF, April 26, 1885, Hooper-Adams Papers, MHS.

"constantly ailing . . . to be called *invalides*": Abba Goold Woolson, *Women in American Society* (Boston: Roberts Brothers, 1873), 189–93.

44   problem in the nervous system: Ellen L. Bassuk, "The Rest Cure: Repetition or Resolution of Victorian Women's Conflicts?" in *The Female Body in Western Culture: Contemporary Perspectives,* ed. Susan Rubin Suleiman (Cambridge, MA: Harvard University Press, 1986), 141–42. Neurasthenia seemed to beset those with a more refined and delicate nature, making it, for those in the middle and upper classes, also a more coveted diagnosis than hysteria, with its implication that the patient was acting out or was uncontrollable. Both men and women were diagnosed with neurasthenia, and cures varied widely. The most popular treatment, the rest cure, developed by Dr. S. Weir Mitchell after the war to treat battle-fatigued soldiers, was nonetheless most often prescribed for women. The patient would be isolated in a sickroom far from the strains of family life and forbidden to read or write; a strict daily regimen had to be followed: enforced rest, a diet of bland fatty foods, and "passive exercise" such as hydrotherapy and massage. Some patients improved and some famously worsened, as dramatized by the narrator of Charlotte Perkins Gilman's 1892 short story "The Yellow Wallpaper." See Nancy Theroit, "Women's Voices in Nineteenth-Century Medical Discourse: A Step Toward Deconstructing Science," *Signs,* vol. 19, no. 1 (Autumn 1993): 8. By 1910, subsequent to the work of Freud, neurasthenia went out of fashion as a diagnosis, replaced by psychoanalytic explanations for the patient's symptoms. See F. G. Gosling, *Before Freud: Neurasthenia and the American Medical Community, 1870–1910* (Champaign: University of Illinois Press, 1987); Barbara Sicherman, "The Uses of a Diagnosis: Doctors, Patients, and Neurasthenia," *Journal of the History of Medicine and Allied Sciences,* vol. 32, no. 2 (January 1977); Gail Bederman, *Manliness and Civilization* (Chicago: University of Chicago Press, 1996), 84–92; Natalie Dykstra, "'Trying to Idle': Work and Illness in *The Diary of Alice James,*" in *The New Disability History: American Perspectives,* ed. Paul Longmore and Laurie Umanski (New York: New York University Press, 2001). "appendage to five cushions": *The Diary of Alice James,* ed. Leon Edel (New York: Dodd, Mead & Company, 1964), 81. See also Jean Strouse, *Alice James: The Life of the Brilliant but Neglected Younger Sister of William and Henry James* (Boston: Houghton Mifflin Company, 1980); and R. W. B. Lewis, *The Jameses: A Family Narrative* (New York: Farrar, Straus, and Giroux, 1991), 380–81.

She was interested in art: Kirsten Swinth documents how women "entered art in unprecedented numbers after the Civil War, flooding art schools, hanging their pictures alongside men's, pressing for critical recognition, and competing for sales in an unpredictable market." Swinth, *Painting Professionals: Women Artists and the Development of Modern American Art, 1870–1930* (Chapel Hill: University of North Carolina Press, 2001), 1. In addition, several colleges had started to admit female students, though not Harvard College. Oberlin College, the first coeducational school, was established in 1833; Mount Holyoke Female Seminary, an all-female college, was founded in 1837; and Vassar College began classes in 1865. Regardless of these developments, in the 1860s, college was not considered a suitable option for a young woman of Clover's social class.

45   a life member: *First Annual Report of the Directors of the Massachusetts Infant Asylum,* 2nd ed. (Boston: Alfred Mudge & Son, 1868), 36.

founding member: *Our Dumb Animals,* vol. 5, no. 1 (June 1872), 305.

"I hope you're not going" . . . "orphan girl to sew": Ellen Tucker Emerson to Ralph Waldo Emerson, August 27, 1868, in Gregg, *Letters of Ellen Tucker Emerson,* vol. 1, 502. This letter is also the source that confirms Clover's involvement with Dorchester's Industrial School for Girls and the Howard Industrial School for Colored Women and Girls in Cambridge.

"perfectly delightful": MHA to Eleanor Shattuck, February 5, 1871, George Cheyne Shattuck Papers, vol. 24, MHS.

"plunged": MHA to RWH, September 15, 1872, *LMHA,* 39. Clover recalled reading through the history with Ida to her father after meeting Professor Mommsen while in Berlin. Clover's copy of Mommsen's book is dated 1865–66.

"full of funny stories": Ellen Tucker Emerson to Ralph Waldo Emerson, August 27, 1868, in Gregg, *Letters of Ellen Tucker Emerson,* vol. 1, 502.

46   "Switzerland in the summer": MHA to Catharine L. Howard, March 3, 1869, *LMHA,* 473.

"mild drizzle" . . . "whispered once": MHA to Eleanor Shattuck, February 5, 1871, George Cheyne Shattuck Papers, vol. 24, MHS.

47   "hot sun" . . . "effect on the brain": MHA to Eleanor Shattuck, March 15, 1871, George Cheyne Shattuck Papers, vol. 24, MHS. Phillips Brooks, first cousin of Henry Adams, became rector of Trinity Church, Boston, in 1869.

CHAPTER 5. Henry Adams

48   "Dr. & Miss Hooper": Facsimile of Henry's engagement book, reproduced in *LMHA,* opp. xiv.

49   "oasis in this wilderness": HA to CMG, May 22, 1871, *Letters,* vol. 2, 110.

"the design" . . . "very steadily": HA to Brooks Adams, March 3, 1872, *Letters,* vol. 2, 132.

"never in his life": T. S. Eliot, "A Sceptical Patrician," *Athenaeum* (May 23, 1919): 361–62.

"The history of my family": As quoted in Paul C. Nagel, *Descent from Glory: Four Generations of the John Adams Family* (Oxford: Oxford University Press, 1983; reprinted by Harvard University Press, 1999), 3.

50   "the only one": Charles Francis Adams, July 4, 1829, in *Diary of Charles Francis Adams,* vol. 2, ed. Aïda DiPace Donald and David Donald (Cambridge, MA: Belknap–Harvard University Press, 1964), 398. For early Adams family history, see especially David McCullough, *John Adams* (New York: Simon & Schuster,

2001); Nagel, *Descent from Glory;* and Stephen Hess, *America's Political Dynasties* (New Brunswick, NJ: Transaction Publishers, 1997), 11–49.

"strange as it may seem": As quoted in *Middle Years,* 316.

He had the habit: For details of how Henry held his hands in his pockets, see "Henry Adams Again," *New York Times,* June 15, 1919.

"very — very bald": HA to CMG, March 30, 1869, *Letters,* vol. 2, 24.

51   Henry had grown up: For a discussion of Henry's early life and education, see Ernest Samuels, *The Young Henry Adams* (Cambridge, MA: Harvard University Press, 1948), 3–52. Henry would be less engaged by Boston's Transcendentalist fervor than many of Clover's relatives were; his family was rooted more in the political than the religious debates of the time. Later, as editor of the *North American Review,* he would sum up his opinion of those "who pondered on the True and Beautiful" in a review of Octavius Brooks Frothingham's *Transcendentalism in New England,* an early history of the movement. Except for Emerson, "whose influence is wider now than it was forty years ago," Henry dismissed most Transcendentalists as those who sought "conspicuous solitudes" and "looked out of windows and said, 'I am raining.'" Henry Adams, "Critical Notices: Frothingham's Transcendentalism," *North American Review,* vol. 123, no. 253 (October 1876), 470–71. Garry Wills rightly notes, however, that Transcendentalism may have "left a deeper mark" on Henry than he acknowledged, given the "nature mysticism of his novel *Esther*" and how his "later admiration of 'Oriental religions' paralleled Thoreau." Garry Wills, *Henry Adams and the Making of America* (Boston: Houghton Mifflin Company, 2005), 39.

"One of us": HA to CFA Jr., December 13, 1861, *Letters,* vol. 1, 265.

52   "a golden time": As quoted in Samuels, *The Young Henry Adams,* 121; "biggest piece of luck": HA to CMG, April 16, 1911, *Letters,* vol. 6, 441.

again worked as a journalist: For a listing of Henry's publications during this time, see Samuels, *The Young Henry Adams,* 317–18.

"it is the teacher": CFA to HA, July 11, 1870, Adams.

"utterly and grossly": HA to CMG, September 29, 1870, *Letters,* vol. 2, 81. Henry protested to President Eliot, "I know nothing about Medieval History," to which Eliot replied, "If you will point out any one who knows more, Mr. Adams, I will appoint him." Samuel Eliot Morison, *Three Centuries of Harvard, 1636–1936* (Cambridge, MA: The Belknap Press of Harvard University Press, 1986), 348.

"greatest teacher": Morison, *Three Centuries of Harvard,* 349.

53   "I allotted to each man": C. E. Schorer, "A Letter from Henry Cabot Lodge," *The New England Quarterly,* vol. 25, no. 3. (September 1952): 391.

"a man of pure intellect": Stewart Mitchell, "Henry Adams and Some of His Students," *Proceedings of the Massachusetts Historical Society,* Third Series, vol. 66 (October 1936–May 1941): 307.

library books on reserve: Morison, *Three Centuries of Harvard,* 348.

"cultivated their genealogies": *Middle Years,* 7.

"makes me so unhappy": Louisa Catherine Adams, as quoted in Nagel, *Descent from Glory,* 206.

54   "fearfully trying": HA to CMG, July 13, 1870, *Letters,* vol. 2, 74.

"too awful to dwell on": Abigail Brooks Adams, as quoted in Edward Chalfant, *Better in Darkness: A Biography of Henry Adams, His Second Life, 1862–1891* (Hamden, CT: Archon Books, 1994), 722.

"one of my trusted supports": CFA, Diary, May 20, 1879, Adams.

"is merely that" . . . "get along somehow": HA to CFA, January 7, *Letters,* vol. 2, 124.

55   "a very uncomfortable week" . . . "everyone's nerves": HA to CFA, January 14, 1872, *Letters,* vol. 2, 125–26.

"I have great reliance": CFA to HA, January 30, 1872, Adams.

"so far away superior" . . . "It is Clover Hooper": HA to Brooks Adams, March 3, 1872, *Letters,* vol. 2, 132.

"happy as ideal lovers": HA to CMG, May 30, 1872, *Letters,* vol. 2, 137; "has a certain vein": HA to CMG, June 23, 1872, *Letters,* vol. 2, 140.

56   Clover's family welcomed: Many years later, Henry would remember with pleasure that he had been made a co-executor of his father-in-law's estate, along with his brothers-in-law, Ned Hooper and Whitman Gurney. HA to CMG, May 10, 1885, *Letters,* vol. 2, 611.

"I am sure" . . . "delighted with": Oliver Wendell Holmes to CFA, March 14, 1872, Adams.

the engagement had "surprised": CFA, Diary, March 2, 1872, Adams.

"Heavens!—no!—": CFA Jr., Memorabilia, May 3, 1891, Adams.

She assured her: MHA to Eleanor Shattuck, March 8, 1872, George Cheyne Shattuck papers, vol. 24, MHS. Clover indicated that Eleanor's younger brother, Frederick, almost got in the way of her engagement. Tell Fred, she wrote Eleanor, "that he nearly stopped all this—that if he had sat one hour longer that fatal Tuesday P.M. this might never have come to pass—so I like him better than ever. Henry outstayed him."

"horrid dream" . . . "put my whole heart into it.": The original of this letter has not been found; quoted in *Mrs. Henry Adams,* 105–6.

57   "One of my congratulatory letters": HA to CMG, March 26, 1872, *Letters,* vol. 2, 133–34.

58   a derogatory term: The term *bluestocking* originated in England in reference to a group of eighteenth-century women intellectuals. It had by the nineteenth century turned into a mocking sobriquet.

"My young female": HA to CMG, May 30, 1872, *Letters,* vol. 2, 137.

found the ceremony "peculiar": CFA Jr. wrote to his father: "The wedding was like the engagement—peculiar." He added: "everyone to his fate." CFA Jr. to CFA, June 28, 1872, Adams.

"We think our wedding" . . . "kindness and assistance": MHA and HA to RWH, June 28, 1872, *Letters,* vol. 2, 141–42. Henry's letter is on the reverse side of Clover's letter to Dr. Hooper.

59   Wedding gifts inundated: MHA to EWH, July 7, 1872, Adams-Thoron Papers, MHS.

"time for seeing Egypt": The Adamses used the 1867 edition. Sir John Gardner Wilkinson, *A Handbook for Travellers in Egypt* . . . (London: John Murray, 1867), 2.

CHAPTER 6. Down the Nile

60   "very beautiful": MHA to RWH, July 26, 1872, *LMHA*, 17.

"cursed the sea" . . . "Think it may have": MHA to RWH, July 9–July 19, 1872, *LMHA*, 14.

61   "gossamer-like web": Henry Adams, review of *Their Wedding Journey*, by William Dean Howells, *North American Review*, no. 235 (April 1872): 444.

"see all we want": MHA to RWH, July 9–July 19, 1872, *LMHA*, 15.

"Often think of Beverly": MHA to RWH, July 9–19, 1872, *LMHA*, 16.

She enclosed with her letter: "Sketch of Stateroom on Board a Ship." Sketch by MHA, July 13, 1872. Copy of photograph from MHA Photographs, photograph number 50.133, MHS.

"scour" . . . "young colts": MHA to RWH, July 23, 1873, *LMHA*, 133.

"We feel": MHA to RWH, July 26, 1872, *LMHA*, 19.

"full of roses . . . were nowhere": MHA to RWH, July 26, 1872, *LMHA*, 18. For a vivid description of Charles Milnes Gaskell, see William Dusinberre, "Henry Adams in England," *Journal of American Studies*, vol. 11, no. 2 (August 1977), 163–86. Dusinberre (178) argues that Henry James used Gaskell as a model for Lord Warburton in *The Portrait of a Lady*.

62   "too ferocious to be liked": *Education*, 207.

"very charming" . . . "gasp": MHA to RWH, August 7, 1872, *LMHA*, 20–21.

"until brains and legs": MHA to RWH, September 8, 1872, *LMHA*, 37.

"pictures in the gallery": MHA to RWH, August 23, 1872, *LMHA*, 25.

"They had never heard": MHA to RWH, August 23, 1872, *LMHA*, 26.

"the role of old married people": MHA to EHG, September 5, 1872, *LMHA*, 30.

63   "Travelling would be": MHA to RWH, August 23, 1872, *LMHA*, 29.

"so rich that I was quite": MHA to RWH, September 8, 1872, *LMHA*, 36.

"bad luck in the matter": MHA to RWH, September 15, 1872, *LMHA*, 40.

"hard" . . . "good fun": MHA to RWH, September 8, 1873, *LMHA*, 37.

"though it's dreary": MHA to RWH, March 11, 1872, *LMHA*, 82.

"to patch up": MHA to RWH, November 17, 1872, *LMHA*, 57; Murray's *Handbook for Travellers in Egypt* (1867) lists three pages of items "useful for a journey in Egypt."

64   Boston had erupted in flames: The city lost over 775 buildings to the fire, which ranged over more than 60 acres. Estimates of total damage were between $70 to $75 million. Twenty thousand people lost jobs and many were left homeless. The exact number of dead and wounded was never made official. See Stephanie Schorow, *Boston on Fire: A History of Fires and Firefighting in Boston* (Beverly,

MA: Commonwealth Editions, 2003); F. E. Frothingham, *The Boston Fire* (New York: Lee, Shepard & Dillingham, 1873).

"rejoiced to hear": MHA to RWH, December 21, 1872, *LMHA*, 63.

"Beverly is certainly": MHA to RWH, August 7, 1872, *LMHA*, 24; "I miss you all": September 8, 1872, *LMHA*, 38; "I miss you very, very much": MHA to RWH, October, 20, 1872, *LMHA*, 52.

"I miss you" . . . "I do very often": MHA to RWH, November 17, 1872, *LMHA*, 58.

"Clover gained flesh": HA to RWH, November 10, 1872, *Letters*, vol. 2, 153.

"dimly lighted streets": MHA to RWH, November 23, 1872, *LMHA*, 59.

65   "competent and faithful": MHA to RWH, March 1, 1873, *LMHA*, 78.

"We saw them": MHA to RWH, December 5, 1872, *LMHA*, 61.

"the air [is] bracing": MHA to RWH, December 21, 1872, *LMHA*, 63.

"tried to write": MHA to RWH, December 5, 1872, *LMHA*, 60.

"One day is so like": MHA to RWH, December 21, 1872, *LMHA*, 63.

"letter-writing is not": MHA to Fanny Chapin Hooper, December 14, 1872, Adams-Thoron Papers, MHS.

not to "show": MHA to RWH, December 21, 1872, *LMHA*, 64.

"which they balance" . . . "miserable": MHA to RWH, January 1, 1873, *LMHA*, 64.

66   "I must confess" . . . "shortcomings": MHA to RWH, January 1, 1873, *LMHA*, 65–66.

"I never seem to get": MHA to RWH, January 3, 1873, *LMHA*, 66.

"How true it is": MHA to RWH, February 16, 1873, *LMHA*, 75. Clover made this statement about herself when she got tired of looking at Egyptian antiquities, frustrated that she didn't understand more about what she was seeing.

Clover and Henry strolled: They also picnicked with the Roosevelts from New York, who were traveling in their chartered *dahabeah* directly ahead; their young son Teddy, at fourteen, had a voice his mother described as "a sharp, ungreased squeak." Quoted in Edmund Morris, *The Rise of Theodore Roosevelt* (New York: Random House, 1979), 36.

67   "The wind is not purer": Ralph Waldo Emerson, October 7, 1839, in *Journals of Ralph Waldo Emerson,* vol. 7, ed. William H. Gilman et al. (Cambridge, MA: Belknap Press of Harvard University Press, 1960–66), 260.

"Dear, sweet Ellen Hooper": Anna Hazard Barker Ward to ESH, August 15, 1848, Swann.

"I doubt if we find": MHA to RWH, January 24, 1873, *LMHA*, 67–68.

"working like a beaver" . . . "we have yet seen": MHA to RWH, February 5, 1873, *LMHA*, 71.

"we waited" . . . "on the river": MHA to RWH, February 16, 1873, *LMHA*, 74, 76.

68   one photograph of Henry: "Interior of Dahabieh 'Isis,'" Photographer unknown, n.d., from HA Photograph Collection, 40.160, MHS.

"bought many nice things" . . . "grows on us": MHA to RWH, March 11, 1872, *LMHA*, 80.

"How much we have lived" . . . "faculty of memory": MHA to Anna Hazard Barker Ward, March 15, 1873, Papers of Samuel Gray Ward and Anna Hazard Barker Ward, MS Am 1465 (5), Houghton. Clover and Henry were in Alexandria on March 10, were sailing on the Mediterranean on March 11, and arrived at the Bay of Naples on Saturday, March 15. See *LMHA*, 80–85.

Henry James apparently did not perceive Clover's troubles on the Nile, but rather thought that she'd gained health from her travels. He wrote to his father in March 1873 from Rome that "the Clover Adamses have been here for a week, the better for Egypt . . . I saw them last P.M., and they are better and laden with material treasures." HJ to Henry James Sr., March 28, 1873, *HJ Letters*, vol. 1, 360.

"sun rise between" . . . "early morning mist": MHA to RWH, March 16, 1873, *LMHA*, 85.

69   "path lying between": MHA to RWH, March 29, 1873, *LMHA*, 89.

"stuffs and accessories": MHA to RWH, April 20, 1873, *LMHA*, 95.

"very clever": MHA to RWH, April 20, 1873, *LMHA*, 96.

"à la française": MHA to RWH, April 20, 1873, *LMHA*, 98.

"very pretty": MHA to RWH, April 20, 1873, *LMHA*, 99.

"swell part": MHA to RWH, May 14, 1873, *LMHA*, 102.

"If I were a boy": MHA to RWH, June 1, 1873, *LMHA*, 108.

"England is charming" . . . "good-humouredly": MHA to RWH, June 29, 1873, *LMHA*, 127.

70   "enjoyed much": MHA to RWH, July 23, 1873, *LMHA*, 134.

Part II: *"Very Much Together"*

CHAPTER 7. A Place in the World

73   "pulled her down" . . . "a small Boston world": HA to CMG, August 12, 1873, *Letters*, vol. 2, 178.

"quite unchanged": EWH to CST, August 19, 1873, Swann.

"I want you to send": MHA to EHG, October 27, 1872, Adams-Thoron Papers, MHS.

74   She and Henry hung many: HA to CMG, December 8, 1873, *Letters*, vol. 2, 183.

They kept a watercolor: HA to Charles Eliot Norton, April 15, 1874, *Letters*, vol. 2, 191.

"excites frantic applause": HA to CMG, December 8, 1873, *Letters*, vol. 2, 183.

"My wife is very well": HA to CMG, October 26, 1873, *Letters*, vol. 2, 180.

75   "nearly all surplus": HA to CMG, June 14, 1876, *Letters*, vol. 2, 275.

"keep the thread": HA, review of *The Constitutional History of England in Its Origin and Development*, by William Stubbs, *North American Review*, vol. 119, no. 244 (1874): 233–34, as quoted in *Middle Years*, 61.

"the reader ought to be": HA to Henry Cabot Lodge, June 25, 1874, *Letters*, vol. 2, 195.

He would read aloud: HA to Simon Newcomb, December 23, 1874, *Letters*, vol. 2, 245.

"while writing before": J. Laurence Laughlin, "Some Recollections of Henry Adams," *Scribner's Magazine*, vol. 69, no. 1 (January 1921): 582.

"I have been hard worked": HA to CMG, June 22, 1874, *Letters*, vol. 2, 193.

76 "farm and woodland": Joseph E. Garland, *The North Shore: A Social History of Summers Among the Noteworthy, Fashionable, Rich, Eccentric, and Ordinary on Boston's Gold Coast, 1823–1929* (Beverly, MA: Commonwealth Editions, 1998), 33.

"into the depths": HA to Sir Robert Cunliffe, July 6, 1874, *Letters*, vol. 2, 199.

77 "our new house is more": HA to CMG, June 14, 1876, *Letters*, vol. 2, 276. I want to thank Harrison Smithwick and his mother, Mrs. Frances Smithwick, who gave me a tour of Clover and Henry's Beverly Farms home, which still has many of its original design elements.

"a footpath" . . . "sunlight of the woods": Mabel La Farge, *Letters to a Niece and Prayer to the Virgin of Chartres by Henry Adams, with a Niece's Memories* (Boston: Houghton Mifflin Company, 1920), 7–8.

78 graduate seminar in history: For a complete listing of Henry's courses at Harvard, see Samuels, *The Young Henry Adams*, 340–41.

"German codes" . . . "colt in tall clover": Laughlin, "Some Recollections of Henry Adams," 580.

"Nothing since I came to Cambridge": HA to Henry Cabot Lodge, June 30, 1876, *Letters*, vol. 2, 280–281.

"long-haired terriers": La Farge, *Letters to a Niece*, 7.

"isolated groups": HA to CMG, February 15, 1875, *Letters*, vol. 2, 216. "I am flourishing as ever and growing in dignity and age. My wife is as well as I": HA to CMG, March 26, 1874, *Letters*, vol. 2, 189; "My wife is flourishing": HA to CMG, June 22, 1874, *Letters*, vol. 2, 194; "my wife flourishes like the nasturtiums which are my peculiar joy": HA to Sir Robert Cunliffe, July 6, 1874, *Letters*, vol. 2, 200; "we are and have been very well and flourishing": HA to CMG, February 15, 1875, *Letters*, vol. 2, 217.

79 "As I've not bored you" . . . "Marian Adams": MHA to CMG, March 29, 1875, Adams.

"toned down": Leon Edel, *Henry James: The Conquest of London: 1870–1880* (New York: Avon Books, paperback reprint 1978; originally published 1962), 375; "had a good effect": Rayburn S. Moore, "The Letters of Alice James to Anne Ashburner, 1873–78: The Joy of Engagement (Part 1)," *Resources for American Literary Study*, vol. 27, no. 1 (2001): 34.

CHAPTER 8. City of Conversation

80 "As for me and my wife": HA to CMG, November 25, 1877, *Letters*, vol. 2, 326.

"my university work": HA to CMG, Sept. 8, 1876, *Letters*, vol. 2, 293.

The October 1876 presidential election: For more on Henry's last issue of the *North American Review* and on his dispute with James Osgood, see Wills, *Henry Adams and the Making of America*, 79–86.

"The more I see": HA to CMG, February 13, 1874, *Letters*, vol. 2, 188.

81 "assume control of everything": HA to CMG, February 15, 1875, *Letters*, vol. 2, 217.

"charming old ranch": MHA to RWH, August 24, 1879, *LMHA*, 170.

"as if we were": MHA to RWH, November 18, 1877, Adams.

"like a gentleman": MHA to RWH, November 18, 1877, Adams; "always amusing": HA to CMG, May 30, 1878, *Letters*, vol. 2, 338.

82 "uncommonly lively": MHA to RWH, January 6, 1878, Adams. Eugenia Kaledin states that Emily and Clover would have a falling out later in their friendship but does not cite where she found evidence for any quarrel or misunderstanding. *Mrs. Henry Adams*, 183. It is somewhat clearer from Clover's letters that she found Emily entertaining and fun-loving but did not feel close to her nor take her particularly seriously.

"the instrument seems like": MHA to RWH, February 3, 1878, Adams.

"a whirlwind had picked up": As quoted in Frank G. Carpenter, *Carp's Washington* (New York: McGraw-Hill Book Company, 1960), 5.

"What had been a most unsightly": As quoted in Kenneth R. Bowling, "From 'Federal Town' to 'National Capital': Ulysses S. Grant and the Reconstruction of Washington, D.C.," *Washington History* (Spring/Summer 2002): 16. For an explanation of the proposal to remove the capital to St. Louis, see Fergus Bordewich, *Washington: The Making of the American Capital* (New York: Armistad, 2008), 272–75.

Washington had always teetered: See Carl Abbott, *Political Terrain: Washington, D.C.: From Tidewater Town to Global Metropolis* (Chapel Hill: University of North Carolina Press, 1999), esp. 2–5. For a description of post–Civil War racial politics, see also Constance McLaughlin Green, *Washington: A History of the Capital, 1800–1950* (Princeton, NJ: Princeton University Press, 1976), esp. 291–338.

83 "a slaveocracry" . . . "her right": MHA to RWH, December 23, 1877, Adams.

"a foul contagion": As quoted in McCullough, *John Adams*, 134.

"always seemed a most iniquitous": As quoted in McCullough, *John Adams*, 104.

"the archbishop of antislavery": HA to CFA Jr., December 26, 1860, *Letters*, vol. 1, 213. CFA had been given the nickname "archbishop of antislavery" by Thomas Corwin, a Republican congressman from Ohio.

84 "no food and no clothes": MHA to RWH, December 9, 1877, Adams.

"only place in America" . . . "complete": HA to CMG, November 25, 1877, *Letters*, vol. 2, 326.

surprisingly "complete": HA to CMG, November 25, 1877, *Letters*, vol. 2, 326.

"City of Conversation": Henry James, *The American Scene* (New York: Harper & Brothers, 1907), 329.

"a lovely path" . . . "in summer": MHA to RWH, December 16, 1877, Adams Papers, MHS.

"Sundays wouldn't come so fast": MHA to RWH, December 16, 1877, Adams.

"new possibilities for us": MHA to RWH, December 23, 1877, Adams.

85   "I've been working" . . . "on opposite stools": MHA to RWH, December 23, 1877, Adams. George Cruikshank illustrated several novels by Charles Dickens, including *Oliver Twist* and *The Old Curiosity Shop*.

"written on the backs" . . . "till now": MHA to RWH, December 16, 1877, Adams.

"a hieroglyphic world": Edith Wharton, *The Age of Innocence*, ed. Laura Dluzyn-ski Quinn (New York: Penguin Group, 1996; originally published 1920), 36.

"Politeness is power": As quoted in Kathryn Allamong Jacob, *Capital Elites: High Society in Washington, D.C., After the Civil War* (Washington, DC: Smithsonian Institution Press, 1994), 73.

"composed, in so great a degree": Madeleine Vinton Dahlgren, *Etiquette of Social Life in Washington* (Lancaster, PA: Inquirer Printing and Publishing Co., 1873), 3–4.

"In this social vortex": MHA to RWH, January 13, 1878, Adams.

86   "a discipline worthy": MHA to RWH, March 3, 1878, Adams.

"I think I'd best announce": MHA to RWH, November 18, 1877, Adams.

"The 'calling' nuisance": MHA to RWH, February 27, 1881, *LMHA*, 271–72.

"sighed for his pines": MHA to RWH, December 9, 1877, Adams.

"It's very cozy": MHA to RWH, November 18, 1877, Adams.

"state secrets": MHA to RWH, December 16, 1877, Adams.

"charming old house" . . . "under her chin": MHA to RWH, December 2, 1877, Adams.

87   "quite nice looking": MHA to RWH, December 2, 1877, Adams.

"a late carouse" . . . "vegetation!": MHA to RWH, December 10, 1878, Adams.

"more agreeable than most": HA to Mary Dwight Parkman, February 20, 1879, *Letters*, vol. 2, 353.

"being the king of 'Vulgaria'": MHA to RWH, December 15, 1878, Adams.

"march to the sea": MHA to RWH, December 10, 1882, *LMHA*, 406–7.

"uproarious laughter": J. Laurence Laughlin, "Some Recollections of Henry Adams," 582.

"so proud of her": Margaret (Terry) Winthrop Chanler, *Roman Spring* (Boston: Little, Brown, and Company, 1934), 303.

88   "Mr. Evarts" . . . "he orates too much": MHA to RWH, December 29, 1878, Adams.

"For a middle aged": MHA to RWH, February 2, 1879, Adams.

"wits for a week": HA to CMG, February 9, 1876, *Letters*, vol. 2, 247.

"So we came home" . . . "superb roses": MHA to RWH, November 25, 1877, Adams.

89   "to report to duty": MHA to RWH, December 9, 1877, Adams.

"Hear me, my chiefs!": Chief Joseph, as quoted in Kent Nerburn, *Chief Joseph and the Flight of the Nez Perce* (New York: HarperOne, 2006), 268; see also Elliot

West, *The Last Indian War: The Nez Perce Story* (New York: Oxford University Press, 2009).

"he saw the Indians" . . . "their bonnets behind": MHA to RWH, December 9, 1877, Adams.

90 "How long Oh!": MHA to RWH, January 26, 1879, Adams.

"A propos to nothing": MHA to RWH, January 13, 1878, Adams.

"charming, most sympathetic" . . . "bearded face": MHA to RWH, April 11, 1880, Adams.

"Mrs. Adams, didn't your husband": MHA to RWH, December 28, 1879, *LMHA*, 223.

"forty-three miles": MHA to RWH, March 3, 1878, Adams.

"midnight cigars" . . . "left to do it": MHA to RWH, July 11, 1880, Adams.

Dr. Hooper wrote back: The reasons why Dr. Hooper's letters to Clover do not survive may have to do with Clover. She wrote to John Hay in 1882, "I do not keep letters." MHA to JH, June 13, 1882, Adams.

91 "stood under" . . . "any feelings": MHA to RWH, December 2, 1877, Adams.

"like a gentleman": MHA to RWH, November 18, 1877, Adams.

"annoying pin" . . . "too old to reform": MHA to RWH, January 6, 1878, Adams.

"Brooks [an] injustice": MHA to RWH, January 13, 1878, Adams.

"never quote" . . . "*Burn* this!": MHA to RWH, January 6, 1878, Adams.

92 "I feel as if": CFA, Diary, October 17, 1877, Adams.

"I have no feelings": CFA, Diary, May 20, 1879, Adams.

Mr. and Mrs. Adams thought: Tension between Clover and her in-laws also may have to do with the increasing misery in the elder Adamses' marriage, which had escalated in the summer of 1876, when Mrs. Adams injured her foot. She went for a cure in the fall at a New York hotel, where her daily treatments included long conversations with her physicians, gentle exercise, and the administration of electricity. Mr. Adams traveled with her to New York but then quickly returned to Quincy and Boston, and in Mrs. Adams's daily letters to him, the first one dated December 1, 1876, she alternately complains about her accommodations, her slow progress, and the horrible winter weather. At one point she wished the doctors would "let the walking alone," declaring that "I don't care one cent about walking—all I ask is freedom from pain."

Lonely and discouraged, she begged her husband to come back, telling him how she longed for nothing but him, scolding him for putting her off, furious with how he announced he was coming to see her but then changed his mind. The more she harangued him, the more miserable she felt. On December 6 she admitted, "This is a horrid letter in all respects, but you won't mind will you? For I love you dearly, even if [I] am old and ugly and lame and homesick." But the next week she felt abandoned and unloved, writing that "I wish you loved me half as well as I do you, such unequal feelings make life an uneven piece of patchwork." After she pulled for his sympathy, she lashed out, and the more she did so, the more Mr. Adams resisted. By December 13, Mrs. Adams wrote in a fury, "It is four weeks today since you left here and I can only say if I had been told that you would let that time pass with such a short distance between us and I here under such circumstances I could not have believed it . . . The weather had nothing to do with my depression for when I don't walk I am better. It was my slow progress and disappointment to your constant delay in coming on." Mr. Adams — patient and encouraging — was also passive and unyielding, admitting in his diary, "My defect is want of flexibility." She could be resigned and realistic — "we are too old to change either your nature or mine." But when they separated again the next April so she could have more treatments, she reacted with rage: "You can't understand my feelings our natures are so entirely different and you are well at home and do not depend in the least on me. It shall never happen again." Abigail Brooks Adams to CFA, December 1, 1876–April 6, 1877, Adams. The early years of the elder Adams marriage are particularly well described by Paul C. Nagel in his *Adams Women: Abigail and Louisa Adams, Their Sisters and Daughters* (Cambridge, MA: Harvard University Press, 1987), 244–77.

"I am told on high authority": MHA to RWH, March 31, 1878, Adams.

"Your postal card": MHA to RWH, April 7, 1878, Adams.

93   "a laconic line": MHA to RWH, February 23, 1879, Adams.

"icing ourselves": HA to Theodore F. Dwight, June 17, 1878, *Letters,* vol. 2, 340.

"winter quarters": HA to CMG, November 28, 1878, *Letters,* vol. 2, 348.

"wild with joy": MHA to RWH, November 3, 1878, Adams.

their "experiment": HA to CMG, September 8, 1876, *Letters,* vol. 2, 327.

"very much together": HA to CMG, November 25, 1877, *Letters,* vol. 2, 327.

"I have myself never cared": HA to CMG, August 22, 1877, *Letters,* vol. 2, 316.

94   "Of ourselves I can": HA to CMG, May 30, 1878, *Letters,* vol. 2, 338.

"springing back to their normal": MHA to RWH, May 11, 1879, Adams.

"prose masterpiece": Wills, *Henry Adams and the Making of America,* 8. Garry Wills argues that one aspect of the *History* that would set it apart is how Henry brought "many kinds of evidence, archival and cultural, that had not before been so deftly interwoven"(388).

"900,000,000 things": MHA to APF, May 18, 1879, Hooper-Adams Papers, MHS.

CHAPTER 9. Wandering Americans

95   "'He who is tired'": MHA to RWH, June 15, 1879, *LMHA,* 140.

"vastness of this London society": MHA to RWH, February 22, 1880, Adams.

"gardens and great trees": HA to Sir Robert Cunliffe, June 15, 1879, *Letters,* vol. 2, 362. Henry relayed what Clover said in his letter to Sir Robert Cunliffe.

"this English world": MHA to RWH, June 22, 1879, *LMHA,* 145.

96   "young and not pretty": MHA to RWH, July 13, 1879, *LMHA,* 154; "refuge": MHA to RWH, June 15, 1879, *LMHA,* 141.

about the art on display: Charles E. Pascoe, "The Grosvenor Gallery Summer Exhibition," *The Art Journal (1875–1887),* new series, vol. 5 (1879), 222–24.

"joke" . . . "face of the public": MHA to RWH, June 15, 1879, *LMHA,* 144. When

Clover met Whistler later that summer, she was even less impressed, telling her father that "his etchings are so charming; it is a pity he should leave that to woo a muse whom he can't win." MHA to RWH, July 27, 1879, *LMHA*, 159. In 1877, Whistler sued John Ruskin for libel, after the English critic disparaged the painting *Nocturne in Black and Gold — The Falling Rocket,* which was exhibited at the Grosvenor Gallery, charging that the artist had flung "a pot of paint in the public's face." Whistler won the suit but was awarded minimal damages.

"pegging away": MHA to RWH, July 20, 1879, *LMHA*, 157.

"sparkle and glitter": MHA to RWH, January 26, 1879, Adams Family Papers.

"whispering gallery": MHA to RWH, January 23, 1881, *LMHA*, 259.

97 Anne felt close to her father and brother: The relationships in Anne's family became clear when Anne had to cut short one of her visits with the Adamses because of a family emergency. "Her father and brother," Clover confided to her father, "are the ones of all her family who are very dear to her." MHA to RWH, February 4, 1883, *LMHA*, 421.

Whatever they did: MHA to APF, August, 9, 1879, Hooper-Adams Papers, MHS. Starting in August 1879, Clover began addressing Anne Palmer by another name in her letters, opening some of them with the greeting "Dear Mrs. Philippa." She and Anne must have shared an inside joke or a story that inspired this role-playing. But when Clover's letters were archived at the MHS years later, those addressed to Anne and those to Mrs. Philippa were put in separate files. Reading the letters together in chronological order, along with Clover's sly references to the ruse, as when she asks Anne if "that hybrid title still pleases you," reveal that Anne and Mrs. Philippa are the same person. MHA to APF, August 6, 1880, Hooper Adams Papers, MHS. My citations make no distinction between those letters that open with "Dear Anne" and those that open with "Dear Mrs. Philippa."

"launched very happily": HJ to Alice Howe James, July 6, 1879, *HJ Letters*, vol. 2, 249.

"intellectual grace": HJ to William James, March 8, 1870, *HJ Letters*, vol. 1, 208.

"become Henry James": Cynthia Ozick, *Quarrel and Quandary* (New York: Vintage International, 2001; first published 2000), 142.

"banishes": As quoted in Edel, *The Conquest of London,* 413.

"wine-and-water": HJ to Mary Walsh James [mother], April 8, 1879, *HJ Letters*, vol. 2, 228.

"plenty of anecdotes": HJ to MHA, November 6, 1881, *HJ Letters*, vol. 2, 361.

"a trifle dry": HJ to Elizabeth Boott, June 28, 1879, *HJ Letters*, vol. 2, 246.

98 "the most complete compendium": MHA to RWH, March 14, 1880, Adams.

"savage notices" . . . "literary reputation": MHA to RWH, April 4, 1880, Adams. For a vivid description of James's reaction to London, see Edel, *The Conquest of London,* esp. 273–75. For an explanation of the controversy surrounding the reception of James's biography of Hawthorne, see 386–91.

"He comes in every day": MHA to RWH, January 25, 1880, Adams.

After reading *A Portrait of a Lady:* Clover told her father that the novel arrived by mail, "which the author kindly set me." She did not say whether he had signed the copy. MHA to RWH, December 4, 1881, *LMHA*, 306.

"It's very nice": MHA to RWH, December 4, 1881, *LMHA*, 306. Clover is quoting a quip made by Thomas G. Appleton, a wit and the brother-in-law of Henry Wadsworth Longfellow, about Appleton's spendthrift younger brother, Nathan Jr.

"half disposed to go": MHA to RWH, August 24, 1879, *LMHA*, 169.

"The second act": MHA to RWH, August 31, 1879, *LMHA*, 171.

99   "a huge shop and restaurant": MHA to RWH, December 21, 1879, *LMHA*, 221.

"better horses, better liveries": MHA to RWH, September 21, 1879, *LMHA*, 179.

"We have quiet mornings" . . . "they seem better": MHA to RWH, September 14, 1879, *LMHA*, 178.

"twenty minutes side by side": MHA to RWH, July 27, 1879, *LMHA*, 159.

"one of the seven wonders": As quoted in Hilliard T. Goldfarb, *The Isabella Stewart Gardner Museum: A Companion Guide and History* (New Haven, CT: Yale University Press, 1995), 8.

"gliding walk, like a proud": Margaret (Terry) Winthrop Chanler, *Autumn in the Valley* (Boston: Little, Brown, and Company, 1936), 35.

100   "breeziest woman": *Town Topics*, December 1, 1887, as quoted in Louise Hall Tharp, *Mrs. Jack: A Biography of Isabella Stewart Gardner* (New York: Congdon & Weed, Inc., 1965), 109.

"who were smiling and bowing": MHA to RWH, January 13, 1878, Adams.

Henry James treated Mrs. Jack: See Edel, *The Conquest of London*, esp. 379–82, for a description of this relationship.

"without exception": HA to CMG, October 24, 1879, *Letters*, vol. 2, 379.

"The sun seems to drive out" . . . "soaked in sunshine": MHA to RWH, October 26, 1879, *LMHA*, 192.

"nothing to wish for," MHA to RWH, November 9, 1879, *LMHA*, 199.

"like enormous lighted candles" . . . *Don Quixote:* MHA to RWH, November 9, 1879, *LMHA*, 202.

"poked about for hours": MHA to RWH, November 9, 1879, *LMHA*, 200.

101   "We are having": MHA to RWH, November 15, 1879, *LMHA*, 206.

"ride was almost": HA to Robert Cunliffe, November 21, 1879, *Letters*, vol. 2, 380.

"most enchanting road" . . . "did me no harm": MHA to RWH, November 16, 1879, *LMHA*, 207.

"one lonely tooth" . . . "great satisfaction": MHA to RWH, November 30, 1879, 212–13.

"Bitterly cold": MHA to RWH, December 11, 1879, *LMHA*, 217. The journal *Science* reported that the 1879 winter was one of the most severe "in a century," and the month of December had been the "coldest on record at Paris." "The Winter of 1879–80 in Europe," *Science: An Illustrated Journal Published Weekly*, no. 3 (April 1884): 485.

The newspapers told: "Cold Weather in Paris: Incidents of the Unwonted Experiences of the French Capital," *New York Times,* January 8, 1880.

102 "like a white frost-bitten ball": MHA to RWH, December 28, 1879, *LMHA,* 222.

"Manuscripts are clumsy": HA to Henry Cabot Lodge, December 20, 1879, *Letters,* vol. 2, 387.

"hard all the evening" . . . "blessed archives": MHA to RWH, January 25, 1880, Adams.

"I hate Paris more and more": MHA to RWH, December 21, 1879, *LMHA,* 221–22.

"a full feast" . . . "so much pleasure": MHA to RWH, December 7, 1879, *LMHA,* 215.

"under a big": MHA to RWH, January 25, 1880, Adams.

"the Adamses are here": HJ to Isabella Stewart Gardner, January 29, 1880, *HJ Letters,* vol. 2, 265.

"every detail charming" . . . "peace and plenty": MHA to RWH, February 1, 1880, Adams.

"mountain of papers": HA to Henry Cabot Lodge, December 20, 1879, *Letters,* vol. 2, 387.

103 "no organized surface": HJ to Mary Robertson Walsh James, January 18, 1879, *HJ Letters,* vol. 2, 210.

"gracious and agreeable": MHA to RWH, February 22, 1880, Adams.

"lovely spring day" . . . "side to side": MHA to RWH, February 8, 1880, Adams.

When a "Mrs. Houkey" . . . "show impatience": MHA to RWH, February 15, 1880, Adams. Clover made no other reference to Mrs. Houkey in her letters, and no corroborating information about her could be found.

"social rapids" . . . "proportion of them": MHA to RWH, March 14, 1880, Adams.

104 "intellectual apathy" . . . "belief in himself ": MHA to RWH, April 11, 1880, Adams.

"burst like a bomb shell" . . . "above criticism": MHA to RWH, May 9, 1880, Adams.

"what a gentleman": HA to JH, October 8, 1882, *Letters,* vol. 2, 474.

"fields of wheat" . . . "stories": MHA to RWH, July 11, 1880, Adams.

"one dinner in six" . . . "new impressions": MHA to RWH, July 4, 1880, Adams.

"Of course" . . . "new impressions": MHA to RWH, July 4, 1880, Adams.

105 "If it proves": HA to Henry Cabot Lodge, July 9, 1880, *Letters,* vol. 2, 403.

"air like champagne" . . . "enchanting": MHA to RWH, August 1, 1880, Adams.

"sunny blue day": MHA to APF, August 6, 1880, Hooper-Adams Papers, MHS.

"crimson moors": MHA to RWH, August 8, 1880, Adams.

"My wife is flourishing": HA to CMG, August 12, 1880, *Letters,* vol. 2, 405.

"wandering Americans": MHA to RWH, January 18, 1880, Adams.

106 "People who study Greek": MHA to RWH, December 28, 1879, *LMHA,* 224.

"15, 361 gowns": HA to CMG, September 11, 1880, *Letters,* vol. 2, 407.

"wee little early Turner": MHA to RWH, June 29, 1879, *LMHA,* 149.

"a wide acquaintance": MHA to RWH, August 20, 1880, Adams.

"more we travel": MHA to RWH, November 2, 1879, *LMHA*, 197.

"Our land is gayer-lighter-quicker": MHA to RWH, August 1, 1880, Adams.

"good American *confidents*": HJ to Mary Walsh James, July 6, 1879, *HJ Letters*, vol. 2, 249.

"inveterate discussions" . . . "those of Europe": HJ to Grace Norton, September 20, 1880, *HJ Letters*, vol. 2, 307.

107 "As I don't expect": MHA to RWH, February 8, 1880, Adams.

"pleasant story" . . . "still is new": MHA to RWH, July 25, 1880, Adams.

CHAPTER 10. Intimates Gone

108 "too fashionable": MHS to RWH, August 22, 1880, Adams. Jerome Napoleon, born in 1830, studied at West Point and served in the French Imperial Army until his resignation in 1871, when he returned to America to marry Caroline Appleton Edgar, the daughter of Samuel and Julia Webster Appleton. Caroline was the granddaughter of Daniel Webster.

"My wife is fairly weary": HA to CMG, January 1, 1881, *Letters*, vol. 2, 416.

109 "didn't realize when": MHA to RWH, November 14, 1880, *LMHA*, 232.

"We are really in": MHA to RWH, December 5, 1880, *LMHA*, 240.

"his house charming": MHA to RWH, January 23, 1881, *LMHA*, 260; "Henry hard at work": MHA to RWH, March 27, 1881, *LMHA*, 279.

"The town is filling": MHA to RWH, November 21, 1880, *LMHA*, 234.

"nice old fellow": MHA to RWH, February 13, 1881, *LMHA*, 266.

"air is full of rumours": MHA to RWH, January 9, 1881, *LMHA*, 255.

110 "pretentious": MHA to RWH, May 14, 1882, *LMHA*, 382.

"it's a gross insult": MHA to RWH, January 9, 1881, *LMHA*, 252.

a "thunder-clap": HA to George William Curtis, February 3, 1881, *Letters*, vol. 2, 418.

"For us it will be most awkward": MHA to RWH, January 9, 1881, *LMHA*, 252.

"one must always": MHA to RWH, January 23, 1881, *LMHA*, 259.

origin of this group moniker: Patricia O'Toole speculates that the name may have been inspired by two other "playing card epithets": Wordworth's "the Five of Clubs" and Clarence King's title of "King of Diamonds." *Five of Hearts*, xvi.

111 Hay first met Henry Adams: William Roscoe Thayer, an early biographer of John Hay, writes that no other person "had so profound an influence on Hay; no other kindled in him such a strong and abiding devotion" as Henry Adams. Though "very dissimilar in temperament," Thayer writes, "their tastes bound them to-gether—their tastes, and their delight in each other's differences." Thayer, *The Life and Letters of John Hay*, vol. 2 (Boston: Houghton Mifflin Company, 1915), 54.

"a handsome woman" . . . "for two": MHA to RWH, February 3, 1878, Adams.

"frivolous and solemn": HA to Mary Cadwalader Jones, January 25, 1909, *Letters*, vol. 6, 215.

"really did say things": Theodore Roosevelt reviewed Thayer's biography of

Hay in the *Atlantic Monthly* in 1915. Roosevelt, "W. R. Thayer's 'Life of John Hay,'" *The Harvard Graduates' Magazine,* vol. 24, no. 94 (1915): 258.

"a touch of sadness": John Russell Young, *Men and Memories: Personal Reminiscences,* vol. 2, 454.

"I am inclined": Hay, as quoted in Michael Burlingame, *At Lincoln's Side* (Carbondale, IL: Southern Illinois University Press, 2006), xiv.

"No matter how": Thayer, *John Hay,* vol. 1, 330.

He later fathered: For a riveting excavation of Clarence King's hidden married life with Ada Copeland, see Martha A. Sandweiss, *Passing Strange: A Gilded Age Tale of Love and Deception Across the Color Line* (New York: Penguin Press, 2009).

112   "a miracle" . . . "better than anyone": *Education,* 297–98.

"resembled no one" . . . "wherever he went": John Hay, "Clarence King," in *Clarence King Memoirs: The Helmet of Mambrino,* ed. the Century Association, the King Memorial Committee (New York: G. P. Putnam's Sons, 1904), 131.

"like the sun": MHA to RWH, March 30, 1884, Adams.

"a basket made": MHA to RWH, February 17, 1878, Adams.

"our prop and stay": MHA to RWH, March 6, 1881, *LMHA,* 274.

the "first heart": HA to JH, April 30, 1882, *Letters,* vol. 2, 455.

113   "a good deal of good talk": MHA to RWH, March 27, 1881, *LMHA,* 278. At some point in 1885, King would give the Adamses a china tea service he'd had made, with cups and saucers in the shape of a heart and a likeness of a clock set at five o'clock sharp.

"Is there disease": MHA to RWH, March 14, 1880, Adams.

"too much" for Fanny: MHA to RWH, May 30, 1880, Adams.

"It's nice to hear": MHA to RWH, August 15, 1880, Adams; "It's nice to have": MHA to RWH, August 22, 1880, Adams.

"increased suffering" . . . "do nothing": MHA to RWH, February 23, 1881, *LMHA,* 269–70.

114   "I've been half expecting": MHA to RWH, February 27, 1881, *LMHA,* 270.

"I want to go on": MHA to RWH, February 27, 11:30 A.M., 1881, *LMHA,* 272.

"how Ned's babies": MHA to RWH, March 6, 1881, *LMHA,* 274–75.

"Unless I am really needed": MHA to RWH, March 11, 1881, *LMHA,* 275.

"deep in history": HA to CMG, February 10, 1881, *Letters,* vol. 2, 419.

"of all the experiences in life": HA to CMG, June 14, 1876, *Letters,* vol. 2, 276.

115   her garden, a "patch": MHA to RWH, April 17, 1881, *LMHA,* 283.

"a bone which will take": MHA to RWH, March 27, 1881, *LMHA,* 279.

telling her father: Clover reported on her voracious reading habits. For instance, she urges her father to get Anatole France's new *The Crime of Sylvestre Bonnard* because she thinks it "charming," December 18, 1881, as is William Dean Howells's recent *Dr. Breen's Practice,* January 15, 1882, *LMHA,* 313 and 321.

"It's read, read, read": MHA to RWH, May 15, 1881, *LMHA,* 288.

The Five of Hearts stayed connected: On November 5, 1881, Hay wrote to Clover that he had "a few sheets of paper made for the official correspondence of The Club and send a sample by mail to you today for your approval. The New

York and Cleveland branches will lunch in a few minutes at the Brunswick and will remember the Residency-Branch with affection tempered with due respect." Theodore F. Dwight Papers, MHS.

116 "In this ever-shifting": MHA to RWH, March 6, 1881, *LMHA*, 273.

"One by one": MHA to RWH, March 27, 1881, *LMHA*, 278–79.

CHAPTER 11. "Recesses of Her Own Heart"

117 "I am much amused" . . . "Clarence King and John Hay!": MHA to RWH, December 21, 1880, *LMHA*, 246–47. Though William Roscoe Thayer in his 1915 biography of John Hay would claim that only Henry "possessed the substance, and style" to have written *Democracy*, it would not be until 1920, two years after Henry's death, that the publisher, Henry Holt, confirmed his authorship.

"except the authorship" . . . "thought of it before": JH to HA, September 17, 1882, Theodore F. Dwight Papers, MHS.

118 "Much as I disapprove": HA to John Hay, October 8, 1882, *Letters*, vol. 2, 474.

"bent upon getting": *Democracy*, 7. Ernest Samuels rightly states that Madeleine's investigation "in its imaginative way" was a "very modest forerunner of *The Education*, a kind of interim report preceding by a quarter of a century the definitive one." *Middle Years*, 70.

"witty, cynical" banter: *Democracy*, 23.

"babbled like the winds": *Democracy*, 55.

"horrid, nasty, vulgar": MHA to RWH, January 31, 1882, *LMHA*, 339.

119 "good enough to make it": HJ as quoted in Edel, *The Conquest of London*, 376. The 1880 review in *The Nation* said that the "main difficulty is that it attempts too much." Review reprinted in *LMHA*, 484. R. P. Blackmur argues that the frame of action in *Democracy* is half "Grimm fairy-tale" and half "Oscar Wilde Comedy," with neither frame completely convincing. Blackmur, "The Novels of Henry Adams," *The Sewanee Review*, vol. 51, no. 2 (1943): 288.

"superficial and rotten": Theodore Roosevelt to Henry Cabot Lodge, September 2, 1905, *Selections from the Correspondence of Theodore Roosevelt and Henry Cabot Lodge* (New York: Scribner's, 1925), vol. 2, 189.

"a favorite haunt": *Democracy*, 5.

"to the tips of her fingers": *Democracy*, 164.

"gave her unchristian feelings": *Democracy*, 11.

like something Clover would say: Clover's Aunt Caroline Sturgis Tappan also suspected her niece was the author. MHA to RWH, February 14, 1882, *LMHA*, 339.

"religious sentiment" . . . "self-abnegation": *Democracy*, 99.

"not known the recesses" . . . "outside the household?": *Democracy*, 182.

120 "A weekly instalment": HA to Justin Winsor, June 6, 1881, *Letters*, vol. 2, 428.

"the social and economical": HA to Justin Winsor, September 27, 1881, *Letters*, vol. 2, 438. The letter enumerates Henry's key interests: "I want to find out how much banking capital there was in the U.S. in 1800, and how it was managed. I want a strictly accurate account of the state of education, and of the practice of medicine. I want a *good* sermon of that date, if such a thing existed, for I cannot find one which seems to me even tolerable, from a literary or logical point of view."

"my eyes ache": HA to CMG, July 9, 1881, *Letters,* vol. 2, 429. HA published *John Randolph* in 1882 and immediately wrote a draft biography of Aaron Burr that, for whatever reason, was never published.

"to their doll cemetery": MHA to APF, May 30, 1881, Hooper-Adams Papers, MHS.

121   "We found the house": MHA to APF, October 28, 1881, Hooper-Adams Papers, MHS.

"road to Damascus": MHA to RWH, December 18, 1881, *LMHA,* 312.

"make all one can": MHA to RWH, January 1, 1882, *LMHA,* 319.

"life is like a prolonged circus" . . . "Medicus": MHA to RWH, January 26, 1882, *LMHA,* 334.

"I really was so driven": MHA to RWH, January 30, 1882, *LMHA,* 334.

"beware of 'partisan' politics": MHA to RWH, February 12, 1882, *LMHA,* 345.

122   "a fatuous fool" . . . "wild toot": MHA to RWH, January 31, 1882, *LMHA,* 338.

"we shall at this rate": MHA to RWH, January 15, 1882, *LMHA,* 321.

"a lady's handwriting": MHA to RWH, January 31, 1882, *LMHA,* 339–40.

"Sir Joshua's pretty": MHA to RWH, June 18, 1873, *LMHA,* 120.

"They are not *first*-rate" . . . "very large": MHA to RWH, January 31, 1882, *LMHA,* 339–41. *Paysages* is French for "landscapes."

123   Mr. and Mrs. Groves: Thomas Woolner to MHA, April 9, 1882, Theodore F. Dwight Papers, MHS.

"genuine Sir Joshuas" . . . "look the other way": MHA to RWH, February 14, 1882, *LMHA,* 348–49. The provenance information in a 1999 catalogue for a Christie's auction reads: "According to Galloway family tradition, [Samuel] Galloway and [Sylvanus] Groves agreed to exchange portraits of themselves and their wives; by descent to Mrs. Anne Sarah Hughes, great-granddaughter of Samuel Galloway, 1877, who took them to Washington and sold them in 1882 to Mrs. Henry Adams . . . Exhibited: Philadelphia, 1876 (Mr. Groves 1093, Mrs. Groves 1094, both lent by Mrs. A. S. Hughes)." *Christie's Important Old Master Paintings,* Auction 29 January 1999, New York, New York (London: Christie, Mason, and Wood, 1999). See also David Mannings, *Sir Joshua Reynolds: A Complete Catalogue of His Paintings, Text, and Plates* (New Haven, CT: Yale University Press, 2000), 171, 229–30.

she found herself feeling drained: In one letter that Clover wrote to her father that spring, she said, "I'm as sleepy as a cat this Sunday morning and as stupid as an owl, so you'll have a sorry letter." MHA to RWH, March 5, 1882, *LMHA,* 358. She concluded another by apologizing that "my mind is as dry as a biscuit today." MHA to RWH, April 2, 1882, *LMHA,* 370.

"an unwise appointment": MHA to RWH, March 12, 1882, *LMHA,* 364.

"had nearly died": HA to CMG, May 2, 1882, *Letters,* vol. 2, 454.

"in these 'bare ruined choirs'": MHA to APF, March 12, 1882, Hooper-Adams Papers, MHS.

"Every fool becomes": MHA to RWH, May 14, 1882, *LMHA,* 382.

"during the months when colic": MHA to APF, June 19, 1882, Hooper-Adams Papers, MHS.

"nightly toothache": MHA to RWH, October 29, 1882, *LMHA,* 394.

"It's quieter here": MHA to APF, July 11, 1882, Hooper-Adams Papers, MHS.

124 "nothing . . . disturbs history": HA to CMG, June 25, 1882, *Letters,* vol. 2, 461.

"bored by our summer": HA to Sir Robert Cunliffe, November 12, 1882, *Letters,* vol. 2, 478.

("like Boston") . . . "tooth finished": MHA to RWH, November 26, 1882, *LMHA,* 403.

"an explicit account": Henry James, *French Poets and Novelists* (London: Macmillan and Co., 1884), 154.

"glad you're reading": MHA to RWH, December 24, 1882, *LMHA,* 410.

"How are you getting on": MHA to RWH, December 31, 1882, *LMHA,* 412.

"bravely acted out": Margaret Fuller wrote of George Sand that she needed "no defense, but only to be understood, for she has bravely acted out her nature." Margaret Fuller, *Memoirs of Margaret Fuller Ossoli,* vol. 2 (Boston: Phillips, Sampson and Co., 1852), 197.

125 "open to *all* experiences": James, *French Poets and Novelists,* 173.

"left out on the whole": James, as quoted in Leon Edel, *Henry James: The Middle Years, 1882–1895* (Philadelphia: J. B. Lippincott Company, 1962), 169.

As much as she found tending: See Anna Howard Shaw and Elizabeth Garver Jordan, *The Story of a Pioneer* (New York: Harper & Brothers, 1915), 154, who write: "Of Abby May and Edna[h] Cheney I retain a general impression of 'bagginess' — of loose jackets over loose waistbands, of escaping locks of hair, of bodies seemingly one size from the neck down. Both women were utterly indifferent to the details of their appearance, but they were splendid workers and leading spirits in the New England Woman's Club."

"Porcupinus Angelicus": John Hay to Augustus Saint-Gaudens, April 12, 1905, as quoted in Thayer, *The Life of John Hay,* vol. 2, 60–61.

126 He said one should treat: Abigail Adams Homans, Henry's niece, remembered that Henry used to express this sentiment. HA-CK Papers.

CHAPTER 12. The Sixth Heart

127 "I make it a rule": HA to CMG, December 3, 1882, *Letters,* vol. 2, 484.

"Birds of Paradise": HA to CMG, May 18, 1884, *Letters,* vol. 2, 540.

128 "Then hate me when thou wilt": Stephen Booth, ed., *Shakespeare's Sonnets* (New Haven, CT: Yale University Press, 1977), 79.

"interlined with purple hills" . . . "nicest men in town": MHA to APF, February

21, 1883, Hooper-Adams Papers, MHS. On Langtry, see HA to Sir Robert Cunliffe, November 12, 1882, *Letters*, vol. 2, 478.

129 "a strong face" . . . "35 cents": From Harold Dean Cater's notes taken on March 15 and 16, 1945, for his book *Henry Adams and His Friends*, published by Houghton Mifflin Company in 1947. HA-CK Papers. Cater interviewed Lady Elizabeth Lindsay, the second wife of Sir Ronald Lindsay, who had first married Elizabeth Cameron's only daughter, Martha, in 1909.

Photographs taken of her: There are five portrait photographs of Elizabeth Cameron taken by Frances Benjamin Johnston archived at the Library of Congress; none are dated. Library of Congress, Prints & Photographs Division, LC–USZ62–124320–124322, LC–USZ62–1891, LC–USZ62–88494.

"a dangerously fascinating": As quoted in Arline Boucher Tehan, *Henry Adams in Love: The Pursuit of Elizabeth Sherman Cameron* (New York: Universe Books, 1983), 10. Tehan does not name this source.

"as fresh and beautiful as ever": Sherman, quoted in Tehan, *Henry Adams in Love*, 19.

"Beauty and the Beast": As quoted in Tehan, *Henry Adams in Love*, 29.

130 They'd rap their umbrellas: MHA to RWH, October 30, 1881, *LMHA*, 294.

"Miss Beale and Mrs. Don Cameron": MHA to RWH, November 6, 1881, *LMHA*, 296.

"If it were not": HA to JH, March 4, 1883, *Letters*, vol. 2, 494.

"I adore her". . . "show *her* kindness": HA to JH, April 8, 1883, *Letters*, vol. 2, 497.

"my dear little friend": HA to CMG, June 10, 1883, *Letters*, vol. 2, 505; "She is still very young" . . . "as I have": HA to James Russell Lowell, May 15, 1883, *Letters*, vol. 2, 500–501.

131 "Our feelings overcame us": HA to EC, May 18, 1883, *Letters*, vol. 2, 501.

"tea every day": MHA to RWH, November 6, 1881, *LMHA*, 296.

"a somewhat ghastly tea": MHA to RWH, March 18, 1883, *LMHA*, 430.

"We've had no gaiety": MHA to RWH, April 1, 1883, *LMHA*, 435.

"a greater grief": Eleanor Shattuck Whiteside to Mrs. George C. Shattuck, October 26, 1886, George Cheyne Shattuck Papers, MHS.

132 "So give me a marriage": MHA to RWH, May 6, 1883, *LMHA*, 447.

"not laughed since you went": MHA to APF, February 8, 1883, Hooper-Adams Papers, MHS.

"and so on & so on" . . . "test his affection": MHA to APF, April 6, 1883, Hooper-Adams Papers, MHS.

"various artists": MHA to RWH, April 8, 1883, *LMHA*, 437.

"very poor" . . . "Philadelphia artist": MHA to RWH, April 15, 1883, *LMHA*, 438.

133 "five pretty" . . . "of attention": "The Society of Artists: Some of the Features of Its Sixth Annual Exhibit," April 8, 1883, *New York Times*.

"pretty and nice" . . . "costume": MHA to RWH, April 15, 1883, *LMHA*, 440.

"The dogs are well": HA to MHA, April 10, 1883, Homans Collection, MHS.

"Henry says he's glad": MHA to RWH, April 15, 1883, *LMHA,* 441.

"my husband": MHA to APF, April 21, 1882, Hooper-Adams Papers, MHS.

"A blessed rain": MHA to RWH, April 22, 1883, *LMHA,* 441.

"It has taken me one week": MHA to APF, April 21, 1883, Hooper-Adams Papers, MHS.

"I long to see": MHA to APF, September 8, 1882, Hooper-Adams Papers, MHS.

134 "nothing but photography": HA to EC, June 26, 1883, *Letters,* vol. 2, 507.

Part III: Clover's Camera

135 "Isn't it odd": Virginia Woolf to Vita Sackville-West, December 25, 1935, *The Letters of Virginia Woolf, 1932–1935,* vol. 5, ed. Nigel Nicolson and Joanne Trautman (New York: Harcourt Brace Jovanovich, 1979), 455.

CHAPTER 13. Something New

137 "We've been riding": MHA to RWH, May 6, 1883, *LMHA,* 446.

"How I wish": MHA to RWH, May 6, 1883, *LMHA,* 446.

"great success" . . . "distance": MHA to RWH, May 13, 1883, *LMHA,* 448–49.

138 "Mr. Pumpelly to tea": MHA to RWH, April 22, 1883, *LMHA,* 442.

The two prints she saved: MHA, May 6, 1883, album #8, 50.50 and 50.51. Marion Langdon was the daughter of Harriett Lowndes Langdon, whose second husband, Philip Schuyler, was a friend to the Adamses. Clover thought her a "perfect beauty." MHA to RWH, March 18, 1883, *LMHA,* 432.

"politics is at the bottom": MHA to RWH, April 1, 1883, *LMHA,* 436.

"as a 'dude'" . . . "not print": MHA to RWH, May 27, 1883, *LMHA,* 451–52.

139 "new machine": MHA to RWH, May 20, 1883, *LMHA,* 451.

Photography itself: *The Philadelphia Photographer* noted in 1882 the rapid growth of amateur photography in this country. The process has been going on for a number of years, but not to any very great extent until, say, within the last year. A great impetus was given to it, of course, by the ability on the part of manufacturers to produce a first-class emulsion plate; and when it was made known by manufacturers of apparatus that such a plate existed, and that apparatus could be had at a reasonable price, the thing took amazingly." *The Philadelphia Photographer,* vol. 19, no. 228 (December 1882): 371. Clover may have used wet plates at first. Of the seven glass negatives at the MHS, three are clearly made by Clover—one of a woman at the beach, which Clover made a print of and put in her album, and two of Henry, one of which she included in her album. The other four glass-plate negatives, three of landscapes and one of a figure in the doorway of a small house, may have been taken by Clover. On four a thumbprint is clearly visible in the upper left-hand corner of the plate, where it had been gripped while being doused with light-sensitive chemicals. Marian Hooper Adams Glass-Plate Negatives, Photo collection 6.2M, MHS.

"have always been employed in": Margaret Bisland, "Women and Their Cameras," *Outing: An Illustrated Monthly Magazine of Recreation,* vol. 17 (October 1890): 38.

140   "amateur photography": Henry Clay Price, *How to Make Pictures: Easy Lessons for the Amateur Photographer* (New York: Scovill Manufacturing Co., 1882), 66. The distinction between amateur and professional photographers has a complicated history that involves economic class, roles of men and women, debates about science, and changing art markets. See especially Jennifer Green-Lewis, *Framing the Victorians: Photography and the Culture of Realism* (Ithaca, NY: Cornell University Press, 1996); Paul Spencer Sternberger, *Between Amateur and Aesthete: The Legitimization of Photography as Art in America, 1880–1900* (Albuquerque: University of New Mexico Press, 2001); Melissa Banta, *A Curious and Ingenious Art: Reflections on Daguerreotypes at Harvard* (Iowa City: University of Iowa Press, 2000). For a history of photography and women after 1885, see Suzanne L. Flynt, *The Allen Sisters: Pictorial Photographers, 1885–1920* (Hanover, NH: University Press of New England, 2002); and *Trading Gazes: Euro-American Women Photographers and Native Americans, 1880–1940,* ed. Susan Bernardin, Melody Graulich, Lisa MacFarlane, and Nicole Tonkovich (New Brunswick, NJ: Rutgers University Press, 2003).

"those whom we love": Oliver Wendell Holmes, "Sun-Painting and Sun-Sculpture; with a Stereoscopic Trip Across the Atlantic," *Atlantic Monthly,* vol. 8, no. 45 (July 1861): 13–29.

"absent loved ones": Mrs. Henry Mackarness, *The Young Lady's Book: A Manual of Amusements, Exercises, Studies, and Pursuits,* 4th ed. (London: George Routledge and Sons, 1888), 214. An earlier edition was published in 1876.

"assist in the ordering": John Ruskin, *Sesame and Lilies* (New York: Wiley, 1886), 137. Kirsten Swinth argues that the link between the arts, refinement, and a woman's social duty intensified in America after the Civil War, as an increasingly industrialized economy seemed to coarsen an earlier vision of American life. "Women began to include the protection and cultivation of art and culture among their duties." Swinth, *Painting Professionals,* 17. See also Erin L. Pipkin, "'Striking in Its Promise': The Artistic Career of Sarah Gooll Putnam," *The Massachusetts Historical Review,* vol. 3 (2001); Erica E. Hirshler, *A Studio of Her Own: Women Artists in Boston, 1870–1940* (Boston: MFA Publications, 2001); Sarah Burns, *Inventing the Modern Artist: Art and Culture in the Gilded Age* (New Haven, CT: Yale University Press, 1996). For a history of the aesthetic movement, popular during the 1870s and 1880s, see Mary Warner Blanchard, *Oscar Wilde's America: Counterculture in the Gilded Age* (New Haven, CT: Yale University Press, 1998); and Roger B. Stein, "Artifact as Ideology: The Aesthetic Movement in Its American Cultural Context," in *In the Pursuit of Beauty: Americans and the Aesthetic Movement* (New York: The Metropolitan Museum of Art, Rizzoli, 1986).

141   It would take Alfred Stieglitz: For a discussion of *Camera Work* and the Little Gal-

leries of the Photo-Secession located at 291 Fifth Avenue, better known simply as 291, see Katherine Hoffman, *Stieglitz: A Beginning Light* (New Haven, CT: Yale University Press, 2004), 213–32.

"There has been some discussion": *The Photographic Times and American Photographer,* vol. 13, no. 149 (May 1883): 207. A photography equipment salesman went further, observing that "the mechanical part of Photography, with modern Dry Plates, is very easily acquired, and presents no serious difficulties to any. It is practiced by very many ladies all over the country . . . It promotes digestion, gives one a taste for healthy exercise." *A Classified and Illustrated Price-List of Photographic Cameras, Lenses, and Other Apparatus and Materials for the Use of Amateur Photographers* (Philadelphia: W. H. Walmsley & Co., 1884), 4.

"a new and small machine": MHA to APF, June 2, 1883, Hooper-Adams Papers, MHS.

The photography manual: Captain W. De Wiveleslie Abney, *A Treatise on Photography* (New York: D. Appleton and Co., 1878).

142   "as soon as the self": Edward Mendelson, *The Things That Matter: What Seven Classic Novels Have to Say About the Stages of Life* (New York: Pantheon Books, 2006), 219.

CHAPTER 14. At Sea

143   "No society this week": MHA to RWH, May 27, 1883, *LMHA,* 452.

"beautiful and swift": MHA to EC, July 26, 1883, Adams.

Henry, four years into: See Edel, *Middle Years,* 221.

"You can never tell what you want": HA to Daniel C. Gilman, March 2, 1883, *Letters,* vol. 2, 493.

"the thermometer": HA to CMG, June 10, 1883, *Letters,* vol. 2, 504.

144   beloved English watercolors: Henry listed this catalogue of artists, writing that they took the art "with us from town every summer." HA to Robert Cunliffe, August 31, 1875, *Letters,* vol. 2, 234.

"On Friday" . . . "tea at 8": MHA to APF, July 23, 1883, Hooper-Adams Papers, MHS.

"husband is working": MHA to EC, July 26, 1883, Adams.

"I've gone in for photography": MHA to Clara Hay, September 7, 1883, Adams.

photographed Pitch Pine Hill: MHA, n.d., album #8, 50.56.

145   three of her older nieces: MHA, August 19, 1883, album #8, 50.75.

The image links: See Erica E. Hirshler, *Sargent's Daughters: The Biography of a Painting* (Boston: MFA Publications, 2009).

Francis Parkman, the American historian: MHA, July 29, 1883, album #8, 50.58 and 50.59. Parkman was in the midst of writing his multivolume work *France and England in North America,* which confirmed his reputation as a leading American historian.

146   "disbelieves in democracy": MHA to RWH, February 24, 1878, Adams.

"ideal woman" in America: MHA to RWH, November 30, 1879, *LMHA,* 213.

photographed Henry's youngest brother: MHA, July 30, 1883, album #8, 50.61.

portrait of Mr. and Mrs. Adams: MHA, July 30, 1883, album #8, 50.60.

147   Mrs. James Scott at Manchester Beach: MHA, August 8, 1883, album #8, 50.63 and 50.64. The beach got its current name—not in wide circulation until the 1890s—because walking across its white sand produces a singing sound. Sarah Cash, "Singing Beach, Manchester: Four Newly Identified Paintings of the North Shore of Massachusetts by Martin Johnson Heade," *American Art Journal,* vol. 27, no. 1/2 (1995–96): 95.

148   This view of the beach: This view was painted by Homer in his 1870 work *Eagle Head, Manchester, Massachusetts (High Tide)* as well as by the American luminist painters Martin Johnson Heade and John Frederick Kensett. Kathleen Motes Bennewitz, "John F. Kensett at Beverly, Massachusetts," *American Art Journal,* vol. 21, no. 4 (Winter 1989): 46–65; Cash, "Singing Beach, Manchester: Four Newly Identified Paintings of the North Shore of Massachusetts by Martin Johnson Heade," 84–98.

Helen Choate Bell: MHA, August 8, 1883, album #8, 50.66.

"infinite longing": E.T.A. Hoffman wrote in 1813 that Beethoven's music "sets in motion the lever of fear, of awe, of horror, of suffering, and awakens just that infinite longing which is the essence of romanticism." Hoffman, "Beethoven's Instrumental Music," in *Source Readings in Music History,* ed. Oliver Strunk (New York: W. W. Norton, 1950), 775.

149   "turned-away figures": The *Rückenfigur,* according to Joseph Leo Koerner, is a figure in the landscape that is turned away from the viewer but which locates the viewer within the landscape, and "functions to infuse Friedrich's art with a heightened subjectivity, and to characterize what we see as already the consequence of a prior experience." The viewer sees what the turned-away figure sees, but always from a distance behind, as if arriving late to the scene. This is part of how Friedrich's paintings produce both identification of the viewer with the scene and a simultaneous estrangement from it, and thus the experience of a terrible Romantic longing. Koerner lists key elements of Romanticism, including "a heightened sensitivity to the natural world . . . ; a passion for the equivocal, the indeterminate, the obscure and faraway . . . ; a nebulous but all-pervading mysticism; and a melancholy, sentimental longing." Koerner, *Caspar David Friedrich and the Subject of Landscape* (New Haven, CT: Yale University Press, 1990), 23, 28.

Though Clover never stated: On her honeymoon, Clover had written to her father that they'd visited Dresden's famed picture gallery. She remarked that "one-tenth part [of the museum] would be enough to try and take in." MHA to Robert Hooper, September 8, 1872, *LMHA,* 36. The gallery catalog published in 1873 lists two paintings by Friedrich, one of which is the well-known 1819 painting of two travelers, with their backs positioned to the viewer, entitled *Two Men Contemplating the Crescent.* His paintings hung in the "modern" gallery. *Complete Catalogue of the Royal Picture Gallery at Dresden* (R. v. Zahn: G. Schonfeld's

Buchhandlung, 1873). Clover was conversant in the history of art, having used Horace Walpole's four-volume *Anecdotes of Painting in England* as a reference while she and Henry amassed their own art collection; she also owned copies of Richard Redgrave's *Century of Painters in the English School* (1866) and Taine's *Philosophy of Art* (1865) and *On the Ideal in Art* (1867). She requested a copy of Walpole's book from Theodore Dwight, Henry's private secretary. MHA to Theodore Dwight, February 3, 1882, Theodore F. Dwight Papers, MHS.

beautifully composed photograph: MHA, August 8, 1883, album #8, 50.65.

"It was charming": MHA to RWH, February 27, 1881, *LMHA*, 272.

CHAPTER 15. *Esther*

151 She photographed Betsey: MHA, August 10, 1883, album #8, 50.67.

She paired a print: MHA, August 10, 1883, album #8, 50.68.

In this second image: MHA, August 10, 1883, album #8, 50.69.

Later in the summer: Clover also took four exposures of Henry in his study at Pitch Pine Hill on August 13, but judged these either "over-timed" or "too dim" to make prints from the negatives.

152 seated Henry at his desk: MHA, August 19, 1883, album #8, 50.71.

The neatly stacked papers: Henry told Lizzie Cameron in late July that he had to correct proof sheets. He was privately printing the first three books of his *History*, both for comments from readers and for safekeeping.

in the next exposure: MHA, August 19, 1883, album #8, 50.52.

Instead, Clover chose: MHA, August 26, 1883, album #8, 50.53 and 50.72. The portrait of Henry, in his light coat, followed by a picture of the umbrella tree, comes first in album #8. Sixteen photographs later, the portrait of Henry in his dark coat is paired in the album with another picture of the same umbrella tree. Clover's August 26 entry in her notebook reads: "August 26 'Umbrella' tree Smith's Pt—large stop—1 second—good—same tree other side 2 sec."

"You judge me": Abigail B. Adams to CFA, December 13, 1876, Adams; "You can't understand": Abigail B. Adams to CFA, April 6, 1877, Adams.

153 "was audacious only": *Esther*, 38.

Part of what Henry did: Ernest Samuels cautions readers to "be wary of treating *Esther* too exclusively as a symbol of his marriage," contending that the "extraordinary emotional fetish that he attached to the book" should not be confused with his state of mind and feeling while writing. *Middle Years*, 225–26. O'Toole, by contrast, sees the novel as Henry's commentary on his marriage, concluding that "in spite of the Adamses' closeness and compatibility, there remained a gap they longed to close." *The Five of Hearts*, 139. But neither of these authors makes explicit note of the connection between Henry writing *Esther* and Clover taking photographs.

"She has a bad figure": *Esther*, 17. Lisa MacFarlane compares Henry's description of Clover during his engagement to his description of Esther in her excellent introduction to the novel.

"hold my tongue or pretend": *Esther*, 128.

"regret at having exposed": CK to JH, July 4, 1886, Clarence King Papers, MHS.

154   But Clover knew: Samuels cites a conversation with Louisa Hooper Thoron, Clover's niece, who "was confident her aunt read the novel." *Middle Years*, 460.

"Poor Esther!": *Esther*, 25.

"You were and are": *Esther*, 7.

"fresh as a summer's morning": *Esther*, 27.

Wharton's battles: See Lisa MacFarlane, *Esther*, xviii, and *Middle Years*, 242–43.

155   "embodied doctrines": William Roscoe Thayer, quoted in *Middle Years*, 237. Patricia O'Toole argues that "the novel reveals less of the author's concern for the relation of man and God than his lifelong perplexity over the relation of man and woman." *Five of Hearts*, 137.

"languid, weary, listless": *Esther*, 89–90.

"saturated with the elixir": *Esther*, 96.

"Some people are made": *Esther*, 159.

"are one" and she is honest: *Esther*, 161.

"in mid-ocean": *Esther*, 17.

156   "a little depressed" . . . "women can't": *Esther*, 67.

"she is only a second-rate": *Esther*, 17.

"I am going home": *Esther*, 70.

"I am almost the last": *Esther*, 131.

"The sea is capricious": *Esther*, 143–44.

157   "Women must take their chance": *Esther*, 25.

"Do you know how": *Esther*, 132.

"in mid-ocean": *Esther*, 17.

"we being chilly folks": MHA to Clara Hay, September 7, 1883, Adams.

"remotest of existences" . . . "droll couple": HA to CMG, September 9, 1883, *Letters*, vol. 2, 510.

158   "cannot deal with": HA to JH, September 24, 1883, *Letters*, vol. 2, 513.

But though Henry Adams: Lisa MacFarlane argues that *Esther* is a hodge-podge of narrative conventions, combining a "roman à clef with a romance, a failed Bildungsroman with a short course in the classics of Western tradition, a novelized debate with an autobiographical confession." *Esther*, vii.

Not surprisingly, the book sold: For a publishing history of the novel, see MacFarlane, *Esther*, viii–x.

"of course" . . . "I could not suggest it": CK to John Hay, July 4, 1886, Clarence King Papers, MHS.

his own "heart's blood": HA to John Hay, August 22, 1886, *Letters*, vol. 3, 34.

CHAPTER 16. Iron Bars

160   "most cordial": MHA to RWH, October 23, 1883, Adams.

photograph of the dining room: MHA, October 24, 1883, album #8, 50.89.

the youngest, Alice Hay: MHA, October 24, 1883, album #8, 50.90.

161 To take their portrait: MHA, October 24, 1883, album #8, 50.91 and 50.92.

could take "views": *The Photographic Times and American Photographer,* vol. 13, no. 145 (January 1883): 658. Meetings were held "on the first Monday of each month," when an essay was read or "a demonstration made relating to and illustrative of photographic art." In addition, "each member contributes monthly a specimen of his work by him exposed, developed, toned, and printed."

"Mrs. Henry Adams is also": *Washington Post,* November 11, 1883.

"two good morning hours": MHA to RWH, November 11, 1883, Adams.

"The children are puffed up": JH to HA, December 7, 1883, Theodore F. Dwight Papers, MHS.

"came to dine Monday": MHA to RWH, December 2, 1883, Adams.

he sits in a chair: MHA, November 27, 1883, album #7, 50.5.

In the second exposure: MHA, November 27, 1883, album #7, 50.6.

162 "I sit all day after": JH to HA, December 26, 1883, Theodore F. Dwight Papers, MHS.

revered American historian: MHA, November 28, 1883, album #7, 50.7.

"Mr. Bancroft is very good": MHA to RWH, December 2, 1883, Adams.

"Mrs. Henry Adams has made": JH to Richard Gilder, December 29, 1883, in *Letters of John Hay and Extracts from Diary,* vol. 2 (Washington, DC: printed not published, copyright Clara Hay), 86–87.

"Please give this": JH to HA, January 3, 1884, Theodore F. Dwight Papers, MHS.

"was amused" . . . "to go with it": MHA to RWH, January 6, 1884, Adams.

163 "Mutual Admiration" . . . "shaping and directing": Howells, as quoted in Rob Davidson, *The Master and the Dean: The Literary Criticism of Henry James and William Dean Howells* (Columbia: University of Missouri Press, 2005), 49. Henry James felt flattered when he first read William Dean Howells's approbation of his fiction in the November 1882 issue of *Century* magazine. But the response of the press, first by London papers and then by other publications, discomfited James, who called it a "truly idiotic commotion." HJ to G. W. Smalley, February 21, 1883, *HJ Letters,* vol. 2, 406.

"I've just written": MHA to RWH, January 6, 1884, Adams.

"We have declined": HA to JH, January 6, 1884, *Letters,* vol. 2, 527.

In rejecting Gilder's offer: Barry Maine argues that Henry abhorred publicity in all its forms in his "Portraits & Privacy: Henry Adams and John Singer Sargent," *Henry Adams and the Need to Know,* ed. William Merrill Decker and Earl N. Harbert (Boston: published by the Massachusetts Historical Society; distributed by the University of Virginia Press, Charlottesville, 2005), 185–86.

"a vile gang": HA to CMG, August 18, 1874, *Letters,* vol. 2, 204. Henry had on his bookshelf Horace Bushnell's *Women's Suffrage: The Reform Against Nature* (New York: Charles Scribner, 1869), which argued that men and women were "unlike in kind" (49). In Bushnell's paternalistic view, women were spiritually superior to men, but grossly unfit for political equality. Suffrage was an "abyss" where a woman "ceases so far to be woman at all" (161).

His only public lecture: The lecture Henry gave at the Lowell Institute on December 9, 1876, was titled "Women's Rights in Primitive History," which he changed to "Primitive Rights of Women" for publication in his book *Historical Essays* (New York: Scribner's, 1891); David Partenheimer notes that the essay "is an elaborate weave of Adams's studies in and engagement with legal history, ethnology, and literary studies." Partenheimer, "Henry Adams's 'Primitive Rights of Women': An Offense Against Church, the Patriarchal State, Progressive Evolution, and the Women's Liberation Movement," *The New England Quarterly*, vol. 71, no. 4 (1998): 635.

164 Equality was based: Ernest Samuels praised Henry for realizing that the "degradation of women grew out of convenient myth . . . As a descendant of Abigail Adams," he knew "woman's capacity for greatness within her sphere." Samuels, *The Young Henry Adams*, 261.

Henry failed to recognize: John C. Orr cites certain polarities in Western thinking as a key to Henry's patterns of thought: "Unity and multiplicity, female and male, body and mind, intuition and reason." According to Orr, Henry's thinking "rotated around these oppositions, and while as with any thinker, he occasionally contradicted himself, on the whole he remained remarkably true to this severe split." Orr, "'I Measured Her as They Did with Pigs': Henry Adams as Other," in *Henry Adams and the Need to Know*, 281.

"The woman's difficulty": HA to Mabel Hooper, May 28, 1898, *Letters*, vol. 4, 596. In this letter to Mabel Hooper, who had embarked on a serious artistic career, Henry tried once more to sort out his thoughts about women. His earlier pessimism, as expressed in *Esther*, had by this time settled into an even starker view: "Women go shipwreck, in ninety-nine cases out of a hundred, from two causes: one is that they cannot hold their tongues; the other is that they cannot run in harness with each other." Instead, he determined that "the woman is made to go with the man," but that "the better [women] are, the purer in character and higher in tone, the more domestic in tastes, and the more irreproachable in life, the more impossible they are with each other." Then he made his diagnosis: "It is the feminine instinct which lies at the bottom of the tangle, and a woman, before thirty, has so little experience of her own instincts that she may be regarded as a child. When she loves, when she hates, when she is jealous, she does not know it until someone tells her, — and then she is furiously angry at being told, and won't believe it. Of course in that respect we are all fools, more or less. The woman's difficulty is that she is fooled by her instincts and her sentiments which are at the same time her only advantages over the man."

"send me photos": MHA to APF, December 24, 1884, Hooper-Adams Papers, MHS.

She also learned about: William Willis, an Englishman, invented the platinum printing process in 1873. The prints "were made on paper impregnated, rather than coated, with light-sensitive chemicals — in this case compounds of iron rather than silver . . . The intense black colour of platinum formed in this way gave the shadows a very rich tone, while the lighter greys had an almost silvery tone." The process also gained a reputation for how little the image deteriorated over time — Clover's platinum prints remain pristine, as if taken yesterday. Brian Coe and Mark Haworth-Booth, *A Guide to Early Photographic Processes* (London: Victoria and Albert Museum, in association with Hurtwood Press, 1983), 80.

"photograph rooms" . . . "only woman": MHA to RWH, December 31, 1883, Adams.

165 "science pure and simple": MHA to RWH, December 31, 1883, Adams.

"My facts are facts": MHA to RWH, November 13, 1881, *LMHA*, 301.

"thin, wiry, one-stringed": HA to Sir Robert Cunliffe, August 31, 1875, *Letters*, vol. 2, 235.

"What is the use": *Esther*, 70.

CHAPTER 17. A New Home

166 "unmanageable" . . ."wag their tails": MHA to RWH, December 16, 1883, Adams.

167 "[John] Hay has bought": MHA to RWH, December 16, 1883, Adams.

"⅓ the price" . . . "73,800": Marc Friedlander, "Henry Hobson Richardson, Henry Adams, and John Hay," *The Journal of the Society of Architectural Historians*, vol. 29, no. 3 (October 1970): 235.

"put up a modest": MHA to APF, December 24, 1883, Hooper-Adams Papers, MHS.

"dark and untenable" . . . $27,000 in her trust: MHA to RWH, December 16, 1883, Adams.

"no more jewelry": MHA to RWH, December 23, 1883, Adams.

"one definite part" . . . "improvements": MHA to RWH, December 26, 1883, Adams.

No other architect: For a discussion of Richardson's career as an architect, see *H. H. Richardson: The Architect, His Peers, and Their Era*, ed. Maureen Meister (Cambridge, MA: MIT Press, 1999).

168 "Richardson was the grand": Frank Lloyd Wright, as quoted by Kathleen A. Curran in "Architect: Henry Hobson Richardson (Gambrill & Richardson)," in *The Makers of Trinity Church in the City of Boston*, ed. James F. O'Gorman (Boston: University of Massachusetts Press, 2004), 61.

"quiet and monumental": James O'Gorman, quoted in Thomas C. Hubka, "H. H. Richardson's Glessner House: A Garden in the Machine," *Winterthur Portfolio*, vol. 24, no. 4 (Winter 1989): 218.

"How I wish I could": MHA to RWH, April 13, 1883, Adams.

"Tomorrow your lamp": H. H. Richardson to HA, February 17, 1883, Theodore F. Dwight Papers, MHS.

"He would charm": Charles A. Coolidge, "Henry Hobson Richardson," in *Later Years of the Saturday Club*, 193.

whom he "valued": *Education*, 65.

169 "can say truly": MHA to RWH, May 7, 1882, *LMHA*, 379. Richardson's out-

sized personality proved at times a trial for his clients. In late January 1883, eight months before his brick mansion was completed, General Anderson complained to his son Larz that Richardson, who had stayed with them several days at their temporary Lafayette Square address, had been "a great deal of trouble. He bullies and nags everybody; makes great demands upon our time and service; must ride, even if he has to go but a square; gets up at noon; has to have his meals sent to his room. He is a mournful object for size, but he never ought to stay at a private house, because he requires so much attention." *Letters and Journals of General Nicholas Longworth Anderson, 1854–1892*, ed. Isabel Anderson (New York: Fleming H. Revell Company, 1942), 207.

"great slabs of Mexican": MHA to EC, July 26, 1883, Adams.

"Nick Anderson's new house": HA to JH, August 10, 1883, *Letters*, vol. 2, 508.

who forwarded one: Anderson wrote his son, "I send you by the same mail a picture of our house, taken by Mrs. Adams." Anderson, *Nicholas Longworth Anderson*, 217.

"excessively" . . . "charming": MHA to RWH, December 2, 1883, Adams.

"Spartan little box": HA to MHA, March 15, 1885, *Letters*, vol. 2, 581.

"sit all day in the library": MHA to RWH, January 11, 1884, Adams.

Henry's study would be: MHA to EC, January 11, 1884, Adams.

a New England coziness: In 1888 Mariana Griswold Van Rensselaer described the Adams house this way: "The chief rooms were to be upstairs, and the ground floor was to be divided longitudinally by a wall — the hall and staircase lying to the right, the kitchen apartments to the left of it, and communication between them being effected only at the back of the house. Richardson clearly marked this division on the exterior by designing his ground-story with two low, somewhat depressed arches with a pier between them. Within one arch is the beautifully treated main doorway, and behind the other, masked by a rich iron grille, are the windows of the servants' apartments, while the door which leads to these lies beyond the arch to the left. Inside, the hall with its great fire-place and its stairway forming broad platforms is as charming as it is individual, and the living-rooms up-stairs are well proportioned, and simple but complete in detail." Van Rensselaer, *Henry Hobson Richardson and His Works* (Boston: Houghton, Mifflin, and Company, 1888), 107.

170 "hurry him up": HA to John Hay, February 20, 1884, *Letters*, vol. 2, 537.

"no stained glass — no carving": MHA to RWH, December 16, 1883, Adams; "fine house" . . . "unusual one": MHA to RWH, March 23, 1884, Adams.

"These I shall put back": Henry Hobson Richardson Drawings (MS Typ 1096), AHW E3j, Houghton.

"worked up" . . . "like a master": HA to MHA, March 23, 1884, Adams.

"I am glad you are pleased": H. H. Richardson to Henry Adams, June 2, 1884, Theodore F. Dwight Papers, MHS.

The first photograph: MHA, January 18, 1884, album #7, 50.11.

a dying lion: Richardson died of Bright's disease on April 27, 1886. He was forty-eight years old. Oudry's drawing was donated to the Museum of Fine Arts in Boston in 1920.

CHAPTER 18. Portraits

171 "expect some very lively tariff" . . . "every day": MHA to RWH, January 13, 1884, Adams.

"add much to us": MHA to RWH, February 17, 1884, Adams. In the same letter, she registered her horror at the tragedy that had befallen Theodore Roosevelt, then a New York assemblyman. He had lost his mother to typhoid fever and his wife, Alice, to kidney failure, both on Valentine's Day. His only daughter was just two days old. Clover recalled to her father how she and Henry had met young Teddy on the Nile twelve years before, remarking that in later years he and his beautiful wife had been "overwhelmingly hospitable" whenever she and Henry had met them in New York.

172 "generosity knew no bounds": Harold Dean Cater, *Henry Adams and His Friends: A Collection of His Unpublished Letters* (Boston: Houghton Mifflin Company, 1947), xlvii–xlviii. Rebecca Dodge vividly recalled meeting the Adamses for the first time: "I passed by the house frequently, for I lived in that neighborhood, and Mrs. Adams, liking my appearance, asked a friend who I was. It happened that this person was a good friend of mine, so we called together one day to see Mrs. Adams . . . I suppose I became an intimate at 1607 H Street."

"always been utterly opposed": MHA to EC, January 11, 1884, Adams.

"a long account" . . . "extremely": MHA to RWH, February 24, 1884, Adams.

"society rabble" . . . "come at all": MHA to RWH, February 3, 1884, Adams.

"a small part": MHA to RWH, January 13, 1884, Adams.

"quiet evenings" . . . "keep out of it": MHA to RWH, February 3, 1884, Adams. She had opened her first album: The first two albums of Clover's photographs were originally archived at the MHS in the wrong order, so that the album numbered #7 in the archive is actually the second album that Clover put together, and album #8 is the first. This is important to know, particularly when trying to consider the images in sequence. Laura Saltz somewhat misreads the photograph collection by basing her otherwise provocative argument in part on the original but incorrect archived order of the albums. Saltz, "Clover Adams's Dark Room: Photography and Writing, Exposure and Erasure," *Prospects: An Annual of American Cultural Studies,* ed. Jack Salzman, vol. 24, 449–90.

173 a notable success: MHA, September 16, 1883, album #8, 50.81, 50.82, and 50.83.

Hegermann-Lindencrone's daughter: The third sitter was Lettita Sargent, the Civil War widow of Lucius Sargent. Clover captured something of a widow's sorrow in the woman's expression, with her head tilted ever so slightly back and her face directed to the light. MHA, September 16, 1883, album # 8.50.84.

Dallmeyer wide-angle lens: MHA, December 28, 1883, album #7, 50.9.

174 "enchanted with it": MHA to RWH, January 6, 1884, Adams.

The Millets, whom Clover had met: See H. Barbara Weinberg, "The Career of Francis Davis Millet," *Archives of American Art Journal,* vol. 17, no. 1 (1977): 2–18.

"different poses as statuary": MHA to RWH, February 10, 1884, Adams.

like a classical: MHA, [February] 1884, album #7, 50.10, 50.21, 50.22, and 50.23.

175 "which one I want" . . . "work": MHA to RWH, February 10, 1884, Adams.

Madame Bonaparte: MHA, March 16, 1884, album #7, 50.20.

"astride a chair" . . . "worth keeping": MHA to RWH, March 16, 1884, Adams.

"photos for nearly two hours" . . . "rumpled it all up": MHA to RWH, February 24, 1884, Adams.

Senator's notable geniality: MHA, February 23, 1884, album #7, 50.18.

176 Clover positioned Gordon: MHA, February 23, 1884, album #7, 50.19.

"It is dim": MHA to RWH, February 24, 1884, Adams.

hung a white sheet: MHA, January 20, 1884, album #7, 50.12 and 50.13.

"funny, dark-haired copy": MHA to RWH, November 25, 1883, Adams.

"a rare chance": MHA to RWH, December 9, 1883, Adams.

177 Oliver Wendell Holmes Jr.: MHA, February 1884, album #7, 50.14 and 50.15.

Clover places Mrs. Field: MHA, 1884, album #7, 50.26.

178 "by long odds": HA to MHA, April 11, 1885, *Letters,* vol. 2, 605.

"Mrs. Bancroft looks" . . . "one eye open": MHA to RWH, May 25, 1884, Adams.

Mrs. Bancroft's portrait: MHA, 1884, album #7, 50.40.

an ancient pine tree: MHA, n.d., album #7, 50.39; Arlington National Cemetery, November 5, 1883, album #7, 50.41.

"how any man or woman dares": MHA to EC, January 11, 1884, Adams.

"a mob almost as un interesting" . . . "rather more solitary": HA to CMG, February 3, 1884, *Letters,* vol. 2, 535.

179 "spelled solitude": MHA to APF, May 1, 1884, Hooper-Adams Papers, MHS.

"Poor little" . . . "not wanted above": MHA to RWH, January 6, 1884, Adams.

"Perdita, perdita" . . . "when you're around": MHA to EC, January 11, 1884, Adams.

"chatter" and "smile": HA to CMG, May 18, 1884, *Letters,* vol. 2, 540.

180 "all in white muslin": MHA to RWH, May 25, 1884, Adams.

"Mrs. Don" . . . "to the sea-side": HA to JH, May 18, 1884, *Letters,* vol. 2, 542.

"or sends for her": *Esther,* 50.

"shipwreck": HA to Mabel Hooper, May 28, 1898, *Letters,* vol. 4, 596.

young woman, Grace Minot: MHA, October 8, 1883, album #8, 50.88.

181 "My wife and I are becoming": HA to JH, August 3, 1884, *Letters,* vol. 2, 547.

"I never feel a wish to wander": HA to Sir John Clark, December 13, 1884, *Letters,* vol. 2, 560.

"the worst part": *Esther,* 117.

"I shall dedicate": HA to EC, December 7, 1884, *Letters,* vol. 2, 559.

19. Part IV: Mysteries of the Heart

CHAPTER 19. Turning Away

185   The past five years: See *Middle Years*, 262–64.

"In you I detect": HA to George Bancroft, January 10, 1885, *Letters*, vol. 2, 568.

which "is disappointing": HA to Henry Holt, January 6, 1885, *Letters*, vol. 2, 567. Henry made arrangements with Holt to have *Esther* published in England together with another American novel, *Among the Chosen*, by Mary S. Emerson. But this idea was dropped by the publisher, Richard Bentley and Son. *Esther* received mixed reviews in the English press.

186   "the only portrait": HA to Royal Cortissoz, May 12, 1911, *Letters*, vol. 6, 443. In one of her old sketchbooks, above a small jewel-toned watercolor painting of a goldfish bowl, Clover jotted down this identification: "February 22, 1885, J. La Farge." MHA sketchbook, Hooper-Adams Papers, MHS. That same day Henry wrote a letter to John Hay, noting that La Farge "is with us again," which indicates that the watercolor may have been painted by the artist while he stayed with the Adamses. HA to JH, February 22, 1885, *Letters*, vol. 2, 575.

"Excuse so much politics": MHA to RWH, June 8, 1884, Adams.

"free-trade Democrat": HA to CMG, September 21, 1884, *Letters*, vol. 2, 551.

there had been "no alternative": MHA to RWH, April 13, 1884, Adams; "tattooed with corruption": MHA to RWH, June 1, 1884, Adams.

"rotten old soulless party": MHA to RWH, April 13, 1884, Adams.

"Grover Cleveland is safely" . . . "windows as from there": MHA to RWH, March 5, 1885, Adams.

187   "'extra' on Thursday" . . . "North Carolina once": MHA to RWH, March 8, 1885, Adams.

"Take care of yourself": MHA to RWH, March 8, 1885, Adams.

188   "Bunged up by the nastiest cold": HA to JH, March 7, 1885, *Letters*, vol. 2, 578.

"nobody wants me": HA to Rebecca Gilman Dodge, April 8, 1885, *Letters*, vol. 2, 600.

"So methinks do": ESH, folio of poems, privately printed by EWH, author's copy.

189   "in despair because Don": HA to MHA, March 30, 1885, *Letters*, vol. 2, 596. The Camerons' travel plans were revised a week later. Don Cameron hoped to go to California for his health, and Lizzie planned to spend the summer in Harrisburg; see HA to MHA, April 9, 1885, *Letters*, vol. 2, 602.

"seated by the library fire": HA to MHA, March 28, 1885, *Letters*, vol. 2, 592.

"low in mind" . . . "glad to see him": HA to MHA, March 21, 1885, *Letters*, vol. 2, 587.

"The day is gloomy": HA to MHA, March 15, 1885, *Letters*, vol. 2, 581.

unspeakably "weary": *Esther*, 89–90.

"for his wife again": HA to MHA, April 12, 1885, *Letters*, vol. 2, 608.

in the third person: Ernest Samuels rightly observes that the tone of the letters is "astonishingly devoid of tenderness, filled with the surface concerns of household and society, visits to the dentist, dinners with Hay and other friends, queries about library fixtures and bells for the new house—all the small talk of a busy household." *Middle Years,* 265.

"unselfish and brave": MHA to APF, April 26, 1885, Hooper-Adams Papers, MHS.

190 "kind heart": As quoted in *Mrs. Henry Adams,* 33.

"You must take good care": EWH to RWH, September 15, 1863, EWH Letters, MS Am 1969 (6), Houghton.

"It seems to me more": MHA to RWH, June 28, 1872, as quoted in *Mrs. Henry Adams,* 115.

"of an anxious make": MHA to RWH, January 15, 1879, Adams.

"as little in his children's": HA to CMG, June 23, 1872, *Letters,* vol. 2, 140.

"No one fills any part": MHA to APF, April 26, 1884, Hooper-Adams Papers, MHS.

CHAPTER 20. "Lost in the Woods"

192 "tired out in mind": MHA to APF, April 26, 1885, Hooper-Adams Papers, MHS. She was curious: "I've no desire to go abroad again, but should like to go in the director's car over that line to the Pacific when the country is a little more settled up." MHA to RWH, April 22, 1883, *LMHA,* 442.

193 they hoped to "camp out": MHA to APF, April 26, 1885, Hooper-Adams Papers, MHS.

"in better condition": HA to JH, April 20, 1885, *Letters,* vol. 2, 609.

In the early spring: Edward Nelson Fell was a British mining engineer and had been born in New Zealand. He and Anne married on May 25, 1885, and they would live in Narcoossee, Florida.

"very glad" . . . "marry only heiresses": MHA to APF, April 26, 1885, Hooper-Adams Papers, MHS. This is the last letter in the long correspondence between Clover and Anne.

194 "on account of the flies": HA to CMG, June 18, 1885, *Letters,* vol. 2, 617.

"a country less known": HA to CMG, June 18, 1885, *Letters,* vol. 2, 617.

195 "flaming yellow" . . . "Appenines": HA to CMG, June 18, 1885, *Letters,* vol. 2, 617. See also Robert S. Conte, *The History of the Greenbrier, America's Resort* (Charleston, WV: Pictorial Histories Publishing Co., 1989).

"so ideally bad": HA to CMG, June 18, 1885, *Letters,* vol. 2, 617.

Clover and Henry had company: Rebecca Dodge would remember the trip many years later, noting she had an "adorable picture of that cottage with Mr. Adams leaning against a post." Rebecca (Dodge) Rae to Louisa Hooper Thoron, June 7 (no year), Unprocessed Thoron papers, *93M–35 (b), Houghton.

The first three photographs: MHA, n.d., album #9, 50.106, 50.107, 50.108.

196 "the ruins of a stone house": MHA to RWH, May 13, 1883, *LMHA,* 448.

She took her first image: MHA, n.d., album #9, 50.111 and 50.112.

197 Henry carefully wrote captions: Lousia Hooper Thoron, MHA's niece, also iden-

tified several photographs at some point. Henry kept the photograph albums in his library, and when his library books were donated to the Massachusetts Historical Society, the albums were donated alongside his books.

not with the trip: MHA, n.d., album #9, 50.96 and 50.97.

198   four photographs: MHA, n.d., album #9, 50.98, 50.99, 50.100, and 50.101.

liked to ride there: General John G. Parke had sent the Adamses the Union army map in 1881. MHA to RWH, November 20, 1881, *LMHA,* 301.

Rebecca Dodge: MHA, n.d., album #9, 50.109 and 50.110.

"we got a long way": HA to CMG, June 18, 1885, *Letters,* vol. 2, 617.

CHAPTER 21. A Dark Room

199   "Whither have you": JH to HA, July 12, 1885, Theodore F. Dwight Papers, MHS.

"a month of rambling": HA to JH, July 17, 1885, *Letters,* vol. 2, 619.

"private opinion" . . . "without fail": Sturgis Bigelow to MHA, July 4, 1885, Unprocessed Thoron papers, *93M–35 (b), Houghton. The letter was dated July 4 and sent to 1607 H Street and forwarded to Beverly Farms on July 25, 1880.

"a gloomy spot": HA to CMG, June 18, 1885, *Letters,* vol. 2, 617.

200   McLean Asylum: The McLean Asylum is now McLean Hospital in Belmont.

"own lips her horror" . . . "take your advice": MHA to RWH, May 9, 1882, transcripts of MHA letters omitted from publication, Hooper-Adams Papers, MHS.

"I cannot bear": MHA to RWH, May 14, 1882, transcripts of MHA letters omitted from publication, Hooper-Adams Papers, MHS.

"taste for horrors": MHA to RWH, December 25, 1881, *LMHA,* 315. When Dr. Hooper warned his daughter, he was trying to protect her. But Clover was defensive about her father's accusation, writing back that wanting to know the social gossip of the Boston circle from her father was motivated "only to save time, otherwise in June I must visit Somerville and ask to see the patients' book, and then explore Mt. Auburn for new-laid graves."

"The insane asylum": MHA to RWH, January 26, 1879, Adams. When Clover's Aunt Anne (who'd been married to Congressman Samuel Hooper) struggled with chronic health complaints, which only got more complicated after the deaths of her son, husband, and daughter, Clover empathized with her father about her horrible fate. "I'm sorry for poor Aunt Anne. You say she 'feels deserted and justly so.'" But she also defended her cousin Annie, Aunt Anne's only surviving daughter, who evidently had been steering clear of her mother. "Annie must have very strong motives for staying away," Clover reasoned. But when Aunt Anne's caretaker and companion, Miss Folsom, apparently quit, and the family was at loose ends about who might be able to take care of her, Clover made it clear she was no candidate. "I decline all responsibility in the matter, especially if Aunt Anne is to be in Beverly Farms," she warned, recommending instead an acquaintance who had served as a companion for another "semi-insane" woman. MHA to RWH, June 11 and May 20, 1882, transcripts of MHA letters omitted from publication, Hooper-Adams Papers, MHS.

She tried to keep up: Clover's niece, Louisa Hooper, remembered that Clover "kept up her riding during the summer and a semblance of her daily round with her family in and out of the house." As quoted in Chalfant, *Better in Darkness*, 497.

201 "Dearest Rebecca": MHA to Rebecca Dodge, September 22, 1885, Unprocessed Thoron papers, *93M–35 (b), Houghton.

"in the gloomiest state of mind" . . . "towards us": Ephraim Whitman Gurney to E. L. Godkin, October 16, 1885, Edwin Lawrence Godkin Papers, MS Am 1083 (350), Houghton. The letter is dated October 16, 1886, in Gurney's handwriting. But it was clearly written the year before, in 1885, when Clover was still alive.

"every reckless" . . . "all of you real!": EHG to Elizabeth Dwight Cabot, envelope dated January 1, 1886, Swann.

"all the dilapidated Bostonians": Brooks, as quoted in Alexander V. G. Allen, *Phillips Brooks: Memories of His Life with Extracts from His Letters and Note-Books* (New York: E. P. Dutton & Company, 1907), 331.

"very bright and full of talk": MHA to RWH, March 11, 1883, *LMHA*, 428.

202 For those surrounding Clover: Clover's sister, Ellen, would later write to a friend, "We did the best we knew how and we know no better now." EHG to Elizabeth Dwight Cabot, January 1, 1886, Swann.

Rebecca remembered: Cater, *Henry Adams and His Friends*, ii.

"It is a common event" . . . "describe adequately": Henry Maudsley, M.D., *Body and Will, Being an Essay Concerning Will in Its Metaphysical, Physiological, and Pathological Aspects* (New York: D. Appleton and Company, 1884), 307. The copy with Henry's marginalia is in the Henry Adams Library at the MHS.

203 "I am peculiarly anxious": HA to Henry Holt, November 13, 1885, *Letters*, vol. 2, 636.

"goes nowhere": HA to Theodore F. Dwight, November 4, *Letters*, vol. 2, 633; "my wife": HA to CMG, November 8, 1885, *Letters*, vol. 2, 635.

"best love": HA to JH, November 4, 1885, *Letters*, vol. 2, 634.

"very low" . . . "before long": John Field to Theodore F. Dwight, November 7, 1885, Field Family Letters, MHS.

"I saw the Adamses": John Field to Theodore F. Dwight, November 12, 1885, Field Family Letters, MHS.

204 "much improved": H. H. Richardson to JH, December 8, 1885, as quoted in Chalfant, *Better in Darkness*, 499.

Maréchal Niel roses: Lizzie Cameron's mother, Eliza Sherman, wrote to her sister, Mary Sherman Miles, on December 21, 1885: "Mrs. Adams called here to see Lizzie on Friday evening, and sent her a gorgeous boquet [*sic*] of Marchineil roses." Quoted in *Letters*, vol. 2, 641–42, n. 1.

The next morning: *Chicago Daily Tribune*, December 6, 1885.

"more patient" . . . "back to life": This retelling of Clover's death is based on her sister's long letter to Elizabeth Dwight Cabot. EHG to Elizabeth Dwight Cabot, envelope dated January 1, 1886, Swann. Some biographers, such as Ernest Samuels, cite the next day's edition of *Washington Critic*, which contended that Henry had met a visitor at the door who wanted to see Clover, and that when he returned to her rooms to see if she was receiving visitors, he found her dead. But Ellen did not include this detail in her letter, and there is no information about the source for the newspaper account. See *Middle Years,* 272.

205 When Henry returned: The exact room in which Henry found Clover is not known.

"Wait till I have recovered": HA to Rebecca Dodge Gilman, December 6, 1885, *Letters,* vol. 2, 640.

Neighbors reported seeing him: General Anderson wrote his son, "Until his family arrived he saw, as far as I can learn, no one whatever, and I can imagine nothing more ghastly than that lonely vigil in the house with his dead wife. Poor fellow! I do not know what he can do." Nicholas Anderson to Larz Anderson, December 9, 1885, in *Letters and Journals of General Nicholas Longworth Anderson,* ed. Isabel Anderson (New York: F. H. Revell, 1942), 252. See also *Middle Years,* 281.

"God only knows": EHG to Elizabeth Dwight Cabot, envelope dated January 1, 1886, Swann.

Rock Creek Cemetery: The vestry of Saint Paul's Church, Rock Creek Parish of the Episcopal Church, owns and operates Rock Creek Cemetery. It is the oldest religious institution in the District of Columbia, established as a mission in 1712. It is a nonsectarian cemetery.

"spring comes early": EHG to Elizabeth Dwight Cabot, envelope dated January 1, 1886, Swann. The internment is listed as December 12, 1885, in the records of the church; copy in Adams-Thoron Papers, MHS.

"a terminal inner loneliness": A. Alvarez, *The Savage God: A Study of Suicide* (New York: W. W. Norton & Company, 1990), 121. Alvarez cautions that suicides present a "profound ambiguity of motives even when they seem clear-cut" (132). If one can often identify the "local and immediate causes" of suicide, he observes, these "say nothing at all of the long, slow, hidden processes that lead up to it" (121). The real motives and reasons belong, instead, to "the internal world, devious, contradictory, labyrinthine, and mostly, out of sight" (123).

206 Creativity can be compensatory: The biographer Hermione Lee argues that Virginia Woolf's art grew out of her sense of loss, the shocks of her childhood, and the early deaths of her parents. While Lee is careful not to narrow Woolf's accomplishments to this, even so, Woolf found deep consolation in her writing, a means of healing, and a way for her to find the "pattern hidden behind the 'cotton-wool' of daily life." Hermione Lee, *Virginia Woolf* (New York: Vintage Books, 1999; originally published 1996), 170. The trope of art's debt to suffering is as old as Sophocles' Philoctetes, the Greek warrior whose festering wound empowered the speed and accuracy of his bow. Philoctetes, for Edmund Wilson, dramatizes how Sophocles thought "a superior strength" was always "inseparable from disability." See Wilson, "The Wound and the Bow," in *Literary Essays and Reviews 1930s & 40s,* ed. Lewis M. Dabney (New York: Library of America, 2007), 271–473.

Things can sometimes go: "For the artist himself art is not necessarily therapeutic," Alvarez warns. "By some perverse logic of creation, the act of formal expression may simply make the dredged-up material more readily available" to the artist so that in dealing with dark themes—sadness, grief, isolation—the artist may discover she is "living it out." Alvarez, *The Savage God,* 53–54.

"go to the Louvre": MHA to EC, July 26, 1883, Adams.

CHAPTER 22. "That Bright, Intrepid Spirit"

207 "I think of you all the time": CK to HA, December 10, 1885, Clarence King Papers, MHS. King went on to tell Henry of his plans to go to Mexico and generously asked if he'd like to come along, to recover and to "hear the waves of the Pacific," promising that he'd "try to bear you cheerful company."

"I can neither talk": John Hay to HA, December 9, 1885, in *Letters of John Hay and Extracts from Diary,* vol. 2, 98–99.

208 "peace that you have reached" . . . "extremity of suffering": HA to Anna Barker Ward, December 22, 1885, *Letters,* vol. 2, 644.

"sympathy has been a relief": HA to Thomas F. Bayard, January 20, 1886, *Letters,* vol. 3, 3.

"What a vast fraternity": HA to Henry Holt, March 8, 1886, *Letters,* vol. 3, 5.

"come out all right": HA to John Hay, December 9, 1885, *Letters,* vol. 2, 641.

"more sorry for poor Henry": Quoted in *The Middle Years,* 166.

"we are anxious" . . . "better than you": JH to HA, December 9, 1885, *Letters of John Hay and Extracts from Diary,* vol. 2, 99.

"You are never out of my mind": JH to HA, December 15, 1885, Theodore F. Dwight Papers, MHS.

"his face steadily": Ephraim Whitman Gurney to E. L. Godkin, December 11, 1885, Edwin Lawrence Godkin Papers, MS Am 1083 (348), Houghton.

209 live "henceforward": HA to EC, December 10, 1885, *Letters,* vol. 2, 641.

"I should have written" . . . "have them still." HA to APF, January 8, 1886, Henry Adams letters to Anne (Palmer) Fell, MHS.

210 "impossible subject": Andrew Soloman, *The Noonday Demon: An Atlas of Depression* (New York: Scribner, 2001), 246.

"succumbed to hereditary": HJ to Elizabeth Boott, January 7, 1886, *HJ Letters,* vol. 3, 107.

"dangerous impression" . . . "Sturgis blood": CFA Memorabilia, May 3, 1891, Charles Francis Adams Papers, MHS. Charles Francis Adams Jr. had recently visited Clover's grave to see the Saint-Gaudens statue for the first time. He wrote that Clover was "a mere child at the time" of Susan's suicide, that she had been with Susan when she took a "fatal dose of arsenic," and that this "made a dangerous impression on her mind; for she was old enough to have some idea of what it all meant." But this is the only direct account of Clover's presence at the Bigelow house at the time of Susan's death. It was entirely possible Clover was there—she often spent considerable time with extended family during the summer months. Subsequent biographers cite this remembrance in the diary but mention no other corroborating evidence, and nowhere did Charles Francis Adams Jr. indicate how he knew the story.

"had been suffering": *Washington Critic*, December 9, 1885; "general depression": Whitman Gurney to E. L. Godkin, October 16, 1886 [misdated year; letter was written in 1885], Edwin Lawrence Godkin Papers, MS Am 1083 (350), Houghton. Current modes of analysis and treatment save many lives and provide a means of understanding experiences that defy reason, but they were not available to Clover. Using them to interpret her condition may be helpful only up to a point. Perhaps interventions of talk therapy and pharmacology would have given her a fighting chance to recover. Perhaps not. Researchers have found that children who lose a parent or a parental figure before the age of eight face a much higher risk for suicide. One study of fifty suicides found in an overwhelming majority of the cases that "'the death or loss under dramatic and often tragic circumstances of individuals closely related to the patient, generally parents, siblings, and mates.'" Alvarez, *The Savage God*, 130.

Mourning can be exceedingly complicated for children. Rage, guilt, and (in the words of William Styron) a "dammed-up sorrow" overflow later as self-destruction. Styron, *Darkness Visible: A Memoir of Madness* (New York: Vintage Books, 1992, first published 1990), 80. Styron ties his catastrophic depression in *Darkness Visible* to "the concept of loss. Loss in all of its manifestations is the touchstone of depression—in the progress of the disease and, most likely, in its origin. At a later date I would gradually be persuaded that devastating loss in childhood figured as a probable genesis of my own disorder; meanwhile, as I monitored my retrograde condition, I felt loss at every hand" (56).

"a bad nervous break-down": Trinity Church Sermon, dated February 7, 1965, Unprocessed Thoron papers, *93M–35 (b), Houghton.

211   "curious impregnability" . . . "unrecognized centre": Alvarez, *The Savage God*, 131–32.

"stoic aspect" . . . "hates to be alone": EHG to E. L. Godkin, June 9, 1886, Edwin Lawrence Godkin Papers, MS Am 1083 (319), Houghton. In an earlier letter to Godkin, Ellen had copied out for him a portion of Clover's last note to her, the same passage she also sent to Elizabeth Dwight Cabot.

"being smashed about": HA to CMG, April 25, 1886, *Letters*, vol. 3, 8.

"a glorious success": HA to JH, June 11, 1886, *Letters*, vol. 3, 12; "who never complains": HA to Theodore F. Dwight, June 28, 1886, *Letters*, vol. 3, 14.

"one of the sights": HA to JH, July 24, 1886, *Letters*, vol. 3, 24.

"as ready to come home": HA to Theodore F. Dwight, September 16, 1886, *Letters*, vol. 3, 41.

"stood in the full centre": HA to CMG, December 12, 1886, *Letters*, vol. 3, 48.

212   "I hope you have all": EWG to Ellen, Louisa, Polly, Fanny, and Mary Hooper, July 24, 1883, Unprocessed Thoron papers, *93M–35 (b), Houghton.

"When I married": HA to CMG, December 12, 1886, *Letters*, vol. 3, 48.

"harvest of thorns": HA to EC, November 19, 1886, *Letters*, vol. 3, 46.

"If the moon were to wander": HA to CMG, December 12, 1886, *Letters*, vol. 3, 48.

"During the last eighteen" . . . "whole relation": HA to APF, December 5, 1885, Henry Adams letters to Anne Palmer Fell, MHS.

213   "I have been sad, sad, sad": HA diary entry, May 20, 1888, reprinted in *Letters*, vol. 3, 114.

CHAPTER 23. "Let Fate Have Its Way"

214   "This little trinket": HA to EC, December 25, 1885, *Letters*, vol. 2, 645.
She would even try: On April 9, 1891, from Washington, Lizzie wrote to Henry, who was then traveling in the Polynesian islands, that she'd been "much to your house lately, using the darkroom . . . Everything looks as if you ought to be there. It is so clean and neat." Henry Adams Papers, microfilm edition of the Adams Family Papers, MHS.

215   Henry's biographer: Samuels, *Middle Years*, 326; Samuels, *Henry Adams* (Cambridge, MA: The Belknap Press of Harvard University Press, 1989), 221.
"liked to flirt": Elisina Tyler, quoted in Tehane, *Henry Adams in Love*, 74.

216   "I read your letters": HA to EC, January 2, 1891, *Letters*, vol. 3, 382; "I need not tell you": HA to EC, February 6, 1891, *Letters*, vol. 3, 406; "My only source": HA to EC, June 3, 1891, *Letters*, vol. 3, 482.
"I shall see you": EC, quoted in Tehan, *Henry Adams in Love*, 124.
"In another week or ten days": HA to EC, September 6, 1891, *Letters*, vol. 3, 538.
"wait only to know": HA to EC, October, 11, 1891, *Letters*, vol. 3, 555.
"A long, lowering, melancholy": HA to EC, November 5, 1891, *Letters*, vol. 3, 556.
"Mrs. Cameron and Martha": HA to Rebecca Dodge Rae, December 5, 1891, *Letters*, vol. 3, 582.

217   "over sodden fields" . . . "Let fate have its way": HA to EC, November 5–November 12, 1891, *Letters*, vol. 3, 556–61. Henry included lines from Elizabeth Barrett Browning, a favorite poet from his days in college: "Know you what it is when Anguish, with apocalyptic *Never* / To a Pythian height dilates you, and Despair sublimes to Power?" Then he referred to Bret Harte's vernacular Gold Rush poem, "The Society upon the Stanislaus," wherein a miner gets kicked in the stomach by another miner and, Henry said, "curls up . . . and for a time does not even squirm." The critic Newton Arvin observed that when writing letters "the discomfort that so often afflicted him elsewhere quite fell away and he became simply a man with a pen—a man for whom, moreover, the pen was a predestined implement. Now he was wholly at one with himself and with his perfect audience of a single person, and all his powers as a writer—powers of sharp attention to people and things, of responsiveness to impressions, of insight and judgment, and above all of expression in language—found themselves in free and unembarrassed play." Arvin, introduction to *The Selected Letters of*

Henry Adams, ed. Newton Arvin (New York: Farrar, Straus and Giroux, Inc., 1951), xiv.

218 "Marry I will not": HA to EC, November 14–28, 1891, *Letters*, vol. 3, 565.

219 "without forgiveness": Edith Wharton, *The Age of Innocence* (New York: The Modern Library, 1999), 34. Henry's relationship with Lizzie Cameron resembled in intensity and chastity the love story at the center of Wharton's *Age of Innocence* (1920). In the "hieroglyphic world" of Old New York in the 1870s, Newland Archer (newly engaged to another woman) and Madame Ellen Olenska renounce their passion for each other, knowing all too well they inhabit a social world that would not forgive impropriety. In fact, the similarities between Newland Archer's passion for Ellen and Henry's attraction to Lizzie are striking enough to raise the question as to whether Wharton was in any way inspired by Henry and Lizzie's relationship when writing her novel. Wharton knew Henry, though the two had never been close friends. She attended social engagements and dinner parties with Henry and Lizzie when they were all in Paris in the early 1910s. Henry wrote to Charles Milnes Gaskell in 1910 that Edith Wharton was "almost the centre" of the "little American family-group" in Paris, which was "more closely intimate, and more agreeably intelligent, than any now left to me in America." HA to CMG, December 14, 1910, *Letters*, vol. 6, 394. Wharton was later a close companion with Lizzie Cameron in Paris during World War I. She would have fathomed the subtext of Henry and Lizzie's relationship, even if Lizzie never laid out its details. See Viola Winner, "The Paris Circle of Edith Wharton and Henry Adams," *Edith Wharton Review*, vol. 9, no. 1 (Spring 1992), 2–4.

his "final approval": HA to Theodore F. Dwight, March 10, 1892, *Letters*, vol. 4, 4.

"Budha [*sic*] — Mental repose": Augustus Saint-Gaudens, *The Reminiscences of Augustus Saint-Gaudens*, ed. and amplified by Homer Saint-Gaudens, vol. 1 (New York: The Century Co., 1913), 361. See also Cynthia Mills, "Casting Shadows: The Adams Memorial and Its Doubles," *American Art*, vol. 14, no. 2 (Summer 2000): 2–25.

"philosophic calm": Saint-Gaudens, *Reminiscences*, 356. Homer Saint-Gaudens, in his interpolations in his father's memoirs, wrote that his father "first sought to embody a philosophic calm, a peaceful acceptance of death and whatever lay in the future"; "beyond pain": Saint-Gaudens, *Reminiscences*, 361. Edith Greenough Wendell, wife of the Harvard literature professor Barrett Wendell, recalled standing before Clover's grave in 1904, when Augustus Saint-Gaudens and John Hay walked up beside her. She asked Saint-Gaudens what he called the bronze figure. "He hesitated and then said, 'I call it the Mystery of the Hereafter.' Then I said, 'It is not happiness?' 'No,' he said, 'it is beyond pain, and beyond joy.'" Quoted in Augustus Saint-Gaudens, *The Reminiscences of Augustus Saint-Gaudens*, vol. 1, 362.

220 "The work is indescribably noble": John Hay to HA, March 25, 1891, Thayer, *The Life of John Hay*, vol. 2, 60–61.

placed no identifying plaque: The fifth point of HA's last will, drafted in 1908, stipulates that "no inscription, date, letters or other attempt at memorial, except the monument I have already constructed, shall be placed over or near our grave." Adams-Thoron Papers, MHS.

"is his own artist": HA to Edgar Dwight Shaw, December 20, 1904, *Letters*, vol. 5, 619. Shaw, managing editor of the *Washington Times*, had written to Henry, asking for the meaning of the bronze statue; "The interest of the figure": *Education*, 314.

"intellectual grace": HJ to William James, March 8, 1870, *HJ Letters*, vol. 1, 208. When he finally arrived: Chanler, *Roman Spring*, 302. Chanler does not specify the exact date when Henry James visited Clover's grave. But James wrote a letter to Edith Wharton, listing Henry's H Street address above his salutation, which briefly mentioned his visit to Clover's grave. HJ to Edith Wharton, January 16, 1905, *HJ Letters*, vol. 4, 340–42. Henry Adams also mentions James's visit in a letter to Louisa Hooper on January 8, 1905, saying, "La Farge and Henry James have engaged rooms with me." HA to Louisa Hooper, January 8, 1905, *Letters*, vol. 5, 625.

221 "very unhappy and sorry": Roosevelt, quoted in Lorena A. Hickock, *Eleanor Roosevelt: Reluctant First Lady* (New York: Dodd, Mead & Company), 92. Blanche Wiesen Cook speculates that in the cemetery's "unmarked holly grove, [Eleanor] forged a healing bond with a stranger that helped to strengthen her to live the kind of life she wished to lead." Cook, *Eleanor Roosevelt, Vol. 1: 1884–1933* (New York: Penguin Books, 1992), 248.

In 1906, Mark Twain visited Clover's grave. There is no record that Twain ever met the Adamses, though they would have known of Twain's writing. After spending time sitting in front of the bronze statue, the author said it was a figure "in deep meditation on sorrowful things." Twain would always keep a small framed photograph of the monument on his mantelpiece. Albert Bigelow Paine, *Mark Twain*, vol. 3 (1912; reprint, New York: Chelsea House, 1980), 1351.

EPILOGUE

223 In the spring of 1901: Ned was attended to first by his private physician for his injuries from the fall, including lacerations, a broken rib, and a punctured lung. But his condition deteriorated. His doctor admitted him to McLean Asylum a month later, where he stayed in a large suite of rooms in the Upham House until his death. The description of what happened in Ned Hooper's last months is based on a family memo shown to the author by a Hooper family descendant.

"I find it hard to express" . . . "nightmares of the past": William James to Ellen Hooper, May 10, 1901, Swann. James wrote this letter from his brother Henry's home, Lamb House, in Rye, England. James was responding to the news of Ned Hooper's hospitalization, but he had not yet heard about Ned's death on June 25. Never before published, the letter reads in its entirety as follows: "In a letter from Mrs. Gibbens which arrived yesterday she says that she has heard that your father has gone to the McLean Asylum. I find it hard to express the sorrow I feel, both for him and for you, for I suppose his condition to have been akin to melancholia, and think it not improbable there may be suicidal impulses. He was such a model of soundness and balance, that this was the last thing I ever dreamed of as possible in his life. But anything and everything is possible for every mother's child of us—we are all in the same box, and not only death but all forms of decay knock at our gate and summon us to go out into their wilderness, and yet every ideal we dream of is realized in the same life of which these things are part, and we must house it and suffer it and take whatever it brings for the sake of the ends that are certainly being fulfilled by its means, behind the screen. The abruptness of your father's case shows well how purely extraneous and disconnected with the patient's general character these cerebral troubles may be. Probably an internally generated poison in the blood which 'science' any day may learn how to eliminate or neutralize, and so make of all these afflictions so many nightmares of the past. I wish that I could see you all and hear about it and talk it over. I hope that before we get home it will be happily ended, and he as well as he was before the fall, though I don't know what effects that may leave on his bodily condition. Dear Ellen, these experiences bring people close to their friends, and I hope that you and all of you are gaining this alleviation. I have known all the branches of your family so long, and have such an altogether peculiar fondness and admiration for them, and owe so much of what has been best in my life to them, that any disaster happening to any of them feels as if it came close to home. Let us all be nearer together after this—I wish I could be nearer still to your dear father—it is only to say this that I have taken up the pen. Alice joins me in a tenderest message of sympathy and so does H. J. Junior who is with us at last. We are doing well, and I so much better that I begin my Edinburgh lecture course next Thursday with a very stout heart indeed. It is cloudy in one place and sunny elsewhere, everlastingly. Love to all of you! Wm James"

224 "For thirty years": HA to CMG, July 3, 1901, *Letters*, vol. 5, 260.
"trinity of fathers": Mabel Hooper La Farge to Wilbur L. Cross, January 1941, as quoted in Tehan, *Henry Adams in Love*, 287.
Lizzie Cameron held a higher rank: From notes taken by Harold Dean Cater, HA-CK Papers.

225 Henry liked to read aloud: *Mont-Saint-Michel and Chartres* was privately printed in 1904 and published commercially by Houghton Mifflin Company in 1913.
"I kept every scrap": EC to HA, December 7, 1915, *Letters*, vol. 6, 704, n1.
"you're not dead": EC to HA, January 27, 1891, Henry Adams Papers, Microfilm edition of the Adams family papers, MHS.
"life is grim": HA to Thomas F. Bayard, January 20, 1886, *Letters*, vol. 3, 3.
bracingly honest: For an account of Henry's great-grandfather, John Adams, and his reputation for honesty, see David McCullough's *John Adams*, esp. 17–20.

226 "I often wonder": EC to Louisa Hooper Thoron, February 18, 1934, Hooper-Adams Papers, MHS.
"I think that now you and I": HA to Rebecca Dodge Rae, December 7, 1896, HA-CK Papers.

"wisdom is silence": HA to APF, December 8, 1889, Henry Adams letters to Anne (Palmer) Fell, MHS. Andrew Delbanco asserts that "irony is the fire of the *Education*. It burns away the personal memories and leaves a floating consciousness trying to slip into phase with the flow of history." Henry left out the years of his marriage and the circumstances of Clover's death because "he could not bear to write about this event in the ironic voice of the rest of the 'autobiography,' as if it had happened at a distance, to be recorded by the bemused observer along with everything else." Delbanco, *Required Reading* (New York: Farrar, Straus and Giroux, 1997), 99.

"to go back" . . . "to Beverly": Cater, *Henry Adams and His Friends*, civ.

"I wander every morning": HA to EC, June 2, 1917, *Letters*, vol. 6, 754.

Later in the summer: HA to EC, August 3, 1917, *Letters*, vol. 6, 763.

227 "My child" . . . "your Aunt Clover": Cater, *Henry Adams and His Friends*, cii.

half-empty vial: According to Cater, after Henry died, Aileen Tone "looked in his desk for possible written instructions as to what he would like to have done in such an event. In the top drawer was the bottle, containing the remainder of the cyanide potassium, as it had been found after Mrs. Adams's suicide." HA-CK Papers. Aileen had been asked by Louisa Hooper to take up the role of secretary and companion to Henry, starting in late 1912. The two women had been friends while in Paris. In Aileen's copy of *Mont-Saint-Michel and Chartres*, Henry had inscribed "to niece Aileen Tone from Uncle Henry."

"Silent while years" . . . "till the end": HA commonplace book, Homans Collection, MHS. Ernest Samuels suggests that Henry thought the "highest wisdom must be the wisdom of silence, the silence of perfected knowledge and being," a value he expressed in his narrative poem "Buddha and Brahma," composed in blank verse in 1891 and published much later in the *Yale Review*. Samuels, *The Major Phase*, 64. See also "Buddha and Brahma," *Yale Review*, vol. 5 (1915): 82–89.

"The thorns he spares": Algernon Charles Swinburne, *Poems and Ballads: Second Series*, 3rd ed. (London: Chatto and Windus, Piccadilly, 1882).

✦

INDEX